STRATEGIC USES OF NATIONALISM AND ETHNIC CONFLICT

T0386248

STRATEGIC USES OF NATIONALISM AND ETHNIC CONFLICT

INTEREST AND IDENTITY IN RUSSIA AND THE POST-SOVIET SPACE

Pål Kolstø

EDINBURGH
University Press

Edinburgh University Press is one of the leading university presses in the UK. We publish academic books and journals in our selected subject areas across the humanities and social sciences, combining cutting-edge scholarship with high editorial and production values to produce academic works of lasting importance. For more information visit our website: edinburghuniversitypress.com

Edinburgh University Press Ltd
The Tun – Holyrood Road
12(2f) Jackson's Entry
Edinburgh EH8 8PJ

First published in hardback by Edinburgh University Press 2022

Typeset in 10/12.5 Adobe Sabon by
IDSUK (DataConnection) Ltd, and
printed and bound by CPI Group (UK) Ltd,
Croydon, CR0 4YY

A CIP record for this book is available from the British Library

ISBN 978 1 4744 9500 4 (hardback)
ISBN 978 1 4744 9501 1 (paperback)
ISBN 978 1 4744 9502 8 (webready PDF)
ISBN 978 1 4744 9503 5 (epub)

Chapters 6 and 9: Research Council of Norway, Project NEORUSS, Project Number: 220599.
Chapter 7: ILOS, University of Oslo, Project 'Discourses of the Nation and the National'.
Chapter 8: Research Council of Norway, Project NEPORUSS, Project Number 228205.

CONTENTS

FIGURES AND TABLES

DIAGRAM

TABLES

PREFACE

The reinvigoration of nationalism studies over the last three decades has, to a large degree, resulted from observations of how post-communist ethnopolitics has unfolded in the former Soviet Union and Eastern Europe: as regimes collapsed, ethnicity came to the forefront as one of the most important factors in politics. One group of observers presented these conflicts as driven by ethnic identities: group membership predetermined both mind-sets and actions. Nationalism and ethnic conflict were perceived as more or less automatically following from such identities. Other observers emphasised how collective allegiances were constructed and actively used by state leaders, ethnic entrepreneurs and rank-and-file members of the groups, pursuing collective or personal goals. Identities could be mobilised for collective action and the politicisation of ethnicity was, to a large extent, interest-driven. This book discusses the relative merits of these two perspectives through one theoretical introduction and eight case studies of Russian and post-Soviet nationalisms and ethnic politics. Expressing these views as a short formula, I claim that collective identities can be and are being used as mobilisational resources to pursue both group and personal interest. Such identities, however, cannot be conjured out of thin air, but must be based on the cultural reservoirs and historical memories of groups.

My book does not purport to contribute to the understanding of the 'essence' of nationalism as such; instead, it takes as a starting point the fact that nationalism is a pervasive feature of politics in the modern world. Various kinds of actors employ nationalist rhetoric and stratagems to further their political agendas and achieve particular goals. A good place to study these processes is the former Soviet Union. As the unitary state collapsed and political authority withered away, ethnic identities, which had already been institutionalised under the communist regime, were used as a mobilisational resource.

The book aims at providing a deeper understanding of contemporary Russian and post-Soviet nationalisms both at the popular level and as a state strategy. It uses different theories for each chapter, since the chapters have different foci. It also aspires to contribute to nationalism theory on a general level by drawing on insights from the various chapters. Each chapter goes deep into the subject matter under scrutiny, while together they give a wide and comprehensive picture of the dynamics of nationalism in Russia since perestroika. I focus on the role of nationalist ideology: ethnic boundary making, the function and usages of symbols, ethnic competition for material goods, in particular jobs, and coalition building in ethnic mobilisation.

Except for Chapter 1, which is new, earlier versions of the chapters have been published in journals or edited volumes: Chapter 2, 'Competing with entrepreneurial diasporians: Origins of anti-Semitism in nineteenth-century Russia', *Nationalities Papers* 2014; 42, 4, pp. 691–707, and 'Sources of Russian anti-semitism in the late nineteenth century: A Socio-economic explanation', *Scando-Slavica* 2009; 55, 1, pp. 43–64; Chapter 3, 'Nationalism, ethnic conflict, and job competition: Non-Russian collective action in the USSR under perestroika', *Nations and Nationalism* 2008; 14, 1, pp. 151–69; Chapter 4, 'The concept of "rootedness" in the struggle for political power in the Former Soviet Union in the 1990s', in Isabelle Côté, Matthew I. Mitchell and Monica Duffy Toft, eds, *People Changing Places: New Perspectives on Demography, Migration, Conflict, and the State*. Routledge, 2019, pp. 347–73; Chapter 5, '*Antemurale* thinking as historical myth and ethnic boundary mechanism', in Liliya Berezhnaya and Heidi Hein-Kircher, eds, *Rampart Nations: Bulwark Myths in East European Multiconfessional Societies in the Age of Nationalism*. Berghahn Books, 2019, pp. 347–73; Chapter 6, 'The ethnification of Russian nationalism', in Pål Kolstø and Helge Blakkisrud, eds, *The New Russian Nationalism: Imperialism, Ethnicity and Authoritarianism 2000–15*. Edinburgh University Press, 2016, pp. 18–46; Chapter 7, 'Symbol of the war – but which one? The St George ribbon in Russian nation-building', *Slavonic and East European Review* 2016, 94, 4, pp. 660–701; Chapter 8, 'Marriage of convenience? Collaboration between nationalists and liberals in the Russian opposition, 2011–2012', *Russian Review* 2016, 75, 3, pp. 645–63; and Chapter 9, 'Crimea vs. Donbas: How Putin won Russian nationalist support – and lost it again', *Slavic Review* 2016, 75, 3, pp. 702–25.

I wish to thank Helge Blakkisrud, Tor Bukkvoll, Johanna Dahlin, Geir Flikke, Elise Giuliano, Henry Hale, Robert Horvath, Marlène Laruelle,

Marthe Handå Myhre, Jardar Østbø, Maryia Rohava and Alexander Verkhovsky for reading and providing insightful comments on draft versions of one or several chapters in this book. I have also received valuable help with copy-editing and layout from Susan Høivik, Trine Skogset Ofitserova and Wendy Lee.

1

NATIONALISMS AND INTEREST-DRIVEN IDENTITIES: THEORETICAL PERSPECTIVES

Siniša Malešević has convincingly argued that, far from being on the wane, nationalism is a stronger force in the contemporary world than ever before. Nationalism, he claims, is 'the dominant form of modern subjectivity' (Malešević 2019, 3). Even so, nationalism attracted far fewer students in the twentieth century than the rival ideologies of liberalism and Marxism. Although the first pioneers of nationalism studies had already published their seminal works by the 1930s and 1940s (Carlton Hayes, Hans Kohn and others), this field of research long remained the preserve of a handful of dedicated experts. The situation began to change when a series of influential books appeared almost simultaneously in the early 1980s – John Breuilly's *Nationalism and the State* (1982), Benedict Anderson's *Imagined Communities* (1983), Ernest Gellner's *Nations and Nationalism* (1983), and somewhat later, Anthony Smith's *The Ethnic Origins of Nations* (1986) – but it was not until the early 1990s that scholarly interest in the topic exploded (Eriksen 1993; Hobsbawm 1991; Mayall 1990; McGarry and O'Leary 1993; Moynihan 1993; Smith 1991; and others).

A major impetus came from the cataclysmic upheavals in the Soviet Union during and after perestroika. As the communist system withered away, strong nationalist movements sprouted almost overnight, setting the political agenda. It is tempting to see this as a consequence of the demise of the communist ideology: when the official worldview that had been foisted upon two generations of Soviet citizens melted into thin air, people craved another coherent narrative to guide their lives. In fact, this perspective is probably not the most fruitful. For most Soviet citizens, the official state doctrine had long since decayed into stale, hollow cynicism, and no longer functioned as an identity anchor.

Far more important was the disintegration of *political authority*. Not only the communist *regime*, but the unitary Soviet *state* exited the historical scene, leaving behind a power vacuum. Politics became a free-for-all: power was up for grabs, to be snatched by those whose ideas and stratagems could command large followings.

For a while, actors mobilising under nationalist banners proved the most influential, although other ideologies and movements might conceivably have filled the post-communist void. The Soviet Union had been established as a workers' state – indeed, independent labour unions made a cameo appearance during perestroika, before being co-opted by the new regimes in the successor states or fading into oblivion. Moreover, religious organisations, suppressed under Soviet rule, were now free to operate and recruit new adherents – which they did, with varying degrees of success. Neither the Orthodox Church nor Islam managed to become strong political actors. No, it was nationalism in various guises – as a programme both for state legitimation and for ethnic mobilisation outside of and against the state – that made itself felt in numerous political arenas. Ethnic identities, already systematically institutionalised under the communist regime (see e.g. Brubaker 1996), were used as a strong resource by various groups – among those in power, and those in the opposition.

This development engendered renewed interest in nationalism studies generally, also influencing the interpretation of conflicts in other parts of the world. For instance, whereas communal strife in Northern Ireland had widely been seen as driven by religious confrontation, it was now increasingly regarded as an ethnic conflict, with the British pitted against the Irish. Also the Basque liberation movement in Spain underwent reinterpretation. The ETA terrorist organisation, Basque freedom fighters who hitherto had sailed under Marxist banners, now stepped forward as defenders of their nation against the allegedly oppressive Spanish state. Nationalism became a dominant mode of political legitimation, increasingly applied as an interpretive template for understanding political movements and dynamics around the globe.

Much energy and sophistication went into the study of the nature of this phenomenon: what exactly is a 'nation'? What should be understood by 'nationalism' (see Balakrishnan [1996] 2012; Beiner 1999; Calhoun 2007; Canovan 1996; Connor 1994; Gellner 1983; Smith [1986] 1991)? Does it have deep or shallow historical roots? Is it primarily a political or a cultural phenomenon? Is there one nationalism or several distinct varieties? – and so on. In this book, I simply accept as a fact that nationalism has become a ubiquitous feature of politics in the modern world. State leaders and 'ethnic entrepreneurs' alike employ nationalist rhetoric to further their political agendas and achieve specific goals. With this as the point of departure, I examine some of the ways in which nationalism has been used as a political strategy, by whom and for what purposes. Instead of 'what' and 'whence', I ask 'for what' and 'by what means'.

The former Soviet Union is an ideal place for studying these processes. Social movement theory has established how popular movements are particularly likely to appear when the 'political opportunity structures' are opening up (see e.g. McAdam et al. [2001] 2008; Tarrow [1998] 2011). By this it is normally meant that the state is moving from a more authoritarian structure towards a more liberal one. However, the Soviet Union and perestroika provided a far more radical kind of opening: the state itself simply disappeared.

In this introductory chapter, first I present some classic and some newer works that discuss the relationship between ideas, identities and interests in nationalism in general, and in the former Soviet Union in particular. Then I narrow in on two specific nationalist strategies and how they can be used to pursue political interests: the construction of boundaries between ethnic/national groups, and the creation and manipulation of national symbols.

Culturalists versus Instrumentalists

The relative weight to be accorded to identities versus interests in nationalist movements is a moot topic in the literature. The *culturalists* fiercely defend the importance of identities, whereas the *instrumentalists* downplay the identity aspect, highlighting instead how people pursue individual and group interests by promoting nationalist agendas. However, the differences between these stances are not necessarily as great as we have sometimes been led to believe. Those who emphasise the importance of culture, history and symbols tend to accept that clarion calls for 'identity' can be, and are being, used to promote certain interests; conversely, instrumentalists accept that most nationalists are not dyed-in-the-wool cynics but are also driven by ideas and ideologies. That being said, however, significant differences of opinion remain. My own research has led me to conclude that we should always look for the interest motives behind the actions of nationalists, and not blithely accept their own idealist justifications for their actions. This brings me closer to the instrumentalists than to their opponents. I agree with John Breuilly, who noted already in 1982:

> [t]o focus upon culture, ideology, identity, class or modernisation is to neglect the fundamental point that nationalism is, above and beyond all else, about politics, and that politics is about power . . . From that departure point we can go on to consider the contributions of culture, ideology, class and various other things. (Breuilly [1982] 1985, 1–2)

Culturalists

Ethno-symbolists such as Anthony Smith, Montserrat Guibernau and John Hutchinson have focused primarily on the historical, cultural, social and psychological mechanisms that lead up to the formation of national identity. Hutchinson denies that interests alone can explain why cultural divisions should act as reference and mobilising points for social and political projects. Rather, in appealing to various class and status groups, the rival symbolic repertoires 'do not so much express sectional struggles as different visions of the nation' (Hutchinson 2005, 87). However, ethno-symbolists also recognise that nationalism has been used as a device for achieving certain political outcomes. For instance, Guibernau notes how the rise of modern nationalism proved 'exceedingly useful' in refocusing people's loyalty away from the monarch towards the modern nation-state ([2007] 2011, 24). She also treats the state as a unified actor which 'employs strategies' in pursuit of a single national identity capable of uniting its citizens (([2007] 2011, 24). This perspective owes quite a bit to constructivism.

Anthony Smith also adopts a moderately constructivist approach to understanding the genesis of the nation and a national identity. He points out that the symbols and traditions, memories and myths of the nation are 'carefully selected' (Smith 2009, 31 and 72) – a use of language which presupposes active agents. However, he also emphasises that nation-builders are not at liberty to choose whichever symbols and traditions they fancy:

> Contrary to those who claim that these traditions are 'invented', ethno-symbolists argue that only those symbolic elements that have some prior resonance among a large section of the population . . . will be able to furnish the content of the proposed nation's political culture. (Smith 2009, 31)

He sees the role of nationalists as important, but more 'circumscribed' than in the schemes of the modernists (Smith 2009, 33 and 116).

To Smith, the deliberate construction of nations has not been uniform, but differs between the 'old' nations of the West and the newer states of Eastern Europe, Asia, Latin America and Africa:

> In Western Europe nations were largely unplanned. Outside the West they were largely the result of nationalist purposes and movements. [. . .] The West acquired nations almost by accident; in other parts of the globe nations were created by design. (Smith 1991, 100)

However, he does not pursue this line of inquiry further to investigate whether or how these various nation-designs have reflected specific material or other interests.

One of the most influential theoreticians within the culturalist school is Walker Connor. In a series of seminal articles from the 1970s to the early 1990s he outlined an original approach to nationalism studies which heavily stressed the non-rational, psychological nature of nationality (later collected in his *Ethnonationalism: The Quest for Understanding*, 1994). He directed a blistering attack against attempts to explain nationalism as a strategy of economic calculations – arguing that, although economic arguments may perhaps act as a catalyst or exacerbate national tensions, economic grievance or the lure of economic gain is not the main motor behind ethno-national conflict (Connor 1994, 145–64). In one of his pithy formulations, man is 'not a rational, but a national animal' (Connor 1994, 196–209); moreover, 'the essence' of nationalism should be sought in the sentiments of the masses rather than in the motives of elites (Connor 1994, 161). At the same time, perhaps unexpectedly, Connor provided several examples of politicians who cynically manipulated nationalist sentiments to their own benefit. For instance, he remarked about Napoleon that he was

> the first major figure to grasp the significance of joining ethnonational and state legitimacy. A Corsican of Genovese descent who fought for Corsican independence as a youth, Napoleon later realized that his personal ambitions could be better fulfilled by the harnessing of the masses' ethnonational zeal to an established state structure. (Connor 2004, 34)

In fact, there is no contradiction here. Precisely to the degree that people have strong, 'irrational' nationalist feelings will it be possible to exploit these sentiments instrumentally for non-national purposes – and Connor also provided several examples of this.

Modernists and instrumentalists

Already in *Thought and Change* (1964) the leading exponent of the modernist school in nationalism studies, Ernest Gellner, had argued that '[n]ationalism is not the awakening of nations to self-consciousness: it invents nations where they do not exist' (Gellner [1964] 1972, 168). This claim was attacked by another prominent theoretician working within the modernist paradigm, Benedict Anderson: 'Gellner is so anxious to show that nationalism masquerades under false pretences that he assimilates "intervention" to "fabrication" and "falsity", rather than to "imagining" and "creation"' (Anderson [1983] 1991, 6). While certain of Gellner's statements may indeed be construed as radical instrumentalism, a more common criticism of his theory is that it is premised on the very opposite: namely, functionalism. The main thrust of Gellner's classic *Nations and Nationalism* is that the phenomenon of modern nationalism is created not by acting individuals, but by impersonal socio-economic forces, industrialisation in particular (see e.g. Hall 1998).

The instrumentalists, we might say, start their quest for understanding where the ethno-symbolists leave off, and place the issue of *interest* at the centre of their inquiry. Paul Brass, perhaps the best-known representative of this school, accords a larger role in the construction of ethnicity and nationalism to elites than do the culturalists. Elites, in his view, 'draw upon, distort, and sometimes fabricate materials from the cultures of the groups they wish to represent in order to protect their well-being or existence or to gain political and economic advantage for their groups as well as for themselves' (Brass 1991 [1996], 8). Like Smith, he emphasises that tradition, memories and myths do not come in ready-made packages that nationalists adopt wholesale; instead, they select certain elements from them. Brass then goes beyond Smith in offering an explanation of *why* and *how* particular traditions are favoured by nationalists while others are discarded: leaders of ethnic movements 'invariably select from traditional cultures only those aspects that they think will serve to unite the group and which will be useful in promoting the interests of the group as they define them' (Brass 1991 [1996], 74).

However, Brass distances himself from what he describes as 'the extreme instrumentalist point of view', according to which ethnicity is to be seen as 'the pursuit of interest and advantage for members of groups whose cultures are infinitely malleable and manipulable by elites' (1991, 73). Indeed, he recognises that, even if new cultural groups may be created for purposes of economic and political domination, this does not mean that the primordialist (culturalist) perspective is irrelevant for *all* groups. Primordialism, Brass maintains, may provide a key to understanding groups with 'long and rich cultural heritages'. Therefore, primordialist and instrumentalist perspectives can be reconciled if we acknowledge that cultural groups differ in the strength and richness of their cultural traditions, he maintains (1991, 74).

The historian Joseph Rothschild is another influential scholar who has discussed the interest perspective in ethno-politics. Like Brass, he attempts to build bridges between culturalist and instrumentalist understandings of ethnicity and nationalism. In his *Ethnopolitics*, Rothschild suggests that the relationship between the 'emotional' and 'interest' component of politicised ethnicity is 'dialectical' (1981, 62). Neither is a mere epiphenomenon of the other, and neither functions alone. 'It is therefore insufficient – though partially correct – to explain the persistence and even the revival of ethnicity into and in the modern era as reflecting a primal "need to belong".' Allegiance to ethnic groups 'can be instrumentally advantageous in the competition and struggle for power, prestige, authority, position, wealth, and income' (Rothschild 1981, 248). Ethnicity is not always and everywhere politicised, but is likely to be so under certain conditions, as when

> those with a conscious interest in maintaining or changing these existing patterns, distributions, and structures determine that it would be instrumentally useful to them to mobilise ethnicity from a psychological

or cultural or social datum into a political resource and lever of action. (Rothschild 1981, 248)

Therefore, Rogers Brubaker would appear to be attacking straw men when he criticises 'instrumentalists' for allegedly adhering to the view that 'elite-driven nationalism is essentially a politics of interest, and that it therefore must be explained in instrumental terms' (Brubaker [1988] 1999, 289). He argues:

> nationalism is not always a subjectively rational or objectively 'successful' political strategy. It is not always possible, let alone easy, to 'stir up nationalist passions'. It is not always possible, let alone easy, to invoke the anxieties, the fears, the resentments, the perceptions and misperceptions, the self- and other-identifications, in short, the dispositions, the cast of mind against the background of which conspicuous and calculated nationalist stance-taking by elites can 'pay off' politically. (Brubaker [1998] 1999, 289)

The problem here concerns the word 'essentially' and the thrice-repeated 'always'. The charge that instrumentalists regard strategic use of nationalist arguments as the 'essence' of nationalism seems misplaced. To argue, as I do in this book, that groups and individuals can, and do, use nationalist rhetoric and stratagems in order to promote particular interests is not the same as saying that this is what they 'always' do, or that this is what nationalism, deep down, really 'is'.

Brubaker does not supply any references to scholars who adhere to the position he attacks, and in all likelihood he would be hard pressed to find anyone who subscribes to this bombastic view. Moreover, his criticism does not rule out that nationalism may 'sometimes' be a successful political strategy; or that, under certain conditions, it may be possible to stir up nationalist passions deliberately. In fact, Brubaker himself espouses such a moderately instrumentalist view, acknowledging that certain people act as 'ethnic entrepreneurs' – as 'specialists in ethnicity' who may live 'off' as well as 'for' ethnicity (Brubaker 2004, 10). Moreover, he sees the elitist, instrumentalist approach as also correct in denying that contemporary nationalist politics is driven by deeply rooted national identities and ancient conflicts. The problem with the instrumentalist view is not that it focuses on interests, but that it does so 'too narrowly' (Brubaker [1998] 1999, 292). To set up a choice between an instrumentalist and an identity-oriented approach to the study of nationalism Brubaker regards as 'a false opposition', since nationalism, he explains, is 'a way of seeing the world, a way of *identifying interests,* or more precisely, a way of specifying interest-bearing units, of *identifying the relevant units in terms of which interests are conceived*' ([1998] 1999, 291, emphasis in the original).

This perspective comes remarkably close to the one defended by an instrumentalist like Paul Brass.

Another instrumentalist researcher, V. P. Gagnon, has used this approach in explaining ethnic violence in the former Yugoslavia. Focusing on Serbian politics under Slobodan Milošević and Croatian politics under Franjo Tudjman prior to the outbreak of the war in Bosnia, he argues that the turn towards violent conflict was not caused by simmering ethnic hatred in the population or by external security concerns, but by the dynamics of within-group conflicts in the Serbian and Croatian political elites. Milošević and Tudjman were faced with challenger elites who sought to mobilise the population in ways that threatened their power. To prevent this, Milosevic and Tudjman used their control over the mass media to create an image of a 'threatened' Serbian and Croatian nation which had to rally around their leaders. Dissenting voices would have to be silenced and society politically homogenised. With a quasi-Clausewitzian turn of phrase (not used by Gagnon), one might say that war (abroad) was the continuation of (domestic) politics with other means.

> [T]he Yugoslav wars of the 1990s were the result of certain parts of the elite creating wars for their own purposes . . . [T]he violence was planned and carried out in very strategic ways by conservative elites in Belgrade and Zagreb, working closely with allies in the war zones . . . By constructing images of external threats and by provoking violent conflict along ethnic lines in their strategy of violence, the elites sought to shift the focus of political discourse away from issues of change toward grave injustices purportedly being inflicted on innocents, thus serving to demobilize – by silencing and marginalizing – those who posed the greatest threat to the status quo: the politically mobilized population. (Gagnon 2004, 179–80)

Generalising from his findings, Gagnon concludes: '[v]iolent conflict described and justified in terms of ethnic solidarity is not an automatic outgrowth of ethnic identity, or even of ethnic mobilization . . . [It] is the result of purposeful and strategic policies rather than irrational acts of the masses' (Gagnon 1997, 166). He maintains that it is far from easy to whip up ethnic hatred – indeed, he argues the exact opposite: ethnic identities are *not* powerful motivating forces, and simply appealing to such identities does not automatically induce a specific political behaviour (Gagnon 2004, xviii). This is precisely why nationalist leaders have recourse to violence to coerce their own population to rally behind the national cause (read: to walk in lockstep behind their leaders). Moreover, such warmongering strategies may be highly dangerous for the nationalist leaders themselves, as illustrated by the miserable denouement of Milošević's career.

Applying the Instrumentalist Perspective to the Soviet Union and its Successor States

During the Cold War there was broad consensus in the research community that the Soviet approach to 'the national question' was, by and large, dictated by manipulative and opportunistic intentions. However, whereas the Soviet Union was indeed an authoritarian state – and under Stalin, at least, a totalitarian one – the knee-jerk reaction of Western sovietologists in detecting hidden motives behind each and every public policy of the Soviet leaders sometimes led them to unreasonable conclusions. In some cases, they regarded the Soviet nationality policies as driven by pure cynicism when there were no grounds for that. Only after the fall of the communist system and the opening of Soviet archives has it become possible to piece together a more nuanced picture (Hirsch 2005; Martin 2001; Slezkine 1994; Suny 1993).

Already in 1903, Vladimir Lenin had insisted on including in the first programme of the Russian Social Democratic Party a clause to the effect that, when the Tsar was toppled, each nation in the Russian Empire should have the right to 'self-determination, up to and including secession' (Conquest 1967, 16; Kołakowski 1978, II, 399–404). This flew in the face of then-standard Marxist thinking that nationalism was a reactionary ideology and should not be tampered with; Lenin's stance on this issue was strongly censored by other communist leaders, such as Rosa Luxembourg (Kołakowski 1978, II, 90–2). Lenin, however, had not abandoned the view that nationalism was the deleterious force; rather, he hoped to exploit its power to recruit the support of the non-Russian nationalities in his struggle against the Tsarist Empire (Carrère d'Encausse 1992, 31; Nahaylo and Swoboda 1990, 351). Lenin never wavered in his adherence to large, non-national states, and he and other Bolsheviks always insisted that to grant the nationalities the right to secede was not tantamount to *endorsing* secession (Conquest 1967, 17). And of course, as long as the Communist Party remained in power in the Soviet Union, secession was not a realistic option for the non-Russians.

Even so, Western experts who insisted that 'commitment to a unitary state with a homogeneous citizenry lies at the heart of all Soviet nationality policies since Lenin' (Huttenbach 1990, 3) presented the Bolshevik approach to nationalism as more consistent and streamlined than it actually was. In the 1920s, the Soviets initiated a policy of *korenizatsia*, which granted a large number of non-Russian nationalities extensive cultural and linguistic rights – far wider, in fact, than virtually all other multinational states at the time. The Soviets pursued a policy of far-reaching 'affirmative action' *avant la lettre* (Martin 2001), and indulged in a national policy that has been described as 'the most extravagant celebration of ethnic diversity that any state had ever financed' (Slezkine 1994, 414). Many analysts, however, interpreted *korenizatsia* primarily as a sinister policy of 'divide and rule'. The development of written standards and codification of dozens of smaller languages should not necessarily be interpreted as a benign policy of liberal multiculturalism, according to Nekrich and Heller; instead, it served to 'prevent the unification of several nationalities around one major non-Russian language' (Nekrich and Heller 1986, 299).

In the standard Western narrative, the fine-grained, ethno-federal structure of the Soviet Union was deliberately designed in order to create ethnic tensions which the central authorities could exploit to increase their control. Paul Goble, for instance, explained that by various stratagems such as 'careful drawing of borders' and 'state-sponsored migration programs', the Soviet nationality policy created 'minority ethnic communities who were dependent for protection on the good will of the central authorities and thus could be counted on to do its bidding'(Goble 1995, 125).

The most detailed and systematic analysis of communist nationality policies – not only in the Soviet Union but also in other communist states – was made by Walker Connor. However, his explanation for the establishment of the ethnically based Soviet Federation as an attempt at deliberate 'gerrymandering' was ill conceived. Connor rightly pointed out that 'in not a single union republic, as originally created, did the titular group account for 90 per cent of the population'. This undermined the nationality principle which the entire structure allegedly was based on, he maintained. Almost equally injurious to the principle of 'one nation, one autonomous unit' was, in his view, the large number of people left outside of the republic bearing their designation: on average, the excluded segment of all groups approximated to 15 per cent of the total (Connor 1984, 303–4). In fact, the lack of ethnic purity in the population of the various Soviet republics was the result not of any 'gerrymandering', but of the great complexity of the national distribution (Kolstø 2013b; Schwartz 1990). The only way the Soviets could have created a greater degree of ethnic homogeneity in the autonomous territories they established would have involved massive population transfers – what we today would call 'ethnic cleansing'.

This should warn us against ascribing some hidden, nefarious motive to every single aspect of Soviet nationality policy. That being said, there can be no doubt that the Soviet leaders on many occasions did have few inhibitions against exploiting national sentiments for their purposes. The most egregious example is perhaps the switch to Russo-centric nationalism which occurred during World War II – in Russian parlance, the Great Patriotic War. In the state propaganda, the standard Marxist–Leninist clichés were suddenly abandoned, and the Soviet media was brimming over with praise of the superior Russian culture and the feats of Russian national heroes in the past. There is no reason to believe that Stalin had suddenly converted to Great Russian nationalism, and the most plausible explanation behind this ideological reorientation was the need to rally the Russian population in the war effort against the

Nazi invaders. Hitler's armies had already occupied large tracts of the non-Russian territories in the west and south – Ukraine, Belarus and Northern Caucasus – and it made sense to appeal specifically to the patriotic spirit of the ethnic Russians. Therefore, although we have no way of knowing with certainty what went on in Stalin's mind, David Brandenburger's cautious conclusion seems reasonable: 'Stalin and his entourage did not aim to promote Russian ethnic interests during these years so much as they attempted to foster a maximally accessible, populist sense of Soviet social identity through the instrumental use of russocentric appeals' (Brandenberger 2002, 4).

Although official state ideology in the Soviet Union was based on the explicitly materialist doctrine of Marxist–Leninism, the study of ethnicity and nationalism in the country, paradoxically enough, was dominated by a culturalist and primordialist paradigm (see e.g. Tishkov 2003). Also, after the breakup of the USSR, only a few scholars have broken with this way of thinking and adopted Western constructivist and instrumentalist approaches. Notably, Viktoria Koroteeva (2000) has analysed the economic factor in ethnic mobilisation in the Soviet Union during perestroika. She finds that post-Soviet nationalism came in both materialistic and idealistic varieties, and that economic motivation was particularly strong in Russian ethno-regions with rich deposits of natural resources, such as Tatarstan and Yakutia. Political leaders in these republics adopted laws and regulations to ensure that the revenues from these resources did not disappear into the federal coffers in Moscow but could be reaped locally (Koroteeva 2000).

The most prominent Russian exponent of constructivism in nationalism studies is undoubtedly Valery Tishkov. In his analysis of the actions of political leaders in Russia's autonomous republics in the early 1990s he adopted a radically instrumentalist position. Usage of ethno-national rhetoric benefited not only the population of the various republics collectively, but also – and even more – their leaders, he maintained. There existed an almost standard collection of arguments and methods that made it possible to mobilise and manipulate rank-and-file members of the nation. Chechen leaders, for instance, were 'a typical example of how political activists can use a collectivist strategy of nationalism to confirm themselves as "leaders of the nation", expressers of "the will of the people", and defenders of its interests' (Tishkov 1997, 217).

Therefore, the best way to forestall the dissolution of the Soviet Union would have been to slake the appetite of republican leaders for vainglory and luxury, Tishkov believed. He relates how, in a personal encounter with former General Secretary Mikhail Gorbachev, he had indicated that the best way to counter the secessionist campaigns in the republics would have been to allow republican leaders to have personal jets for business flights. Then they would not have had to pursue secessionism in order to satisfy their vanity and greed. That was a suggestion presented in all earnestness, he insists (Tishkov 1997, 44).

Tishkov argued that regional leaders soon learned that challenging the centre could prove far more effective and legitimate when framed in the language of ethno-national demands (1997, 242) – but, he noted, the ethno-nationalist weapon was nevertheless not brandished everywhere. The large number of autonomous republics in Russia provides ample material for comparisons, and Tishkov believed that he could detect clear patterns. Ethno-nationalist rhetoric was unlikely to be wielded in two quite different situations: on the one hand, when it was a futile strategy unlikely to succeed; and, on the other, when it was unnecessary, since the objectives of the ethnic elites could be also achieved without using it. For instance, in Karelia, Komi, Yakuta and Buryatia, the titulars comprise less than one-third of the population; here it seemed too risky to inscribe strong ethno-political demands into official texts. On the other hand, in republics such as North Ossetia, the titular nation enjoys such a strong demographic preponderance that there was no need to provide additional safeguards for their political dominance through provocative statements. In between these two extreme, however, were a large number of republics with a rough demographic balance between titulars and non-titulars – and here fierce ethno-political struggles erupted:

> Thus, the language of ethnonationalism proved to be an instrumentalist tool used mainly in highly competitive situations when the proportion of titulars to the rest of the population lay around 40/60, and where power dispositions made it possible to impose political ethnonationalism through formal legal procedures. (Tishkov 1997, 58)

In the early 1990s, Tishkov belonged to a group of advisers around Boris Yeltsin on ethnic and national affairs, and it could arguably be said that he lacked the necessary academic distance to pass judgement on these cases. However, Western scholars who have studied post-Soviet nationalist conflicts support his assessments, at least up to a point. Philip Roeder (1998), for instance, has documented how ethnicity was used as a resource in centre–periphery struggles in the late Soviet and early post-Soviet periods. The political leadership in the republics consisted disproportionately of titulars who had built up what Roeder calls 'ethnic machines' – a retinue of co-ethnics who made up their power base and who in return were provided with lucrative positions and career possibilities. As long as the Soviet communist system remained intact, this entire structure was dressed in a cloak of communist rhetoric – but when the unitary state began to crumble, the republican leaders, with dazzling alacrity, switched their rhetoric from communism to ethnic nationalism, using that as leverage to achieve full independence for their republics.

As Roeder points out, there were also 'ethnic entrepreneurs' in the republics outside the corridors of power. However, even if they used more stringent nationalist language than the former communist elites, these outside challengers seldom managed to oust the powerholders (Roeder 1998, 97–8). Ethnicity proved to be an extremely valuable resource in the republics' struggle against the central Soviet authorities, but ethnic outbidding *within* the republics rarely succeeded. The ethnic card was played most effectively by those already in positions of power.

However, analysing the civil war in Moldova in 1992, Stuart Kaufman (2001) found an asymmetry with regard to the mobilisation on the two warring sides: right-bank Moldovan mobilisation was mass-led and fuelled by popular chauvinism, but in Transnistria, he maintains, the initiative behind the confrontation was taken by the economic and political elites. They used their influence to stir up hostility towards the cultural policies of the Moldovan nationalists in right-bank Moldova, in particular against the new language law, which would require them to conduct their business in the new state language, Moldovan. The left-bank Russophone elites had much to lose – their jobs, influence and perquisites – but also much to gain by fanning a violent conflict, such as increased power and career opportunities for themselves (Kaufman 2001, 146). Moldovan nationalists had, in fact, designed the new language law in such a way that it exempted ordinary Russophone workers from its most onerous requirements – but the Dniestr elites, with their control of the local media, whipped up ethnic fears to ensure that the local rank and file fell in line behind them in resisting it.

In her *Constructing Grievance: Ethnic Nationalism in Russia's Republics* (2011), Elise Giuliano scrutinised much of the same material as Tishkov had discussed and reached similar, albeit more nuanced, conclusions. Like him, she found significant differences among the republics: while large crowds rallied under nationalist banners in Tatarstan, Tuva and Chechnya, and to some degree in Bashkortostan and Yakutia, mobilisation among titular nationalities failed to get off the ground in Chuvashia, Mari El or North Ossetia. To account for these differences Giuliano examined various parameters, and concluded that most of them had low explanatory value: demographic composition, for instance, which Tishkov had regarded as decisive, did not account for much in her view. And while attempts have been made to explain Chechen secessionism by pointing to how the population had been collectively deported from their homeland in the Caucasus under Stalin, this traumatic history was shared by various other peoples, like the Balkars and Karachais, who remained quiescent. Only by focusing on *the content of the nationalist messaging* did Giuliano find significant correlations: those titular leaders in the republics who focused on economic grievances managed to rally large parts of the population under their banners, whereas those who concentrated on language, history and other cultural issues failed.

Successful nationalist leaders, whom Giuliano, like Roeder, refers to as ethnic and nationalist 'entrepreneurs', created stories about economic inequalities along ethnic lines: members of their ethnic groups allegedly faced obstacles to economic achievement caused by the dominance of ethnic Russians in the most prestigious and well-paid jobs. Local Russians in the republic enjoyed access to desirable resources, while titulars were presented as being concentrated in low-status occupations and in the rural economies. There was some truth in this, Giuliano acknowledges, but it was only one part of the picture: while titulars were indeed underrepresented to some extent in white-collar jobs compared to Russians, an equally powerful story could also be told about non-Russian empowerment and socio-economic advances over the last generations. There continued to be structural economic gaps between Russians and titulars in many republics, but the gaps had been closing and there was no reason to think that this trend should not continue. There were no 'blocked opportunities', but ethnic grievances could be 'constructed' by elites who imbued economic conditions and structures with ethnic meaning.

In Giuliano's view, ethnic entrepreneurs cannot construct group grievances 'utterly divorced from objective conditions' (Giuliano 2011, 17). What made the narrative about a relative deprivation of titulars particularly credible in the early 1990s was the general collapse of the Soviet economy at the time, which created immense job insecurity for millions of Soviet citizens. Even if economic hardships hit virtually everyone, irrespective of ethnicity, this could be – and was – given an ethnic spin. While the titulars' share of the pie might not be shrinking, the size of the pie itself was. It was a rational strategy for titulars to try to exploit the power vacuum created by the weakening of the central authorities under Gorbachev and Yeltsin to support ethnic parties and movements that would help them achieve a larger slice of the pie in the future.

Giuliano, however, warns against viewing nationalists as exclusively strategic actors, cynically manipulating issues they know would strike a chord in the population. 'They often earnestly believe in the ideas they articulate . . . In Russia, nationalist leaders acted both expressively *and* strategically' (Giuliano 2011, 18, emphasis added). Giuliano's analysis has proven fruitful and has been applied by, among others, Marc Dorpema, in a reinterpretation of 'ethnic war' in Abkhazia as an exercise in 'imbuing . . . economic conditions and structures with ethnic meaning' (Dorpema 2021, 3).

* * *

In the early part of this book, I show how an interest perspective on ethnic strife in Russia and the Soviet Union can add important insights that are easily overlooked in a traditional identity perspective. In Chapter 2, I argue that the conventional understanding of the emergence of Russian anti-Semitism in the second half of the nineteenth century is faulty. Xenophobia, obscurantism and religious bigotry have normally been adduced to explain the emergence of the anti-Jewish agitation; however, although these factors no doubt played a certain role, I find that far more mundane, economic motives were more important. Also, the most common materialistic explanation, according to which the anti-Semitism started with peasants who were being fleeced by greedy Jews, is misconceived. In reality, pogroms almost invariably started not in the countryside but in the towns and cities, and the main instigators were artisans, merchants and others who plied the same trades as the Jews, later also professionals such as lawyers. Whipping up anti-Jewish hatred was a means of getting rid of troublesome competitors. Indicatively, one of the most important aspects of discrimination against the Jews was the introduction of quota restrictions limiting their admission to institutions of higher learning. The religious factor, as well as racism imported from Western Europe, should not be entirely dismissed, but the main driving forces were economic interests and professional rivalry. This can be documented from the writings of Russian anti-Semites themselves; it is also how most Jews at the time understood the situation.

In Chapter 3, I show how the job competition dynamics which Elise Giuliano explained so forcefully in her book did not play out according to her script in some parts of the Soviet Union during perestroika and in the 1990s. In Central Asia, rather than rational political nationalism geared towards capturing a larger share of the most prestigious parts of the labour market, there were seemingly irrational ethnic riots, often victimising hapless, weak minority groups. In my interpretation, this ethnic frenzy was, to a large extent, caused by growing mass-level unemployment – an unprecedented phenomenon in the postwar USSR – due to extremely high population growth in this region. In the more developed European part of the Soviet Union, however, there was a job competition situation more in line with Giuliano's pattern. In the Baltics, titulars had low fertility rates and very high levels of education. Here, there were enough menial jobs to go around – indeed, often a dearth of applicants – but, as in virtually all societies, fierce competition for the most prestigious and well-paid positions. Therefore, I argue, ethnic conflict in these two very different parts of the USSR was driven by distinct sociological developments: population growth in the Asian republics, and increasing educational levels in Ukraine, Moldova and the Baltics.

To be sure, the rhetoric used by titulars in Estonia and Latvia was different from what Giuliano had found in Tatarstan: since these republics had been independent states in the interwar period, the titulars here could use legal arguments about state reconstitution which were not available to the Tatars – but many of the ethno-social dynamics were similar.

As Tishkov, Roeder, Giuliano and many other researchers agree, in most former Soviet republics the titular ethnic groups gained the upper hand in inter-ethnic conflicts (Moldova, as studied by Kaufman, was an exception). The concept of 'titular', however, was rarely used in the nationalist rhetoric, although it was known. '*Titul'nyi*' is a calque from English, regarded as an alien concept and not carrying much legitimacy: strictly speaking, it merely indicates that the name of the republic/state and that of this particular ethnic group is the same. The titulars themselves have preferred another term, '*korennoi narod*': 'those with roots' in the area. In Chapter 4, I examine how this concept was put to good use by titulars in interethnic competition in the 1990s.

The obverse concept of '*nekorennoi*' implies that persons or groups do *not* have local roots; they are 'alien' and somehow 'do not quite belong' – at best, they are 'guests'. The rootedness card was mostly played in those places where other factors, such as language proficiency or demographic preponderance, could not so easily be used as an argument for titular prerogatives in politics and in the economy. Such was the situation in Kazakhstan, for instance, where the titular urbanite elite was much more fluent in Russian than in the 'titular' language, Kazakh – but they could claim to be the 'sons of the soil': their forebears had been living on the Kazakh steppes for centuries, in contrast to the Slav settlers who had migrated there later. In Bashkortostan, an autonomous republic in Russia, the titulars made up less than a quarter of the total population but, as I document, managed to monopolise politics to an astonishing degree, not least by posing as the '*korennoi*' – 'autochthonous', 'indigenous' – group.

STRATEGIC BOUNDARY DRAWING

In 1969, the Norwegian anthropologist Fredrik Barth wrote an article which fundamentally changed our understanding of how ethnic groups and social identities are constituted (Barth [1969] 1998; see also Cohen 2000; Kolstø 2005b; Vermeulen and Govers 1994; Wimmer 2013). The traditional view had been that groups are held together by the 'cultural stuff' they have in common, but this had proven problematic, for various reasons. The common-culture approach implicitly ignored cultural differences within groups, made it difficult to explain cultural change, and did not allow sufficiently for cultural overlap and continuity between and among groups. Barth saw the boundary between groups as the locus of identity formation and differentiation. As a social anthropologist, he focused on the role of boundary markers – or diacritica – in relations between ethnic groups. Later researchers have expanded this approach to include the study of nationalism (Conversi 1995; Eriksen 1993), macro-regions (Neumann 1999) and social groups in general (Jenkins 1996).

According to Barth, it is in the contrast and interaction with outsiders, with 'the Other', that group identity is constructed and maintained. Indeed, without such interaction, identity formation would hardly take place at all. As Barth's younger colleague, Thomas Hylland Eriksen, has expressed it, 'if a setting is wholly mono-ethnic, there is effectively no ethnicity, since there is nobody there to communicate cultural difference to' (Eriksen 1993, 34).

Like all pioneering works, Barth's new approach has been readjusted and refined by later scholars. He had focused primarily on material and visible objects as boundary markers: however, boundaries of the kind we are discussing here are not something 'out there' but are located in 'the minds of their beholders', Anthony Cohen points out (Cohen [1985] 2008, 12; see also Guibernau 2013, 37). This also means that 'boundaries perceived by some may be utterly imperceptible to others' (Cohen [1985] 2008, 13). As Mach argues (1993, 57), almost all features of culture may become the substance of the boundary if they divide one's own group from the other.

Moreover, the ethnic boundary should not be regarded as a self-functioning mechanism that perpetuates itself without human interference. Boundaries are social constructs that require active maintenance. Barth called the boundary markers that delineate groups 'diacritica'. Such diacritica are selected from a group's available fluctuating and diverse cultural repertoire. 'An imagined community is promoted by making a few such diacritica highly salient and symbolic, that is, by an active construction of the boundary.' This will always be the joint work of two differentiated groups, Barth points out, but stronger groups will normally be better able to impose and transform the relevant idioms (Vermeulen and Covers 1994, 16).

Boundary maintenance, then, is a matter of *power relations*, and hence of politics. Almost invariably, leaders of putative political groups justify their claims in terms of cultural and national difference. For this reason, 'much of the activity of political innovators is concerned with the codification of idioms: the selection of signals for identity and the assertion of value for these cultural diacritica, and the suppression or denial of relevance for other differentiae' (Barth [1969] 1998, 35).

Daniel Posner (2005) emphasises that group boundaries are not only contingent and malleable but also multilayered. All members of society belong to several different groups; which potentially salient cleavages are activated in each situation, he explains, will depend on the benefits to be drawn from affiliating with it. In her self-identification, a citizen may move up or down the scale and identify with groups of different size. In this game of strategic identity, where the context defines the contours of the optimal group, an individual may activate membership in several different groups simultaneously. Changes in the boundaries of the political arena generate changes in the dimensions of ethnic identity that are mobilised (Posner 2005, 143). This general framework Posner applies to an analysis of politics in Zambia.

The Zambian population consists of a high number of ethnic groups, and although virtually all politicians insist that communal identities should not interfere with politics, they nevertheless do. The ethnic landscape, however, can be divided up in two very different ways, and the concept of ethnicity as Posner employs it (not in frequent use in Zambia) denotes two different kinds of identities: language and tribe. The language groups are large and few – roughly four or five – whereas there are more than five dozen tribes, all of which belong to one of the larger, overarching language groups. Using terminology from rational choice theory, Posner explains that the ultimate goal of identity selection in Zambian politics is to create a 'minimum winning coalition'. The optimal outcome for politicians, as well as their followers, is to belong to a group which is just large enough to prevail in the electoral district to which one belongs, but not so large that the spoils have to be shared with more people than necessary. Therefore, in national elections it makes sense to identify with the entire region of residence in order to get 'one's own people' elected, but in local elections it would be rational to scale down and identify with one of the subgroups within the region. This means that in national elections you will naturally vote for candidates who belong to your language group, but in local elections information about language is normally irrelevant, as most voting districts are basically monolingual.

The physical boundaries of political units need not change in order for the boundaries of the effective political arena to be altered, Posner argues (2005, 145). This may also occur with a change in political institutions, in the rules of the game, such as a change from one-party rule to multiparty rule (or vice versa). In a multiparty system, voters have more information about the candidates than in a one-party system, and must take into account the (ethnic) profile not only of the individual candidates but also of the party to which they belong.

Posner adopts an unabashedly instrumentalist approach. Identity choices are the product of deliberate decision designed to maximise payoffs. These payoffs may be material but also immaterial, such as prestige, social acceptance or protection. At the same time, Posner wants to move beyond a purely elitist account and incorporate the mechanisms behind the identity choices of rank-and-file members of a community. Whereas most instrumentalist accounts, he claims, tell a story about the passive socialisation of the masses, he wants to emphasise their 'active, strategic investment' (Posner 2005, 24).

Like Posner, Andreas Wimmer (2013) underscores how people behave strategically in their identity choices. 'They try to align themselves with certain individuals rather than others; they promote certain types of classification – of defining who is what – rather than others; and they do so in an attempt to gain recognition, power, or access to resources' (Wimmer 2013, 44). More than Barth, Wimmer focuses on *agency*, the *making* of the ethnic boundary, whether by political movements or through the everyday interactions of individuals.

However, Wimmer warns against exaggerating the hegemonic power of the dominant modes of ethnic boundary-making, pointing out that counter-discourses always exist. A plurality of rival boundary projects, then, are normally available, and 'an actor will pursue the particular strategy and the level of ethnic differentiation that she perceives to further her interests, given her endowment with economic, political, and symbolic resources' (Wimmer 2013, 93). Actors relate to existing boundaries by trying to change them, or to de-emphasise them and enforce new modes of categorisation.

Wimmer distinguishes between two basic types of boundary change: *boundary expansion* and *boundary contraction*. In the first case, an actor may attempt to shift the existing boundary to a more inclusive level. As the most common variety of boundary expansion he mentions nation-building, which is a strategy for amalgamating all ethnic groups within a country under one national identity. Individuals of varying ethnic backgrounds may accept the offer of assimilation and cross the boundary into the 'nation' (Wimmer 2013, 99). In a second, opposite strategy, the identity boundary is moved to a lower level in multitiered systems of ethnic specification. Contraction, he explains, is particularly attractive for individuals and groups who do not have access to the centres of a political arena. Wimmer does not refer to Ernest Gellner's par-able of 'Megalomanians and Ruritanians', but his model has a strong affinity to Gellner's understanding of the two venues open to minorities in a multi-ethnic state: either assimilation into the majority culture (through Wimmer's 'boundary expansion'), or secession and the establishment of a smaller separate nation-state (through 'boundary contraction') (Gellner [1983] 1990, 58–62).

Building on Wimmer's model, I would emphasise – referring back to Barth's original conception – that boundary drawing is the outcome of a 'joint effort' between those on the putative 'inside' and those on the 'outside'. My self-image is strongly influenced by how others see me, and this is also true for groups. Auto-images and hetero-images are closely linked to each other: identity forma-tion is an action–reaction process, and the outcomes of these dynamics are not easily predictable. The members of the weaker cultural group may accept the invitation to become a part of the larger community – or this invitation may be perceived as an intolerable encroachment, an attempt to obliterate their 'self'. The latter reaction leads to what Wimmer refers to as 'counter-discourses' and 'resistance' (2013, 95). We encounter an example of this in Chapter 5, where I discuss how nationalists in Ukraine, Belarus and Georgia have reacted to Rus-sian overtures to see themselves as part of a larger Russia-dominated culture.

Second, I hold that inclusion and exclusion may be combined by the same actors as two aspects of the same strategy.[1] In a typology developed in *Myths and Boundaries in South-Eastern Europe* (Kolstø 2005b, 16–27), I identified four frequent boundary-making myths: myths of *sui generis*, of *martyrium*, of *antiquitas* and of *antemurale*. To claim that 'we' are *sui generis* is to say that we are unique, and have nothing in common with our neighbours. A myth of *mar-tyrium* is based on the claim that we are the victims of discrimination or atroci-ties committed by others – an extremely powerful legitimation strategy in the modern world. A myth of *antiquitas* we have encountered above in the claim among some titular groups in former Soviet republics of being the country's *korennoi* or original people; and, as I will show in Chapter 5, the *antemurale* myth has been employed in Ukraine, Belarus and Georgia, where the titular culture shares many features with Russia.

Historically, the *antemurale* concept derives from the designation of certain Central and Eastern European countries in the late Middle Ages and early modern era, such as the Habsburg monarchy, Venice and Poland, as *antemurale Christianitatis*. The first to use the concept were popes who wanted to rally support for concerted Christian mobilisation against the Ottomans in order to evict the Muslims from Europe. The *antemurale* message addressed the frontline countries bordering on Muslim areas that would inevitably be heavily involved in this battle. Often, however, the religion to be defended was more narrowly defined as Western Christianity, or Roman Catholicism in particular, rather than Christianity as such. The Poles, therefore, also defended their country and the civilisation it represented against another Christian nation, the Orthodox Muscovites (Mach 1993, 185; Lawaty 2015). Similarly, the Croats often viewed the position of the Orthodox Serbs as highly suspect. In many cases they were placed 'beyond the Pale' or 'outside the gates' (see e.g. Žanić 2005, 35–76).

One might think that in today's secularised Europe the very concept of being *antemurale* would be anachronistic: however, while most Western Europeans may not profess any strong religious identity, the *antemurale* mental frame is flexible enough to be adapted to new historical circumstances. For instance, in the twentieth century many anti-communist Poles updated the anti-Russian *antemurale* myth, directing it against Soviet atheists. In most contemporary versions, the concept of being 'European' has been retained, but is now more related to secular values – individualism, entrepreneurial spirit, respect for human rights and so on – which the *antemurale* nation claims to represent against the allegedly non-European neighbours.

An *antemurale* group regards itself as occupying a frontier territory of *a larger civilisation* confronted by hostile aliens 'outside the gates'. This self-perception has been a major boundary-creating mechanism in the self-perception of Ukrainian, Belarusian and Georgian nationalists, defining their country's position between Europe, on the one hand, and Russia, on the other. They present themselves as belonging to a qualitatively different civilisation from the Russians, even though they are close neighbours, have belonged for long periods to the same state, and have traditionally adhered to the same religion – Eastern Orthodoxy. Even so, the *antemurale* ideology presents these peoples as frontline defenders of European civilisation against the allegedly 'non-European' Russians. This myth tears down the boundary between their nation and a large, positively valued civilisation in one direction – westwards – while building a solid 'wall' (*murus*) towards the East, vis-à-vis the Russians.

The Russians have not reciprocated this kind of thinking by erecting a similar mental boundary as regards the Ukrainians, Belarusians or Georgians. On the contrary, they often *de-emphasise* or even *deny* any differences in identity between themselves and their Orthodox neighbours. This asymmetry reflects power relations. Weaker and smaller groups, and groups with unclear or weak collective identity, are likely to employ *antemurale* arguments to distinguish themselves from stronger, overweening neighbours, whereas stronger groups (larger, with more material resources, with a robust self-awareness), will de-emphasise their identity distance from culturally similar neighbouring groups, subsuming them under their own instead. Indeed, many Russians regard Ukrainians and Belarusians as merely subgroups of a larger 'Russian' nation.

But among some Russian nationalists too a redefinition of boundaries has taken place since the dissolution of the Soviet unitary state. Historically, Russian nationalism has been linked to the state: Russians in general, and Russian nationalists in particular, have primarily identified with the vast and multinational Russian Empire. While they have been conscious of the difference between 'Russians' and 'non-Russians', ethnicity was not their main identification criterion. Instead, the outer boundary of their collective identity coincided with the borders of the state. This self-perception continued into the Soviet period but, as I show in Chapter 6, slowly began to change after the dissolution of the unitary state in 1991. Whereas Soviet nostalgia and a hankering for the lost empire continued to be a strong force in the 1990s, after the turn of the millennium a new generation of Russian nationalists came to the fore. Rather than the state, the focus of their identity and loyalty has been the cultural group of ethnic Russians – a significant contraction of the imagined national community.

There were probably three main reasons for this reorientation. First, as discussed in Chapters 3 and 4, titular nationalism in the non-Russian republics since perestroika had been predominantly ethnic; when parts of the Russian nationalist movement fell in line with this general trend, they were affected with a 'contagion' from other nationalist movements in the former Soviet Union. Second, after the breakup of the Soviet Union, Russians had become citizens of a state that was far more ethnically homogeneous. Their group, the Russians, now made up the vast majority within this state– around 80 per cent, as against 50 per cent in the Soviet Union. Third, ethno-nationalism in the new Russian nationalist movement was propelled by migrant anxiety, as Russia after the turn of the millennium experienced an influx of 'guest workers' from Central Asia and the South Caucasus: a cultural underclass regarded by many Russians as alien, although they came from countries that had belonged to the same state as Russia, the Soviet Union.

The reorientation of many Russians from a Soviet to a Russian identity linked to the Russian Federation can be regarded as an exercise in nation-building (Kolstø 2000). Andreas Wimmer, as we saw, considered nation-building as resulting from boundary expansion, and indeed, when many local ethnicities are amalgamated into one larger, national culture this is the case.

However, nation-building can also follow from boundary contraction, when larger, multiethnic states are divided into smaller, more homogenous entities. That is what we could observe in the post-Soviet states after the dissolution of the USSR, including Russia.

After around 2010, some of these new Russian ethno-nationalists declared that, if they came to power, they would be prepared to embrace Western-style democracy – including the full package of minority rights for non-Russians. The new 'democratisation' of Russian ethno-nationalism was based on highly pragmatic reasoning: as the non-Russians had now been reduced to some 20 per cent of the population, they did not threaten the ethnic quality of the state, and a liberal minority policy would not jeopardise the dominant role of ethnic Russians in 'their own' country.

SYMBOLS AND RITUALS AS NATION-BUILDING INSTRUMENTS

Among the most important diacritica in ethnic and national boundary-making we find various kinds of symbols, myths and rituals (Armstrong 1982, 8–9; Kolstø 2005b, 16–34). The crucial role of symbols and rituals in the construction of any society has been recognised at least since Emile Durkheim's seminal study, *The Elementary Forms of Religious Life* (1912). While primarily concerned with the social origins and consequences of religious beliefs and practices in premodern, religious societies, Durkheim assumed that the dynamics he had identified lived on in secularised forms in modern societies as well:

> There can be no society that does not experience the need at regular intervals to maintain and strengthen their collective feelings and ideas that provide it coherence and distinct individuality. This moral remaking can be achieved only through meetings, assemblies, and congregations in which the individuals, pressing close to one another, reaffirm in common their common sentiments. Such is the origin of ceremonies that, by their object, by their results, and by the techniques used, are not different in kind from ceremonies that are specifically religious. (Durkheim [1912] 1995, 429)

Lars Erik Blomqvist has claimed that 'history had produced no single society where the power of symbols has not been recognised' (Arvidsson and Blomqvist 1987, 7). Similarly, Abner Cohen ([1974] 1976, 30) writes: '[s]ocial relationships develop through and are maintained by symbols. We "see" groups through their symbols. Values, norms, rules, and abstract concepts like honour, prestige, rank, justice, good and evil are made tangible through symbols.' Or, as Kertzer puts since it, 'Far from being window dressing on the reality that is the nation, symbolism is the stuff of which nations are made . . . Without rites and symbols, there are no nations' (1988, 6 and 179).

There is, however, considerable disagreement as to precisely how this effect is produced, and to what degree symbols really contribute to the production of social cohesion and national unity.

As argued by Gabriella Elgenius (2011b, 397), '[s]ocial life is a repository of symbols, whether in the form of flags, ceremonies, heroes, icons, capitals, statues, war memorials, museums or football teams, which – at their core – will mark, celebrate and glorify social groups'. However, she warns against a functionalist Durkheimian interpretation that sees this as always and everywhere producing consensus and unity.

In contrast to other kinds of signs, such as signals and indexes, symbols have no fixed meaning. Abner Cohen ([1974] 1976, 23) defines symbols as 'objects, acts, concepts, relationships or linguistic formations that stand *ambiguously* for a multiplicity of meanings, evoke emotions, and impel men to action' (emphasis in the original). The meaning of a symbol cannot be deduced. Symbols have value and meaning only for those who recognise them. The inherently ambiguous character of symbols makes them eminently usable for nation-building purposes (Abner Cohen [1974] 1976, 36–7; Anthony Cohen 2008, 23; Guibernau 2013, 38 and 97; Kertzer 1988, 11; Mach 1993, 30 and 51.)

According to David Kertzer (1988, 11), 'the same symbols may be understood by different people in different ways. This trait is especially important in the use of ritual to build political solidarity in the absence of consensus.' This understanding also lies at the core of Anthony Cohen's celebrated study of the symbolic construction of society. He maintains that 'symbols do not so much express meaning as give us the capacity to make meaning' (Cohen 2008, 15). Because symbols are malleable, they may be made to 'fit' the circumstances of the individual. The range of meanings in concepts such as patriotism, duty, love and peace 'can be glossed over in a commonly accepted symbol – precisely because it allows its adherents to attach their own meanings to it. They share the symbol, but do not necessarily share its meanings' (Cohen 2008, 15). However, this view, I will argue, overstretches the ability of symbols to 'sweep differences under the carpet' through their ambiguity. It presupposes that members of society are unaware of, or at least ignore, the fact that their fellow citizens attach rather different, sometimes even opposite, meanings to the symbols from those they do themselves. That assumption is unwarranted, for the simple reason that people communicate not only through (non-verbal) symbols but also through (the verbal symbol of) *language*. An example which Kertzer (1988, 92) uses brings this out clearly: 'The American flag can be as valuable to the civil rights marchers as to the Ku Klux Klan in defining what is good for the community.' We may legitimately ask to what degree the flag, in such a situation, can be said to contribute to social solidarity and recognition among the various flag bearers of belonging to the same community.

National symbols, Michael Geisler (2005) reminds us, are heatedly contested just as often as they are embraced. It therefore seems more fruitful to regard nations, as John Hutchinson does (2005), as 'zones of conflict'. Within nations, 'cultural wars' are waged between groups that see themselves as members of the same nation but uphold different visions of what that nation is or ought to be. '[T]hese rival symbolic repertoires, in appealing to multiple class and status groups, do not so much express sectional struggles as different visions of the nation' (Hutchinson 2005, 87).

Symbols are extremely important as boundary markers between groups, especially when they are enacted through rituals:

> The consciousness of forming a community, such as the nation, is created through the use of symbols and the repetition of rituals that constitute and strength the belief in a common identity shared by its members. By bringing about occasions on which they can feel united and by displaying emblems – symbols that represent its unity – the nation establishes the boundaries that distinguish it from others. (Guibernau 2013, 37)

Rituals can be regarded as performed symbols. They are particularly powerful emotionally for several reasons:

- Rituals engage more than one sense, not only sight but also hearing and even smell and touch (Cerulo 1993).
- Rituals engage the participants directly; you are asked not merely to watch a flag being hoisted from afar, but to carry the flag yourself, in your hands (Kolstø 2006).
- Rituals are performed together with others, often in large groups who are in agreement with each other; contested interpretations of the symbols are held at bay. Of course, sometimes counter-demonstrators challenge the same symbols on the same day, even on the same spot, lining the route of the parade or demonstration with hecklers. But this arguably can function as an additional boost to identity-building among the original group of demonstrators. (Guibernau 2013, 104).
- For that reason, participating in a ritual means that your sympathies are out in the open. They are no longer something you can hide: it becomes a testimony to the world (or, with a ritual performed in a closed society, a testimony to the other members of the group) (see e.g. Guibernau 2013, 105; Zuev and Virchow 2014).

However, Elgenius (2011a, 13) maintains that, although rituals such as national days may 'provide a unifying narrative, cohesion and solidarity do not necessarily follow their introduction. Whereas national day ceremonies are expressions of societal worship and affirmation of values, the effect of this worship continues to be assumed rather than proved.'

Guibernau (2013, 105) distinguishes between rituals of 'inclusion' and 'exclusion'. I feel that this distinction is neither necessary nor helpful. It would be more fruitful to distinguish between the *exclusionary and inclusionary aspect* or *exclusionary and inclusionary usages* of all rituals: they exclude precisely through the process of including some, but not all. That is what boundary-making is all about.

Barth's concept of the boundary can be extended to a study not only of national and ethnic groups but also of social groups *within* the putative nations (see also Bourdieu 1991, 120–4). It can fruitfully be employed to study contentious politics among various groups who engage in struggles to define 'the nation' – what Hutchinson calls 'cultural wars'. Symbols will also appear here as both weapons and bones of contention. The contentious issues in nation-building struggles may be religious (secular versus clerical, or competing confessional orientations); linguistic (which idiom should be the basis for the standard national language, or state monolingualism versus bi- or multilingualism); class wars; rivalry between regions; or political (rightists vs. leftists) (see e.g. Ross 2009).

The most powerful institutional actor in the modern world is the state. As Andreas Wimmer notes, state institutions 'are in a privileged position to make their preferred ethnic distinctions politically relevant, publicly acknowledged, and culturally legitimate through commemorative holidays and public rituals' (Wimmer 2013, 64).

National symbols perform an important function not only as catalysts for the formation and maintenance of national identity but also in 'fusing a *nation* to a *state*' (Geisler 2005, xv, emphasis in the original; see also Edelman 1985; Wilentz [1985] 1999). As pointed out by Michael Walzer, 'the state is invisible; it must personified before it can be seen, symbolized before it can be loved, imagined before it can be conceived' (1967, 194, quoted in Kertzer 1988, 6). Symbols provide such visual and auditive identification anchors (Kolstø 2006). As Kertzer (1988, 5) has observed, we are ruled by power holders whom we never encounter except in highly symbolic settings: 'Through symbolism we recognize who are the powerful and who are the weak, and through the manipulation of symbols the powerful reinforce their authority.' Elgenius (2011a, 16–17) argues that 'symbols and ceremonies have come to constitute tools through which nationalist regimes attempt to mobilize populations in pursuit of power.' The Putin regime has been very adroit in handling this tool.

In Chapter 7, I show how the Putin regime has used symbolic innovation to strengthen its emotional grip on the Russian population by inventing a new emblem, the orange–black ribbon of St George. This symbol has a dual provenance, as it is based on both a Tsarist and a Soviet military order – which makes it possible to sell to different ideological camps in Russian society, ranging from monarchists and Orthodox Christians to Soviet nostalgics and Stalinists. At the same time, this symbol functions as a boundary marker against the Western-leaning liberal intelligentsia, who reject this symbol precisely because it is an important pillar in the legitimation strategy of the Putin regime. In that way, the St George ribbon functions as a symbol of both inclusion and exclusion.

The emotional power of the ribbon symbol is enhanced by being combined with a new ritual, the 'Immortal Regiment'. In this ritual, ordinary citizens march through the streets of Russian cities carrying portraits of their deceased relatives who fought in the Great Patriotic War, very often adorned with ribbons in orange and black. In this way, their family histories are drawn directly into the victory celebrations. These marches started as a civil society initiative in 2005 but were soon hijacked by the state authorities. They have become extremely popular, with annual participation exceeding all expectations.

During the 2011/12 'winter of discontent', Russian oppositionists of various hues tried to unite in a concerted effort to topple the Putin regime. In mass demonstrations in Moscow and other Russian cities, socialists and other leftists marched under red banners, liberals under the Russian tricolour, and nationalists under the Tsarist golden, white and black flag. As an attempt to signal unity among these very different ideological groups many of them also displayed a White Ribbon on their breast lapel. That symbol carried a dual meaning: on the one hand, it was an explicit alternative and challenge to the St George ribbon and hence marked the protesters off from the Putinites; on the other, it was intended to express unity among the opposition since 'white is the sum of all colours'. As I discuss in Chapter 8, however, this most ambitious attempt to mobilise against Putin proved to be an uphill struggle and eventually petered out. After Putin's re-election as President in March 2012, the regime reconsolidated, and adopted a range of laws and other measures that made it even more authoritarian and more menacing than before.

Opinion polls showed that, as a result of the turmoil in 2011–13, support for Putin among the Russian population took an abrupt downward turn, but then swung steeply upwards again in spring 2014, primarily as a result of the annexation of Crimea in March, a surprise move that was immensely popular in Russia. It bolstered the regime considerably, but this success was threatened by the bloody war in Eastern Ukraine that followed immediately afterwards. This was not a bloodless show of strength like the Crimean operation, but took a heavy toll on civilian lives – on both sides of the frontline. As I show in Chapter 9, Russian nationalists had cheered when 'little green men' – a moniker for Russian soldiers with no insignia – invaded Crimea, seemingly without effort; however, they began to waver in their faith in the wisdom of the national leader in the Kremlin. Astute

Western observers at the time surmised that Putin's Ukrainian policy might be 'self-defeating' (see Popescu 2014). Stephen Fish (2014) was of the opinion that Putin's attempt to play the game of Russian nationalism with his 'Ukrainian gambit' could backfire.

Putin has managed, however, to retain the confidence of the vast majority of the Russian population. An important victory was won in the battle for the minds and hearts of the Russians by sending St George into the breach. The knight, with his black-and-orange ribbon that resonated so well among the Russian populace, was massively exploited by the rebels in Donbas and their supporters in Russia to give a positive spin to something that was, to all intents and purposes, a war of aggression. The fact that the Ukrainian media not only fiercely rejected the ribbon symbol, but dehumanised all who identified with it, only made it easier for Russian officialdom to present Kyiv-loyal Ukrainians as implacable foes.

Concluding Remarks: The Interest Aspect of Identity, and the Identity Aspect of Interest

Traditionally, politics has been understood in terms of the struggle for (material) interests, as in Harold Lasswell's classic formulation: 'who gets what, when, how' (Lasswell 1935). In the 1970s and 1980s, however, political scientists increasingly focused on other less pragmatic motivations such as 'authenticity', 'recognition' and 'identities' (see e.g. Taylor 1994). Identities were contrasted with interests in order 'to highlight and conceptualize *noninstrumental* modes of social and political action' (Brubaker 2004, 33).

However, interests and identities should not be dichotomised. They are closely intertwined and, as Goldstein and Rayner point out, it often makes little sense to try to determine which of the two is primary and which secondary: 'What I want is in some sense shaped by my sense of who I am. On the other hand, in clarifying my interests I may sometimes begin to redefine my sense of self' (Goldstein and Rayner 1994, 367–8). The relationship is reciprocal:

> Just as economic interests influence our affiliations, for instance, so do those affiliations shape our senses of economic interests. The same person might conceive of her most politically salient identity as a worker, or as a white worker, or as a female worker, or as an American worker, or as a global work force member. She is likely to define her economic interests differently and to pursue distinct political courses depending on which conception she favors. (Smith 2004, 304)

These observations, originally made by Rogers Smith with regard to the individual level, can also be extended to the group level. It is simply impossible to fight for group interests unless one has an understanding of who and what constitute that group. A group without some kind of collective identity is not a group but a statistical category, and categories are not and cannot be political actors. Interest politics and identity politics are not 'the same' – but, I maintain, every instance of interest politics has an identity aspect, and vice versa.

All this has consequences for how we understand ethnic conflict and nationalism. As Umut Özkırımlı argues:

> we need to discover which political interests are secured in and by particular constructions of nationhood. If nations do not have essential identities and if they all contain groups that have different constructions of the nation, then every identity conceals a particular relationship of power. Thus we need to decode the relationships that create and sustain national identities. We need to explore how a particular representation of the nation comes to dominate others, who stands to gain by it and which other projects are marginalized or eliminated in the process. (Özkırımlı 2005, 177)

Nationalism is mobilisation to promote the interests of an identity group, the imagined community of 'the nation'. These interests may be material or immaterial. For some members of the nation (however that is understood), immaterial goods, such as the possibilities to practise one's culture and language, may be paramount, whereas others hope to reap more practical, mundane rewards. The benefits of successful mobilisation may vary considerably within the national or ethnic group. Some, the leaders in particular, may gain a lot, while others end up with less. Precisely in situations when large numbers of people are caught up in nationalist enthusiasm, some may tap into this fervour, basing their careers on it. Some of the winners may be true believers themselves, whereas others are simply riding with the tide.

As Daniele Conversi notes in his introduction to a book on the role of ethno-symbolism in nationalism studies, Anthony Smith, the leading interpreter within the school of ethno-symbolism, did not deny that ethnicity, as an independent variable, can be abused and manipulated. National myths cannot be created from scratch – but elites can distort and dramatically alter them. Therefore, 'instrumentalism is not necessarily incompatible with ethno-symbolism. Indeed, in order not to remain on the surface and avoid "descent into discourse", ethnosymbolism would need to be supplemented by a robust dose of instrumentalism' (Conversi 2007, 25–6). A similar position is taken by Brandon O'Leary. In a basically critical article on instrumentalism, he judiciously concludes:

> All instrumentalist theoretical traditions have their place in any attempts to explain nationalist phenomena. This is so, as long as they are accompanied by accounts, which give due weight to the independent consequences

of ideas and identities in shaping human conduct. It is possible, after all, to believe in the importance of both ideas and interests, or to believe in the importance of interests and identities. (O'Leary 2001, 152)

NOTES

1. A combination of strategies can be found in some nation-building projects that are both assimilatory and exclusivist at the same time, but vis-à-vis different groups. Brubaker mentions the nationality policy of the Polish state in the interwar period, which was geared towards enforced assimilation of Ukrainians and Belarusians and exclusion of the Jews (1996, 84–106).

2

COMPETING WITH ENTREPRENEURIAL DIASPORIANS: ORIGINS OF ANTI-SEMITISM IN NINETEENTH-CENTURY RUSSIA

In the last decades of the nineteenth century anti-Semitism emerged as a mass phenomenon in Russian public debate. Various explanations have been given to account for the rise of anti-Jewish sentiment: religious bigotry, racism, state policy and class enmity. In this chapter I agree with the latter theory that socio-economic factors were most important, but in contrast to it I argue that Russian anti-Semitism was not generated by a confrontation between two different classes; instead, the main impetus was economic competition within the same social segments. This can be shown by a close reading of contemporary Russian anti-Semitic texts. Their authors often complained that the Jews exploited poor Russians by charging extortionate prices for their goods, but a closer look reveals that, much more often, the opposite charge was made: the Jews were selling their goods *too cheaply*. This was a problem, of course, not for the Jews' customers, but for their competitors.

It is generally believed that anti-Jewish pogroms originated among the peasants, partly as a result of religious bigotry, partly as a reaction against alleged Jewish exploitation. In actual fact, pogroms almost invariably started in towns and cities, and the main instigators were artisans, merchants and other people who plied the same trade as the Jews.

The Jews could be targeted for persecution because they were a diaspora group and did not enjoy the same protection as the indigenous population. Thus, even though the Tsarist regime can be cleared of any suspicion that they deliberately whipped up the pogroms, they did contribute to them by failing to give the Jews the same rights as other subjects of the Empire.

As the socio-economic position of the Russian Jews changed, so did the social support bases of Russian anti-Semitism. When the Jews began to acquire higher education and qualified for ever new professions, pressure built up to restrict their entrance into high schools and universities.

Nineteenth-century Russia was notorious for its widespread and undisguised anti-Semitism. A number of laws were specifically directed against the Jews and designed to restrict their freedom of movement and occupational opportunities. A system of *numerus clausus* limited their access to institutions of higher learning. Starting in 1871, a series of violent pogroms erupted, during which the mob went on the rampage, with indiscriminate killing of innocent Jews. What caused this official discrimination and popular frenzy?

Russian anti-Semitism has been accounted for by different explanations. Some see it basically as religiously motivated. Religious anti-Semitism had been strong in medieval Europe and modern Russian judophobia is often regarded as a continuation of this tradition. And indeed, some nineteenth-century Russian anti-Semites continued to harp on the same themes as their medieval forerunners, such as the allegation that the Jews killed Christian boys in order to use their blood for ritual purposes. A second possible explanation behind the growing Russian anti-Semitism was racism. In the second half of the nineteenth century racist ideas developed in Western Europe, and racist books were also imported into and read in Russia.

Finally, socio-economic circumstances have also been adduced to account for the rise of Russian anti-Semitism. This explanation has been popular among Marxists and other materialists who regard religion as an epiphenomenon and look for the causes behind this ideational current in the social and economic structure of society (see e.g. Kautsky 1906). Accustomed to think in terms of classes and class conflict, they have debated whether or not Jews constituted a separate economic class or not (see e.g. Brutskus 1904).

All of these three explanations have some merit, and none of them should be dismissed out of hand. Traditionally, most has been made out of the religious perspective, but socio-economic factors are, in my opinion, the most important. The standard materialistic understanding, however, barks up the wrong tree by trying to squeeze the phenomenon of anti-Semitism into the rigid schema of class war. In this chapter I argue that Russian anti-Semitism was generated not by a confrontation between two different classes, but by *economic competition within the same social segments*. This means that we ought to look for its instigators not among the peasants, who were allegedly exploited by the Jews, but among those groups who filled the same occupational niches as the Jews. As the socio-economic position of the Russian Jews changed over the hundred years prior to the Russian Revolution, so did the social support bases of Russian anti-Semitism. In this article, I give a broad analysis of Russian anti-Semitic texts to substantiate this view.

I first discuss the alternative explanations of Russian anti-Semitism – the religious and racial approaches – before I present my own. I then trace the socio-economic transformations of Russian society in the nineteenth century as they affected relations between Jews and Gentiles. Finally, I present an analytical overview of anti-Jewish texts published in Russia in the nineteenth century and the first decade of the twentieth century.

The Religious Explanation

In the European Middle Ages, hatred towards the Jews was primarily propelled by – or at least cloaked in – religious enmity: the Jews had killed Jesus and were regarded as the enemies of the Christian God. Such premodern sentiment is often referred to as anti-Judaism rather than anti-Semitism (e.g. Laqueur 2006, 39–70). A corollary of this worldview was that conversion to Christianity would expiate the Jew of the collective guilt of his/her people. This attitude prevailed as late as the fifteenth century in Spain, when Jews could escape persecution by adopting the Christian faith, while by the time of the massacres in the Cossack Hetmanate in Ukraine in 1648–9, this was no longer the case. Importantly, too, as Walter Laqueur argues, in earlier times religious bigotry does not seem to have been the sole motivating factor. The widespread plundering of Jewish property which accompanied the First Crusade at the end of the eleventh century suggests that 'economic motives must have been involved' (Laqueur 2006, 38).

Among Russian authors writing against the Jews in the nineteenth century we find several who adopted a religious position and who primarily, or ostensibly, were concerned about combating the pernicious influence of the Mosaic faith. The number of books they produced was relatively small compared to the total corpus of Russian anti-Semitic writings of the time, but some of them consisted in voluminous and seemingly very erudite theses. Most of this literature dissected the classical Jewish religious texts and claimed to find in them a message of unmitigated hatred towards the *Goyim*. Weird theories about Jewish bloodthirstiness were not the innocuous ramblings of deranged fanatics, but could result in so-called blood libel cases. Most notoriously, in 1913, the hapless Jewish factory worker Mendel Beilis was accused of having murdered a Christian boy for religious purposes and taken to court. Although he was acquitted, the jury nevertheless concluded that a ritual murder had indeed been committed, although the perpetrator/s had not been found (Rogger 1966, 620).

A typical text in this genre of Russian religious anti-Semitic literature is *The Secrets of Talmud and the Jews in their Relation to the Christian World*, published in 1880 by V. Mordvinov. Mordvinov starts by stating that he will not write about the unscrupulous and scandalous Jewish exploitation of the Russian peasantry or the enormous monetary losses which the Jews inflict upon Russian society, for all that it is already too well known. Instead, he will concentrate on the root causes of the Jews' ill treatment of their Christian neighbours, which he finds in the Talmud. Two-thirds of this collection of Rabbinical texts has an antisocial message, Mordvinov asserts. Thus, for instance, the Talmud distorts the Mosaic prohibition against theft into meaning that it is permissible to steal from Christians. The Seventh Commandment means only that it is not allowed to steal from 'people', but for the Jews Gentiles are not humans; they are 'cattle' and the Mosaic ban does not apply (Mordvinov 1880, 4, 48, and 146).

Interestingly, Mordvinov sees enlightenment (*prosveshchenie*) as the best remedy against Jewish barbarism (Mordvinov 1880, 8 and 158–230). That apparently means that Mordvinov would welcome – perhaps even want to force – Jews into secular schools and institutions of higher learning. If this is correct, his practical advice is the very opposite of what we can find among most Russian anti-Semites two decades later. At the turn of the century it had become a paramount concern for reactionary Russians to keep the Jews out of high schools and universities, and to bar them from most intellectual professions.

By far the most prolific contributor to the library of religiously oriented Russian anti-Semitic texts is Ippolit Liutostanskii (1835–1915), a defrocked Catholic priest who converted to Orthodoxy. Liutostanskii wrote a three-volume book on *The Jews and the Talmud* (1879, second edition 1902), plus a slightly smaller treatise on *The Jews' Use of Christian Blood for Religious Purposes*, in two volumes. Like Mordvinov, Liutostanskii often veers into the realm of socio-economic analysis. Almost the entire second volume of the latter book, ostensibly devoted to matters relating to 'blood libel', in fact deals with more secular crimes attributed to the Jews. This is because the Talmud, in Liutostanskii's interpretation, is primarily a Jewish handbook on how to behave towards the Gentiles. 'Exploitation of the Christians is the historical and most characteristic trait of Jewry, as established in the Talmud' (Liutostanskii 1880, II, 250). The Jew is driven by two equally irrepressible desires: religious fanaticism and greed. Even in Russian anti-Semitic literature supposedly concentrating on religious subjects, then, a grudge against the alleged social and economic harm caused by the Jews constantly cropped up.

The Russian anti-Semitic texts that I have examined show that a religious attitude towards converts is reflected in some of these writings. Thus, for instance, one of the most extreme Russian anti-Semites, S. Rossov, proposed a long list of discriminatory regulations specifically targeting the Jews (see below), but also argued that all rights should be granted to second-generation Jewish converts. Interestingly, Rossov would also allow miscegenation and let Jews marry Christians, provided that their children were baptised and given a Christian upbringing (Rossov 1907, 101–2).

THE RACIALIST EXPLANATION

In the second half of the nineteenth century traditional, religiously motivated anti-Judaism gradually lost out in Western Europe to a new anti-Semitism based on racialist ideas. The books of Arthur de Gobineau, Houston Stewart Chamberlain, Eugen Dühring and other modern racists were also read in Russia and several scholars have pointed out that racialist and racist Western ideas influenced the Russian public and officialdom to a significant degree (Poliakov 1974, 125; Tolz 2019).[1]

The litmus test for whether or not an anti-Semitic author is motivated by racism is his (they all seem to be men) attitude towards converts. If he treats baptised Jews as if they have shed their Jewishness, that would indicate the non-racist character of their anti-Jewish sentiments. If, on the other hand, converts to Christianity are regarded as if their change of religion did not affect their Jewishness, that would suggest that race rather than confession is the real issue.

Eli Weinerman (Weinerman 1994) basically refutes the racialist explanation. He has studied the arguments put forward by those Russian anti-Semites who insisted that anti-Jewish legislation should affect not only those who professed the Mosaic faith but also Jewish converts to Christianity. The most commonly cited reasons behind this demand, Weinerman points out, was not that the Jews kept their harmful genes after conversion but that it was necessary to eliminate Jewish economic and professional competition.

> Black Hundreds' periodicals frequently published the names of converts who served in the state bureaucracy. Although these offices, as a rule, had no connection with national security, extreme anti-Semites complained that converts should be dismissed from them because hiring converts deprived ethnic Russians of the means of gainful employment. (Weinerman 1994, 463)

Jewish converts to Christianity were no less resourceful or socially ambitious than other Jews; if anything, the opposite was the case. Hence, the need to keep the converts down was greater, not smaller. Weinerman concludes that although some narrow groups of Russian nationalists did accept racist anti-Semitism, '[t]he Russian legislation against converts was motivated by concerns other than racial bias' (Weinerman 1994. 474). In any case, the Tsarist authorities never closed the entrance to state service to Jews who had converted.

Other historians, however, have reached different conclusions. Hans Rogger documents that in late Tsarist Russia increasing pressure was exerted to exclude baptised Jews from various schools and professions. In his view, 'this racial component cast doubt on the view that official discrimination was based on religion' (Rogger 1986, 36). Eugene Avrutin points out that Russian officialdom made it almost impossible for Jewish converts to Orthodoxy to blend into mainstream

Russian society by marking 'of Jewish origin' (*iz evreev*) next to their name in official documents. (Such a mark was not required for Jewish converts to other Christian denominations.) Moreover, Avrutin found that the 684 baptised Jews who returned to Judaism shortly after the 1905 Edict on religious freedom did so because conversion to Christianity 'had done little to unburden them of their innate Jewishness' (Avrutin 2007, 34 and 36).

As we shall see below, racialist reasoning was used by some, albeit far from all, Russian anti-Semites. But for those who did have recourse to such arguments they often serve as auxiliary props in support of what was basically a socio-economic agenda. If the main concern of the anti-Semite was to keep Jews out of certain niches of the economy and to limit socio-economic competition, it made perfect sense to define Jewishness in racial and not religious terms and to include Jewish converts too.

Hans Rogger has suggested that 'the government's often-expressed fear that the Jews posed an economic threat to their less adaptable Russian competitors' may be one of the real driving forces behind official Russian anti-Semitism (Rogger 1986, 38). Another leading expert on Russian policies towards the Jews, John Klier, has remarked that the theme that Jews would dominate state service or a particular profession or field of endeavour 'almost invariably appeared first in the Pale, and may have represented real fears by the local intelligentsia at the growing economic and intellectual might of a modernized Jewish elite' (Klier 1995, 365–6). If these authorities are right, Russian anti-Semitism must be regarded, to a large extent, as being motivated by socio-economic factors. This is the track I will explore here.

THE SOCIO-ECONOMIC EXPLANATION

One of the most consistent and thorough attempts to give a socio-economic explanation for Russian anti-Semitism is Heinz-Dietrich Löwe's book *Anti-Semitism and Reactionary Utopia* (Löwe 1978). Löwe sees the rise of Russian anti-Semitism as a reaction against the rapid socio-economic modernisation that Russia underwent over the last decades of the nineteenth century and the beginning of the twentieth century. The Jews were regarded as one of the driving forces behind the new economy and for that reason became a convenient target for all anti-modernist forces. Löwe identifies the nobility as the greatest losers in the modernisation and consequently regards this estate as the main wellspring of anti-Semitic sentiment.

As Löwe himself points out, however, it was illogical to associate the Jews with the phenomenon of modernisation. The vast majority of them continued to be linked to the traditional economy and way of life. Therefore, Löwe remarks, 'the image of the Jews as a spearhead of capitalism which the Russian conservatives created was more an artificial ideological construction than a reflection of real conditions' (Löwe 1978, 39).

I share Löwe's conviction that economic conditions and social transformation were indeed behind the emergence and spread of Russian anti-Semitism. In contrast to him, however, I believe that the anti-Semites were not lashing out at the Jews at random or due to some misconceived ideas about the Jews' actual socio-economic condition. Instead, I believe that they well knew what they were doing and whom they were attacking. They were hitting out at people whose economic activity represented a real threat to their own. This means that the motor of Russian anti-Semitism should be located among the urban classes, and in particular among the social groups that were in direct competition with the Jews.

In traditional, premodern Russian society Jews had been restricted to certain occupations: in particular, trades, arts and crafts, stewardship on nobles' estates, and the production and sale of alcohol. As a result, the main instigators of Russian anti-Semitism were, for a long time, found primarily among Gentile practitioners of these same trades. In the last decades of the nineteenth century, however, the Jews, as well as other population groups in Russia, were caught up in the processes of modernisation. Reduced infant mortality led to rapid population growth. Another important consequence of modernisation was a marked increase in education, both at the basic level and in higher education. Young people left the Russian villages, as well as the Jewish *shtetls*, in droves, the majority ending up in the larger towns and big cities. Here, some found employment at the new factories that were sprouting up under Russia's crash industrialisation, while many tried to enrol at the universities. This created a scramble for university slots and, in turn, competition for white-collar jobs among university graduates. These processes exported anti-Semitism to ever new professional groups at various levels of society.

To be sure, not only Jews and Russians were caught up in the whirlwind of modernisation. Other ethnic groups in the Empire also participated in the new educational boom. There were, however, several factors that explain why the xenophobia created by the new competition for jobs should manifest itself first and foremost as anti-Semitism.

First, the Jews had the highest level of urbanisation of all the ethnic groups in Russia. Second, for a number of reasons, they embodied what has been called 'an achievement-oriented culture' (Lewis et al. 1976, 87–96). This was not perhaps so much a result of the Jewish religion – although the heavy emphasis on scriptural studies in Judaism may have played a part – as it was a culture they shared with other diaspora groups around the globe, and hence can be explained as a result of 'the diasporic condition'.

Third, Jewish competition was particularly resented by other job seekers since Gentiles were used to regarding Jews as poor and powerless underdogs. When they started to penetrate new and more prestigious segments of the labour market – and frequently succeeded in them – their Christian neighbours were threatened by a status reversal. To be bettered by a Jew was regarded as a greater affront than to lose out to, for instance, a German or a Pole, two ethnic groups who had historically had a large upper class in Russia and been highly overrepresented in the Tsarist bureaucracy.

Finally, the attitude of the Russian authorities was clearly important. It has been convincingly proven that the Tsars and their ministers cannot be saddled with direct responsibility for the pogroms, but they clearly were guilty of anti-Semitism. On numerous occasions the Tsarist state gave in to pressure from the Jews' competitors and adopted anti-Jewish legislation. By doing so, they signalled to the populace that the Jews in a sense stood outside the law. As long as the authorities did not treat the Jews as fully-fledged members of society, the mob felt free to deal with them as they pleased, as least in periodic killing sprees.

Job competition and diaspora groups

Jews and Armenians are prototypical examples of achievement diaspora groups. The successes of Jewish bankers or Armenian merchants, however, have nothing to do with biology or ethnic culture as such. In a global comparative study Robin Cohen (1997, 25) found that members of a number of different diasporas – not only Jews and Armenians, but also Lebanese, Chinese and Indians – tend to do far better than their co-ethnics who stay at home. The explanation for the social advancement of the diaspora members, then, should probably be sought in the diasporic condition itself. One possible reason is that diasporians tend to have all the odds stacked against them in their host society: they simply have to strive harder and do better than others in order to survive. Another possible explanation is historical. Already in premodern times, many diaspora members were engaged in professions in which economic calculation and competitive spirit were important assets, at least more so than in the subsistence agriculture in which the majority of the indigenous population were engaged (Sombart 1913; Slezkine 2004).

While some diaspora groups are grafted on to their host society at the top, others end up somewhere towards the bottom. John Armstrong distinguishes between a mobilised and a proletarian diaspora. The former is 'an ethnic group which does not have a general status advantage, yet which enjoys many material and cultural advantages compared to other groups in the multiethnic polity'. Among the latter we find, *inter alia*, labour immigrants to Western countries from the third world, 'a disadvantaged product of modernized polities, a nearly undifferentiated mass of unskilled labour'. Rather than gradually bettering their lot, they tend to enter a downward spiral, Armstrong argues. Their upward mobility is blocked, and they 'tend to become progressively more distant culturally and in physical appearance from the dominant ethnic group and to suffer more discrimination' (Armstrong 1976, 393 and 406).

Armstrong's dichotomous typology has not been universally accepted and may, in fact, be rather misleading. Cohen points out that Poles and Italians in the interwar USA, two groups that Armstrong identifies as proletarian diasporas, have actually done quite well (Cohen 1997, 58–9). Jörg Hüttermann documents how many members of a typical 'proletarian' diaspora, such as Turkish *Gastarbeiter* in Germany, have moved out of the ghetto and into the middle class, and this has caused tension:

> For members of the autochthonous group the advancing Stranger becomes a problem, and in a sociological perspective a social offense because in their everyday experience they have overcome the status boundaries that had been taken for granted, and thus put in question the identity-affirming ranking order in society. (Hüttermann 2000, 275)

In such a situation of 'structural assimilation', the Peripheral Stranger in the perception of the autochthonous mutates into a threatening Advancing Stranger, and the likelihood of ethnic conflict increases. Job competition between members of the autochthonous group and diasporas involves not only material matters of income and daily bread, but also crucial issues of status and status anxiety (Hüttermann 2000).

The modernisation of Tsarist Russia

Until a few decades before the demise of the Russian Empire the social distinction of estate (*soslovie*) overruled any distinction based on culture or ethnicity in Russian society. Russians constituted the largest ethnic group but they were not favoured by the state authorities. Non-Russians and in particular Germans were strongly overrepresented in the higher echelons of the state bureaucracy. For a long time this did not produce any strong feeling of resentment among ethnic Russians, simply because there was a surplus of such jobs. If a Russian with the necessary qualifications applied for a position, he could be pretty sure to get it, not because he was Russian but because he was qualified. As Andreas Kappeler points out, reports from the Russian ministries bristled with laments over *maloliudstvo*, or lack of qualified personnel to fill the vacancies (Kappeler 1993, 111, 115 and 136). Russian nobles often possessed an excellent education and impressive language skills, but many of the best qualified among them did not bother to serve (obligatory state service for the nobility was abolished by Peter III in 1762). They were wealthy enough to live a life of leisure and very often preferred to do so. In such an environment, ethnically based competition for elite jobs could not arise.

In the last thirty or so years of the nineteenth century, however, things began to change. Nationalism gradually became a factor to be reckoned with in Russian politics and social life. Now, for the first time, a state-sponsored programme was set out to base the Russian state on Russian culture and the Russian language. The non-Russians were supposed to participate in this culture by undergoing Russification. Several circumstances seem to have contributed to this change of policy: bureaucratic standardisation and centralisation; a desire to emulate the more 'progressive' European nation-states; nationalist mobilisation during the 1876–7 Russo-Turkish war; and finally, fear of revolution, in particular after the assassination of Tsar Alexander II by terrorists in 1881 (Kappeler 1993, 226–8).

One important aspect of the new Russian nationalism did not fall into this pattern, however, and that was the policy towards the Jews. In the last three or four decades of the Tsarist era, anti-Semitism developed into one of the most crucial ingredients of Russian nationalism, both official and popular. *This* policy, however, was not a programme for Russification; on the contrary, it was aimed at the *isolation* and rejection of the Jews as 'aliens'. Why were the Jews treated differently?

The simple but misleading answer to this question is that the Jews *were* different, and therefore had always been treated differently. While this is basically true, official Russian policy on the so-called 'Jewish Question' had, right up until the 1870s, been aimed at *the very opposite of isolation*. The problem, it was felt, was that the Jews had isolated themselves, and they had to be brought out of their self-imposed seclusion and into the mainstream of society, with equal rights and equal obligations to the Tsar's other subjects (Rogger 1986; Klier 1998). Sometimes this goal was pursued through a benign policy of integration and emancipation, at other times through a coercive policy of assimilation. These policies were fiercely resisted by the religious establishment within the Jewish community, but in the last decades of the nineteenth century they were nevertheless beginning to bear considerable fruit. Jewish youth left the *shtetls* in large numbers, looking for jobs and education in the towns and cities. But as soon as this happened, the emancipation/assimilation policy towards the Jews was not only abandoned, but *reversed*. This strange paradox can be understood only against the background of the demographic and educational development of Russia at the time. As the most achievement-oriented minority group in Russia, these modernised Jews became direct competitors of the dominant Orthodox–Slavic groups on the labour market.

Between 1860–4 and 1909–13 the population of the Russian Empire increased from 74 million to 164 million, an average rise of 1.6 per cent per year. Except for typical immigrant countries such as the USA, Canada and Australia, this was the highest population increase experienced by any country in the world in that period (Gatrell 1986, 50). Some of this figure may be accounted for by the annexation of new territories, but most of it was caused by declining death rates in an environment of continued high fertility. Part of the demographic pressure was taken off the overcrowded Russian villages by rural–rural migration to periphery regions and some overseas migration from the western provinces. Most of those who left the Russian villages, however, filled up the rapidly expanding cities. Between 1855 and 1913 the population of Moscow increased three times; that of St Petersburg, four times; and that of Kiev, eight times. Many typical industrial cities such as Baku grew even more quickly.

In relative terms, the Jews contributed more than any other ethnic group to this population boom in the last decades of the nineteenth century. Jews were encouraged by cultural traditions and communal pressures within the *shtetls* to marry early and have many children, in spite of the prevailing poverty. In combination with relatively low child mortality this resulted in a rapidly expanding population. The Jewish population had always been urban, but in this period they clustered in towns and large cities to an even higher degree than before (Orbach 2004, 139). Already in the early 1880s Jews made up more than half of the town population in eight *guberniias*: Mogilev, Volhynia, Minsk, Kovno, Podolsk, Vitebsk, Grodno and Vilnius (Demidov 1883, 63). In the 1897 census Jews were by far the most urbanised group.

While only 0.2 per cent of the Russian population in the 1897 census had higher education that group nevertheless amounted to the substantial figure of 238,000 individuals. In addition, another 1,245,000 men and woman had full secondary education (Shanin 1985a, 61). Most of the new school graduates stemmed not from the nobility but from the new middle-layer or *raznochintsy* group. They were men and woman of strictly limited means and could not afford a life of leisure such as the scions of the nobility enjoyed. Hence, the *maloliudstvo*, or lack of qualified people for the state bureaucracy, was eliminated.

Roots of official Russian anti-Semitism

There is no doubt that both Alexander III and Nicholas II, as well as a number of their advisors and ministers, were inveterate anti-Semites, and during the nineteenth century numerous laws and regulations were adopted that restricted the legal position and economic rights of the Jews. Even so, the Russian state seems to have played a more passive than proactive role in the development of Russian anti-Semitism than has often been assumed. It can be demonstrated that when anti-Jewish legislation was passed, this often came about as a result of pressure from various lobby groups, in particular from professional groups that felt threatened by Jewish competition.

From an economic point of view, the state had nothing to gain from restricting the movement and rights of any particular group in society, and certainly not when this group contained a strong element of experienced merchants and artisans. When it did, therefore, the state acted against its own economic interests. By far the most important institution that regulated the position of the Jews in the Russian Empire was the Pale of Settlement. This special residence zone was established in 1791 to restrict the movements of the Jewish population in the newly acquired western provinces in today's Belarus, who had become Russian subjects after the first partition of Poland in 1772. Later, with the new territorial gains in the eighteenth century, the Pale was extended to cover most of the western and southern parts of the Empire. The motives behind the establishment of this special zone were complex, but the most important were clearly economic. By limiting the Jews' permitted area of residence, the imperial powers tried to ensure the growth of a non-Jewish middle class in the other parts of the Empire (Klier 1986, 75–7). The first demand for the establishment of a restricted zone of movement for Jews came from Russian merchants, who complained that their Jewish competitors engaged in shady business such as smuggling, tax evasion and 'selling goods at bargain prices' (Avrutin 2010, 5).

For the state, the economic benefits of the Pale were mixed at best. The provinces outside the Pale suffered economically from the lack of a mercantile class of Jews while the population within the Pale had far more merchants and craftsmen in many trades than they needed (Klier 2004). As a result, the Pale of Settlement had to be supplemented over time by a host of other regulations and palliative measures intended to mitigate its negative consequences.

The vast majority of the Jews were incorporated into the Russian estate system as petty bourgeoisie (*meshchane*) while the richer merchants among them were classified as *kuptsy* – merchants – and enrolled in one of the three merchant guilds. Catherine II subjected them to the same rights and restrictions as other members of these two estates. Initially, Catherine II 'scrupulously ensured that the Jews really were allowed these news rights, as this was of great importance for their activity as merchants and craftsmen' (Gessen 1906, 25). Later, however, under pressure from Christian merchants and *meshchane*, these rights were gradually reduced (Klier 1986, 67–8).

Even so, the Jews continued for a long time to enjoy the support of the government for their economic activities, since this benefited the country as a whole, and a number of exceptions were made to the new restrictive regulations that were passed. Nicholas I introduced some new restrictive policies but, notes Iulii Gessen, 'the government was so dependent on the merchant and artisan activities of the Jews that it was forced to partially reverse several of the new restrictive regulations' (Gessen 1906, 26).

Under the liberal regime of Alexander II, a number of special Jewish restrictions were eased or abolished. This new liberality, however, lasted only until the so-called May Laws of 1882 limited the rights and movement of Jews in numerous new ways (Klier and Lambroza 2004, 41). These laws had been prepared by the minister of interior, Count N. Ignatiev, a notorious anti-Semite, who presented them as a counter-measure to combat the revolutionaries who, the year before, had managed to kill 'the liberator Tsar', Alexander II.

It soon became clear, however, that Ignatiev's measures created more problems than they solved. This was recognised by the so-called Pahlen Commission, which was established in 1883 to examine virtually all aspects of the 'Jewish Question'. After five years of laborious work, it came up with surprisingly liberal recommendations, as summarised by Hans Rogger. The constant enlistment of state aid by the competitors of the Jews had to stop: 'if in free competition [the Russians] were the losers it was because they were less agile, less parsimonious, less sober and less enterprising than the Jews and too dependent on the state' (Rogger 1986, 65). None of the recommendations of the Pahlen Commission, however, was implemented.

Many decisions to restrict the activities of the Jews were made by local authorities. This was normally the case when, for instance, it was decided to evict the Jews from a certain town or city. Their self-government organs were often controlled by the Jews' economic competitors. In 1891, some 30,000 Jews, mostly artisans, were expelled from Moscow and sent back to the Pale. This constituted more than 85 per cent of Jews living in the city (Pinkus [1988] 1989, 31). Elsewhere, Jewish artisans were allowed to make up only a certain percentage of the total number of artisans in a given corporation.

In many cases of expulsion from a city only a specific group of Jews was targeted, such as when all Jewish students of pharmacy, medical attendance (*feldsherstvo*) and obstetrics were denied the right of residence in Moscow in 1897 (Gessen 1906, 22). This decision was linked to a growth in the number of Gentile practitioners in these professions in the capital. Benjamin Nathans maintains that '[w]ithout denying the state's readiness to discriminate against Jews and other minorities . . . the decisive impetus for such action increasingly came from within the Russian public itself' (Nathans 2004, 364).

One professional group that was specifically targeted was Jewish lawyers. The struggle to keep the Jews out of the legal profession became one of the most embittered battlefields in the war against Jewish occupational rights (Shmakov 1906, 333–6; Rogger 1986, 35; Nathans 2004, 340–66). In 1889 a report in the journal of the St Petersburg Juridical Society pleaded with the authorities to restrict Jews' entrance to the Bar: 'Here, as elsewhere, free competition between Jews and Christians is dangerous and even simply impossible.' The reason for this was that the Jewish people allegedly had 'a resourcefulness that stops at nothing' (quoted in Nathans 2004, 352). The plea was heard, and that same year a decree required every admission of a non-Christian to the Bar to receive the personal approval of the minister of justice. As a result, the number of Jewish lawyers fell precipitously (Nathans 2004, 355–61). Later, new and even tighter restrictions were introduced. In 1915 it was decided to limit the number of Jewish lawyers to 15 per cent in Warsaw, Vilnius and Odesa, 10 per cent in St Petersburg and Kiev, and 5 per cent elsewhere (Löwe 1978, 166).

Restrictions in higher education

The Russian state's changing attitudes towards Jewish higher education nicely illustrate its complete volte-face on the 'Jewish Question' in the last decades of the nineteenth century. The Statute on the Jews from 1804 had stated that all Jewish children should be allowed entrance into all Russian educational institutions, including gymnasiums and universities. In 1841 the Ministry of Education reported that 'the acceptance of Jews into our civil schools has so far had no negative consequences'. In 1844 and again in 1859 the right of all Jews to send their children to general state schools was reconfirmed (Kosven 1904, 168–9).

In traditional Jewish society, bookish learning (for boys) was regarded as a sacred duty, but this education should be conducted at the Jewish religious community schools, the *chederim*, and concentrate on the study of the Torah. Jewish community leaders regarded attempts to attract Jewish students into regular state schools with great scepticism, and as a concession to Jewish concerns the state established certain schools and colleges that were reserved for Jewish students, where they could study without mingling with their Gentile coevals. In 1873, however, these specialised Jewish colleges were closed. 'This devastating blow, however, had some positive effects,' explains the renowned Jewish historian Iulii Gessen. 'The liquidation of specialized Jewish colleges, together with the general renewal of the Jewish life that took place at the time, stimulated interest among Jewish youth for general institutions of higher learning' (Gessen 1906, 107).

One important impetus behind the decision of an increasing number of Jewish youth to take up higher education was clearly the desperate economic situation in the Pale. There was simply no room for more Jewish goldsmiths, cobblers or shopkeepers, and some of the Jewish artisans' many sons had to seek another livelihood. Higher education opened up new and promising prospects for them. In 1861 – the same year as the Russian peasants were emancipated – Jews with higher education had been allowed to settle in any part of the country. This measure was in line with the Enlightenment spirit of Great reforms and aimed at the gradual and selective assimilation of the Jews.

The *shtetl* Jews responded with alacrity. In twenty years the number of Jewish gymnasium students rose from less than 1,000 to more than 7,500, while the number of university students increased by more than fourteen times. In 1886, there were 1,856 Jewish students in the country, comprising no less than 14.5 per cent of the total student body, up from 129 in 1865 (Nathans 2004, 218).

The enormous success of this educational policy, however, brought about its own undoing, and in the early 1880s a backlash set in. In March 1880 the conservative newspaper *Novoe vremia* published a letter to the editor under the title 'The Yid is Coming!' The anonymous author lamented the fact that the Jews were flooding the universities:

> In another decade or so, we will see that in certain areas of Russia, Jews will dominate not only the practical professions, but also the so-called liberal professions, that is, they will hold in their hands both the material and the intellectual power.

Employing a zero-sum kind of reasoning, the author claimed that 'Every Ioshka and Hershka who passes through a gymnasium, prevents a poor Russian from doing the same' (quoted in Nathans 2004, 259).[2] The article triggered a wide debate and became one of the most influential anti-Semitic texts published in Russia in the nineteenth century.

A year later, in March 1881, Alexander II was killed, and a general backlash against the Enlightenment and liberalism set in. In a move intended primarily to stem the recruitment of students to the ranks of the revolutionaries, Alexander III decided that higher education ought to be a prerogative of the upper classes, and in 1887 the Ministry of Education prohibited the 'children of coachmen, menials, cooks, washerwomen, small shopkeepers and the like' from studying in gymnasiums (Nathans 2004, 267). The same year, a decree from the Ministry of Education restricted the number of Jews enrolling in gymnasiums in the Pale of Settlement to 10 per cent of the total, 3 per cent in Moscow and St Petersburg, and 5 per cent elsewhere. In 1901, these quotas were reduced to 7 per cent, 2 per cent, and 3 per cent, respectively. In 1908 this *numerus clausus*, which hitherto had been an administrative rule, was given the force of law. Haggling over the size and application of the quotas continued, however, and in 1909 they were also extended to private schools. The next year, one of the last loopholes was closed when the *numerus clausus* was applied to 'external' students who took exams without following the usual teaching sessions (Rogger 1986, 96). However, in most institutions the *numerus clausus* was never fully enforced, and the Jewish share of the student body exceeded the norms year after year (Nathans 2004, 270–1).

One of the arguments that was used to ease the introduction of the *numerus clausus* was fear of revolution. This was part of the official justification offered for the decrees but the measure was certainly counter-productive. The best way to drive competent and ambitious Jews into the arms of the revolutionaries would be precisely to block their access to education and social advancement.

As another argument, Russian anti-Semites claimed that 'Jews who acquire education – and the rights that go with it – bring the gravest possible harm to society', since the Jews invariably lower the ethical standard of whichever profession they enter (Tutkevich 1906, 55). There is reason to assume that the

Russian authorities were not swayed by such disingenuous claims, however. Whatever other reasons the authorities might have had, it seems clear that they were also giving in to pressure from non-Jews who wanted to reduce competition from well-qualified 'aliens' on the job market (Rogger 1986, 110). It was felt that the Jews were 'assimilating too well'.

As Jews with higher education found entry into state service or public employment increasingly difficult, they tended to cluster in those professions where restrictions were fewer or difficult to enforce. This is probably part of the reason why so many of them ended up as lawyers or as part of the humanistic intelligentsia. As a result, remarks Viktor Kel'ner, at the turn of the century anti-Semitism also began to spread among the Russian intelligentsia, which had hitherto been rather immune to such attitudes. A noticeable shift could be detected among Russian writers, artists, journalists and people in the so-called free professions as soon as they acquired many Jewish colleagues: 'In the new circumstances, their previous Judeophilia smoothly but quite naturally (*zakonomerno*) flowed into the opposite sentiment' (Kel'ner 2004, 77).

Who was behind the pogroms?

The most sinister expressions of anti-Semitism in Tsarist Russia were the pogroms. In the older scholarship on the history of the Jews in Russia, and also in the popular understanding, the causes of and dynamics behind the pogroms were poorly understood. In recent decades, newer and more scrupulous research has identified and dispelled at least three serious misconceptions around the issue:

1. Pogroms were a frequent, indeed perennial, occurrence in Russian history.
2. Pogroms were a rural phenomenon involving mainly peasants seeking to take revenge for alleged Jewish exploitation.
3. The state authorities instigated the pogroms.[3]

In actual fact, the pogroms almost invariably started in the cities and only later spread to the surrounding villages. Furthermore, no major pogrom took place in the first eighty years after the partition of Poland, which, for the first time, gave Russia a large Jewish population. The first large pogrom erupted in Odesa in 1871.[4] Later, a new wave of pogroms swept the country at fifteen-year intervals on average, in 1881–3, in 1903–6, and finally during the Russian civil war, in 1918–20. With each recurring sequence, the violence tended to become more gruesome and claim more lives. Finally, the newest studies have acquitted the Tsarist authorities of the charges of active involvement in the planning and execution of the pogroms. While many highly placed persons clearly nourished anti-Jewish prejudices, their visceral distrust of 'the mob' was equally deep, and their basic law-and-order instinct prevailed over any temptation to incite the 'dark' masses (Rogger 1986, 28–31; Aronson 2004, 55–6). But if not the authorities, who was behind the pogroms, and what were their motives?

The answer to these questions is not the same in all cases and with regard to all perpetrators. We must distinguish between individuals and groups who created a pogromist atmosphere for their own reasons prior to the actual outbreak of violence, and the people who smashed Jewish shops, raped Jewish women and killed their husbands. These people were normally recruited from very different social groups. Moreover, there were important local variations: the 1918–20 pogroms in particular, which were far more lethal than the earlier ones, seem to have been driven by very different dynamics. While casualties in the earlier pogroms ran into tens or hundreds, during the civil war *tens of thousands* of Jews perished. In contrast to previous cases, the violence this time was, to a large extent, a rural phenomenon (Budnitskii 2002; Kenez 2004).

A common element in all the first waves of anti-Jewish violence was the involvement of Christian merchants and other social groups who saw Jews as dangerous competitors. In the 1871 Odessa pogrom the turmoil started when a rumour spread that a cross had disappeared from a Greek church; allegedly, it had been stolen by Jews. Most commentators agree that the rumour had been put out by Greek merchants who feared Jewish competition. The early 1870s was a transition period during which Jewish merchants were establishing themselves in the city in competition with Greek firms (Morgulis 1910, 63–4; see also Klier 2004, 15–16; Weinberg 2004, 251).[5]

When new and much more widespread pogroms broke out in a number of southern towns and cities ten years later, the highly respected Russian lawyer, Prince Pavel Demidov San-Donato, a member of the Pahlen Committee, gave the following explanation for the rapid spread of the violence:

> In major trade and production centres such as Odesa, Kiev, Rostov-na-Donu and others, [the pogrom] movement found an especially propitious soil, for several reasons. A significant part of the population in these cites were merchants and manufacturers who were hostile towards the Jews due to the extremely dangerous competition they faced from them in virtually every branch of trade and industry. Secondly, in such large trade and production centres there are an assorted group of uncultured and benighted (*temnye*) people, who covet other people's goods, as well as workers, mostly migrants who are known for their tempestuous instincts. The downtrodden and despised Jews represent the most convenient element upon which they can take revenge for their various grievances, without risking either resistance from the victims, or rebuff from the local population. (Demidov 1883, 79)

This view is corroborated by modern scholarship (Aronson 1990, 108; Aronson 2004, 47–9). I. Michael Aronson also points out that the number of artisans who participated in the pogrom was relatively high and attributes this to economic and professional rivalry. Finally, he surmises that the Jews' well-to-do business competitors – merchants, industrialists and professional people – while not participating actively in the pogroms themselves, may have contributed by spreading rumours and the like.

The most vicious pogrom in the third cycle of violence broke out in Kishinev in 1903. The riots themselves seem to have been started by a loosely organised bunch of hooligans whose original goal was to 'teach the Jews a lesson', but contemporary observers, as well as modern researchers, agree that there had been a deliberate prior campaign to whip up anti-Jewish feeling, orchestrated by the notorious editor of the Kishinev newspaper *Bessarabets*, P. A. Krushevan. Articles in *Bessarabets* demanded that Jews be fired from municipal jobs to make room for non-Jews (Lambroza 2004, 196). One of Krushevan's closest collaborators cherished his reputation as a spokesman for Christian working men in their alleged struggle against Jewish competition and exploitation. Another was a businessman who had found himself in serious competition with several Jewish contractors. 'Unable to better the Jews in open competition, he tried a different tack: he began using his wealth and influence to undermine the Jewish community through political intrigue and public slander' (Judge 1992, 33 and 37; see also Löwe 1978, 63). Some Kishinev burghers clearly had a vested interest in the pogrom.

Another serious pogrom in the 1903–6 cycle, that taking place Ekaterinoslav in 1905, has been studied by Gerald Surh, who focuses on the alleged role of industrial workers in the riots. Suhr concludes that the term 'workers', used by contemporary observers as well as by historians, was misleading. The *pogromshchiki* were *not* factory workers from the suburbs. Instead, they were disproportionately recruited from among the artisans, labourers and clerks in small factories and small businesses: that is, 'from among those in direct competition with Jewish workers' (Surh 2003, 160).

In October 1905 Odesa was once again the site of a viscious pogrom, far more deadly than the previous ones, and more than 800 Jews were killed. As explained by Weinberg, this time non-Jewish day labourers, more than any other group, filled the ranks of the pogromists. They competed with unskilled Jews, who made up roughly half of the workers at the docksides and in the railway depots. During the quiet October month in the off-season, barely half of the dockworkers were able to find employment. These workers were 'especially prone to anti-Jewish violence (Weinberg 2004, 263–4 and 272). Idle and hungry, they vented their anger and frustration at the Jews as soon as the possibility presented itself.

It might seem incongruous to try to explain such violent and uncontrollable actions as pogroms – involving so much wanton and indiscriminate destruction – in terms of economic interests. In a global comparative study in which she analyses precisely how hatred of economically successful minorities fuels violence in the modern world, Amy Chua makes an explicit exception for East European anti-Semitism and claims that 'economic grievances certainly had nothing to do with the numerous pogroms directed at poor shtetls in Russia and Eastern Europe' (Chua 2003, 201). Pogroms, however, are not a subject Chua had studied in detail and her opinion on this matter simply indicates that the legacy of the older research tradition as regards pogroms continues to influence secondary sources. More meticulous and updated studies from recent years suggest otherwise: the pogroms cannot be *reduced* to a mere function of economic competition, but nevertheless they certainly have *much* to do with economic grievances.

A Jewish lawyer from Odesa, who witnessed the 1871 pogrom in the city, gave the following explanation for what happened.

> The lawyer who loudly proclaims that the mob that loots the Jews are acting legally and naturally, is in fact interested only in the Jewish lawyers who know their profession better than he does himself, the ones who enjoy more confidence among the public – even among the Christian public – and as a result can take away a significant part of his practice. He does not dare to act in a similar way vis-à-vis, for instance, German lawyers who in similar ways hurt his business, since he knows that the Germans enjoy the same rights as he does himself. But when a Jew, whom he since the days of his childhood has been used to regard only as a day worker and a petty salesman, has the temerity to become his equal and even surpass him, he inevitably regards this as a scandalous infringement of his national rights . . . It turns out, then, that each citizen hates only that Jew who prevents him from monopolizing his business. But since it is shameful to admit openly to such a crude egotism, he has resort to the well-known and age-old subterfuge which is practised by people all over the world: they mask their personal concerns behind loud words about the common weal. (Orshanskii 1877, 167)

Thus, as we see, this Jewish commentator explains the hatred of the Jews in Russian society not by any peculiar Russian character traits, but with reference to universal human nature and general laws of psychology and sociology: in this case, dynamics of individual feelings of shame and mob psychology. This account also suggests that the contribution of the authorities to the pogrom was very indirect, but no less important for that: by depriving the Jews of certain rights they suggested to the populace that the Jews stood outside the law and were free targets that no one would be punished for attacking.

THE ARGUMENTS OF THE ANTI-SEMITES

Complaints about the pernicious influence of Jews on the economy were a recurrent theme in the many books and pamphlets produced by nineteenth-century Russian anti-Semites. An irate writer from 1890, Ivan Chernoiarov, explained that Jews nourish the most virulent envy and hatred towards Christians. They wage an eternal, bitter struggle, the aim of which is to 'destroy the Christian faith, dissolve all morals, corrupt and defile, encroach on the welfare of Christians, and finally to drive them into bankruptcy and take over all the wealth in the world'. To this end, many of the Jews even adopted the Christian faith; baptised Jews are wolves in sheep's clothing and even more dangerous than ordinary Jews, Chernoiarov insisted.

Another favourite Jewish way to outwit and deceive the Christians is to acquire education, Chernoiarov explains:

> The Yids regard educational qualifications and diplomas as means to increase their power and might in order to carry out their criminal-minded, Yid-like acts . . . . Therefore, an educated Jew cannot be a statesman or a public figure; he cannot be an honest and useful citizen, neither a science-loving doctor, nor a faithful pharmacist, not a judge or an honest lawyer, and not a member of a town council or a provincial council dedicated to the common good. No! He always remains a Yid, an enemy of Christ and a follower of the Talmud. (Chernoiarov 1890, 11)

This list of professions which the Yids cannot fill amounted to an outright plea for *Berufsverbot* (professional ban) for educated Jews.

In a pamphlet published in 1894 under the title *The Jewish Question*, another author, V. Iarmonkin, assures his readers that he is no enemy of the Jews. The only kinds of people Russians cannot stand are those who exploit others (*liudoiedy*). But this is precisely the variety of the human species so often found among the Jews (Iarmonkin 1894, 15). Well, not necessarily all Jews, Iarmonkin concedes, just the rich ones. The wealthy Jew has only one religion and that is money. He exploits everyone, even his own co-religionists. At this point Iarmonkin seems to become embroiled in contradictions. While, on the one hand, he claims to be attacking only one small group of Jews, the cut-throat fleecers among them, at the same time he explains that 'exploitation is in *the nature* of the Jew'; 'The Jewish calling in life is exclusively to sweat the Christian' (Iarmonkin 1894, 9 and 13).

Based on this analysis, Iarmonkin puts forward a list of specific recommendations.

- Repeal the existing legislation that allows the richest Jewish merchants – 'the 'merchants of the first guild' – to settle anywhere in the Russian Empire.

- Allow the Jews to hire as many workers as they want, but only their co-religionists. Hiring Christians should be strictly forbidden to them.
- Give all Jews free access to higher education, without restrictions, on the condition that, upon graduation, they live and work only among other Jews and not among the Christian population. Purely scientific pursuits should be absolutely free (Iarmonkin 1894, 19–20).

This programme may be regarded as a precursor of South African apartheid, or the ideology of 'separate but equal' that dominated White supremacist thinking in the American South until the rise of the civil rights movement. An interesting anomaly is the proviso that pure science should be exempted from this regimentation, an indication that scholarly professions had not yet become a field of competition.

One of the most prolific anti-Semitic Russian writers at the turn of the last century was the Moscow lawyer Aleksei Shmakov, the author of several bulky and rather incoherent volumes containing accusations against the Jews. Shmakov had received a classical education and relished Latin quotes and references to ancient history. His main concern, however, was closer to home. A common theme in several of his books is the need to keep the Jews out of the legal profession. In a 500-page anti-Semitic diatribe published in 1897 Shmakov declares that 'We must keep *Russia for Russians*, and in particular, the profession of lawyers in Moscow must remain *Russian*' (Shmakov 1897, 62, emphasis in the original). Nine years later, he returned to the same theme. Particularly worrying is the fact, he claims, that the process of Yidification of the Bar was strongest in St Petersburg: that is, in the city where the highest state organs of the Empire were located. Thus, Shmakov intimates that Jewish lawyers represented a threat not only to the interests of their Gentile colleagues, but also to the state (Shmakov, 1906, cccxxxvii). Shmakov also specifically points out that baptised Jews should have no more rights in the judiciary than Mosaic believers.

To combat the Jewish problem, Shmakov suggests, one should nip it in the bud: that is, one should restrict the right of Jews to acquire higher education. As a predominately urban group, the Jews, if not checked, would flock to the universities in droves. 'Higher education is the ground where they will inflict on us the very hardest blow.' A novel idea in Shmakov's book is the thought that Jews should not only be denied access to state universities above a certain quota but also be forbidden to establish their own private institutions of higher learning (Shmakov 1906, cccxxxiv).

In 1907 one of the most militant Russian anti-Semitic authors, S. Rossov, published a book on *The Jewish Question*, in which he presented a long list of harms allegedly caused to Russian society by the Jews. Some of his accusations sound remarkably 'modern', such as the allegation that the Jews engaged in pornography and trafficking: 'The Jewish trade in living goods' allegedly included 'the export of beautiful women to Alexandria, Port-Said and even Calcutta' (Rossov 1907, 57). While such descriptions no doubt might appeal to the lurid fantasy of some of Rossov's readers, this is not the section of his book in which we should look for his main message. We come closer if we focus on what Rossov called Jewish 'Exploitation and usurpation'. His understanding of 'exploitation', however, was quite peculiar; in fact, it basically covered what most of us today would call 'economic competition'. Rossov lamented that Jews had invaded the best towns and cities in the Empire. Even in Moscow and St Petersburg they had wormed their way in. Everywhere they drive Russians out of business.

> Wherever the Jews arrive, the business of Russians grows noticeably weaker. For instance, factory owners in Moscow are losing money due to the fact that pushy Jews turn up at the hotels, where they intercept and adroitly ensnare the wholesale dealers as they come to town, and offer to deliver goods below factory price. (Rossov 1907, 43–4)

No Russian can compete with the Jews, Rossov explains, since the Jews always and everywhere are preoccupied with one thing only: how to make a profit. His suggested solution to the 'Jewish Question' is simple and direct: they should be told to leave the country, and if necessary be removed by force. Rossov realised, however, that the Russian authorities would not agree to such drastic measures, and therefore proposed a long list of half-measures that could, if not eliminate, then at least mitigate the harm caused by the Jews. Among them we find, *inter alia*,

- Limit the number of Jewish trade establishments to a certain percentage of the total.
- Prohibit them from serving as middlemen. The Jews should be given no state contracts or assignments.
- Do not allow the Jews, as foreigners, to sit in the state Duma, on town councils, or in any other popular assemblies.
- Forbid the Jews to engage in stock exchange and banking business, as well as in publishing, or to run newspapers, journals or print shops.
- Deny Jews entry into all intermediate and higher Russian educational institutions. They may, if they want, study in their own schools.
- Forbid Jews to serve as doctors or lawyers for Christians.
- Send all Jews who have settled outside the Pale back to where they came from.
- Forbid Jews to take Russian or Christian names. (Rossov 1907, 99–101)

Rossov's proposal for anti-Jewish legislation is the most detailed and restrictive I have come across. Compared to the suggestions forwarded by Iarmonkin and

Chernoiarov in the 1890s, the thumb screws have been tightened considerably. The theme of the stock exchange is introduced for the first time, and the complete banishment of Jewish students from Russian schools is also a novelty.

Another Russian anti-Semitic publicist writing at the same time as Rossov, D. V. Tutkevich, confided that, in his personal experience, 'there is not a single sphere of life where the Jews are not harmful' (Tutkevich 1906, 11). Perhaps not every Jew is a crook, but the honest people among them are fewer than the number of righteous in Sodom and Gomorra at the time of Lot. To prove this, Tutkevich points to the activities of Jewish artisans. It is often claimed that they perform a useful service to Russian society, but that view is utterly misconceived.

> The Jewish artisans ruin the trade: they use unsuited, poor quality materials and are sometimes not even disposed to pay for them. In that way they can produce their goods very cheaply. An honest and conscientious artisan cannot and will not behave in that way, and due to the competition from Jews and the inclination of the customers to buy as cheaply as possible, the conscientious artisan is driven out of business. Therefore, it is not surprising that in the Pale of Settlement the Jews are more and more taking over all the trades. (Tutkevich 1906, 23–4)

This, however, did not mean that the Pale should not be repealed; on the contrary, it ought to be enforced more vigorously (Tutkevich 1906, 73).

It is often assumed that the most common economic accusation levelled against the Jews was that they defrauded the innocent population by charging extortionate prices. Indeed, such accusations may sometimes be found in Russian anti-Semitic tracts, but much more often, as in Tutkevich's diatribe, the *opposite* charge was made: the Jews were selling their goods *too cheaply*, at dumping prices. This was a problem, not for the Jews' customers, of course, but for their competitors.

CONCLUSIONS

Walter Laqueur warns against monocausal explanations for the phenomenon of anti-Semitism. 'In different times and places different factors were at play' (Laqueur 2006, 37). This warning we should heed. But this also means that in specific times and places, certain motivations played a larger role than others, and as I argue in this book, in nineteenth-century Russia social economic competition was a major driver.[6]

Underdog groups that begin to advance will often be considered as particularly threatening since they challenge not only the income security of other groups but also their social status and self-esteem. Typical underdog groups are diasporas: that is, groups which have, or can be construed to have, weak historical roots in the country. Groups that can present themselves as 'indigenous' can denounce the diasporas as 'aliens', 'intruders' and so on. Diasporas are also favourite targets since they normally have little political power.

The causes behind the economic competitiveness of the Jews are complex. The Jews of Russia (as well as most other countries) specialised in crafts, trade and other 'middleman' jobs, and filled different economic niches from the majority of the indigenous population. From a global perspective this social position was not unique, but rather one which the Jews shared with numerous diasporas around the world.

Few kinds of enmity towards 'the Stranger' have been regarded as more irrational and less interest-driven than anti-Semitism (see e.g. Benz 2004, 10 and 237). Stephen Bronner believes that, among the factors behind anti-Semitism economic jealousy is 'only the most superficial' (Bronner 2003, 34). Denis Prager and Joseph Telushkin insist that Jew hatred is 'unique'. It is triggered not by any socio-economic factors but by the Jews' superior religion and higher quality of life, they maintain (Prager and Telushkin 2003). My study, however, is based on the premise that anti-Semitism is *not* a unique phenomenon. I believe that the way Russians and other European nations have reacted against the Jews in their midst can, to a large extent, be explained by the social position occupied by the latter, and this is a position which the Jews have shared with many other diaspora groups around the world. I have not, however, attempted in this chapter to formulate a new catch-all theory of nationalism or anti-Semitism. No doubt many other factors besides job competition influence the crystallisation of xenophobic sentiments and movements.

To explain Russian anti-Semitism in the nineteenth century as interest-driven is, of course, not to condone it or 'explain it away'. Economically motivated anti-Semitism is no less and no more reprehensible than anti-Semitism driven by racism or religious bigotry. Historically, no doubt, these other varieties have also existed, but it is my contention that economic factors have been more important than most histories of anti-Semitism have often led us to believe.

NOTES

1. Remarkably, in the early twentieth century, some influential Jewish intellectuals such as Vladimir (Ze'ev) Jabotibinskii also started to characterise Jewish ethnic and cultural specificity in racial terms (Mogilner 2019).
2. Nathans (2004, 257–307) points out that Russian students of the time were radicals politically and did not push for the expulsion of Jews from the universities.
3. Typical examples of older scholarship are Vishniak 1942, 79–110; Dubnov 1975 vol. 2, esp. 247–83; and Pinkus [1988] 1989, esp. 27–9. For a critical assessment of this scholarship, see Aronson 1990, 1–15.
4. Smaller pogroms, or anti-Jewish riots which claimed no lives, had taken place in 1821 and 1859.

5. The Greeks were, of course, a diaspora no less than the Jews, but as Orthodox Christians they were less 'alien'.

6. Also, in the Soviet Union, attempts to eliminate Jewish competition for white-collar jobs seems to have been a major factor behind widespread anti-Semitism. The system of ascriptive nationality, with official ethnicity enshrined in the internal passports, was often exploited to weed out Jewish applicants for entry into institutions of higher learning. See Voslenskii 1984, Ch.7.14: 395–9). In the present chapter, I do not have space to discuss expressions of anti-Semitism in the Soviet period; interested readers are referred to Pinkus [1988] 1989and Gitelman [1988] 2001.

3

NATIONALISM, ETHNIC CONFLICT AND JOB COMPETITION: NON-RUSSIAN COLLECTIVE ACTION IN THE USSR UNDER PERESTROIKA

During perestroika, ethnic and national conflicts erupted all over the Soviet Union, but not in uniform ways. In Central Asia, virtually all republics experienced interethnic riots, frequently with deadly outcomes. In the Baltics, however, developments unfolded very differently: here, the titular nationalities – the Estonians, Latvians and Lithuanians – organised peaceful protests with hundreds of thousands of participants. Moreover, the local Supreme Soviets adopted increasingly radical legislation geared towards enhancing the sovereignty of the republics. Those few scholars in the Brezhnev years who had predicted the dissolution of the Soviet state, pointed to Muslim regions as the potential catalyst for this. However, it turned out that mobilisation in the European parts of the country – and in the Baltics in particular – was far more effective, and the Balts were the ones who led the march of the non-Russians towards independence. How can this best be explained?

In this chapter, I maintain that the factor of job competition, which, as we saw in the previous chapter, played such a major role in the emergence of Russian anti-Semitism, is also an important part of the explanation behind ethnic conflict and nationalism under Gorbachev. I argue that rapid demographic increase leads to competition for blue-collar jobs while an increase in the number of graduates from higher education leads to competition over elite jobs. In the first case, people risk unemployment, in the second, blocked career opportunities. Mass-level unemployment may lead to anger-driven mass riots, while an intelligentsia will be able to formulate more rational strategies to eliminate threatening competitors from the labour market. One such strategy is to insist that the state ought to be a national state, in which the national elites will be in control.

The Soviet educational system had been producing greater numbers of highly educated people than even the overgrown Soviet bureaucracy could absorb. In the republics, Russians and titulars competed for the same positions; and by making knowledge of the titular language a mandatory requirement for entry into higher education and top-level employment, titulars gained a competitive edge. While questions of identity no doubt may also have enormous mobilising power in times of national resurgence, identity issues are normally intertwined intimately with interest politics. These mechanisms are traced in the history of ethnic mobilisation in the Soviet Union and the post-Soviet states during and after perestroika.

*   *   *

The sudden upsurge of national mobilisation and ethnic conflict in the USSR in the 1980s had not been foreseen. One of the few experts who, as early as the late 1970s, had predicted a collapse of the Soviet state was Hélène Carrère d'Encausse, but her argument was ill conceived. She explicitly discounted Baltic nationalism as a possible motor in this process. The Baltic nations, she believed, had a high degree of national consciousness but were nevertheless 'condemned by circumstance to weakness, even extinction' (Carrère d'Encausse 1979, 267). The circumstance she referred to was unfavourable demographic trends: low fertility and high immigration of non-Balts to the Baltic republics. In contrast, Central Asia was, in her view, the most likely place for the decline of the Empire to start, due to rapid population increase in the region. In Central Asia, she argued, 'ethnic consciousness and demographic vitality go hand in hand' (Carrère d'Encausse 1979, 267). As we now know, the drive for political independence among the Soviet republics started in the Baltics, and the Balts were pivotal in keeping up the momentum of the independence struggle throughout the perestroika period. In the end, the Central Asian republics too declared independence, in the autumn of 1991, but this was done very reluctantly and only when it was plain for all to see that the Soviet Union could no longer be salvaged.[1]

This is not to say that Central Asia remained tranquil throughout the perestroika period. On the contrary, some of the earliest cases of violent ethnic conflict took place here. Contemporary commentators were often at a loss to explain this frenzy. In Fergana in June 1989, for instance, it appears that the killings started with a mere trifle, when a Meskhet-Turk complained about the price of a box of strawberries at the marketplace (Carrère d'Encausse 1993, 98). This seemed to confirm the viewpoint of those who insist that ethnic collective action is basically irrational.

If ethnic riots in Central Asia were seen as emotion-driven, the Baltic 'singing revolutions' were generally regarded as pure cases of identity-driven mobilisation. The sources of mass support seemed to stem from an urge to regain national dignity, rectify historical injustices, and save the national language and culture from extinction. No doubt such cultural concerns were central to the independence struggle, not only in the Baltics but in many other Soviet republics as well. Even so, more mundane considerations, I will insist, also played their part. Many Balts were convinced – with good reason, as it turned out – that their countries would become much more prosperous as soon as they left the planned economy behind and introduced capitalism in its place. In addition, Balts with higher education could hope that national independence would affect their personal career opportunities by curbing or eliminating Russian competition on the job market. This issue was not a central part of the nationalist propaganda, but, as I will show in this chapter, several strategies adopted by the non-Russian nationalists during perestroika, as well as laws enacted by the new states after independence, clearly had that effect.

In my view, economic competition is one of the most important factors that can explain the different trajectories of interethnic development in the various Union republics in the USSR under perestroika. It is certainly not the only factor, but it is one which has often been overlooked or downplayed. Combining insights gleaned from the theory of nationalism and the theory of ethnic conflict, this chapter argues that two related but distinct socio-economic dynamics contributed to two different kinds of job competition and two types of ethnic collective action in the Soviet Union during perestroika:

- Hypothesis 1: Demographic growth > mass-level job competition > grassroots-level non-political ethnic conflict
- Hypothesis 2: Educational growth > elite-level job competition > articulate political elite nationalism

In both cases the dynamic will not be unleashed before the labour market has reached a certain saturation point.

Central Asia was the only Soviet region that experienced high levels of general unemployment in the late Soviet period. In all other parts of the USSR there was, on the contrary, a very tight labour market, due to low labour productivity and declining birth rates. The overheated labour market in Central Asia was clearly one important factor behind the ethnic riots in this region. For reasons that will be explained below, elite competition for jobs did not become an issue in Central Asia, with the partial exception of Kazakhstan. In the Baltics and Moldova, on the other hand, important actors perceived such competition to be acute and this decisively influenced the trajectories of ethnic politics in these republics.

In a standard account of nationalist mobilisation under perestroika Mark Beissinger found that several structural factors correlated with regional differences in mobilisation, including the formal status of the various national autonomies; degrees of linguistic assimilation; population size; and urbanisation. As a supplement to a structuralist explanation he proposes an 'eventful' approach that highlights how mobilisation comes in tidal waves. Beissinger concluded that 'tide and structure were intertwined in the ways in which separatist action materialised across time and space' (Beissinger 2002, 233). This is a balanced and reasonable conclusion but is, in my view, weakened by Beissinger's failure to discuss two structural factors commonly identified as crucial for nationalist mobilisation: levels of education and levels of underemployment in the intelligentsia, and how they relate to each other.

Hale (2000) does examine whether levels of education might explain the propensity for secession in the Soviet federal units, and finds a certain but very weak correlation. Far more important are regional wealth, regional autonomy status and ethnic group distinctiveness. Hale tests two very different theses about how educational levels might affect national mobilisation, neither of which he finds convincing. The first suggests that groups possessing elite skills tend to have strong interests in preserving a union state, while the other, on the contrary, claims that such groups will be most separatist since only they can build viable independent states (Hale 2000, 50). The argument put forward in this chapter differs from both of these theories and hypothesises instead that individuals with higher education will tend to be attracted by nationalist programmes when they feel that their career ambitions are being frustrated and they perceive these frustrations as somehow linked to their ethnic identity. As Elise Giuliano has pointed out, 'framings' and perceptions of the job market are just as important as the 'objective' job situation (2006, 289–91). One person may spurn a job offer that another with the same qualifications will gladly accept.

In this chapter I will not conduct any rigorous mathematical testing of my twin theses, but instead examine the utterances and actions of members of titular groups in the republics. Do they express job-related grievances? Do they mobilise collectively in reaction to perceived discrimination on the labour market? Do they make any moves to redress the situation when they have the power to do so after independence?

HYPOTHESIS I: THE LABOUR FACTOR IN THE RISE OF ETHNIC CONFLICT

Ethnic division of labour is a commonly observed phenomenon in many parts of the world. This system may have diverse roots and take various forms. Sometimes it is regarded as beneficial to all parties involved, at other times it has the character of oppressive ethnic stratification (Horowitz 1985, 105–31; Barth [1969] 1998, 27–8). In premodern societies ethnically stratified systems may be quite stable. Children learn their trade from their parent or some other close family member, and socio-professional patterns are perpetuated through the ages. The professional lore is transmitted through and remains within the ethnic group. This stability, however, may be upset by various forms of social, economic and ecological change. One of the most important is the interrelated processes normally referred to as modernisation.

Two aspects of modernisation are particularly pertinent to the present study: population growth and job equalisation. In the early stages of modernisation higher hygienic standards and better nutrition lead to decreased mortality in an environment of continued high fertility, and birth rates soar (only in the later stages of modernisation will family planning lead to a drop in fertility). In addition, industrial society has a much higher degree of job standardisation than traditional society. While the number of different types of jobs certainly multiplies, the basic skills needed to fill them are more similar than before (Gellner [1983] 1990, 24–8). The barriers between the guilds break down, and people from different backgrounds, also different ethnic backgrounds, compete for the same jobs. Modernisation combines local markets into industry-wide markets, and the likelihood of competition between members of different ethnic groups for the same occupation increases.

These processes have been studied by Fredrik Barth ([1969] 1989) and Susan Olzak (1992), among others. In *Ethnic Groups and Boundaries* Barth maintained that ethnic identities are not based on the cultural repertoire of each group, but are produced on the boundaries between them. The character of relations between groups depends to a large extent on the character and degree of their competition. As long as they occupy separate ecological niches, the relationship between groups may be quite stable, while niche overlap increases the level of competition and potential for conflict (Barth [1969] 1989, 20).

Barth discussed premodern societies only, while Susan Olzak has extended his theory to modern industrial societies by applying it to ethnic competition in the USA around the turn of the last century. She found that, as long as an ethnic group occupied a separate economic sector in a stratified labour market, it could escape the unwanted attention of other groups. This view ran counter to the theories of 'a cultural division of labour' and 'split labour market', as developed by Michael Hechter and others. Hechter (1975) saw a high degree of economic ethno-stratification as leading to a crystallisation of national consciousness and a trigger for ethnic conflict. Olzak, on the contrary, found that the likelihood of ethnic hostility and conflict grew when the cultural division of labour broke down and niche overlap increased.

Olzak explored this dynamic along four parameters: immigration and migration; economic contraction; increases in ethnic group resources; and political challenges to ethnic dominance. She found that levels of ethnic violence correlated with levels of immigration, but not always in the way she had expected. While one would assume the violence to be directed against the most recent arrivals, Olzak (1992, 36) found that, in some cases, other groups, and in particular those with the least capacity to retaliate, became the target of hostility. She did not study the impact of different birth rates on interethnic relations, since in an immigrant society like the USA the effects of these differentials on demographic development was dwarfed by the effect of immigration and migration. In Soviet Central Asia the situation was very different. The Central Asian republics reached the early stages of modernisation only in the 1960s and 1970s, and birth rates soared. Soviet-style industrialisation with low productivity created many new jobs, but not enough to prevent a severe labour surplus. This was the most important reason behind the persistently high unemployment in this region. To apply competition theory to ethnic conflict in Central Asia, then, is to extend Barth's model a second time, via Olzak's application to modern societies to a study of modernising societies.

Elise Giuliano, as we saw in Chapter 1 (pp. 13–14), has employed a competition model in an analysis of nationalist mobilisation in the non-Russian autonomous republics in the Russian Federation after 1989. Giuliano argues that there was a close correlation between economic and political trends. Republics with high levels of educational and job competition for white-collar jobs, such as Tatarstan and Sakha-Yakutia, experienced higher levels of nationalist mobilisation than republics with lower levels of such competition, such as Mari-El and Mordovia (Giuliano 2005, 6; 2006; 2011).

Up to a point Giuliano follows Susan Olzak's reasoning, but she takes issue with her for allegedly being overly structuralist: while job competition in Olzak's scheme is more or less sufficient to trigger ethnic turmoil, a structural battle for jobs does not spontaneously determine who will become the victims of street attacks or political campaigns, Giuliano argues. 'Ethnic mobilization motivated by job competition cannot be adequately understood apart from politics; or more specifically apart from a process in which intentional actors attempt to define a grievance in order to achieve particular political goals' (Giuliano 2005, 15).

I believe that Giuliano's disagreement with Olzak stems, at least in part, from a confusion between the two levels of conflict analysed in the present chapter: non-political, inarticulate ethnic violence related to mass-level job competition, on the one hand, and political nationalism related to increases in higher education and competition for top-level jobs, on the other. Olzak deals primarily with the former and Giuliano primarily with the latter. In the former case, we should not expect to find many articulations of grievances in the form of political programmes and explicit nationalist strategies from identifiable parties and pressure groups.

Wilkinson (2004) has studied regional variations in ethnic violence in India, and concludes that the most important explanation behind it is related to politics and not to socio-economic factors. His findings run counter to my assumption that political nationalism and grassroots-level ethnic riots have separate causes. Wilkinson (2004, 163) does occasionally show that job competition can be a contributing factor behind a riot, but the most persistent pattern he finds is related to election cycles and party constellations in Indian democracy. It is worth noting, however, that Wilkinson hardly ever claims that regional leaders *instigate* violence; instead, he points out that some of them abet or fail to prevent riots whenever they believe that ethnic polarisation may boost their election campaign. In those Indian states where state government is weak in ordering their police to prevent violence, local economic and social factors will often be important in determining the location and scale of ethnic riots, Wilkinson acknowledges (2004, 20).

Hypothesis 2: The Labour Factor in the Rise of Elite Nationalism

In contrast to ethnic rioting, successful mobilisation for nationalist political goals clearly presupposes some kind of organisational framework and recognised leaders with a programme. Most studies of nationalism agree that the emergence of such programmes is related to the advent of modern society. An important consequence of modernisation is increasing levels of education in the population. At the basic level, illiteracy goes drastically down, while at the top of society the universities churn out an immeasurably higher number of graduates than before who are qualified for prestigious and well-paid jobs. Although a modernising society is often also characterised by a rapidly expanding state bureaucracy, as well as a burgeoning business sector that may absorb a growing number of the university candidates, the coveted top jobs will normally be far fewer than the number of people who are formally qualified to fill them.

The social mechanisms unleashed by increased levels of higher education are different from those produced by population growth. The strength of the competition will vary with the number of *qualified* applicants, and tend to increase when the educational system produces more qualified job seekers than this segment of the labour market can absorb, particularly if some groups believe that they are systematically discriminated against when the best jobs are filled. Whereas ethnic riots at mass levels may be regarded as unarticulated and haphazard expressions of ethno-economic frustration, ethnic job competition at elite levels engenders articulate nationalism: that is, political demands for a nationalisation of the existing state or the establishment of a new, national state. This is one important reason why the proper place to look for the genesis of nationalism is the elites. Karl Mannheim's idea of the intelligentsia as *'freischwebende'* – 'free-floating' and 'interest-free' – simply does not stand up to scrutiny. No less than other groups, academic and cultural elites pursue a value that in most societies is in short supply: a well-paid and interesting job (since most readers of this book belong to the academic elite they should be able to confirm this with experience from their own life).

In *Thought and Change* ([1964] 1972) Ernest Gellner presented the first formulation of his theory of nationalism as caused by the uneven spread of industrialisation and education in modern society. Sociologically, Gellner identified the intelligentsia and the proletariat as the two 'prongs' of nationalism. Both of these groups can be mobilised by the nationalist cause, but what they can gain by an independent national state differs wildly: the proletariat may exchange hardships-with-snubs with the possibly greater hardships-with-national identification, while

> [for] the intellectuals, independence means an immediate and enormous advantage: jobs and very good jobs. The very numerical weakness of an 'underdeveloped' intelligentsia is its greatest asset: by creating a national unit whose frontiers become in effect closed to foreign talent (except in 'advisory' short-term capacity), they create a magnificent monopoly for themselves. (Gellner [1964] 1972, 169)

In *Nations and Nationalism* Gellner developed this argument into his wonderful parable of Ruritania versus Megalomania ([1983] 1990, 58–70). In this book Gellner claimed that his theory of nationalism had been misunderstood: One need not assume any conscious long-term calculation of material advantage or social mobility on anyone's part behind the drive for a national state. Instead, the people of Ruritania had been taught 'to be aware of their culture, and to love it' (Gellner [1983] 1990, 61). However, in *Thought and Change* Gellner had written about 'a more or less *spurious* concern for local culture' ([1964] 1972, 171, emphasis added), so rather than correcting a misunderstanding of his theory, Gellner seems to have decided to restate the first bombastic formulation of it in a less reductionistic way.

Eric Hobsbawm similarly underscored the importance of job competition for the emergence of nationalism while at the same time hedging against reductionistic interpretations of his theory:

> I do not wish to reduce linguistic nationalism to a question of jobs ... Nevertheless it cannot be fully understood, and the opposition to it even less, unless we see the vernacular language as, among other things, a vested interest of the less examination-passing classes. (Hobsbawm 1991, 118)

These assumptions Hobsbawm saw confirmed in the development of, among others, Finnish, Flemish and Tamil nationalism.

Clearly, there is no one-to-one relationship between elite job competition and nationalism, or between mass-level job competition and ethnic riots. For one thing, people compete over many more material goods than just jobs. In parts of the world lack of water and land is what triggers the fiercest conflicts; these two issues severely exacerbate the Palestinian Question and the Darfur crisis, for instance. Sometimes conflicts that seem to be job-related may, in fact, be linked to competition for other scarce goods. Thus, the organised import of Russian blue-collar labour to the Baltic states in the late Soviet period was greatly resented by the local population, but not so much because they took jobs that the Balts wanted for themselves. In most cases they did not, and Hypothesis 1 did not apply. Instead, the most controversial issue was the distribution of flats: 'The immigrants often received the scarce housing for which Estonians had been waiting for years. Newcomers sometimes would simply invade newly finished apartments – no Estonian official would dare to evict them and risk being charged with nationalism' (Taagepera 1993, 96). Similarly, in the bloody anti-Armenian pogrom in Sumgait in Azerbaijan in February 1988, some of the rioters seem to have been motivated by a desire to take over the flats of the Armenians who fled (de Waal 2003, 29–44). Job competition, then, should be regarded as an aspect of a more general competition for scarce resources among ethnic groups.

Moreover, people do not fight over material resources only, but also over immaterial goods such as the right to use their own language and to preserve their culture, and such imponderables as national dignity and prestige. No doubt questions of identity may have an enormously mobilising power in times of national resurgence, and during perestroika the language issue in most Soviet republics was certainly at the very top of the political agenda. However, while the desire to expand the use of one's own language may be, and for many people no doubt is, a motivating force in its own right, I will nevertheless maintain that this issue is often intimately intertwined with interest politics.

It is often easy to demonstrate that a language revival opens up new job opportunities for members of the indigenous ethnic groups, through the sacking, demotion and semi-voluntary outmigration of members of non-indigenous groups. What we cannot demonstrate so easily is the direction of the causal links. Were the new job opportunities a fortuitous windfall from the cultural battles, or were they a prime goal of the language struggle?

My Hypothesis 2 attempts to explain the behaviour of nationally minded educated *elites* only. During perestroika, many nationalist rallies in the non-Russian republics drew hundred of thousands of participants, and clearly, far from all of them belonged to the intelligentsia. It is beyond the scope of this chapter to try to explain how the elites are able to convince the masses to follow under their nationalist banners when they, as Gellner ironically expressed it, 'exchange hardships-with-snubs with the possibly greater hardships with national identification', as so often turned out to be the case in the post-Soviet states too.

ETHNIC RIOTS IN CENTRAL ASIA

In the late 1980s there was no general unemployment in the Soviet Union as a whole, primarily due to a combination of two circumstances: low fertility rates and extremely low labour productivity. Often, it took three persons to do the same job as one person, or a machine, would do in the West. This created a situation in which labour was in constantly short supply. Only in Central Asia was the situation different. Here, productivity was no higher – in fact, it was only 50 per cent of the Soviet average and one-third of productivity in the Baltic republics – but this factor was offset by very high fertility rates (Rumer 1990, 111–12). While the average gross reproduction rate in the Slavic parts of the USSR in the mid-1970s had dropped to 0.98–1.08, in the Central Asian republics it was in the range of a staggering 2.33–3.07 (Rywkin 1979, 2). Such figures not even the labour-intensive Central Asian economy could absorb. Attempts to induce the Central Asians to move to other parts of the Soviet Union to find work produced meagre results. Central Asia, then, was the only place in the Soviet Union where riots related to unemployment and mass-level job competition could, and did, erupt.

The ethnic riots in Central Asia in the perestroika period started in 1986 and lasted to 1990, with 1989 as the peak year.

- In June 1986 several thousand Tajiks in Dushanbe attacked everyone who looked foreign. Countless people were wounded.
- In December 1988, February 1989 and April 1989 students and workers in Tashkent attacked foreigners with iron rods and some light arms.
- In May 1989 the mob destroyed cooperatives owned by Armenians and other Caucasians in Ashgabat in Turkmenistan.
- In June 1989 the Fergana Valley exploded after the famous strawberry quarrel. The death toll ran to roughly 100 people, while more than 1,000 were wounded.
- In June 1989 clashes between Kazakhs and immigrant workers from Chechnya and Azerbaijan in the Kazakhstani oil town of Novy Uzen left half a dozen dead and 200 wounded, in addition to considerable material damage.
- In June 1990 more than 200 people died in fighting between ethnic Kyrgyz and Uzbeks in the southern Kyrgyz city of Osh (Fuller and Bohr 1989; Carrère d'Encausse 1991, 96–100).

Soviet authorities initially blamed the disturbances on 'youth hooliganism' and underplayed the fact that the victims had almost invariably been non-indigenes. The riots were not, however, cases of indiscriminate xenophobia. One important group of non-natives was virtually always spared: the Russians.[2] This may reflect the fact that the Central Asians perceived the Russians as somehow associated with the Soviet authorities in Moscow and realised that their economic wellbeing was dependent on transfers from the central Soviet budget: you don't bite the hand that feeds you. But just as important, probably, was the fact that Central Asia had a split labour market: the indigenous groups were heavily concentrated in agriculture and the Russians in industry (Rumer 1990, 105–22). Thus, they were not in direct competition for jobs at the mass level.

The causes of the violence were complex and not necessarily the same in all instances. In the Osh killings, members of two indigenous Central Asian groups confronted each other – one being the titular nation in Kyrgyzstan, where Osh is located, the other, the titular nation in neighbouring Uzbekistan just across the border. In all other cases, the victims, almost without exception, belonged to small diaspora groups. Some of them had been deported to the region under Stalin – Meskhets, Chechens – while others had arrived there in search of work (Tiskhkov 1997, 80). Many of them had done reasonably well in their new place of residence, often against heavy odds, and were considered to be better off than the indigenous population. The propensity of the mob to go after small and vulnerable groups conforms with the patterns Olzak observed in the USA.

In some cases, such as the Dushanbe riots, the housing shortage seems to have been the trigger, as rumours circulated that refugees from Armenia were being given the best flats in the city (Brown 1991). In most cases, however, the mob accused the intruders of taking jobs from the locals. In Novy Uzen: 'Many of our young lads don't have a job. . . . The anti-Caucasian moods are caused by the rumours that many Caucasians who came here get good jobs, bring their relatives, get their domicile registration using bribes' (Numanov and Sidorov 1989). One journalist in Fergana was told that 'the Meskhetians, the Crimean Tatars, the Jews and the Germans are financially better off and have greater opportunities than the Uzbeks' (Bohr 1989, 24). In Osh: 'Local Uzbeks and Kirgiz came to blows as a result of tensions engendered in part by the Uzbeks' perception that they were underrepresented in the local government and the Kirgiz view that the Uzbeks took all the best jobs in the retail and consumer sector' (Anderson 1997, 68).

To say that economic grievances were an important factor behind the ethnic frenzy in Central Asia in the late 1980s is, of course, to claim that it was (at least in part) interest-driven, but not that it was a rational strategy to improve the lot of the indigenous population. Clearly, it was not. When the mobs demanded the exodus of 'foreigners', they got much more than they had bargained for. Not only did the targeted diaspora groups leave in droves, but also an increasing number of ethnic Russians and other Russophones began to feel the earth shaking under their feet. In the heated atmosphere of interethnic hostility many decided to leave before it was too late (Kolstø 1995, 200–29). The first to leave were often Russians with higher education since they could more easily find a new job in the Russian Federation. As a result, the local industry and infrastructure lost key technical and administrative personnel that could not be easily replaced.

Coming on top of the general depression that set in in the Soviet Union under perestroika, this brain drain forced many local industries in Central Asia to close down. Hence, fewer, not more, job opportunities opened up for the locals. In 1990 there were estimated to be 650,000 unemployed in Tajikistan and 1 million in Uzbekistan (Kaiser 1994, 240).

POLITICAL NATIONALISM IN THE WESTERN REPUBLICS

In the postwar period, higher education in the Soviet Union reached unprecedented high levels. From 1960 to 1980, the number of students increased from 2.4 million to 5.2 million, or by almost 120 per cent. The rise in enrolments far outstripped population growth with the result that the number of students per 10,000 inhabitants rose from 111 to 196 over the same period. This was one of the highest participation rates in industrialised countries (Avis 1987, 202).

For a long time, only a few national minorities – the Jews and the three major South Caucasian nationalities – had levels of higher education comparable with or surpassing those of the Russians. Most of the others trailed far behind. In 1987 George Avis (1987, 217) predicted that these imbalances would be perpetuated into the next decade as no further expansion of the student body was foreseen in the current five-year plan. However, a few years later, twenty nationalities had a higher rate of higher education than the Russians. While the number of Russian students had dropped from 213 to 190 per 10,000 inhabitants between 1974 and 1989, it had increased by 13 for Moldovans, 24 for Latvians, 36 for Kazakhs and 37 for Estonians (for more comprehensive figures, see Kaiser 1994, 232; Arutiunian 1992, 118).

The main reason behind this unexpected trend seems to have been ethnic favouritism. A special quota system for the education of non-indigenes in the republics had already been established in the 1920s (Martin 2001), and in the post-Stalin period the preferential treatment arrangement was intensified (Zaslavsky 1993, 35–6). In her seminal study, *Ethnic Relations in the USSR*, Rasma Karklins (1986, 63–6 and 218–21) found that both formal and informal systems of affirmative action were operating in the republics (see also Karklins 1984). The locals aggressively insisted that they had a right to preferential access to higher education in their republic. In 1978, Kazakhs at the Kazakhstan State University used knives to attack Russian students, whom the Kazakh felt were too heavily represented in the student body. Karklins concluded that

> perceptions of unequal access to socio-economic and occupational status play a role not only on the macro level of group relations, but on the micro level as well. . . . Job dissatisfaction tends to be transposed into more negative ethnic views, which is bound to be even more pronounced

when direct ethnic competition at work is involved. Several sources note that this is especially true for professionals and white-collar personnel, who in addition also tend to be the strata most concerned about the flourishing of native cultures. (Karklins 1986, 220)

Bohdan Krawchenko has given an account of the emergence of Ukrainian nationalism that repeats almost perfectly Gellner's story of Ruritanians coming to town. The improvement in the level of education among the Ukrainians, he explains, resulted in new job aspirations and in an intense desire to leave the confines of the village. This led to competition between Ukrainians and Russians. 'At stake in this rivalry were higher status and better paying jobs, political and economic power and influence. In this competitive process, Russians enjoyed considerable advantages' (Krawchenko 1985, 185). This, Krawchenko believes, was one of the underlying factors behind the recrudescence of Ukrainian nationalism.[3]

Nicholas Dima points out that, already during the 1960s, the 23 per cent Russio-Ukrainian share of the Moldavian population held some 65 per cent of the urban/industrial jobs in the republic. It appears that some Romanians/Moldavians demonstrated their discontent concerning the situation. 'With a small but strong pro-Soviet and pro-Russian leadership at the top, and with an increasing middle class drawn probably toward traditional Romanian values and interests, the ethnic stability of Moldavia is very delicate to say the least,' Dima argued (1991, 89).

Robert Kaiser saw no reason why 'those nonindigenes (and particularly Russians) who migrated to the growing urban/industrial centres in the past will voluntarily make room for the socially mobilised and increasingly educated indigenes'. The increase in indigenous higher education would therefore create 'growing international [= interethnic] competition for the resources of the republics, including high-status occupations' (Kaiser 1994, 235).

In Latvia, the vice-chairman of the Latvian Movement for National Independence, Mirdza Vitole, complained in 1990 that 'the demographic crisis in Latvia is heavily influenced by the processes of migration. Latvians do not have any hopes for a better life while the immigrants are settled in fast and comfortably, at the expense of the indigenous population' (*Sovetskaia Molodezh*, 4 July 1990). Rebutting allegations that Russians were discriminated against in independent Latvia, Latvian MP Vilis Zarins maintained in 1992 that in the Soviet Union *Latvians* had been discriminated against. The 1989 census showed that 71.5 per cent of agricultural workers in Latvia were ethnic Latvians, while only 17.3 per cent of the male employees in administrative structures in Riga at that time belonged to the titular nationality. 'So which people is being subjected to discrimination and squeezed out of the important positions in the state structure and economy?' Zarins asked rhetorically (*Diena*, 20 June 1992). Another

Latvian MP, Dzintars Abikis, claimed that as late as in 1993 ethnic Latvians still carried out most of the heavy manual work in their country. The reason for this he saw in the 'unequal possibilities for education, and discrimination against Latvians in the Soviet cadre policy' (*Diena*, 26 March 1993).

To what extent did these persistent perceptions of job discrimination against non-Russians reflect the realities? Different rates of employment in elite positions among ethnic groups do not by themselves prove that any group is being discriminated against; such figures may instead stem from unequal levels of education. The crucial issue is whether a person with higher education in a given group will be able to get a job in accordance with his or her qualifications. Very little statistical data on this are available, but the volume *Russians: Ethnosociological Essays*, published by a team of researchers from the Institute of Ethnology and Anthropology in Moscow in 1992, provides some insights. These researchers combine data from Soviet job centres with census data and calculate that, in the mid-1980s, 85–86 per cent of Russians in Central Asia with higher or medium specialised education were employed in jobs where their level of education was required, while among the titular groups the number of persons employed in such jobs *exceeded* the number of people who were qualified to fill them. In Estonia the educational qualifications of ethnic Russians and ethnic Estonians were utilised by 68 per cent and 85 per cent, respectively, meaning that 32 per cent of Russians and 15 per cent of Estonians with high or medium specialised education were working in positions where their education was not needed. The corresponding figures for Latvia were 20 per cent for Russians and 6 per cent for Latvians (Arutiunian 1992, 121). These figures suggest that competition for elite jobs was much fiercer in the Baltics than in Central Asia. The fact that titulars everywhere were better off than the Russians did not in itself give them any reason not to press for even more. In the opinion of David Laitin, titular nationals seeking social mobility would not be satisfied with a share of top jobs that corresponded to their share of the total population, but would attempt to achieve 'a near monopoly on high-status cadre jobs' (1991, 168).

In Central Asia, as pointed out above, very many of the Russians and other Russophones who emigrated belonged to the intelligentsia and had held top positions in public administration, education and other institutions that could not simply be shut down. As a result, as Robert Kaiser reported, 'skilled job vacancies are increasing so rapidly that they cannot be filled by the number of trained indigenes even though this number also grew substantially during the 1980s' (Kaiser 1994, 240–1). The competition for white-collar jobs in Central Asia during perestroika was won by the titulars by default, as it were, as the non-indigenous office-holders gave up their positions without a fight. From the western republics, however, outmigration of Russians and other Russophones was considerably smaller. Most of them opted to stay and did not step down from their positions unless various kinds of pressure were put on them to do so. The adoption of new language laws and other legislation contributed massively to that result.

On the face of it, language demands must be classified as a typical 'identity issue'. Language was the most important ethnic identity marker in the Soviet Union, and an enhanced status for the titular language would entail an enhanced status for the eponymous ethnic group too. In the course of 1988–90, all non-Russian republics passed laws making the titular language the 'state language' of the republic, virtually everywhere in the face of fierce Russophone resistance. The first laws adopted were, in most cases, very liberal, at least on paper, and contained seemingly solid guarantees for the continued usage of minority languages. Russian was given a status as 'language of interethnic communication'. This was the case, for instance, with most of the laws adopted in the Central Asian republics. Since the Russians were already leaving en masse from this region, no linguistic pressure was necessary to make them give up their prestigious positions. On the contrary, in Kyrgyzstan there was concern that the outflow of Russophones might seriously hurt the economy, and the language legislation was amended in 1995 to raise the status of Russian and to encourage the Russians to stay (Landau and Kellner-Heinkele 2001, 120).

In most western republics too the first language laws adopted during perestroika gave Russian a status as the 'language of interethnic communication'. What that would mean in practice was far from clear since the legislators could not, of course, regulate which language two persons with different ethnic backgrounds would use as a 'means of communication' when they met on the street. Many Russians felt that such clauses were meaningless and just a smokescreen to conceal the main aim of the law, which was to remove the Russophones from public life and the top echelons of the labour market. In a major comparative study of the language laws adopted in the Soviet republics under perestroika, the Russian[4] sociolinguist Mikhail Guboglo (1993, 162) saw growing competition for key positions in the administrative structures in the *nomenklatura* and later also for prestigious jobs in the culture and the sciences, as one of the driving forces behind the adoption of the language laws in many republics. In most of the laws the true objectives were hidden, he maintained. Nevertheless, in virtually all cases 'the non-linguistic "sore thumb" stuck out: to ensure the competitiveness of the groups in the titular nation that had a command of the state language' (Guboglo 1998, 222).

The language laws would have had no bite unless they also included some clauses about implementation. It was generally felt that the Russophones would sabotage the new language requirements and not learn the new state language unless non-compliance carried with it credible threats of penalties. Thus, in many republics employment in certain jobs was linked to proficiency in the state language at a certain level.

In Moldova the parliament adopted a language law in 1989 which stipulated that the sole state language was Moldovan, and that this language was to be used in all public administration (with translation into Russian as necessary). Under the Popular Front government in 1990–2, however, a system of language attestations was instituted that went far beyond anything that was envisioned in the language law. In many offices and institutions, Russian speakers who failed the sometimes rather arbitrary language tests either lost their jobs or were not granted promotion.

In a detailed study Petr Shornikov has documented that, in the early 1990s, firings were carried out in Moldova in virtually every profession. In the medical profession alone more than 1,000 doctors and 1,500 other medical personnel were fired with reference to the new language law (Shornikov 1997, 52–4). Shornikov – who wrote in a double capacity as a scholar and an activist on behalf of the Russophone group in Moldova – concluded that cadre policy was at the heart of the nationality policy of the national–radicals who held sway in Moldovan politics in the early 1990s. 'The actual function of the legislation about the language regime was to ensure a legal basis for ethnic cleansing in the prestigious and advantageous spheres of activity' (Shornikov 1997, 75).

Latvia is another case. A liberal language law from 1988 was replaced after independence by new and much stricter legislation. Under the 1992 law it was forbidden even for private firms to use anything but the state language in their business correspondence and in the minutes of their internal meetings. A State Language Inspectorate was established to ensure compliance with the new law. Its staff conducted language tests of the workforce and issued a statute according to which all who did not pass the test could be fired.

By the end of 1995 some 250,000 persons had been language-tested. Although many failed the test, few were actually fired, but there were some cases of mass notice being given. The most important effect of the law, instead, was that no one was hired for a job unless the language requirement was met. This was enforced with special rigour in the most prestigious positions (Kolstø 2000, 116). According to Antane and Tsilevich, 'a multitude of new jobs were created in the organs of government. The vast majority of the officials who filled these positions were ethnic Latvians' (Antane and Tsilevich 1999, 132).

Should the employment clauses in the language legislation be regarded as a means to raise the status of the titular language or a means to squeeze non-titulars out of prestigious positions? It clearly contributed to both, and the legislators could well have had both effects in mind when they passed the law. The only situation in which we might determine which of the two concerns – protection of the national language or elimination of job competition – is more important would be if they were at cross-purposes and the nationalists would have to choose between them. Such a situation did, in fact, exist in Kazakhstan. From this republic the Russophone population did not leave at the same pace as from the other parts of Central Asia. By 1994 only some 10 per cent of the Kazakhstani Russians had left, as compared with 20 per cent in Kyrgyzstan and 40 per cent in Tajikistan (Pilkington 1998, 9). In addition, some Russians who left other Central Asian republics initially resettled in Kazakhstan rather than in Russia. In this situation, it was temping for educated Kazakhs to follow the Latvian example and reserve certain jobs for speakers of the titular language. Since, according to the 1989 census, less than 1 per cent of the Russians had a command of this language, such a clause would effectively reserve these jobs for Central Asians.

The problem, however, was that most of the indigenous Kazakh elite itself, from the entourage of President Nursultan Nazarbaev and downwards, had a better command of Russian than of their putative native tongue. Only a small group within the cultural Kazakh intelligentsia felt more comfortable speaking Kazakh than Russian. In this situation the current political leadership would frustrate their own career possibilities if they decided to make proficiency in the titular language a prerequisite for employment in prestigious jobs.

In 1996 Bakhytzhan Khasanov (1996), director of the Centre for Language Development Strategy in the Kazakhstani Academy of Sciences, told the newspaper *Kazakhstanskaia Pravda* that, for the last six years, he had been engaged in the compilation of a list of such jobs. However, no such list was ever adopted by Kazakhstani authorities. When a new language law was promulgated in 1997, it declared that 'it is absolutely necessary' that every citizen of Kazakhstan learns the state language. Still, the law was quite innocuous as it also stated that 'Russian can still be used in all organs of the state and in local administration'. At least part of the explanation for this liberal attitude was rather obvious: the current power holders would shoot themselves in the foot if they should institute a requirement for the top positions in society that they themselves and their children would have difficulty fulfilling (Kolstø and Malkova 1997, 1 and 3–4).

In Latvia and Estonia, the new state authorities have also had another legal instrument besides language requirements with which they may regiment the labour market along ethnic lines. After independence, these two countries reserved original citizenship for only those persons who had been citizens of the interwar republic and their descendants. This provision excluded the vast majority of the Russians and other Russophones who had arrived in the Baltic republic during the Soviet period, as well as their children, even those who had been born in Latvia/Estonia and lived there their entire life. Non-citizens who were unable to fulfil rather stringent naturalisation requirements were entitled to a status as permanent residents only.

In most countries, permanent residents are denied the right to vote but otherwise enjoy most or all civil and economic rights. In the case of Latvia, however, permanent residents also have limited property rights, social rights and rights on the labour market. As documented by Opalski et al. (1994), legislation adopted in Latvia in 1991–3 confined the following jobs to citizens only: customs officers, national militia service, police service, judges, public prosecutors, state security officers, diplomatic and consular service, fire officers, lecturers and researchers at the medical academy, land surveyors and afforestation inspectors. In the last four categories in particular it is hard to see how these restrictions can be dictated by a concern for national security, the national language or any other national issues.

Erik André Andersen (1999) has studied the effects of economic reform in Estonia after independence from an economic perspective and found evidence of systematic differences between Russians and Estonians in how well they fared under the privatised economy. He examined these processes on two levels: legislative, and on the basis of social and economic statistics. In all laws, he found rules that favoured Estonians over Russians to a smaller or larger degree, and these differences became even more visible when he investigated the actual consequences of privatisation on a statistical basis (Andersen 1999, 404). Specifically, the privatisation of large enterprises led to a marked change in leadership positions. 'The non-Estonians almost completely disappeared from management positions in all the counties of Estonia' (Andersen 1999, 409).

Conclusions

This chapter has, I believe, explained why Helene Carrère d'Encausse, while remarkably correct in her general prediction about the future of the Soviet Union, nevertheless was violently wrong in the premises upon which this prediction rested. The rise of nationalism in the Soviet Union was not related to demographic imbalances, as she thought, but to educational imbalances.

I have argued that, on the labour market, competition on the supply side is caused by two distinct social processes: demographic increase and increase in the number of graduates from higher education.[5] In the first case, this leads to competition for unskilled jobs and blue-collar jobs; in the second, to competition for white-collar elite jobs. In the first case, people risk unemployment; in the second, blocked career opportunities. A person with higher education may well feel frustrated even if he or she finds a job, if this is a job for which they feel overqualified.

In the next step of the analysis, the chapter hypothesised that mass-level unemployment or underemployment may lead to anger-driven riots with unclear, apolitical goals, while the intelligentsia will be able to formulate more rational strategies to eliminate from the labour market groups that are considered as threatening competitors. One such strategy is to insist that the state ought to be a national state, in which the titular culture shall be hegemonic and the national elites shall be in control.

The job issue is not equally important in all places and all contexts. Much depends on local variations in ethnic makeup, employment patterns and other socio-economic factors. Thus, for instance, in a study of economic nationalism in the ethnic republics in the Russian Federation, Viktoria Koroteeva found economic competition to be a far more decisive factor behind nationalist mobilisation in Tatarstan than in Yakutia. The latter republic had a much more segregated job market (Koroteeva 2000, 148).

The structural factors identified by Mark Beissinger, Henry Hale and others are indispensable for any explanation of differences in ethnically based collective action in the Soviet Union during perestroika. In particular, the various ethnic units' placement in the Soviet federal structure was clearly crucial. The job competition theory can, however, explain some unforeseen differences between federal units that were located on the same autonomy level.

While this chapter argues that nationalism is strongly influenced by socio-economic structures, it does not favour structure over agency. Structures do not shape nationalism and ethnic mobilisation directly, but only by influencing the perceptions and decisions of individuals who adopt more or less rational strategies to enhance their life-chances.

NOTES

1. Mark Beissinger (2002, 210–11) has counted the number of participants in separatist demonstrations in the various Soviet republics in 1987–92. In the Baltic republics they ranged from 1.2 million in Estonia to 4.4 million in Lithuania. Also Ukraine, Moldova and the three Transcaucasian republics were mobilisational successes in Beissinger's coding. By contract, mobilisational figures for the Central Asian republics ranged from 96,000 in Tajikistan to 0 in Turkmenistan.
2. Only in one incident were Russians victims of mob violence. This took place in the republic of Tuva (not in Central Asia, but in Southern Siberia) in August 1990 (Sheehy 1990).
3. Krawchenko's view has been criticised by Alexander Motyl (1987, 53–70), who believed that political rather than socio-economic factors were decisive in fuelling Ukrainian nationalism.
4. Guboglo is an ethnic Gagauz, but writes from a Russian perspective.
5. On the labour demand side it will naturally be influenced by development in the economic sphere, such as business cycles and labour productivity.

4

THE CONCEPT OF 'ROOTEDNESS' IN THE STRUGGLE FOR POLITICAL POWER IN THE FORMER SOVIET UNION IN THE 1990s

Jockeying for positions and political power was no doubt a major impetus behind non-Russian ethnic mobilisation in the USSR during perestroika. Titulars in the republics could use the heightened value of ethnicity under perestroika to outmanoeuvre non-titulars in the struggle for material goods such as housing, but even more so for prestigious jobs and university admission. The Soviet educational system had been churning out greater numbers of highly educated people than even the overgrown Soviet bureaucracy could absorb. In the republics, Russians and titulars competed for the same positions; and by making knowledge of the titular language a mandatory requirement for entry into higher education and top-level employment, titulars gained a competitive edge.

When Mikhail Gorbachev's perestroika policy opened up the political space in the Soviet Union and the non-Russian republics began to push for more rights, they also enhanced the status of their titular (eponymous) ethnic group. In common Russian parlance, this group was described as '*korennoi*', meaning 'rooted'. Allegedly having deeper roots in the 'soil' of the republic than other groups, they felt entitled to a privileged position. As pointed out in Chapter 3, as a first practical step the republics upgraded the titular language to 'state language' on the territory of the republic (Guboglo 1994). Since usage of the Russian language under Brezhnev had gradually expanded all over the Soviet Union at the expense of the minority languages, this could legitimately be presented as a defensive cultural policy.

However, the new language laws were – not without reason – also perceived as weapons in a battle for status, jobs and political power, and the titular group's claim to 'rootedness' represented the sharp edge of that weapon. An uneasy feeling spread among the non-titulars that they were being reduced to second-rank citizens in their own land (perhaps not so different from how many non-Russians had felt before the rules of the game shifted under perestroika).

This new mood of despondency and helplessness among many Russians in the republics was captured in a cartoon in the Soviet satirical magazine *Krokodil* in autumn 1989. A fire has broken out in the flat of a Russian couple in a city in one of the non-Russian republics but when the husband tries to call the fire department, he is told that he has to 'call back, using the "the language of the *korennoi* population"' (*Krokodil* 1989). *Krokodil*'s readers understood that the non-Russian fireman who received the telephone message was a fluent Russian speaker, as were all educated people in the Soviet Union. By demanding a call in 'the language of the *korennoi* population' he was flexing his new powers, with potentially disastrous consequences for the caller. However, the cartoon was not only hyperbolical – as are all cartoons – but slanderous, since no non-Russian fireman would act like that, not least because in all the republics Russian was still designated a status as the official 'language of interethnic communication'. What the cartoon can tell us, then, about the reaction of the *Russians* is more important and probably more accurate. The expressions of the hapless fire victims are not anger, but bewilderment and despair. They are losers who know that they are losing, yielding to 'the sons of the soil' almost without a fight.

LATE ARRIVAL DATE AS A DEFICIENCY

The concept of 'sons of the soil' (SoS) conflicts was first formulated by Myron Weiner in his 1978 study of a specific type of communal conflict in post-independence India (Weiner 1978). Such conflicts, he explained, erupt when well-educated and resourceful migrants from other parts of a state move into less developed regions and compete with locals for the same jobs, land and other resources. Having less education or fewer other formal qualifications, the locals tend to lose out. In order to protect their livelihoods from tough outside competition, they argue that those already long established in the area should have privileged access. Since they represent the 'sons of the soil', the given province in a certain sense 'belongs' to them. If that argument is not accepted by the newcomers, local protests may unleash rowdy demonstrations and other violence.

A common factor in such SoS conflicts is that the newcomers are not *im*migrants from abroad. As they hold the same citizenship as the locals, they cannot be stopped by passport regulations or visa restrictions. Other arguments must be employed to hold them back, and so the length of residence of the various groups in the area is used as a moral argument. The fact that the SoS population settled there first entitles them to special rights, as they see it.

Such conflicts can be found in many places, particularly in large, multicultural countries with considerable internal migration. Ethnic groups within the same country often have different internal social structures and modernise at different paces. Early modernisers tend to be more socially and geographically mobile, moving out from the core regions of their group's settlements to establish themselves as elites in peripheral areas, on what the locals regard as their ancestral lands. Such was the case in the Russian Empire and the Soviet Union (Lewis et al. 1976; Kolstø 1995, Chs 2 and 3).

While the situation in the Soviet Union was, in many ways, similar to what Weiner described in India, there was one major difference: with very few exceptions, confrontations in the USSR and its successor states did not become violent. For the Soviet period this may be explained by the presence of the omnipotent Communist Party, which held all other social forces in check – but even when this control system unravelled during perestroika, few major inter-ethnic clashes and upheavals took place. True, there was ethnically motivated violence in some republics, but the conflict lines did not follow the pattern described by Weiner. Communal riots in Central Asia pitted locals not against Russians or other Russophones, but against smaller, vulnerable, non-indigenous groups like Armenians, Chechens or Meskhet Turks (Carrère d'Encausse 1991; Chapter 3 in this volume). The violent conflicts between titulars and Russians/Russophones that had been predicted in many republics failed to materialise. In this chapter I argue that conflicts of the type identified by Weiner are indeed real and widespread around the world, but they may have varying outcomes – both violent and non-violent.

Below, I discuss how the SoS argument was employed in two post-Soviet political entities – Kazakhstan and Bashkortostan – in the 1990s. The *korennoi* discourse was actively used in both places. In addition, a third entity, Tatarstan, is introduced as a contrasting case: while many of the demographic and political circumstances there have similarities to the two first cases, the Tatars' struggle for sovereignty and republican rights was fought without the *korennoi* argument. In the 1990s, Tatarstan, like neighbouring Bashkortostan, pursued a determined and successful policy of amassing local power at the expense of Moscow (Toft 2003; Giuliano 2011) – but using a very different rhetoric.

All three republics have sizable contingents of Russians and other non-titulars in the population, and at the time of the last Soviet census in 1989 the titular nation did not comprise a majority in any of them. While Kazakhstan, as a former Union republic with the formal right to secede, became an independent state in 1991, Bashkortostan and Tatarstan were autonomous republics within the Russian Federation, and have remained so.[1] In other words, a seat at the United Nations (UN) is not a necessary condition for a titular group to play the SoS game successfully.

In this chapter, I document not only how, in the 1990s, the indigenous Bashkir and Kazakh intelligentsia and political elites employed this argument in order to marginalise the ethnic Russians politically, culturally and in the labour market, but, even more importantly, how the Russians and other Slavs themselves accepted the titulars' view on the importance of length of residence. I see this as an important reason why violent conflicts between titulars and Slavs were avoided in these two political entities.

Institutionalised Nationhood, Soviet-Style

The disintegration of the Soviet Communist Party created a power vacuum. Since the communists had made sure that no civil society existed independent of the party, few other organisations or social structures were ready to fill that vacuum: there were no independent trade unions, and the churches and other religious organisations had long since been cowed into subservience and could not pose as an alternative source of authority, as the Catholic Church did in Poland, for instance (Strayer 1998, 171).

This absence of autonomous societal structures was one reason why ethnicity became so acutely politicised during the collapse of the Soviet state (Posen 1993). No independent ethnic organisations had existed during the communist period, and 'nationalism' was regarded as a pernicious, reactionary ideology – but ethnicity (*natsional'nost'*) as a category of identification was a different matter altogether. People were not only *allowed* to keep their ethnic identity under the communist system, they were *required* to have one: it was enshrined in their internal passports, which they received on reaching maturity at age sixteen (Zaslavsky [1982] 1994, 91–129; Brubaker 1996, 31–2). Changing this official, ascriptive identity was extremely difficult, even for those who might not subjectively feel that they belonged to it. Moreover, these identities often formed the basis for unofficial hierarchies: some ethnicities were more equal than others (Karklins 1986).

In the USSR, ethnicity was institutionalised not only on the individual, but also on the collective, territorial–administrative level, in the form of an ethnic federation consisting of fifteen ethnically defined Union republics, in addition to a host of lower-level autonomous units inside some of these republics. This arrangement reflected Soviet understanding of the principle of 'self-determination of nations' (Connor 1984; Pipes [1954] 1997). Within their respective republics, members of the titular nation could send their children to schools that gave instruction in their vernacular; newspapers were published in their language; theatres performed native-language dramas, and so on. At the same time, all Soviet citizens – irrespective of ethnic identity – were allowed to move into all republics and settle there. Such migration took place, on a massive scale. Already in the nineteenth century millions of people moved from their traditional settlement areas; after the October Revolution these migratory currents picked up further speed (Lewis et al. 1976). By the time the Soviet state disintegrated in 1991, as many as 25 million Russians, in addition to several millions belonging to smaller, linguistically Russified non-titular groups, were living outside 'their' republics (Kolstø 1995; Melvin 1995; King and Melvin 1999).

With the exception of the special cultural arrangements provided for titular groups, all denizens of the republics were supposed to have the same rights. In practice, however, informal mechanisms ensured that titulars often had privileged entry to institutions of higher learning, as well as access to prestigious jobs and leading positions in the party and state apparatus (Jones and Grupp 1984; Karklins 1984; Brubaker 1996, 38). According to Rasma Karklins (1984, 49), the titulars had 'a strong notion of being the proprietors of their respective republics and of being naturally entitled to a dominant cultural, economic, social and political role.'

With the collapse of the unitary state in 1991, the Soviet successor states inherited this dual legacy: on one hand, full formal equality among all citizens; on the other, power structures skewed in favour of the titular group. In the more liberal political climate of perestroika, and even before the departure of the Communist Party of the Soviet Union (CPSU) from the scene, movements and organisations claiming to act on behalf of various ethnic groups began struggling for power in the Union republics and autonomous republics. In these struggles for supremacy, material resources were not enough: the contestants needed a convincing narrative to back up their claims. Their arguments did not necessarily have to be logically coherent or supported by hard facts – the main point was that their version was accepted by the other groups, even if with their fists clenched in their pockets. Otherwise, what started out as political struggles could easily turn violent, along the lines of Weiner's argument.

The Soviet successor states embarked on a nationalising policy built around the symbolic supremacy of the titular groups (Smith et al. 1998; Kolstø 2000). These new states were not ethnocracies in the strict sense of the word – all permanent residents generally received citizenship if they wanted it, together with the accompanying political and civil rights – formally, at least. In practice, the titular groups managed to retain and even expand the informal prerogatives they had enjoyed under the communists. Democracy was proclaimed – but the state was a nation-state 'of and for particular nations' (Brubaker 1996, 46). The same nationalising policies were also pursued in some of the constituent republics of the Russian Federation, with considerable success (Tishkov 1997; Gorenburg 2003).

The equanimity with which non-titulars in the Soviet successor states in the ethnic republics of the Russian Federation acquiesced in the nationalising policies of the early 1990s was remarkable. Particularly puzzling was the passivity of the generally resourceful, educated and numerous Russian diaspora groups in the non-Russian republics (Kolstø 1999b).

Interestingly, in post-Soviet ethnic discourses the concept of 'titularity' rarely featured; when it was used, the word was frequently placed in inverted commas, to indicate its strangeness and/or the author's ironic distance. One reason might be that the term 'titular' (*titul'nyi*) sounded foreign. It was a calque from English, brought into the Russian language not by nationalists or other activists, but by scholars. The alternative term, *korennoi*, was more 'substantive' than *titul'nyi* and had the added value of carrying normative overtones. The implicit message was that long-term residence gives grounds for group claims. A cluster of related terms like 'masters (*khoziaeva*) of the land' and 'our primordial land' (*nasha iskonnaia zemlia*) were also used to bolster the SoS argument.

Migrants from other parts of the Soviet Union were referred to as *nekorennye* ('non-rooted') or *prishlye* ('foreigners'). To be sure, not all non-titulars in the various republics were latecomers or settlers. Some were small, marginalised, indigenous groups who had maintained traditional lifestyles until recently. Occasionally, in the nationality discourses, these groups were included in a category of *korennye*, plural of *korennoi*. However, the concept of rootedness was generally used in the singular and referred to the same group as those whom scholars called *titulars*.

To complicate matters further, in the Russian language the term *korennoi* is used to denote a very different category of peoples from the 'titular nations'. *Korennoi* is the standard Russian translation of the English 'indigenous', as used in international legal texts. ILO Convention No. 169 (1989) on 'Indigenous and Tribal Peoples Convention' describes 'indigenous people' as groups characterised by

> traditional life styles; a culture and a way of life different from the other segments of the national population, e.g. in their ways of making a living, language, customs, etc.; their own social organization and political institutions; and living in historical continuity in a certain area, or before others 'invaded' or came to the area. (Convention 1989)

This description might fit the situation of some of the smaller ethnic minorities in several former Soviet republics, but not their titular nationalities. It is true that some of the post-Soviet titulars modernised late, and until recently followed a 'traditional' lifestyle: the Bashkirs and the Kazakhs remained predominantly nomadic well into the twentieth century. However, they certainly have not tried to create or develop 'their own' social organisation and political institutions: on the contrary, they strive for domination over the *national/republican* institutions. While this terminological coincidence breeds confusion, for titular activists it also represented an opportunity: the rights of indigenous, *korennye*, peoples as set out in international conventions were, implicitly or explicitly, transferred to the titular group. As the Bashkir scholar D. Zh. Valeev, speaking at the First International Congress (*Kurultay*) of Bashkirs in Ufa in 1995, declared:

> When we discuss the renaissance of ethnic groups and their culture, the content of the concept of *korennoi* is important. In international law, this concept has a very specific meaning, but in spite of that, in Russian political literature it is often incorrectly replaced (*podmeniaetsia*) by the inadequate term of 'titular'. (*Pervyi vsemirnyi* 1998, 339)

Valeev went on to claim that, as the *korennoi* people of Bashkortostan, the Bashkirs are entitled to all the rights granted to indigenous peoples by ILO Convention No. 169. He acknowledged that the concept of 'indigenous peoples', as used in that convention, is sometimes understood as applying solely to 'very small peoples with a tribal life-set'. This interpretation Valeev regarded as 'one-sided'. In support of his view, he referred to Article 1 of the Convention, where it is stated: 'Self-identification as indigenous or tribal shall be regarded as a fundamental criterion for determining the groups to which the provisions of this Convention apply.' On the basis of that article, Valeev claimed, somewhat disingenuously, that the ethnic Bashkirs would be covered by this convention from the moment they declared themselves as an indigenous people (*Pervyi vsemirnyi* 1998, 339).

The Bashkirs had been a minority in 'their' republic ever since it was established in 1919. Bashkiria (as Bashkortostan was called then) was the first of the ethnic autonomies established by the Bolsheviks, who at the time were hard pressed by the counter-revolutionary White Army of Admiral Kolchak in Western Siberia and the Urals, and desperately wanted the Bashkirs to remain neutral in this conflict (Pipes [1954] 1997, 161–3). Therefore, the Bolsheviks magnanimously granted the Bashkirs an ethnic territory with very liberally drawn boundaries. Virtually all ethnic Bashkirs ended up inside Bashkiria – as did many non-Bashkirs too. In no Soviet-era census did Bashkirs comprise more than 24 per cent of the republican population. In 1994, the figure was down to 21 per cent: the Bashkirs were not even the second-largest category in Bashkortostan – ethnic Russians made up 40 per cent, and ethnic Tatars 28 per cent (Tishkov 1997; Gabdrafikov 1998). Tatars, Chuvashs, Maris and Udmurts living in the republic could claim to have 'roots' there, just as easily as the Bashkirs.[2] This argument did not sit well with Bashkir nationalists.

Under Putin, most of the prerogatives of Bashkortostan, Tatarstan and the other ethnically defined republics in Russia have been chiselled away through centralisation of state power, but in the 1990s the ethnic republics enjoyed a formal status that elevated them above the other Subjects of the Federation. In the 1993 Constitution they were designated as 'states' (*gosudarstva*) – even as they were constituent parts of another, larger state, Russia. They had a considerably higher degree of self-rule, formally and in practice, than the normal, non-ethnic federation subjects, the *oblasti* and *krai* (Tishkov 1997).

The Kazakhs had a somewhat different demographic history. In the early twentieth century they made up a decisive majority in the Kazakh SSR – more than 60 per cent – but by the late 1950s their share of the total population had been halved. This was due primarily to two demographic shocks: first, the enforced sedentarisation of Kazakh nomads during the collectivisation of the 1930s that decimated the ethnic Kazakh population; later, the influx of Slavic settlers in the northern parts of the country under Khrushchev's Virgin Soil scheme in the 1950s. After that, the number of Kazakhs increased through high birth rates, but by the time of the last Soviet census – in 1989 – they still made up less than 40 per cent. Unlike in Bashkortostan, the non-titular populations in Kazakhstan were basically non-*korennoi*: the indigenous minorities – Uzbeks, Kyrgyz, Uighurs and others – were numerically very small (Kolstø, 1999a, 31).

BASHKORTOSTAN: MINORITY SoS RULE AGAINST ALL ODDS

With its demographically weak position, Bashkortostan had what most observers would see as a hopeless starting point for introducing ethnic minority rule after the collapse of the Soviet Union. And yet, the degree to which the ethnic Bashkir elite was able to monopolise positions and influence in the republic was quite remarkable. The emphasis on special rights for SoS in official rhetoric has ebbed and flowed, but has informed public and official discourse to a greater extent than in most other Russian federal subjects.

The first and most blatant attempt to introduce ethnocracy in post-Soviet Bashkortostan was a legislative initiative taken in 1992 by the Bashkir National centre 'Ural', which, in the early 1990s, was an extremely influential non-governmental organisation (NGO) in Bashkortostan (Gorenburg 2003, 59). 'Ural' presented the republican parliament with a draft law, 'On the *korennoi* people of the Republic of Bashkortostan' ('Zakon', 1992) which it claimed was based on the understanding of ethnic rights as established by the UN Sub-Commission on Prevention of Discrimination and Protection of Minorities. The draft law was intended to counteract the alleged 'deformation (*deformirovannost'*) and erosion (*razmytost'*) of the Bashkir people due to the assimilatory influences of larger nations'. However, this draft law was never voted on in parliament.

The Constitution of Bashkortostan that was adopted three years later, in 1995, was balanced between a multiethnic and an ethnic approach to nationhood, veering slightly in the direction of the latter. According to Article 69, 'the Republic of Bashkortostan has been formed as the realisation of the Bashkir people's right to self-determination and defends the interests of the entire multinational people of the Republic' (*Konstitutsiia* 1995, 27). The word used for

'Bashkir' here is unambiguously ethnic. Ethnocratic thinking can also be found in abundance in academic discourses, as well as in public statements by top political leaders, including President Murtaza Rakhimov (in office 1993–2010).

Although ethnic Bashkirs comprised only slightly more than 20 per cent of the total population in Bashkortostan, they captured 41 per cent of the seats in the State Assembly of the Republic elected in 1995. For the ethnic Russians the situation was the reverse: they gained only 20 per cent of the seats, although they made up 40 per cent of the total population (Tishkov 1997, 257; Gabdrafikov 1998, 35).[3] Such election results were extraordinary in a republic that is a constituent part of a larger state – Russia – where ethnic Russians dominate both politically and demographically.

This electoral preponderance of the Bashkirs was the result of an active and determined policy pursued by the Bashkir political elite around President Rakhimov (Tishkov 1997, 257; Gorenburg 2003, 96–103). This included effective utilisation of executive and juridical powers, but also manipulation and control of the nationhood discourse, and the power to define key terms like *korennoi*.

On several occasions, President Rakhimov employed the concept of '*korennoi* people' in his speeches and other statements. In one interview, he used the term in the plural, talking about the *korennye* peoples of Bashkortostan. Unlike the Bashkir popular movement 'Ural', Rakhimov (1998, 266) here included not only the eponymous Bashkir nation, but also other ethnic groups local to the Volga–Ural region in this concept. In the same interview, he vehemently denied all claims that non-Bashkirs, *in casu* Tatars, were being squeezed out of positions of power in the republic, dismissing this insinuation as a fabrication produced by 'extremists'. As 'extremism' is punishable under Russian penal law, this was a serious allegation. On other occasions Rakhimov also used veiled threats to get his message across. In one text he declared:

> Even so, this is the only place in the world where the *korennoi* Bashkir people enjoy statehood, here is their historical Fatherland. Arab as well as European travellers mentioned them as being here from the 9th–10th centuries of our era. . . . If the *korennoi* people should be forced to express its concern for the fate of their language and culture in a harsh manner (*v rezkoi forme*), this will pose a direct threat to our friendship and stability. (Rakhimov 1998, 346)

The message could not be misunderstood: the Bashkirs (read: the Bashkir elite) would not be deterred from pursuing their exclusive ethnic rights in 'their' republic; if anybody tried to stop them, that could lead to instability and an end to 'the friendship of the peoples'.

In 1999 a state-appointed working group elaborated a 'State Programme for the Peoples (*Narody*) of Bashkortostan', which attempted to square the circle: on the one hand, it proclaimed equal rights for all ethnic groups, while at the same time according special prerogatives and rights to one group, the Bashkirs. The various editions of this document show how the authors struggled to find politically correct terminology, in particular as regards the controversial '*korennoi*'. The draft version stated that in the nationality policy of a state:

> *korennye* peoples, naturally, enjoy and will enjoy special attention. What this means is that the state as its immediate goal should search for a general balance between an equality among the citizens of the Republic of Bashkortostan [on the one hand], and the sovereign statehood of the Republic as a national–territorial protection of the *korennoi* nation, in this case the Bashkirs [on the other]. (*Gosudarstvennaia programma* 1999, 26)

The final version of this programme included a minor but significant change to the text: while the claim about 'the sovereign statehood of the Republic as a national–territorial protection of the *korennoi* nation' was retained, '*korennoi*' was now placed in inverted commas! ('Narody Bashkortostana' 1999, 51). Evidently, the members of the working group had concluded that the term *korennoi* was problematical as a legal concept.

Few, if any, non-Bashkir politicians in Bashkortostan have ever tried to challenge the political hegemony of the eponymous group. Ethnic Bashkirs continue to dominate political life in the republic. On the level of NGO mobilisation and academic defence of non-titular rights, the second-largest group – the ethnic Tatars – have been more active than the largest one – the Russians. One reason may be that, unlike the Russians, they have historical roots in the region and feel more acutely deprived of a status as *korennoi* people. Local Russians in Bashkortostan more readily accept that they are actually *prishlye* – migrants or settlers – even if their forebears arrived in the Volga–Ural region centuries ago.

KAZAKHSTAN: PROMOTING THE *KORENNOI* PEOPLE BEHIND A CIVIC NATION-STATE VENEER

Under the Nazarbayev leadership, the Kazakhstani state authorities have shied away from direct ethnocratic language. Kazakhstan has been promoted as a civic but also a multinational nation-state with equal opportunities for all ethnic groups. Local residents as well as foreign observers, however, have had no difficulty discerning the ethnic agenda behind this rhetoric; the statistics speak for themselves.

After independence, the predominance of ethnic Kazakhs in positions of power in the republic increased well beyond Soviet-era levels. In 1994, 60 per cent of the parliamentary seats were filled by Kazakhs, with only 28 per cent Russians. In 1995, 26 Kazakhs and 12 Russians were elected to the Senate, while 42 Kazakhs, 19 Russians and 5 representatives of other nationalities took seats in the Lower House (Dave 1996, 5). Also the ethnic composition of the top echelons of executive officials in two key bureaucracies – the apparatus of the Cabinet of Ministers and the Presidential apparatus – showed stark ethnic discrepancies (see Galiev et al. 1994, 43–8; Kolstø 1998).

In the opinion of Anatoly Khazanov, this situation contributed to a 'general deterioration of interethnic relations in the Republic' (Khazanov 1995, 164–5). Other observers in the mid-1990s also offered dire predictions of interethnic clashes in Kazakhstan (Bremmer and Welt 1996; Kaiser and Chinn 1995). However, looking back at the 1990s, Bhavna Dave (2007, 141) concluded in 2007 that the Soviet-installed national elites in Kazakhstan had succeeded in accumulating power and resources, and pushing out rival ethnic contenders – curtailing, in particular, the political and economic influence of the Russians, with 'apparent ease'.

Most legal documents adopted in Kazakhstan in the 1990s, such as the language laws, avoided ethnocentric terminology. In contrast to the rhetoric adopted by President Rakhimov in Bashkortostan, President Nursultan Nazarbaev's speeches and other statements were couched in civic language (Nazarbaev 1993; 1995). This does not necessarily mean that the post-Soviet leadership in Kazakhstan would pursue an inclusive nationality policy. The ethnic Kazakhs preponderant in Nazarbaev's entourage had no intentions of letting more than a handful of token Russians and other Slavs into leadership positions, but it was difficult for them to use language legislation for keeping the Russian speakers out. Products of the Soviet incubator, they themselves were far more comfortable speaking Russian than Kazakh, whereas several ethnic Kazakh opposition leaders who hailed from the countryside were far more fluent in Kazakh than they were. If a restrictive language law were adopted, the opposition could use that as a lever to evict the Nazarbaevites from their positions. The solution was to adopt an ostensibly restrictive law which made Kazakh the only state language, but which contained so many loopholes that it had no real effect (Kolstø 2003).

Many Kazakh scholars in the 1990s gave ethnocratic interpretations of Kazakhstani statehood. Distinguishing between the *korennoi* nation and the non-*korennye* peoples in Kazakhstan became established practice in the state-building discourse. Thus, for instance, professor of philosophy Raushanbek Absattarov claimed that 'the [ethnically] Kazakh people are the legal heirs (*naslednik*) of this country' (Absattarov 1996, 3). Another scholar, associate professor of sociology Murat Tulepbaev, denounced an initiative taken by some Russian Cossacks to rename certain villages and streets in the southern Semirech'e region of Kazakhstan and give them Slavic names. Even if these settlements had been founded by Cossacks this would be an historical injustice, he maintained, since they had been established on 'primordial (*iskonnoi*), *korennoi* Kazakh land' (Tulepbaev 1996).

Writing in the leading theory-oriented journal 'Thought' (*Mysl'*) in 1994, S. Sabikenov distinguished between 'national sovereignty' and 'popular sovereignty'. He claimed that

> As the *korennoi* nation, the Kazakh nation has the right to realize on its own territory (*na svoei sobstvennoi territorii*) its historical and unalienable right to self-determination. It goes without saying that such a state will have a national character, in this state the national traits of the *korennoi* nation, the Kazakhs, will be displayed. (Sabikenov 1994, 9)

Sabikenov's use of the reinforcing possessive adjective *sobstvennoi* ('own') made it clear that he saw the ethnic Kazakhs as the (exclusive) owners not only of the Kazakhstani *state* but also of the territory on which that state had been established.

In an overview of the political system in Kazakhstan, Kazakh political scientist Zhalnylzhan Kh. Dzhunusova used the *korennoi* concept in an original way to justify strong presidential rule in the country:

> As is well known, the peculiarity of Kazakhstan's polyethnic composition is the fact that the *korennoi* ethnos – the Kazakhs – make up only approximately one half. The other *ethnoses* cannot be united under one single national idea. Historical experience shows that [in such a situation] only a party, a front, or a political leader can become such an integrating force. . . . Unification of society by means of a political leader does not contradict the mentality of the peoples of Kazakhstan, which has no traditions of parliamentary democracy. (Dzhunusova 1996, 57)

In other words, given the demographically weak position of the ethnic Kazakhs, it would be dangerous to introduce Western-style democracy in the country, an argumentation employed to legitimise Nazarbaev's autocratic rule.

In an article in the political science journal *Saiasat*, Makash Tatimov, a senior expert in the presidential Informational–Analytical Centre, described the Kazakh nation as 'young' in the dual sense, referring to a people that has just recently acquired its own statehood, and simultaneously to a nation where the younger age-cohorts predominate. Russians, Balts and Ukrainians in his typology were 'old nations'. He predicted that, in a 'psychological cold war' for control in Kazakhstan, the Kazakhs would eventually win, due to their higher birth rates. The ethnic battle would be fought in the bedchamber, as it were, where the Kazakhs would inevitably be victorious (see Kolstø 1998). The Kazakhstani state authorities should actively bolster natural trends through 'an effective demographic policy, supporting and promoting the full manifestation of the historically objective tendencies in the development of our population'. Such a policy, wrote Tatimov, would enjoy the full backing of the international community, and pointed out that the UN had declared 1995–2004 'a *Decade of the World's Indigenous Peoples*'. Exploiting the ambiguity of the concept of *korennoi* in post-Soviet parlance, he claimed:

> The decision of the United Nations to proclaim an International *Decade* of the World's *Indigenous (korennykh)* People enhances the chances of a young state – the Republic of Kazakhstan – to improve the demographic position of its *korennoi* population after long and brutal colonialism. (Tatimov 1995, 23)

How did the non-Kazakh population in Kazakhstan react to the Kazakhs' use of the *korennoi* concept? Broadly speaking, a shift in attitudes can be observed, from initial resistance in the 1990s towards growing acceptance of the concept of *korennoi*. In the first years after independence was proclaimed in 1991, some Russians and other Slavs desperately sought to refute the claim that the Kazakhs were the (sole) indigenous population in the country. In 1992, a Russian historian from the northern city of Ust'-Kamenogorsk, Aleksandr Feoktistov, wrote a booklet about *Russians, Kazakhs and Altai* to counter Kazakh claims that their nomadic forebears were the indigenous population of Kazakhstan:

> You cannot adjust history to fit a desire. Around the world there are many young nations: Argentinians and Mexicans, Australians and Canadians, Cubans and Guatemalans, whose history starts from the 16th century, and they are not offended by their short history. (Feoktistov 1992, 16)

In particular, Feoktistov saw the claim that the Kazakhs were the *korennoi* people in his own part of the country, the northwestern Altai region, as almost ridiculous. 'The terms often used in the periodical press about these regions, "*korennoi* people" and "*korennye* inhabitants", are *not correct*. Which people is *korennoi* in the Altai Mountains? The Huns, Turks from various periods? Mongols, Kalmyks, or the Russians who came here 300 years ago?' (Feoktistov 1992, 40, emphasis for 'not correct' in the original).

Another Russian author, I. A. Averin, attempted to turn the tables on the Kazakhs by accepting the distinction between *korennoi* and alien (*prishlie*) peoples, and using it against them. He argued that in the north of Kazakhstan the Russians – the Ural Cossacks in particular – represented the *korennoi* population, whereas the Kazakhs were latecomers (Averin 1995, 161). It is symptomatic that this article was published in Moscow, not in Kazakhstan.

A congress organised in 1998 by the then leading political oppositional forces in Kazakhstan – both Kazakh and Russian – accepted the concept of 'primordial Kazakh land' that was used in the 1995 Constitution, but warned against drawing any distinctions on that basis between the *korennoi* Kazakh people and the non-*korennoi* groups:

> [T]he territory of Kazakhstan is the 'primordial land' of the Kazakhs, it is their historical motherland. However, over the course of the centuries Kazakhstan has become the motherland also of many other peoples – Russians, Germans, Ukrainians, Belarusians, Uzbeks, Koreans, Uighurs, and others. Therefore, we are against a division of the citizens into *korennye* and non-*korennye*. (*Kongress* 1999, 122)

However, Russians and other Europeans who discussed interethnic issues in Kazakhstan increasingly began to use the concept of 'the *korennoi* people' as a synonym for the ethnic Kazakhs, in the same way as ethnic Kazakh publicists did (see e.g. Dokuchaeva 1994; Giller and Shatskikh 1993; Loginova 1995, 40), even when criticising the nationality policy of the Kazakhstani state. As expressed by the leader of the Kazakhstani Polish Cultural Centre, 'Motherland is where you have the deepest roots,' which led her to conclude sadly that the Polish minority in Kazakhstan would 'never be *korennoi* anywhere' (Voitkevich 1997).

Some Russian authors in Kazakhstan not only accepted the division of the population of the country into an indigenous Kazakh and a non-indigenous part, but even embraced the negative valorisation of the settlers and the claim that the indigenous status of the ethnic Kazakhs made them the legitimate owners of the country. Thus, in a booklet titled *The Cossacks and the Cossack Hosts in Kazakhstan*, Andrei Sergeevich Elagin claimed, 'Already in the 1930s the [Soviet] authorities recognized the nomadic Kazakhs in Semirech'e as the masters (*khoziaeva*) of this region' (1993, 66). He referred to the ethnic Kazakhs not only as *korennye* (Elagin 1993, 67 and 74), but even as 'aborigines' (*aborigeny*, Elagin 1993, 71).

The SoS discourse in Kazakhstan seems to be characterised by a certain division of labour between politicians and scholars. In their writings and public statements Nazarbaev and his entourage generally avoid referring to the Kazakhs as a *korennoi* people with special rights, whereas Kazakh political scientists and other scholars loyal to the regime exhibit far fewer inhibitions about using such language. The term is also widely used in newspaper articles and popular publications, and neither Kazakhs nor non-Kazakhs have any doubts whatsoever that 'the *korennoi* people' is a code-word for the Kazakhs as the hegemonic nation of Kazakhstan.

TATARSTAN: REPUBLICAN SELF-ASSERTION AND ETHNIC PREDOMINANCE WITHOUT SOS RHETORIC

The contrast between Bashkortostan and its immediate neighbour, Tatarstan, regarding usage of the *korennoi* concept is noteworthy. Tatars and Bashkirs are closely related linguistically and otherwise, but there are also significant differences between the two groups. The Tatars became settled and urbanised much earlier than the Bashkirs, and have traditionally had a greater proportion of middle-class, educated people (Gorenburg 2003). Ethnic Tatars also comprise a higher share of the total population of the eponymous republic – in the early 1990s, roughly 50 per cent. When the drive for republican self-determination commenced under perestroika, Tatarstan and Bashkortostan led the 'parade of sovereignties', seemingly in tandem, but the methods and the rhetoric employed were markedly different. Dmitry Gorenburg has documented that

> [w]hereas in Tatarstan, only radical nationalists called for the establishment of an ethnic Tatar state, the right of ethnic Bashkirs to have such a state was a fundamental aspect of the mobilizing frames that were formulated by the mainstream Bashkir nationalist movement. (Gorenburg 2003, 102)

In a booklet published in 1993, Rafael Khakim, political scientist and advisor to Tatarstan's President Mintimer Shaimiev, discussed the concepts of national minorities, *korennoi* people, and migrants. Defining a *korennoi* people as 'an ethnos which has been formed on a given territory and retains its ethnic specificity', Khakim claimed, is consistent with UN terminology. In his view, 'the most important criterion for being regarded as a *korennoi* people is the fact that it has been conquered by another people' – therefore, 'in most parts of Russia the Russians must be regarded as non-*korennoi*' (Khakim 1993, 26).

This would seem to lead up to an ethnocratic treatment of the national question in Tatarstan but, somewhat surprisingly, Khakim did not draw that conclusion. In Tatarstan, he claimed:

> The concept of *korennoi* people does not play a political role but remains a purely ethnic concept. It does not bestow upon the Tatars as a *korennoi* people any prerogatives; on the contrary, by giving the Russians the same rights as the Tatars, it can secure the successful self-determination of Tatarstan as an independent state. (Khakim 1993, 28–9)

Even more surprisingly, the Ittifak Party too, regarded in the 1990s as the most ethnocentric movement in Tatarstan, denied that any nation should enjoy special rights as a *korennoi* people. Admittedly, the party's position here was not quite clear. On the one hand, its political programme proclaimed that 'the nation-state does not give any social prerogatives to the basic, indigenous (*osnovnoi, korennoi*) nationality', but at the same time it maintained that 'the state is obliged to defend the language of the indigenous, basic nation as well as its culture and spiritual heritage' ('Programma tatarskoi' 1991, 19). Furthermore, Ittifak held that 'the international community is obliged to find the legal and economic mechanisms necessary to guarantee that each nation is "allotted" its "primordial" (*iskonnoi*) territory' ('Programma tatarskoi' 1991, 16–7).

When Tatars began to mobilise in the republic of Tatarstan in the early 1990s, they also expressed concern for their co-ethnics in neighbouring Bashkortostan. In its 1991 Political Platform, the Tatar Public Centre (TOTs), the dominant social movement in Tatarstan at the time, declared: 'the Tatars who live in the territory of Bashkortostan are just as much a *korennoi* nationality as the Bashkirs', and should therefore be entitled to 'self-determination as a *korennoi* nation' ('Platforma' 1991, 24). However, while TOTs was a force to be reckoned with in Kazan, it had no clout in Ufa.

One factor that may explain the unwillingness of the Tatars to play the *korennoi* card is their settlement pattern within the Soviet Union. While hefty majorities of the other two groups examined in this chapter resided within their eponymous republic – the Bashkirs 60 per cent and the Kazakhs 80 per cent in 1989, according to the last Soviet census – only 26 per cent of ethnic Tatars lived in Tatarstan (*Natsional'nyi* 1991, 5, 34, 38 and 102; Toft 2003, 57). Even if many Tatars resided in the Volga–Ural region just outside the borders of their eponymous republic, hundreds of thousands, perhaps millions, were living in Moscow, Leningrad and other cities far afield, and also in the other Union republics, where they could, by no stretch of the imagination, claim *korennoi* status. As a result, the Tatar leaders developed a strong diaspora policy, but a weak SoS one.

CONCLUSIONS: YIELDING TO THE SOS

In this chapter we have seen how, after the breakup of the USSR, a discourse on 'the indigenous (*korennoi*) nation', understood as the 'titular' or 'state-bearing' ethnic group, has been used as an instrument in a policy geared towards keeping social control and ethnic hegemony in two former Soviet federal subjects, one Union republic and one autonomous republic. In neither of these cases did the titular group comprise a majority of the population in their respective republics – in Bashkortostan, not even a plurality. Nevertheless, they managed not only to retain social peace but also to entrench a political system with elements of ethnocracy.

Around the time of the dissolution of the Soviet Union, many pundits prophesied that ethnic tensions would unleash considerable social and political upheavals. Violent conflicts did indeed occur – but generally confined to certain peripheral regions, bypassing some states which, according to Western conflict theory, should have been the most likely candidates for civil war. For instance, in his influential *Ethnic Groups in Conflict* (1985) Donald Horowitz had singled out 'centrally focused systems'– bipolar states where two numerically more-or-less equal groups vie for control over the central state apparatus – as more volatile than multinational states with numerous overlapping and cross-cutting conflicts (Horowitz 1985, 38ff). Kazakhstan clearly fitted Horowitz's description – and yet it avoided massive turbulence (see Kolstø 1999a).

Another political situation which might be expected to unleash violence would be attempts by a minority to take control of the state. That the Bashkortostani leadership under Murtaza Rakhimov managed to get away with flagrant favouritism in favour of the numerically very weak ethnic Bashkirs is an astonishing instance of undemocratic avoidance of conflict. This is particularly remarkable since, according to Isabelle Côté and Matthew Mitchell, SoS conflicts generally have 'a much lower threshold of violence than other kinds of communal and ethnic conflicts' (Côté and Mitchell 2017, 337).

One feature of those two cases which might explain the absence of violent confrontations is the structuring of the ethnopolitical debates in the republics as 'Sons of the Soil versus migrants'. This is the kind of conflict that Myron Weiner pioneered in analysing, but the post-Soviet cases had a different outcome from those of India. Weiner showed that, when confronted with migrants from other parts of the country who were better able to compete for jobs, positions and political influence, locals played the SoS card. Then, if the newcomers refused to accept the argument that the locals should be given preference in appointments and access to resources, violence ensued. The major difference between Weiner's cases and those studied in this chapter is the fact that, in the post-Soviet cases, the SoS argument was accepted by the newcomers themselves.

Monica Duffy Toft has pointed out that, in ethnic conflicts, urban populations are especially weak on what she calls the 'legitimacy dimension', or faith in their own cause. 'They are usually recent immigrants who, unlike concentrated majorities and minorities, lack a strong sense of attachment to the land they occupy' (Toft 2003, 25). This description fits the Russians in the former Soviet republics quite well. In all Union republics, and also in the autonomous republics within the USSR, they were clustered in the major cities, especially the capitals (Arutiunian 1992; Kolstø 1995, 49–50). These cities had a far more 'Soviet' character than the countryside, and their residents tended to identify with the Soviet Union as a whole and not so much with the republic where they were living.

As David Laitin and James Fearon point out, 'A [SoS] conflict may be violent, but it need not be' (Fearon and Laitin 2010, 200). They call attention to the role of the state in shunting the conflict in one direction or the other: if the political authorities side with the migrants against the locals, the chances are greater that violence may break out than if they support the locals. Being more mobile and less attached to 'the soil', the migrants usually have the option of just quitting the region, giving victory to the locals by a 'walkover', as it were. This, in fact, was the case throughout Soviet Central Asia, where return migration of Europeans to Russia and other Slav regions had already started in the 1970s and picked up considerable speed after independence (Kolstø 2005a). In Bashkortostan the situation was slightly different: here, there were two 'states', one within the other in a Russian *matrioshka*-doll fashion. The outer doll – the Russian Federation – supported the non-titulars (but not very energetically), while the doll inside – Bashkortostan – was controlled by the titular locals. From this region, return migration of Russians has been limited – but still no violence has occurred.

Dmitry Gorenburg is no doubt correct in regarding the defeatist attitude of the non-titulars in the non-Russian regions as a legacy of the Soviet nationalities policy. Even if the Soviet Socialist Republics were intended to be more form than content (and were largely perceived as such by the outside world), the Soviets

> not only succeeded in convincing the Soviet people that the ethnic forms were authentic, they also fostered the belief that these ethnic forms should be imbued with ethnic content. Most importantly, the state convinced both titular *and Russian inhabitants of the ethnic regions* that these regions belong to the titular ethnic group. (Gorenburg 2003, 84, emphasis added)

In a comparative study of three countries with potentially volatile, bipolar ethnic structures – Malaysia, Fiji and Guyana – R. R. Milne (1981) found that, in all cases, the ethnic groups able to claim the deepest 'roots' in the country prevailed over those who could be branded as 'latecomers'. In all three states, the argument was eventually accepted by all groups that arrival time in the country was politically relevant. It had effect even in Guyana, where neither of the two major ethnic groups (the Africans and those from India) could claim to be autochthonous – but the Africans had immigrated (or rather, were brought there) earlier than the Indians and were thus more 'settled' (Milne 1981, 15–39). The Africans won out, despite being far less numerous than the Indians (31 per cent versus 52 per cent). In Malaysia, the SoS argument was invoked explicitly: ethnic Malay were declared *bumiputra* – roughly equivalent to 'SoS' – a term that entered the official Malaysian lexicon as a basis for special indigenous rights.

Like the cases in India analysed by Weiner, Malaysia, Fiji and Guyana have all experienced ethnic turmoil, especially around the time of achieving independence from the British. The political hegemony of the indigenous group was accepted by the latecomers, albeit grudgingly and belatedly. Therefore, the peaceful outcomes of the ethnic controversies in Bashkortostan and Kazakhstan stand out – but they are not unique. My co-workers and I have found similar ethnopolitical structures with peaceful outcomes in other post-Soviet countries, Latvia and Abkhazia (Kolstø 1999a; Kolstø and Blakkisrud 2013).[4] It seems reasonable to assume that in the post-Soviet cases there were some common circumstances that set them apart from other SoS situations – most likely the ethnopolitical structure of the Soviet Federation, which had accorded certain formal and informal rights to the titulars. And so, when the communist unitary state collapsed and new states were established, non-titular, non-indigenous groups were mentally prepared for a subservient position. As some of Bhavna Dave's informants in Kazakhstan explained to her, 'we accepted that this was how it had to be . . . . Many . . . Russian inhabitants felt that they were left with little choice but to live with the institutional framework that favoured titular entitlement for quotas and promotions' (Dave 2007, 82–3).

NOTES

1. Now called simply 'republics'.
2. Author's interviews, Ufa, 1999.
3. Ethnic Tatars were represented in the Assembly roughly in accordance with their demographic strength.
4. Confrontations between the titular Abkhaz and the largest ethnic group, the Georgians, ended in civil war in the early 1990s, but when the Georgians had lost and fled, the other minorities accepted the political dominance of the Abkhaz, even though they were a minority.

5

ANTEMURALE THINKING AS HISTORICAL MYTH AND ETHNIC BOUNDARY MECHANISM IN EASTERN EUROPE

The Myth of Being *Antemurale*

As discussed in Chapter 1, ethnic groups and nations are differentiated from each other not on the basis of the 'objective' cultural content in each of them, but on how they contrast themselves with the others. This does not, however, mean that 'anything goes', that boundary drawing is entirely arbitrary. The elements which are singled out for self- and other-identification – the 'diacritica', in Fredrik Barth's terminology – must belong to the available repertoire, meaning the existing language, religion, food habits, family structures and so on which are commonly found within the group. Virtually all features of the group's culture may become the substance of a boundary if they distinguish one's own group from surrounding groups. This was emphasised by one of Barth's earliest disciples, the US political scientist John Armstrong (1982, 8–9), who saw various kinds of *symbols* and *myths* as equally important for the drawing of ethnic and other cultural boundaries as the material *diacritica* that Barth had focused on (see also Mach 1993, 57; Kolstø 2005b, 16–34).

Armstrong did not develop his ideas on the construction of ethnic myths in any great detail, but over fifteen years ago I made an attempt to flesh them out in a rudimentary typology of boundary-constituting myths. I identified four different historical myths (Kolstø 2005b, 16–34):

- the myth of *antiquitatis* (being those who had arrived first in a particular territory and therefore having a particularly strong claim to it);

- the myth of being *sui generis* (being in possession of a unique culture not shared by anyone else);
- the myth of *martyrium* (having been chronically victimised throughout the ages and thereby able to claim the moral high ground);
- the myth of being *antemurale* (being the defenders of a larger civilisation faced with outside assailants).

The list is not exhaustive; other myths can no doubt be identified. Moreover, these four are not mutually exclusive: members of a group may draw on several myths simultaneously, even when that might seem logically impossible. In particular, the two last myths – *martyrium* and *antemurale* – often go hand in hand. Nor is this surprising: the valiant guardians defending a larger civilisation against the enemy at the gates – or the frontline defenders of Civilisation as such against barbarism – will naturally incur suffering and death in the course of their battles.

Typologically, the myth of *antemurale* differs greatly from the myth of being *sui generis*. Rather than insisting on the uniqueness of the group, as the *sui generis* ideologues do, the group is now included in some larger and allegedly superior cultural identity that enhances its status vis-à-vis the other groups that do not belong. Rather than drawing a border around the group, equally strong on all sides, the differences that distinguish the group from one specific neighbour are magnified out of all proportion, while boundaries in other directions are de-emphasised.

Antemurale myths may be symmetrical or asymmetrical. We can find instances where both opposing groups agree that a civilisational wall separates them but at the same time hold diametrically opposed views as to just who represents the forces of cosmos and of chaos. At other times one group may de-emphasise – perhaps even deny – the cultural difference between themselves and a neighbouring group, while this neighbour will do its utmost to erect an identity barrier between them, even going to ludicrous lengths to 'prove' the insuperable differences. While asymmetrical myths are probably more common, Europe versus the Islamic world in the Middle Ages was an example of a symmetrical *antemurale* myth. The Muslim Arabs and Ottomans were, no less than the Christian Europeans, convinced that they represented a superior civilisation, the only true one: they were defending the 'true faith' against the barbarians of the North. As Bernard Lewis explains,

> in this holy war, Europe was a frontier to which the Ottomans, and indeed many other Muslims, looked in much the same way as Europeans were to view the Americas from the 16th to the 18th century. Beyond the northern and western frontier lay rich and barbarous lands to which it was their sacred mission to bring religion and civilization, order and peace. (Lewis 1982, 29)

However, in most situations, as is the case with Ukraine, Belarus and Georgia that I will present below, they are asymmetrical: only one side sees itself as a frontier civilisation vis-à-vis their neighbour.

In most instances, *antemurale* mythmaking is obviously an instrument of politics – as, indeed, are all historical myths – designed to strengthen the in-group in question vis-à-vis other groups that are seen as threatening. To call it a political device is to emphasise the element of power and power relations. *Antemurale* myths are normally invoked by smaller and vulnerable groups in order to enhance their relative power in one direction by latching on to a larger, powerful group in another direction. They try to enlist the support of stronger groups by claiming that they share with them not only a common identity/culture/history, but also *a common enemy*. This is often a crucial method of recruiting allies. If the frontline states are the ones that will have to bear the brunt of the battle and suffer more human loss as the defenders of the gate, reasons of equity and 'burden sharing' dictate that nations safely located to the rear, far removed from the danger and the Wall, must contribute more otherwise. Power politics is by no means a matter of counting cannons, manpower and economic strength only: it also includes strategies of legitimisation (Barker 2001).

Contemporary Applications of the *Antemurale* Myth to Eastern Europe: Erecting a Wall Between Western and Eastern Christianity

Some of the most striking examples of *antemurale* mythmaking today may be found in Eastern Europe and, remarkably, the tropes and categories employed are often quite similar to the medieval prototype. The Wall is frequently invoked by using religious language, even if the setting has become thoroughly secular. An example of this is the article 'The Tragedy of Central Europe', which Czech novelist Milan Kundera published in the *New York Review of Books* in 1984, when the Cold War was at its coldest. As 'Central', Kundera defined the parts of Europe which belonged culturally to 'the West' but which, after World War II, had ended up politically in 'the East'. Kundera has often been interpreted as making a plea for the acceptance of 'Central Europe' as an old and well-established but little-recognised geographical subunit of Europe. Some of his remarks do allow for such an interpretation, but that was not his main message. Instead of a tripartite Europe consisting of West, Central and East, Kundera's vision of the continent was bifurcated. There are only two Europes – West, and East:

> 'Geographic Europe' (extending from the Atlantic to the Ural Mountains) was always divided into two halves which evolved separately: one tied to ancient Rome and the Catholic Church, the other anchored in Byzantium and the Orthodox Church. After 1945, the border between the two Europes shifted several hundred kilometres to the west, and

several nations that had always considered themselves to be Western woke up to discover that they were now in the East. (Kundera 1984)

The fact that, at the time when Kundera was writing, there were *three* Europes he considered a historical aberration and the result of a political crime. Europe had been divided twice over: by a centuries-old cultural fault and now by a new political 'iron curtain'. In Kundera's ideal world, one of them – the political (and physical) wall – could and should be done away with; the cultural divide would remain.

According to Kundera, this cultural divide of Europe follows religious lines: the 1054 Great Schism between Orthodoxy and Catholicism established an insurmountable barrier. Only the Catholic and Protestant parts of the communist bloc would qualify for inclusion in his category of 'Central Europe'. In his essay Kundera was exclusively occupied with Russia as Central Europe's 'constituting Other' (Neumann 1993) and brushed aside the fact that the traditional faith in many parts of the region that ended up to the east of the Iron Curtain after 1945 has long been Orthodox Christianity. This was the case with Romania and Bulgaria, while Yugoslavia (according to Kundera's religious criterion) would be cut in two parts: the northern regions adhere to Roman Catholicism; further south and east, Orthodoxy predominates, along with Islam. Southeastern Europe was conspicuously absent from Kundera's mental map; this region did not fit into his dichotomous model and was simply ignored (Kolstø 2016).

In 1989 Kundera's dream was realised: the Berlin Wall came tumbling down, and with it the entire political bifurcation of Europe. Certain half-hearted attempts were made to create new Central European regional collaboration structures, but with few results. Instead, the Catholic countries of 'the new Europe' (Donald Rumsfeld's phrase) all strove to be included in Western political structures – NATO and the EU – as rapidly as possible, and they eventually succeeded. With their newly acquired Western-ness, their Central-ness could be tossed aside as a stepping stone. After the EU accession of Poland, Hungary, Slovakia and the Czech Republic, 'Central Europe' lost its *raison d'être* as a political programme (Le Rider 2008; Todorova 2009, 190). The concept continued to be used as a loose geographical designation, but was infrequently evoked in political discourse.

In 1993, another famous article, this time by US political scientist Samuel Huntington, made waves by employing analytical frames remarkably similar to those of Kundera (Huntington 1993). Huntington, who had earlier written a euphoric book (1991) on the unstoppable march of democracy throughout the world, had turned pessimist and no longer expected 'the West' to be able to export its societal model to other continents. Using a geological metaphor, he now divided the world into cultural 'tectonic plates', each of which represented one of the world's great civilisations. World civilisations were doomed to collide at the edges: metaphorical volcanoes and earthquakes erupted, producing dangerous and volatile conflict zones. Huntington predicted that the most deadly violent conflicts worldwide would explode precisely along the 'fault-lines' – another geological metaphor – between civilisations.

Historically, as pointed out above, civilisations have been defined mainly through religion, and this is also how Huntington (Huntington 1996, 28) saw them. Most of his categories had religious designations – Islamic, Hindu, Buddhist. However, some macro-regions did not fit readily into this pattern, so the civilisational categories of 'Latin America' and 'Africa' were defined along other lines, or not defined at all (Kirkpatrick 2013, 51–4). And, oddly, Huntington split Christendom up into two subgroups, 'Western' and 'Orthodox'. It was not immediately apparent why this division should be more fundamental than, for instance, the distinction between Shia and Sunni in Islam; nor was the fact that Protestantism and Catholicism should be lumped together in one category, while Eastern Orthodoxy – which, in many theological and ethical questions, has more in common with Catholicism than has mainstream Protestantism – was separated.

A remarkable consequence of Huntington's model was that Eastern Christians were presented as having more in common with Muslims than with their Western co-religionists. His civilisational map of Europe features a thick line running between 'Western Christianity circa 1500' to the west, and 'Orthodox Christianity and Islam' to the east (Kirkpatrick 2013, 159). This line, which follows precisely the line that Kundera had drawn one decade earlier between East and West, represents the 'Eastern boundary of Western civilization', according to Huntington. Even more than Kundera's idea of a captured Western Europe, Huntington's conception illustrates how old religious categories can be manipulated to fit contemporary political needs.

Not surprisingly, Huntington's model was enthusiastically embraced by politicians and intellectuals in the frontline states (as he defined them) – Estonia, Latvia, Lithuania, Poland, Slovakia, Hungary and Croatia.[1] All of them ended up on the western side of the civilisational 'fault-line'. The fact that, on his map, they also became *antemurale* states was an important extra bonus. Their exposed position as outposts bordering on alien civilisations to the east could be exploited for all it was worth to lobby for economic support from the stronger and richer nations that belonged to the same civilisation: the West.

For the political leaders in Ukraine, Belarus and Romania, however, the situation was more problematic. During the Counter-Reformation, 'Uniate' churches – that is, churches that recognise the authority of the Roman pope but have an Orthodox liturgy –had been created in the western parts of all of them, and so the civilisational fault-line on Huntington's map ran straight through these countries. He chose to ignore – or was ignorant of the fact – that the Uniate churches in Ukraine and Belarus today cover only a very small part of the population. Even so, Huntington insisted that, not only historically but even today, 'Ukraine . . . is a cleft country with two distinct cultures. The civilizational fault-line between the West and Orthodoxy runs through its heart and has done so for centuries' (Huntington 1996, 165). Apparently contradicting himself, however, two pages further on he declares: 'if civilization is what counts, . . . violence between Ukrainians and Russians is unlikely. These are two Slavic, primarily Orthodox people who have had close relationships for centuries and between whom intermarriage is common.' For many Ukrainians this analysis was hardly reassuring: it left them in limbo, as neither East nor West.

Moving the Wall Further East: *Antemurale* Thinking in Orthodox Countries Towards an Orthodox Neighbour

Huntington had offered his model not as a blueprint for aggression but, on the contrary, as an invitation to Russia to 'live and let live'. Indeed, the very concept of *antemurale* presents the frontline population as *defenders* of a religion/ civilisation, not as attackers. The logic behind both the Great Wall of China and the Berlin Wall – and behind the entire Iron Curtain – was to leave the Outsiders alone as long as they left the people on the Inside in peace. Typically, Huntington was highly critical of NATO expansion too far eastwards. Only those parts of Europe which rightfully belonged to the West by dint of historical religion ought to be invited in:

> NATO expansion limited to countries historically part of Western Christendom . . . guarantees to Russia that it would exclude Serbia, Bulgaria, Romania, Moldova, Belarus, and Ukraine as long as Ukraine remained united. NATO expansion limited to Western states would also underline Russia's role as the core state of a separate, Orthodox, civilization, and hence a country which should be responsible for order within and along the boundaries of Orthodoxy. (Huntington 1996, 162)

The losers in this 'spheres of interest' thinking were those Serbians, Bulgarians and others who identified themselves with 'Europe' (or simply wanted to partake in the higher standard of living in the West) and sought to be let in. For them, this kind of civilisational thinking was simply a sellout, especially if they also saw Russia as an overhanging threat to both their security and their national identity. Precisely because they shared a common historical religion with Russia – and often also spoke similar Slavic languages – many Russians tended to regard them simply as 'little brothers'. The looming shadow of Russia was particularly ominous where there was a common border with Russia and where the territories which now made up their nation-states had historically been part of the Russian Empire. This was the case with three nations: Belarusians, Ukrainians and Georgians.

The Georgians could take some comfort in the fact that they speak a non-Slavic language; they could thus be more secure in their self-identity and in their cultural distance from Russia and all things Russian. They are also separated topologically from Russia by the high Caucasian range. Ukraine and Belarus, however, are located on the same vast plain as Russia with no obvious geographical borders, and even more importantly, no 'hard' cultural differences. The Belarusians and Ukrainians are keenly aware that many Russians denied the existence of separate Belarusian and Ukrainian identities altogether. In the pre-revolutionary Russian Empire, the people whom we today call 'Russians' were referred to as 'Great Russians' – *Velikorossy*. The concept of 'Russians' was also used, but as a collective noun that comprised three branches: the Belarusians and the Ukrainians, in addition to the Great Russians (Plokhy 2017, 124).[2] The same triune way of thinking is reflected in much contemporary Russian political rhetoric, as when, in one and the same speech, it can be claimed that 'Ukrainians and Russians are brotherly people,' and also that 'Ukrainians and Russians are *one* people' (see below).

Confronted with the threat of being gobbled up by their overwhelming eastern neighbour, some Belarusian, Ukrainian and Georgian intellectuals and politicians in different periods of nation-building have sought refuge in *antemurale* mythologisation. They insist that a massive civilisational chasm separates them from the Russians. This boundary cannot be defined by religion – Eastern Orthodox on both sides – so it must be demarcated by something else. Typically, that is a rather vague notion of 'Europeanness', to which they claim to belong. However, this identity will separate them from the Russians only if the Russians can be firmly excluded from this same European civilisation – a corollary they are normally prepared to draw.

Exactly which civilisation Russian culture is held to belong to may differ in these narratives. Sometimes Russia is said to be a continent unto itself, a separate entity between East and West – a notion which many Russian intellectuals have toyed with throughout the ages (see e.g. Riasanovsky 1952). At other times, Russia is said to belong to a Eurasian civilisation, benefiting from its intermediary location between Europe and Asia and drawing impulses from both of them. This is a position shared by some Russian intellectuals, first developed by the 'Eurasianists' in European exile in the 1920s and picked up again by Russian neo-Eurasianists like Alexander Dugin today (see e.g. Laruelle 2008; Bassin and Pozo 2017). And finally, Russian culture can be depicted as being primarily or essentially Asian/Oriental, behind a deceptive European mask. This viewpoint does not find any supporters in the Russian identity debate but is not infrequently set forth by anti-Russian *antemurale* thinkers in the neighbouring states.

I now turn to some *antemurale* ideas presented in the identity debates in the three Orthodox countries that flank Russia to the west and south – Belarus, Ukraine, and Georgia. No claim is made that they represent a dominant narrative in their respective countries: quite the contrary, a strong case can be made that in Belarus, in particular, such perspectives are rather marginal.[3] In Ukraine and Georgia they are more widespread, but here also these ideologemes have fluctuated, reflecting the ups and downs of political relations with Russia and, not least, the military confrontations between these countries and Russia. No doubt, the connection between action and discourse is dialectical: antagonistic discourse and demonising narratives about 'the Other' may precipitate violent actions – but conversely, warfare leading to suffering and death will inevitably be reflected in perceptions of the enemy, whoever that may be.

The task of constructing, interpreting and manipulating worldviews normally falls on intellectuals. They are the ones who provide the vocabulary and the arguments for particular ideologies. However, intellectuals may pursue their own agendas, which do not necessarily coincide with the interests of the state as the current state leaders define them, or even with the perceptions of the average member of the public. State leaders may draw on the services of the mythmaking intelligentsia whenever they feel this may be useful, and then discard them as a nuisance when the intellectuals come up with utopian or crackpot ideas that cannot be harnessed to power politics. If and when intellectual *antemurale* ideas fail to resonate in the corridors of power as well as among the population at large, the mythmakers consign themselves to cultural isolation even in their own countries, as 'voices crying in the wilderness'.

BELARUSIAN *ANTEMURALE* THINKING

Belarusian national identity is generally regarded as quite vague and insecure, the country being squeezed in between two nations with a long cultural history and robust self-confidence – Poland and Russia (Vakar 1956; Marples 1999; see also Bekus 2010). Any attempt the Belarusians might make to distance themselves from the Poles would risk throwing them into the embrace of the Russians, and vice versa. Therefore, the dominant tendency in Belarusian identity-building has focused on the *sui generis* myth: to carve out an identity that differs from *both* the eastern and the western neighbour, focused on the Belarusian language and the Uniate Belarusian Church (Zaprudnik 1993).

Historically, Polishness has probably exerted a stronger pull on Belarusian intellectuals than has Russian culture; in 1863/4, for instance, many of them made common cause with the insurrectionaries in the second Polish rebellion. All this changed, however, in the second half of the twentieth century, when Belarus was rebuilt after the devastations of World War II and brought back on its feet in a Sovietised Russian mould. An increasing number of Belarusians in general and intellectuals in particular traded in their Belarusian language in favour of Russian, and in the secularised Soviet society the religious tradition of Uniatism could no longer function as a bulwark against Russian influence. Perestroika, however, saw the emergence of a fledgling Belarusian nationalist movement, modelled on similar movements in the Baltics and in Ukraine, and attempts were again made to construct a unique Belarusian national identity. Spearheaded by the Belarusian Popular Front (*Belaruski narodny front*, BPF), these attempts yielded meagre results. The BPF rhetoric then grew increasingly shriller, and relied on stark *antemurale* tropes.

A typical exponent of the strident and uncompromising BPF language was Genad Saganovich (Hienadz Sahanovich), who in April 1993 wrote an article in the Belarusian newspaper *Narodnaia gazeta* (Saganovich 1993). Under the title 'The Russian Question from the Viewpoint of a Belarusian', he argued that the Russians had never managed to formulate a national idea or to develop a national consciousness. The medieval doctrine of 'Moscow as the third Rome' had rapidly been transformed into an imperial ideology; being God's 'chosen people' became a Russian national idea. Under Soviet rule this imperial consciousness was strengthened even further.

If someone living in Russia previously saw himself first and foremost as a subject of the tsar, then under the new conditions he identified himself with the state powers and its organs – the army, the police and other oppressive structures. This had dire consequences for Russia's relationship with Belarus. As Saganovich saw it, for two entire centuries, war had defined the relationship between the two neighbouring peoples. Anticipating Huntington's article by a few months, Saganovich proffered an analysis quite in line with the clash-of-civilisations thesis:

> Whenever I look to the past, each time I become convinced that at least from the beginning of the 13th century and until the annexation of the Belarusian region, each century drove us further apart . . . So, yes, I dare to say that these were two different worlds, two different societies. The defining quality of the former was democracy and freedom, of the latter, totalitarianism and despotic rule. (Saganovich 1993)

Similar ideas were also propounded by the leader of the BPF, Zianon Pazniak (Zenon Pozniak), who in 1993 participated in a roundtable discussion organised by the Belarusian journal *Neman* (Pozniak 1993). Pazniak's main message was that 'a national state is the highest cultural and social value achievable', and 'without a national consciousness no independent, free, and strong state is possible'. This should be the ultimate aim of all Belarusians, he maintained.

Pazniak saw Belarus as occupying an important geopolitical position between East and West, but he rejected as dangerous nonsense any talk about a national mission as 'a bridge between Europe and Asia'.

> Belarus is not a 'bridge', but a country of the eastern part of Europe with a European people with a specifically European history and culture. It was torn from the structures of European civilization by force and experienced horrible destruction, but now we again stand before the possibility of resurrecting as a nation and returning to the fold of its historically, traditional cultural–national life. Belarus is Europe. (Pozniak 1993)

Pazniak's reasoning here echoed Kundera's 1984 article – with the important difference that he had moved the civilisational wall through Europe considerably eastward.

Russia was decidedly *not* part of Europe, but not exactly Asia either, Pazniak maintained. In his view,

> if only what we had found to the east of Belarus had been Asia, I think things might have been easier for us. The difficulty consists precisely in this: that we are confronted with a peculiar country and a peculiar phenomenon – *Aziachina* (Asianness) dressed up in European clothing.

This made it more difficult to detect the true nature of Russia and created an extremely sinister situation. In the view of the BPF leader, the border between Belarus and Russia represented a classical civilisational boundary: Belarus was a prototypical frontline state, an *antemurale* nation.

The next year, Pazniak (Pozniak 1994, 15–17) repeated many of the same points in an article in *Narodnaia gazeta*, this time with rather transparently racist overtones. Explaining why Russia represented a deadly threat to Belarus, he resorted to historical determinism. An imperial state with an imperial public consciousness, an imperialist expansive policy and a multinational structure, he argued, can never become democratic:

> Democracy and imperialism are incompatible. They are antipodes. The existence of the Russian state is dramatic for the Russian society itself primarily because as a result of its imperial content no full-fledged [*polnotsennaia*] European Russian nation has been formed. This is a scrappy [*loskutnyi*] people with no clearly delineated national territory, interspersed with Finno-Ugric, Turkic, Mongolian and other enclaves. (Pozniak 1994)

This article brought a flurry of irate rebuttals, and may well have administered the *coup de grâce* to BPF-type nationalism.[4] The Belarusian population at large was not receptive to BPF's ideas – as indirectly acknowledged by Pazniak himself. For instance, he pointed out that since independence was achieved in 1991, the publication of books in the Belarusian language had been severely curtailed but 'hardly anybody seems to notice'. Belarusians clearly preferred to read books in Russian. So much for that massive civilisational gap between Belarusness and Russianness.

Since the turn of the century, the anti-Russian discourse in Belarusian nationalist circles has become less shrill, but some of the same arguments nevertheless remain. In 2017, for instance, the independent Belarusian TV station 'Belsat' featured a series of programmes with historian Alexander Kravtsevich on 'The Riddles of Belarusian History'. In one of his lectures he set out to explain why Belarusians are Europeans, and listed such characteristics of Belarusian history as individualism, the treatment of women (who had inheritance rights), and religious and spiritual tolerance: on the last point, Kravtsevich argued, Belarusians were more European than most nations in Western Europe since they had never had an Inquisition. But more importantly, their historical experience distinguished the Belarusians from their eastern neighbours, the Russians.

> Russian statehood is a statehood of an Asian type. The tradition of Russian statehood is that the human being is a brick with which to build the state . . . In Russia, life does not count for much. That is their tradition. Ours is European. ('Pochemu' 2017)

Therefore, Belarus is not only different from Russia, Kravtsevich maintained, but the main bulwark against this alien civilisation:

> We joined Western Europe after the Mongol–Tatar attack and the aggression of the Teutonic orders. We belong to this Europe and were the outpost of Europe on its border with Russia. We were the shield of Europe. Not Poland but Belarus was the shield of Europe . . . Then we were for a long time pulled toward the east, but in our mentality remained in the West. ('Pochemu' 2017)

'Outpost' and 'shield' are military metaphors, and this is undiluted *antemurale* rhetoric.

UKRAINE AS AN *ANTEMURALE* COUNTRY

The Canadian historian Volodymyr Kravchenko has pointed out that even though Ukraine for centuries represented the border region between the Catholic, Orthodox and Muslim worlds, *antemurale* historical mythology did not develop in eighteenth-century or early nineteenth-century Ukraine, primarily because Ukraine was subsumed under the larger Russian world (*russkii mir*) concept. *Antimurale* crept into Ukrainian historiography only with the writings of Mykhailo Hrushevsky in the early twentieth century (Kravchenko 2019). For Hrushevsky the important identity wall was not against the Crimean Tatars, Ottomans, or other

Muslim groups but against another Orthodox people and fellow Slavs, the Russians. Since then, *antemurale* perceptions have permeated Ukrainian nationalism, and always with the sharpest edge against the Russians.

Andrew Wilson has described Ukrainian nationalism as 'a minority faith' (1997). Even so, nationalism in Ukraine is clearly a stronger societal force with deeper historical roots than anything we can find in Belarus. In the interwar period, some right-wing Ukrainian intellectuals propounded an illiberal variety of nationalism which is often referred to as 'integral nationalism' (Armstrong 1955; Motyl 1980; Shkandrij 2015).[5] One of the most influential and prolific of these writers was Dmytro Dontsov (1883–1973), who later exerted considerable influence on several Ukrainian nationalist parties and movements, particularly in western regions (see e.g. Rudling 2013).

Dontsov expounded his ideas in various books, the most important of which was *The Foundations of Our Politics* ([1921] 1957). Here, he presented Ukraine as squeezed in between two fundamentally different mental worlds – Europe and Russia. To say that this was a clash between two 'civilisations' would be inaccurate, since Russia, in his view, did not represent any kind of civilisation but the opposite – barbarism. Even worse, Russia was obsessed by a messianic mission to impose its barbarous culture upon the outside world: in earlier times, through the idea of 'Moscow as the third Rome', and later, through the Third International. The formidable task placed upon the Ukrainian nation was to be at the forefront in the battle to stem the advances of Russia:

> This our eternal struggle against the chaos from the East, in defense of the entire culture of the West – through our own statehood and culture – precisely this defines the Ukrainian national idea, and this must be the foundation of our entire political program. And truly, which of the two principles on this continent that will be victorious – the European or the Muscovite – will depend upon the part Ukraine will play in this battle. (Dontsov [1921] 1957, 87)

Dmytro Dontsov belonged to the extreme right, but *antemurale* thinking in Ukraine is not restricted to integral nationalists. After independence from the Soviet Union, the political elite across the board agree that, in order to build a Ukrainian nation-state, Ukraine needs a unique and separate national culture and identity, and this can be created only by emphasising the cultural distance from Russian culture and language. That is the main reason why virtually all Ukrainian politicians at the national level – even those from the Russian-speaking east – have rejected all demands to elevate Russian as a second state language as soon as they achieve positions of power in Kyiv.[6] The best example is perhaps Leonid Kuchma from the eastern city of Dnepropetrovsk (today, Dnipro), who, during the presidential elections in 1994, campaigned on a ticket to elevate the status of Russian, a pledge which made him popular among voters in the eastern parts of the country. However, when he was installed in office in Kyiv, this promise was soon forgotten ('Leonid Kuchma' 1994). Precisely because the cultural distance between Ukraine and Russia is so short, it seems vitally important for Ukrainian state leaders and intellectuals to exaggerate it out of all proportions.

These attempts at cultural disentanglement may become rather ludicrous, as when certain linguistic differences between the two languages are adduced as evidence that 'there exists no European nation more different from the Ukrainian than the Russian'.[7] But in the 1990s, a scholarly publication called *Politychna dumka* ('Political Thought') also published articles aimed at underpinning an understanding of Ukrainian culture as significantly more European than the Russian. Discussing 'Ukraine and Russia in the context of European values', an article in that journal in 1993 claimed that the basic Russian ideas were 'primitive collectivism and equality, as well as illusions of social equity and justice, and hatred towards the rich'. The Ukrainian people, by contrast, had luckily avoided the influence of the peasant community – the *mir* – and had instead developed concepts of the free life derived from the Cossack philosophy and Cossack free spirit, as well as from the Magdeburg laws found in earlier times in some west Ukrainian cities. Therefore,

> It is Ukraine (more than Russia) that is the carrier of a European mentality, which has been forming for centuries as the foundation of Ukraine's history, traditions, system of values and of everything else that reflects the spirit of a nation. (Polokhalo et al. 1993, 140)

The same kind of rhetoric can be found today. In 2016, political scientist Nikolai Mikhalchenko, a former advisor to President Leonid Kravchuk, published a thick book on 'The Great Civilisational Explosion at the Turn of the 21st Century'. Here, he presents a detailed but rather one-sided version of Russian history from the earliest days until Putin's regime. Mikhalchenko explains that the anti-civilisational essence of the Muscovy state was present from the very beginning, when the first Russian conquistadors 'got lost in the marshes and forests, ran wild among the local population, and removed themselves from European civilization' (Mikhalchenko 2016, 6). Russians are not Europeans – in fact, not even Slavs. The Russian language may superficially be regarded as Slavic but, Mikhalchenko insists, it is based on a combination of Fenno-Ugric and Turkic languages 'in which the Slavic admixture is insignificant'. For most linguists, this discovery would probably as come as a surprise, but for Mikhalchenko it serves as a basis for the claim that 'there are no historical or linguistic or "blood" reasons to regard Russia as an heir to the medieval Rus' state' (Mikhalchenko 2016, 6).

The Cossack Hetman Bohdan Khmelnitskyy made a colossal mistake when he linked the fate of Ukraine to the Russians with the Pereyaslav Treaty in 1654. It turned the country into a Russian colony, in which most of the population became Russified, but now Ukraine had a new chance:

> now we have to work out a new national consciousness adequate for a Central European country with its corresponding policies, economy, and way of life. It will not be easy to acquire a new civilizational thinking and consciousness, but the first steps in that direction have already been taken. (Mikhalchenko 2016, 9)

One might be tempted to dismiss this quasi-history as the ramblings of a marginalised crackpot, but a certain echo of it can also be found in more authoritative statements by Ukrainian politicians. Thus, in spring 2015, President Petro Poroshenko claimed on several occasions that Ukraine is an 'outpost' (*forpost*) of European civilisation in the struggle for freedom and democracy ('Ukraina seichas' 2014; 'Ukraina iavliaetsia' 2015). Exactly in which direction the frontline between European Ukraine and its un-European enemy is running is not quite clear from Poroshenko's statements. On one occasion, he refers simultaneously to Ukraine's participation in World War II, when the enemy was Nazi Germany, *and* to the ongoing war in Eastern Ukraine. With its heroism and its sacrifices in the struggle for the liberation of Europe, Poroshenko declared, the Ukrainian people had made an invaluable contribution to the victory over in Nazism in 1939–45, adding: 'and today Ukraine is also an outpost of European civilization in the struggle for freedom, democracy and European values'. Ukrainian sacrifices in World War II – when Ukrainians were fighting in the ranks of the Soviet army – and in the most recent war on Ukrainian territory are presented as two sides of the same coin.

> Ukraine is defending not only its own country but also the Eastern world frontier (*rubezh*) of democracy and freedom. Ukraine today is a genuine outpost of Europe. Therefore, we selflessly uphold our right to be an inalienable part of European civilization.

Poroshenko's choice of words here make sense only if we assume that he is excluding Russia from European civilisation.[8]

As far as I can see, the civilisational discourse has been toned down in official Ukrainian under President Volodymyr Zelenskyj and has been relegated to the far right. Still, it continues to inform statements of spokespersons of, for instance, the rightist movement Pravy Sector. In February 2020, one of its leaders, former member of the Ukrainian parliament the Supreme Rada Boryslav Bereza, claimed that Ukraine was engaged in a 'civilisational war' against Russia:

They have inherited the Soviet traditions. A technological civilization, which is indifferent to civil freedoms and rights . . . For Russia, the citizens are a resource which can be sacrificed to achieve results . . . We have chosen another path. The path of cultural, spiritual development in which the state serves the people, not the other way around. This is the European version. (Bereza 2020)

Georgia

In Georgia we can find two discourses on Georgian–Russian relations, one focusing on the similarities between the two countries while the other underlines the differences. The emphasis on dissociation dominates, while voices stressing the common features of Russian and Georgian cultures represent a self-critical opposition.[9] Former President Mikheil Saakashvili is among those who, on occasion, have handed out sweeping characterisations of the entire Russian people, in commenting on the actions of the Russian state. For instance, at a joint press conference with US Secretary of State Condoleezza Rice after the August War in 2008, Saakashvili called the Russian troops 'coldblooded murderers and barbarians' ('Russkie voiska' 2008).

The Russians behave as if they lived in the 18th or 19th century. The only difference is that in the past there were no stock exchanges or live television. But their habits, expressions, and passion for alcohol remain the same. In the past, no-one took pictures of their robbery while today, the TV footage shows how they load toilets onto their tanks. One might think that they are barbarians from a bygone century. (Smolar 2008)

While it is not difficult to understand why negative portrayals of Russians and Russia would proliferate after the August War, it is worth noting that they could also be found in Saakashvili's utterances earlier. Thus, for instance, in 2006 many Russians became upset when it was reported that, at the XVI Economic Forum in Poland, Saakashvili had compared the Russians to the nomadic Huns who had invaded Europe from Asia in the fourth century ('Saakashvili depicted' 2006). At other times, however, Saakashvili emphasised Russia's strong cultural traditions. In an interview with Belarusian television in 2010 he remarked: 'I am perhaps the last, or penultimate, Georgian president who can quote Pushkin, Lermontov, Brodsky, and Esenin' (Petrov 2010).

Negative characteristics of Russians dominate in the Georgian media discourse. For instance, under the headline 'Russia – the Womb of Evil', the writer and academician Nodar Koberidze quoted novelist Grigol Robakidze, who once warned, 'the Russian is a Scythian with Mongolian eyes, a horrible, wicked race, hateful towards all that is human'. This animosity towards humanity, Koberidze claimed, stems from the inferiority complex which the

Russians cannot rid themselves of. 'When they came out of the woods, they realized that they were not up to such things as administering a state, and called in the Scandinavians, the so-called Varangians [to do it for them]' (Koberidze 2008). In October 2008, some two months after the August War, the Georgian movie director Otar Ioseliani told the Ukrainian newspaper *Ezhenedelnik 2000* ('Weekly 2000'):

> Russia has never psychologically grown out of serfdom even after it was abolished. First and foremost Russia represses its own people, who continue to live in slavery . . . We will never have peace with Russia! If previously we felt contempt for them, now a feeling of hatred has appeared. (Quoted in Rutkovskii 2008)

At the same time, it has been important for most Georgian intellectuals to emphasise that Georgia, in contrast to Russia, is a *European* country through and through. In April 1999, the Georgian Prime Minister Zurab Zhvania declared from the rostrum of the Council of Europe: 'I am a Georgian, consequently I am a European' (Scholtbach and Nodia 2006).

In 2006 Saakashvili maintained that the Georgians have been Europeans ever since Prometheus was chained to a rock in Georgia and since the Argonauts came to the country in search of the Golden Fleece ('Saakashvili ustanovil' 2008). Saakashvili often pointed to Georgia's Christian identification, stressing how Georgia had received the Gospel long before most contemporary West European nations: 'We are not the new Europe or the old Europe; we are the ancient Europe' (Quoted in Tarasov and Ermolaev 2008). Avto Dzhokhadze, executive director of the Caucasus Institute for Peace, Democracy and Development, points out that in the Georgian self-perception, its geographical position makes the country a 'forward boundary of Christian Europe', a kind of *antemurale Christianitatis* (2007).

While concepts of Georgia as a European country have dominated the political discourse in Tbilisi after independence, alternative views exist as well. Some scholars and analysts argue that Georgia lies at a crossroads of civilisations, straddling the border between East and West. For instance, Gigi Tevzadze (2009), Rector of Ilia Chavchavadze State University, has stressed the importance of the idea of a crossroads of cultures in Georgian cultural and intellectual self-identification. Similarly, historian Nino Chikovani of the Department of Cultural Studies at Tbilisi State University has argued that 'Georgia has always been a contact zone, a crossroads of Western and Eastern civilizations' (Chikovani undated). In the 1990s, the idea of a crossroads was promulgated by President Eduard Shevardnadze (Tevzadze 2009): the history of Georgia was formed by the Silk Road, he explained, while another type of East–West connection, the pipelines, symbolise Georgia's future.

RUSSIAN ATTITUDES TOWARDS THEIR ORTHODOX NEIGHBOURS

Identity formation not only is relational, it is also reciprocal. How Russia's nearest Orthodox neighbours perceive Russia is strongly influenced by how Russia views them.

As in Georgia, we can find in Russia two discourses, one emphasising dissociation while the other highlights shared features of Russian and Georgian cultures. However, whereas the former discourse dominates in Georgia, Russians tend to stress commonality. In Russia the message that Russia and Georgia are closely related, fraternal peoples – *bratskie narody* – has been officially endorsed by both Dmitry Medvedev and Vladimir Putin. The 2008 August War is presented as a regrettable but temporary aberration from what has been and should remain a 'fraternal relationship' between the two countries. However, no one in Russia has any doubts about who is the older and who is the younger of these two 'brothers'.

Already in his first statement after the start of the August War Putin declared, 'In Russia we have always had an enormous respect for Georgia. The Georgian people we regard as fraternal.' Prime Minister Putin expressed the conviction that this positive attitude would survive 'in spite of the criminal policy of the current leadership in this country' (Putin 2008).

This conciliatory message was soon repeated by other Russian officials,[10] becoming a standard ingredient in political statements. In a meeting between Russian civil society activists on 19 September 2008, then President Medvedev declared:

> [T]o us it is axiomatic that the Georgian people are of course not to be blamed for the aggression and the genocide [on the South Ossetian people]. This is the guilt of the criminal and irresponsible regime which unleashed this war . . . For centuries relations between our peoples have been fraternal . . . . ('Stenograficheskii otchet' 2008)

The *bratskie narody* metaphor is a cliché from the Soviet terminological repertoire, but should be recognised as more than a knee-jerk reaction inherited from the communist past. It also reflects the inequality in the relationship between Russians and Georgians, and between Russians and Ukrainians, which should sensitise us to the importance of power relations in the study of reciprocal identity formations. Towards the Ukrainians, Russian leaders employ the same kind of fraternal terminology as towards the Georgians, but go one step further, denying any difference between the two peoples. In his landmark speech on 18 March 2014 in the Kremlin, celebrating the incorporation of Crimea into the Russian Federation, President Putin (Putin 2014a) employed the brotherly peoples metaphor. However, he also made another claim, apparently very similar but in fact radically different: Russians and Ukrainians, he maintained, are '*one people*'. It is not clear how this should be interpreted, but it sounds very much like a throwback to the pre-revolutionary concept of the tripartite Russian nation, with its 'Great Russian', '*Malorosskii*' and 'Belorussian' branches – with no doubt as to which group naturally takes the lead in this trinity. By subsuming the Ukrainians under a common national identity umbrella, Putin effectively wiped the separate Ukrainian nation out of existence. Interestingly, this element in his rhetoric predates the 2014 Ukrainian crisis. Already in September 2013, Putin made the same claim: 'we [Russians and Ukrainians] are one people (*odin narod*)' (Putin 2013). This claim was repeated in an interview with TASS in February 2020: 'The Ukrainians may like it or not but we are one and the same people' (Putin 2020). It is against this background that the Ukrainians' insistence on an identity wall separating them from their mighty northern neighbour must be understood.

Conclusions

The *antemurale* myth is a boundary-defining mechanism. The understanding of the world as being populated by antagonistic civilisations – most famously associated with US political scientist Samuel Huntington – easily lends itself to *antemurale* thinking. However, whereas Huntington saw religions as the main ingredients of world civilisations, I contend that no 'objective' religious difference is necessary in order to construct an *antemurale* boundary. Indeed, political and cultural activists may employ *antemurale* arguments to distinguish their group or their country from a neighbouring group or country that traditionally adheres to the same religion. This is not to say that *antemurale* boundary-drawing is totally haphazard, or that all kinds of mental maps and identification structures are equally probable. Certain patterns can be discerned, but they seem to be influenced more by *power differentials* between groups than by religious or other cultural differences.

Identities are always relational. You define who you are through a contrast with the Other. *The boundary* is the locus of identity formation – with individuals as well as with collectives, including ethnic groups and nations. Furthermore, as Iver Neumann (Neumann 1999) has pointed out, in these processes the neighbours you want to dissociate yourself from are more important than the ones you want to emulate. Therefore, *antemurale* theories tell us not only something about how a nation or ethnic group perceives one of its neighbours, but also something about their self-perception.

Identity relations, like other relations, involve power. Russia is a much larger, stronger and more populous state than its Orthodox neighbours and has, to a considerable degree, influenced their history, while they have generally played far more limited roles in Russian history.

In conflict situations involving two culturally related nations, the larger and more powerful nation will tend to underscore similarities and downplay differences, whereas the smaller and weaker one will normally insist that the boundary between the two is strong and real. The larger group has an interest in subsuming its neighbours under some common identity since this may legitimise continued hegemony, while the weaker part may fall back on a combination of two different strategies (Kolstø 2005b, 19–20). It may claim to be unique, *sui generis*, one of a kind. But those who stand alone in the world are vulnerable and exposed, so a *sui generis* identity is often supplemented with the claim that 'our nation' is indeed a member of a larger community – but that is a *different* community from the one dominated by the (former) hegemon. For some politicians and intellectuals in Georgia, Ukraine and Belarus this alternative community is Europe. Their political leaders have gone out of their way to stress how their countries belong to European civilisation and that they have an important contribution to offer to this value community. They should be recognised as outposts of European civilisation towards the east, defenders of the gate, or, as they were called in medieval and early modern Europe, nations *antemurale* (Kolstø 2005b, 24–5).

If the *sui generis* myth is a strategy of dissociation, *antemurale* thinking represents a new association. Of course, membership in the new community cannot shield the country from the former hegemon if the hegemon also belongs to it. With Georgia, Ukraine and Belarus, *antemurale* thinkers in these countries must convince their fellow Europeans – and themselves – that Russians are *not* Europeans and do not belong inside the gates.

The myth of being *antemurale* is a boundary marker created so as to emphasise the cultural distance between groups. It maximises the effect of this boundary by claiming that it represents a civilisational divide. The evidence mustered is cultural: historical, religious, linguistic and so on. As I see it, however, it is not these cultural differences *per se* that drive the mythogenesis, but concerns about power and power relations. Whatever else the *antemurale* myth has been in the history of European nations, it is primarily a weapon in the hands of weak nations confronted by what they perceive as strong and aggressive neighbours.

Notes

1. For instance, Huntington's book was translated into Estonian in 1999 with a Foreword by the then-Minister of Foreign Affairs, Toomas Ilves (Huntington 1999). A leading Estonian intellectual, sociologist Marju Lauristin, referenced Huntington to underpin her assertion that ethnic nationalism was not the most decisive factor in the dissolution of the Soviet Union. Instead, she claimed, it was 'precisely the civilizational conflict between the Russian-Soviet Empire, the "New Byzantium" of the twentieth century, and the Baltic and other East-European nations, representing the Western traditions of individual autonomy and civil society' (Lauristin and Vihalemm 1997, 29). By contrast, in Russia, Huntington's ideas were received with a strong dose of scepticism. See e.g. Afanas'ev 2009; Govorun 2015.

2. In official Russian statistics, the Ukrainians were referred to as *Malorossy*, or 'Little Russians'.
3. In 2000, 42.6 per cent of the respondents in a survey in Belarus agreed with the statement that 'the Belarusians are a part of a triune Russian people'. See Bekus 2010.
4. In Kolstø 2000, 163–7, I argue that the demise of BPF was caused by 'self-inflicted wounds' rather than by 'murder'.
5. 'Integral nationalism' ('nationalisme intégral') was first developed in France in the late nineteenth and early twentieth centuries by intellectuals such as Charles Maurras. Among its defining characteristics were statism, militarism and anti-individualism. It is often regarded as proto-fascist.
6. I argue this point in Kolstø 2000, 168–93.
7. Author's interview at the headquarters of the Ukrainian Popular Front (RUKH) in Kyiv, September 1994. For instance, while the most common Ukrainian word for 'leader' is *holova*, meaning 'head', a typically Russian term for the same is *predsedatel'*, derived from the Russian word for 'to sit'. According to my Ukrainian informant, this proved which part of the body was more important for Ukrainian and Russian leaders, respectively!
8. A similar rhetoric was used by Ukrainian Minister for European and Euro-Atlantic Integration Ivanna Klimpush-Tsintsadze. See 'Klimpush-Tsintsadze' 2017. For the wider ramifications of the war in Donbas on the Ukrainian identity debate, see Zhurzhenko 2018.
9. This section builds on my co-authored article with Alexandr Rusetskii (Kolstø and Rusetskii 2012).
10. See e.g. the statement by the Russian ambassador to Estonia (Uspenskii 2008).

6

IMPERIALISM AND ETHNOCENTRISM IN RUSSIAN NATIONALISM

The trajectory of Russian nationalism under Putin illustrates two important mechanisms in the strategic use of nationalism. First, we can observe how ethnic nationalism, which previously had been a rather marginal phenomenon, moved to centre-stage. As long as Russia was a large, multinational empire under the tsars or commissars, Russians tended to link their collective) identity to that state rather than to their ethnic group. With some time lag, this changed when the USSR was consigned 'to the dustbin of history' (to use Trotsky's expression): Russians – not only professed nationalists but also the population at large – increasingly identified more with the (somewhat) smaller state in which they were now living – the Russian Federation – as well as with their ethnic group. This is a clear example of what Andreas Wimmer calls 'boundary contraction': when the disappearance of the large state seemed irrevocable, they identified instead with the realistic alternative, the state in which they actually live. This could also be seen as reflection of what rational choice theorists call 'the sour grapes syndrome': they acted like the fox in the Greek fable who realised that he was unable to reach the delicious high-hanging fruits, and therefore convinced himself that he did not want them because they were probably sour. In more common parlance, one could say that this boundary contraction reflected a 'reality check'.

Second, the fate of Russian nationalism since the turn of the millennium shows how political leaders can tap into and exploit popular nationalist sentiments for their own purposes. Although Vladimir Putin at one point claimed that

'I am the biggest nationalist in Russia' (Putin 2014c), this should not be taken at face value. 'Nationalism' is, to all intents and purposes, a four-letter word in the official Russian lexicon. Putin and his entourage very much prefer to call themselves 'patriots' and so do the majority of Russians (Blum 2006; Bækken 2021; Sanina 2017; Goode 2018). Only people who are both strongly nationally minded and in opposition to the powers-that-be prefer to call themselves nationalists. Even so, Putin and the Kremlin ideologues have had no inhibitions about switching to nationalist rhetoric when the occasion has called for it. Such was the situation in 2014, when Russia, in a surprise move, decided to invade the Ukrainian peninsula of Crimea. This flagrant breach of international law needed a justification, and Putin for a while latched on to parts of the rhetoric of the Russian nationalists. A confluence of a number of circumstances made this a suitable strategy. For three years, nationalism had been on the rise in the Russian population, propelled by, among other things, an influx of migrant workers from Central Asia, which created strong xenophobic sentiments in parts of the Russian population. Second, the flawed parliamentary elections in December 2011 had unleashed unprecedented waves of disgust and even hatred about the lack of real democracy in the country and brought trust in the Putin regime to a low ebb. By posing as 'the biggest nationalist in Russia', Putin managed to hijack the nationalist agenda and side-line his nationalist critics. As argued by Yuri Teper, the Kremlin's approach toward Russian ethno-nationalism was 'predominantly utilitarian' (Teper 2016, 380).

Many of the arguments used by Putin in his landmark speech on 18 March 2014, when Crimea was solemnly accepted into the Russian Federation, were vintage Putin rhetoric. To the Russian Federal Assembly he explained how this move was necessary to build and defend a strong Russian state, Western criticism of it reflected Western double standards in international relations, and so on. A novel motif in his talk, however, was his references to the Russian people as an ethnic entity. He claimed that, with the dissolution of the Soviet Union, 'the Russian people has become one of the largest divided nations in the world, if not the largest' (Putin 2014a). By 'the Russian people' Putin was clearly referring not to 'the (multiethnic) people of Russia', but to 'ethnic Russians' – wherever they may live, even abroad. The expression he used was *russkii narod*, a concept which, in the modern Russian political lexicon up until then, had been used in the ethnic sense only, not to refer to the political nation. For the latter entity, the Yeltsin administration had introduced the term *rossiiskii narod*. It is true that, in the Tsarist era, the terms *rossiiskii* and *russkii* had often been used interchangeably (Tishkov 2013), and arguably Putin was trying to resurrect the pre-revolutionary terminology. In the same speech he also referred, for instance, to 'Russian Armenians', 'Russian Tatars' and 'Russian Germans', concepts which make sense only if they are translated as 'Armenians, Tatars and Germans in Russia'. However, the claim that 'the

Russian people has become one of the largest divided nations in the world' clearly presupposes an ethnic understanding of 'the people'. As long as 'the Russian people' is understood as 'the total population of Russia', full stop, it cannot, by definition, be divided among several states.

Ever since Putin took office he has regularly been characterised in the Western media as a 'nationalist'. His original brand of nationalism, however, was clearly of the statist kind, *derzhavnichestvo*, with a strong emphasis on the *state*, the *derzhava*. In his article 'Russia between two millennia', which was published on New Year's Eve 1999, the day before he was appointed acting President, Putin (1999) strongly emphasised the centrality of a strong state for Russian identity and discussed at length the cultural foundations of Russian statehood (Kolstø and Blakkisrud 2005). Remarkably, at this stage he did *not once* use the adjective '*russkii*'. In a long section Putin discussed what he regarded as 'traditional Russian values', but he consistently referred to them as '*rossiiskie*' values, even if these values, for the most part, were exactly the same ones that numerous authors before him had singled out as typical of ethnic Russians and not necessarily of other peoples of Russia. At this stage, Putin still toed the terminological line of his benefactor and predecessor, President Yeltsin. Later, the term *russkii* gradually crept into his speeches.

The substitution of one word for 'Russian' with another in Russian political discourse, I will argue, was not just a matter of phrasing, but reflects a perceptible shift in nationalism and national identity which has taken place in Russia over the last decades, from statist to ethno-nationalist positions. This change can be detected at various levels, societal and political. I will demonstrate that before it found its way into Putin's speeches, it could be detected in oppositional public discourse. Among the first to adopt an ethno-nationalist understanding of the Russian nation were certain Soviet dissidents, most famously Alexander Solzhenitsyn in the 1970s. His little band of likeminded Russian culturalist thinkers, however, remained isolated voices in the wilderness as long as the Soviet Union existed. Most Soviet citizens took great pride in the fact that their state was one of the world's two superpowers and, indeed, the largest country on the planet. Moreover, the available evidence suggests that Russians, more than other Soviet nationalities, linked their identity to the state and not to ethnicity.

Whence, then, the new ethnic turn in Russian self-understanding? The simple answer would be that it is linked to the collapse of the USSR, but while this is obviously true, it is far from the whole story. Under Yeltsin both the regime and its critics espoused various brands of state-focused nationalism: the hard-line, so-called red–brown opposition were Soviet nostalgics who longed for the defunct superpower while the Yeltsinites tried to the best of their ability to inculcate in the population loyalty to the truncated Russian state, the Russian Federation. At the time, the ethno-nationalists were few and far between; they came later.

A Typology of Russian Nationalisms

Numerous books and articles have been written about Russian nationalism: under the Tsars (Riasanovsky 1959; Seton-Watson 1986; Tolz 2001; Tuminez 2000), in the Soviet Union (Brudny 2000; Carter 1990; Dunlop 1983; Dunlop 1985; Mitrokhin 2003; Simon, 1991; Yanov 1978), under perestroika (Drobizheva 1998; Dunlop 1993; Szporluk 1989) and in the post-communist period (Laruelle 2008; Laruelle 2009; Tolz 2001; Tuminez 2000). These analyses have argued that nationalism has influenced the worldview of Russian thinkers and politicians and shaped events in Russia. Nikolai Mitrokhin, for instance (2003, 41), has claimed that in the USSR, Russian nationalism was 'a rather widespread phenomenon', while John Dunlop (1985, 92) expressed the view in 1985 that Russian nationalism was well positioned to replace Communism as state ideology. In contrast to this, Alexander Motyl (1990, 161–73) claimed in 1990 that Russian nationalism was a marginal phenomenon in Russian society – indeed, a 'myth' – while Rowley (2000) ten years later followed up by asserting the *absence* of nationalism in Russian history.

As it turns out, however, the apparent discrepancy among those who assert and those who deny the significance of Russian nationalism stems from the authors' different definitions. Rowley and Motyl claimed that most of what has passed for Russian nationalism turns out on closer scrutiny to be *imperialism*, and, argues Motyl (1990, 163) 'nationalism and imperialism are polar types'. Scholars who adhere to this view equate nationalism with *ethno-nationalism* but while this no doubt is an extremely important variety of this -ism, it is not the only possible one. The pioneers of nationalism studies such as Karl Deutsch (1966) and Ernest Gellner (1983) regarded as nationalism all strategies to homogenise a country's population, and on that basis create a common identity among them attached to the state. The 'ties that bind' do not necessarily have to be ethnicity or a myth of common descent.

It is only if we equate nationalism with ethno-nationalism that political, state-based nationalism in multiethnic states becomes a contradiction in terms (Kolstø 2019). One reason why Rowley and Motyl did so with regard to Russia, I surmise, is that the nationalisms of the other small and medium-sized nations in the Russian Empire and the Soviet Union, almost without exception, belong to the ethno-nationalist variety (see e.g. Simon 1991, Carrère-d'Encausse 1993). This is not surprising. As long as there was no Belarusian, Uzbek or Chechen state, nationalism among Belarusians, Uzbeks, Chechens and so on focused on the ethnic group rather than on the state. Indeed, in a typology attributed to Hans Kohn (1971),[1] nationalism among stateless, state-seeking groups has been characterised as 'Eastern' in contradistinction to 'Western', state-focused nationalism. While this distinction has some potential for explaining the trajectory of nationalism among stateless nations in the eastern part of Europe, it is unsuitable for an analysis of nationalist thinking in East European nations that identify with one of Europe's old states, such as the Poles, the Hungarians and the Russians.

Marlène Laruelle (2009, 3) argues that since ethnocentrism and nationalism are not synonymous terms, 'there can be no question here of excluding from "nationalism" so-called imperialist or statist currents'. Vera Tolz likewise believes that the word nationalism, as it is used in Western scholarly literature, is applicable to the Russian case because, in the nineteenth century, the Russians themselves, 'when they talked about the Russian Empire they thought they were talking about the Russian nation-state' (Tolz 2001, 18). Emil Pain and S. A. Prostakov (2014) also think that, in a Russian context, the expression 'imperial nationalism' is not necessarily an oxymoron. I will follow these researchers and include in my definition of nationalism both state-centred and ethnocentric nationalisms.

Laruelle (2014c, 59) believes that it does not make sense to try to distinguish between imperialist and ethno-nationalist currents in Russian nationalism since 'the main ideologues and politicians can use at the same time both imperialist and ethnonationalist arguments'. In my view, however, it is important to keep these tendencies analytically apart. Even if virtually all 'real existing nationalisms' in Russia historically or today are of a mixed kind, clear differences with significant political consequences appear when we ask which of these two concerns is the driving motor behind it: the interests of the state or the interests of the Russian ethnic group. The most important distinction, I argue, runs between those that focus on ethnicity versus those that focus on the state. But since the borders of the Russian state have changed, we must also hold apart those nationalists who identify with the current Russian Federation, and those who orient themselves towards one of its much larger predecessors, whether this is the Tsarist Empire or the USSR. For these purposes I will use a two-axes model proposed by Sven Gunnar Simonsen in 1996.[2] The two axes should not be understood as dichotomies but rather as continuums, and the four boxes as ideal types in a Weberian sense.

Territorial orientation	Primarily statist A	Primarily ethnic B
I 'Empire'-oriented	1 Empire-saving nationalism	2 Supremacist nationalism
II 'Core'-oriented	3 Russian Federation nationalism	4 Ethnic core nationalism

Diagram 6.1 A typology of Russian nationalisms

Until around 1988–9, almost all Russians, including virtually all nationalists, took for granted that 'the state' in question was the USSR. It was only when this state was reeling under the increasing onslaught of non-Russian nationalism that the term became ambiguous. In a seminal article in 1989, Roman Szporluk (1989, 16) described those Russians who wanted to preserve the USSR as 'empire-savers' while those few who were willing to contemplate a breakup of the unitary state and see the Russian Soviet Federative Socialist Republic (RSFSR) as a Russian nation-state – or as a territorial area that could be developed into such an entity – he referred to as 'nation-builders'.

Today, some three decades after Szporluk wrote his article, the USSR has ended up in the dustbin of history and a new generation of Russians has grown up who have never known any other 'homeland' than the Russian Federation. This is not to say that the 'empire-savers' have quietly left the scene. They are still around, now in the guise of various kinds of 'empire-nostalgics' or so-called Eurasianists. Acrimonious quarrels between empire-nostalgics and ethno-nationalists mark one of the most important fault-lines in Russian nationalist discourse today.

On both axes intermediate positions can be found. With regard to territory, it is not uncommon to hear among contemporary Russian ethno-nationalists that while the Soviet Union is irredeemably lost and should not be resurrected, the two Slavic republics of Ukraine and Belarus, plus perhaps the Russian-populated part of Kazakhstan, ought to be incorporated into a Russian nation-state. The main motivation behind this stance is ethnic commonality among the Eastern Slavs rather than any harking after a big and strong state. As Oxana Shevel (2011) has pointed out, some Russian ethno-nationalists also include the Ukrainians and the Belarusians among those whom they regard as 'Russians' alongside the Great Russians, or 'Russians proper'.

Below, I trace the historical trajectory of Russian nationalism and argue that a discernible movement has taken place from A to B positions on the x-axis in my typology and from I to II positions on the y-axis. This development did not pick up speed until after the breakup of the Soviet Union and can be linked to two issues that both resulted from this dissolution: the so-called 'new diaspora' issue in the 1990s and the flow of unskilled labour from former Soviet Republics into Russia after the year 2000.

RUSSIAN NATIONALISM BEFORE THE NATION-STATE

Tsarist Russia was an empire in name and self-understanding, as well as in actual fact. Regime legitimation – often called 'Official nationality' (Riasanovsky 1959) – was of a dynastic, statist kind, emphasising loyalty to the Emperor. Virtually all nationalist currents among the intelligentsia were also located on the I axis in my matrix, for the most part in quadrant 1.

Geoffrey Hosking (1998, 19) claims that the huge efforts expended on building the vast Russian Empire impeded the attempt to create a Russian nation. Likewise, Tuminez (2000, 25) argues that since 'the state developed as a multi-ethnic, authoritarian empire, the idea of nation both in ethnic and civic terms never gained widespread influence'. Only towards the end of the nineteenth century did the Russian state introduce a policy of Russification toward some of its non-Russian subjects, but the effect was limited. 'Russia remained a state where the sense of nation (both ethnic and civic) was weak, and nationalism that bound state and society did not exist' (Tuminez 2000, 39).

After the first Russian Revolution in 1905 we see for the first time the emergence of a Russian nationalism with a strong emphasis on blood, descent and ethnicity. The extremist pro-Tsarist groups often referred to as the 'Black Hundreds' 'defined membership in the nation chiefly in ethnic terms – only ethnic Russians were bona fide members of the nation' (Tuminez 2000, 126; see also Laqueur 1993). At the same time, such moderate great power nationalists as Petr Struve and Petr Stolypin tried to combine a civic and ethnic strategy of nationalism (Struve 1997; Tuminez 2000, 128; Hosking 1998, 32). As we know, this did not save the Empire.

The Bolshevik regime that took over in 1917 professed an anti-nationalist ideology, internationalist Communism. Writing in 1986, Seton-Watson (1986, 28) believed that 'the Soviet leadership, from 1917 to the present day, has not been inspired by Russian nationalism'. Frederick Barghoorn (1980, 57–8), however, insisted that, for Stalin, a 'new Soviet Russian ethnocentrism' was central to his 'socialist patriotism', while Brezhnev was 'a Russifier and exponent of neo-Stalinist Russian ethnocentrism' (see also Barghoorn 1956). The truth should be sought somewhere in between Seton-Watson's and Barghoorn's one-sided claims. The least we can say is that Stalin consciously appealed to Russian national sentiments during and after World War II to bolster support for the regime (Brandenberger 2002). Brezhnev, for his part, gave a certain leeway to Russophile ideas within the party apparatus as well as among the cultural intelligentsia (Brudny 2000; Duncan 2000; Dunlop 1983; Mitrokhin 2003; Yanov 1978). Researchers have been able to identify a number of different strands and currents within the spectrum of state-tolerated Russian nationalisms: some veered towards aggressive statism, replete with vehement anti-Westernism and rather transparent anti-Semitism, while others, such as the so-called village prose writers, were far more concerned with the preservation of Russian cultural values. One of the things they had in common was that they took the continued existence a Soviet unitary state for granted.

The same was true with Russian nationalism as it developed in Russian émigré circles in the interwar period. The two parallel movements, National-Bolshevism and Eurasianism, were often at loggerheads, but on many crucial issues they advocated very similar brands of nationalism. Both were strongly committed to the preservation of the unitary Russian state within the old borders. The main difference between them was that while the National-Bolshevists trusted the Bolshevik regime to carry out this task (Agurskii 2003), the Eurasianists developed their own ideology for a post-Bolshevik, unified Russia. This ideology should build on values that were common to all residents of this state, but also, somewhat contradictorily, on Russian Orthodoxy as the sole state religion (Bassin et al. 2015). While Eurasianism paid considerable attention to cultural matters, the concerns of the state were nevertheless paramount for them, and Laruelle (2008, 29) sees their movement as 'an extreme form of statism'.

John Dunlop (1983, 1985) identified the vast majority of Russian nationalists in the postwar dissident movement as culturalists (or *vozrozhdentsy*, from 'renaissance', in his terminology) rather than as 'National-Bolsheviks'). They were strongly preoccupied with the preservation of Russian cultural traditions and monuments, concerned about the decaying of the Russian countryside and – some of them at least – professed the Orthodox faith. Other researchers found a much larger element of statism and aggressive Messianism, even proto-fascism and fascism among anti-regime Russian nationalists (Yanov 1978; Laqueur 1993; Duncan 2000, 82–96; Shenfield 2001, 40–4). In any case, neither the dissident statists nor the culturalists questioned the territorial integrity of the Soviet state – with a few notable exceptions. Best known is Alexander Solzhenitsyn and his appeal to the Soviet leaders to let go of Central Asia and concentrate the resources of the state on the development of the Russian north (Solzhenitsyn [1973] 1980). It is true that Solzhenitsyn under no circumstances envisioned any relinquishing of the demographically Slavic parts of the Soviet state such as Ukraine, Belarus and northern Kazakhstan. However, by combining an ethnic reasoning with a readiness to forego state grandeur he nevertheless anticipated the later development of Russian ethnic core nationalism (quadrant 4 in my matrix).[3]

RUSSIAN NATIONALISM AFTER THE DISSOLUTION OF THE UNITARY SOVIET STATE

The collapse of the USSR was a major watershed in Russian history in the twentieth century, and inevitably also affected the trajectory of nationalist thinking (Dunlop 1993). As Leokadia Drobizheva observed, 'when perestroika unleashed an explosion of national feeling among the non-Russian peoples . . . many Russians responded by reorienting their sense of group identity away from this imperial mass consciousness' (Drobizheva 1998, 132). If Russians until then had identified with the Soviet state as a whole and not with the RSFSR, they were now asked to transfer their allegiance to this smaller entity. According to Georgiy Mirsky, this almost immediately led to two separate, major reorientations in Russian perceptions: towards an ethnic Russian nationalism, on the one hand, and towards a non-ethnic loyalty towards the Russian Federation, on the other.

> It would not be an exaggeration to say that it was at that juncture that Russians, for the first time in decades, became really conscious of their national identity. Now it suddenly appeared that they belonged not to a great multinational empire transcending ethnicity but to a smaller Russian state. *The fact of being an ethnic Russian, formerly just taken for granted, became salient overnight . . . And it was at this juncture that ethnic Russian nationalism came to the fore.* Russians began to feel that they were left all alone, that they were not *Rossiyanie*, but *Russkie*, a purely ethnic community . . . . Ethnicity became a sanctuary for people lacking other outlets for self-fulfillment. This is the first, and major, cause of the rise of Russian nationalism. (Mirsky 1997, 165–6, emphasis in the original)

In Mirsky's view, the fourth quadrant in my matrix, hitherto inhabited by a few quirks only, suddenly became the abode of millions of Russians. At first, however, ethnic solidarity was eclipsed by another stronger sentiment, Mirsky asserts: a feeling that all nations, regardless of their ethnic background, belonged to Russia. This was the basis for the new nation-building project launched by the Yeltsin administration in the 1990s (Mirsky 1997, 165–7). The third quadrant, characterised by non-ethnic Russian Federation-focused nationalism, for a while attracted many Russians.

As Mirsky saw it, post-Soviet Russian nationalism has moved through three stages in a remarkably short time, from a subdued feeling of Russianness over-shadowed by an overall Soviet loyalty, via a *rossiiane* period, marked by non-ethnic loyalty to the Russian Federation, to a 'genuine Russian ethnic nationalism with chauvinistic overtones' (Mirsky 1997, 167). While Mirsky's observations are important, I think he errs on two accounts. First, the two varieties of Russian Federation-focused nationalism should not be seen as *stages* in which one sup-plants the other, but as co-existing phenomena. It is true that ethnic orientation has indeed grown stronger over time at the expense of the civic or Westernising variety, but this development, I will argue, has taken place *since* Mirsky published his book in 1997. Second, Mirsky downplays too much the enduring strength of the Soviet-focused varieties of Russian nationalism (axis I in my matrix). Indeed, it can even be argued that, during perestroika and throughout the 1990s, the empire-focused nationalisms initially gained strength, becoming *more* articulate and better organised – as 'empire-saving' – and in its immediate aftermath – as 'empire-nostalgia'.

Below I will present the four major trends in post-Soviet Russian nationalism in the categories defined above.

USSR-focused statism

The unprecedented upsurge of ethnic nationalism among non-Russians during perestroika did not initially trigger a similar movement among ethnic Russians. Instead, as the nationalist effervescence led to demands for secession in the Union republics, ethnic Russians responded by creating organisations aimed at preserving the unitary state. Pointedly, in many republics these organisations were called '*intermovements*', short for 'international movements', a name chosen in deliberate contrast to the nationalist movements among the non-Russians (Kolstø 1995). In the Congress of People's Deputies – the new superparliament established by Mikhail Gorbachev in 1989 – the 'Soiuz' (= Union) group of deputies fought tooth and nail to keep the Soviet Union together (Dunlop 1993, 147–51).

In his heated disputes in the 1980s with Alexander Yanov about the character of Russian nationalism John Dunlop had claimed that the 'culturalists' were the stronger force and would carry the day. Alexander Yanov (1978, 19), for his part, predicted that the anti-regime culturalists (or nationalism 'A', in his terminology) would eventually be won over by hard-core anti-Western isolationists ('nationalism B') and finally merge into military imperialism ('nationalism C'). Perestroika and its immediate aftermath seemed to prove Yanov right. In the late 1980s and early 1990s, several Russian nationalists whom Dunlop (1985, 88) had identified as leading culturalists, such as Vladimir Osipov and Igor Shafarevich, made common cause with the 'empire-savers'. In 1992, both of these former dissident anti-communists were among the signatories when the leading red–brown organisation, the National Salvation Front, was established. Their names appeared alongside hard-line imperial nationalists such as Alexander Prokhanov, Albert Makashov and Sergei Baburin, all of whom have been characterised by Stephen Shenfield (2001) as 'fascists'. The same appeal was also signed by 'red' statist nationalists such as Communist Party leaders Gennadii Ziuganov and Aman Tuleev ('Obrashchenie' 1992).

The most important aim of the so-called 'red–brown' coalition – first against Mikhail Gorbachev, later against Boris Yeltsin – was indeed not to preserve the communist ideology or the planned economy but to hold the Soviet Union together as state. In a public appeal the organisers of the National Salvation Front used high-strung language:

> Dear *rossiiane*! Citizens of the USSR! Fellow citizens! An enormous, unprecedented misfortune has befallen us: the motherland, our country, a great state, which has been given us by history, by nature, and by our glorious forefathers, is perishing, is being broken apart, is being buried in darkness and non-existence. ('Slovo k narodu' 1992)

The National Salvation Front pledged to 'work consistently for the restoration of the state unity of our country'.

The 'red–browns' failed in their bid for power in October 1993, when the besieged Russian parliament, which they controlled, was shelled into surrender by Yeltsin-loyal troops. After this defeat, the 'red' and the 'brown' statists drifted apart, and important differences in their thinking came to the fore. Even so, both factions continued to adhere to a basically ethnicity-neutral variety of statism. Ziuganov and his red nationalists generally eschewed ethnicity in their argumentation (Simonsen 1996, 103), while Vladimir Zhirinovsky and his Liberal-Democratic Party are somewhat more difficult to pin down. According to Marlène Laruelle, Zhirinovsky cannot reasonably be classified as belonging to either an 'imperialist' or an 'ethno-nationalist' party. On the one hand, he campaigned for a self-sufficient regime in which ethnic Russians shall enjoy legal primacy, but at the same time 'he refuses . . . to provide a racial definition of Russianness, emphasizing instead a linguistic and cultural sense of belonging to a Russian world' (Laruelle 2009, 100).

A more ethnocentric orientation could be expected from the Congress of Russian Communities (KRO), which was explicitly devoted to the support of Russians in 'the near abroad'. The adjective 'Russian' in the name of the movement was indeed *russkii*, not *rossiiskii*, but according to Alan Ingram (1999, 688), KRO 'rejects an ethnic nationalism based on blood and descent, but neither is its nation fully civic, embracing all regardless of culture and identity' (see also Tuminez 2000, 191).

In the mid-1990s, neo-Eurasianism became one of the strongest currents of Russian nationalism, if not *the* strongest (Bassin and Pozo 2017). Like their interwar namesakes, most latter-day Eurasianists adhered to a non-ethnic definition of the nation. Aleksander Panarin, for instance, warned that 'the logic of ethnic sovereignty takes us back to pre-medieval times and jeopardizes Eurasian unity' (Laruelle 2008, 96), while Aleksander Dugin denounced ethno-nationalism and called for 'a rational, dispassionate nationalism' instead (Laruelle 2008, 128). Dugin proclaimed the coming of 'a new Eurasian stage in Russian history in which the traditional expansion of the historical mission of the state will reach its final limits'. In this state, 'the preservation of each and every people and ethnos will be regarded as a highest historical value' (*Nash put'* 1999, 32 and 134–5).

Russian supremacist nationalism

While the majority of the Empire-oriented Russian nationalists steer clear of ethnocratic thinking, certain groups nevertheless do adhere to what I have called supremacism here. These are groupings that more or less consciously stand in the tradition of the pre-revolutionary Black Hundred movements. First and foremost this was the case with the *Pamiat'* movement, which gained notoriety under perestroika for its combination of monarchism, stringent Orthodoxy and fascist-inspired symbols and ideology elements (Laqueur 1993). The same tendency is found in a number of smaller groups which, at various points in time, splintered off from *Pamiat'* but kept its Russian supremacist orientation, such as the People's National Party (PNP), the Russian National Union (RNS) and the National-Republican Party of Russia (NRPR) (Shenfield 2001, 225–44). NRPR leader Nikolai Lysenko initially declared that his party would lean heavily on the ideas of Alexander Solzhenitsyn; evidently, it was Solzhenitsyn's emphasis on Russian ethnic concerns that appealed to him. However, Solzhenitsyn's rejection of imperial aspirations was not to his liking and, in the end, NRPR's ideology became a combination of Russian ethnic nationalism and great power imperialism (Shenfield 2001, 233).

While all of the three above-mentioned parties were minuscule and ephemeral, a fourth suprematicist movement, Russian National Unity (RNE), for a while became the largest Russian national organisation. At its apogee, this militant and militarised movement had between 50,000 and 200,000 members and 350 regional chapters (Laruelle 2009, 56). RNE leader Aleksandr Barkashov took a definite stance against state patriotism in favour of ethnic Russian nationalism. Nationalism means loving one's nation and recognising it as the highest value, he proclaimed. Everything else, including the state and its political and economic system, must be subordinated to the goal of achieving the highest possible creative manifestations of the nation (Barkashov 1993, 2). RNE displayed a number of Nazi-inspired symbols, such as a variety of swastika, and clearly must be characterised as a fascist movement ('O simvole' 1993). In its opinion, the state ought to become 'an ethnic entity at the service of the titular Russian people' (Laruelle 2009, 55). However, RNE more or less disintegrated in the early 2000s and while there are still organised fascist groups in Russia, only some of them continue in the supremacist–imperial tradition of RNE.

Russian Federation-centred civic nationalism

During the power struggle between Mikhail Gorbachev and his nemesis, Boris Yeltsin, in the late perestroika period, the Yeltsinites secured control first over the RSFSR legislature in June 1990 and over the newly established RSFSR presidency in June 1991. As a result, Yeltsin and his group of supporters began to identify with and promote the interests of the Russian Republic over the Union centre (Dunlop 1993). From this fortuitous starting point the transformation of the RSFSR into a democratic nation-state based on civic nationalism, the Russian Federation (RF), commenced (Breslauer and Dale 1997, 315–17; Kolstø 2000, 194–202).

In the 1990s it was widely predicted that the phenomenon of the 'new' Russian diaspora in 'the near abroad' would become a major impetus behind a revitalisation of Russian ethnic identity. News about discrimination against their fellow Russians in the other Soviet successor states would lead to an outburst of ethnic solidarity (Melvin 1995, 127; Zevelev 2001, 5). However, while the diaspora issue figured prominently in the Russian media for a while, no large-scale mobilisation around this issue took place, neither in Russia nor among the diaspora communities themselves (Kolstø 2011). There were clearly a number of reasons for this, but probably most important was the attitude of the Russian government at the time. Little support for the diaspora was forthcoming, either rhetorically or financially, and crucially, the official policy was coached in deliberately non-ethnic terms (Zevelev 2001). The diaspora – Russians as well as others with roots in the RSFSR – were referred to as *sootechestvenniki*, fellow countrymen, an emphatically political, 'civic' term (*Gosudarstvennaia Duma* 1999).

The theoretical underpinnings of the Russian Federation nation-building project are practically the work of one man, Valerii Tishkov, director of the Institute of Ethnography and Anthropology at the Russian Academy of Sciences. In contrast to most of his Russian colleagues, Tishkov is a convinced constructivist who believes that nations are the product of nationalists, not the other way around. He likes to quote the nineteenth-century Italian nationalist Massimo D'Azeglio, who allegedly said, 'We have created Italy – now we have to create Italians' (Tishkov 1992). Tishkov saw no reason why Russia could not develop into a modern nation-state with the same kind of identity and the same attributes as other European states. The structural as well as the cultural preconditions are in place: 'Russia is more culturally homogenous than many other large and even small countries considered to be nation-states' (Tishkov 1995, 49). Tishkov acknowledged that Russia indeed is a multiethnic federation but the ties that bind the various groups together are strong. The all-encompassing knowledge of the Russian language throughout the country's population provides the means for pervasive social communication and facilitates the development of a strong, common, supraethnic national identity as *rossiiane*. Tishkov strongly urges the depolitisation of ethnicity in Russia, but he does not challenge the existing system of ethno-territorial autonomy. As Oxana Shevel (2011, 183) has remarked, it may therefore be difficult to see exactly how his *rossiiskaia* nation concept differs from the more traditional concept of the multinational *rossiiskii* people.

Tishkov (1995, 48) noted with satisfaction that some of his notions found their way into official Russian statements and documents in the Yeltsin era, in particular in the President's Address to the Federal Assembly in February 1994, when Yeltsin (1994) defined the nation as 'co-citizenship' (*sograzhdanstvo*). Tishkov eventually became disappointed with Yeltsin's lack of ability to follow through with these ideas but he regained hope when Vladimir Putin took over. Putin, Tishkov today declares, is finally realising his, Tishkov's, *rossiiskii* nation project.[4] Tishkov (2010; 2011; 2013) has published a number of books in which he declares that the *rossiiskii* nation (*natsiia*) or the *rossiiskii* people (*narod* – Tishkov uses these two concepts interchangeably) is already an established fact. No need for any Russian D'Azeglio after all, then. Indeed, Tishkov (2010, 7) pushed the genesis of the *rossiiskii* nation far into the past: both the

Romanov state and the Soviet Union were nation-states, he now insists. The fact that the official name of this nation has undergone alterations over time and, in the communist period, was reference was made to 'the Soviet people' should not confuse us: the main thing is that, also in its Soviet version, 'the people' was a supraethnic concept.

Ethnic core nationalism

Tishkov's civic nationalism does not, however, seem to carry the day in Russia. In Putin's second presidential term (2004–8), ethno-nationalism, which had earlier been a rather marginal phenomenon even in the Russian nationalist movement, increasingly came to the fore. Writing in 2009 Aleksandr Verkhovsky (2009, 89) claimed that '[n]either civic nor even imperial, today's Russian nationalism is instead almost exclusively ethnic.' This may be an exaggeration, since 'imperial' groups like Dugin's Eurasianists were still active, but the tendency Verkhovsky identified was obviously correct. The leading nationalist organisation at the time was the Movement Against Illegal Immigration (DPNI). Although DPNI's programme in many respects reflected a multinational stance, for instance by supporting the reintroduction of a nationality entry in the Russian passport, it also specifically demanded that the Russian (*russkii*) people should be recognised as the 'state-bearing' or 'state-forming' (*gosudarstvoobrazuiushchii*) nation in the Russian Federation, 'the people which has created this state and which makes up the majority of the country's population'(Programma, not dated).

In December 2010 DPNI was banned by the Russian authorities, only to re-emerge as one of two founding organisations of a new movement, '*Russkie*', which explicitly called itself an 'ethnopolitical association' (see http://rusnat. com/). Former DPNI leader Aleksandr Belov-Potkin explained that

> with the dissolution of the Soviet Union a national reawakening took place among all ethnic groups in the country, but most markedly among the Russians since their ethnic identity had been very weak. A new nation is being born today, a new identity, a new self-understanding. I myself was raised with a Soviet identity, but my son has a very different identity, an identity as a Russian. The empire disappears as a distant historical memory.[5]

In the '*Russkie*' movement former DPNI members collaborate with former members of the Slavic Union (*Slavianskii soiuz*), another banned organisation. Slavic Union had a number of neo-fascist features, but in contrast to similar organisations in the past decades, such as *Pamiat'* and Russian National Unity, it was oriented towards Russia and not the former Soviet Union (Demushkin et al. 2004).

At the same time, the new ethno-national current in Russian nationalism also includes a number of parties and personalities who represent pro-Western and pro-democracy leanings. This is particularly true of the large segment which is increasingly referred to as 'the national democrats'. This loose group includes both thinkers who veer in the direction of ethnocracy and those who believe that Russian nationalism can be combined with democracy. In the former category we find Alexander Sevast'ianov, who has declared that 'national democracy is democracy within the framework of the nation. And I emphasize time and again that *nation* in this context means the *ethnonation* and nothing else' (Sevast'ianov 2013, 203, emphasis in the original). This view is rejected by most other leading national democrats, who insist that in a future Russian nation-state full democratic rights can and shall be extended to all citizens irrespective of ethnicity.[6]

The demographic predominance of ethnic Russians is a result of the collapse of the USSR. Commenting on this epochal event, Alexander Sevast'ianov (2010, 139) waxes lyrical:

> for our country the pseudoimperial epoch is now coming to an end. Having lived for three centuries in a multinational empire Russians we suddenly find ourselves in new realities, in a mononational state, a state in which Russians make up almost 9/10. This is truly good fortune!

Even if it was hard to accept the dissolution of the unitary state at the time, explains Sergei Sergeev (2010, 236),[7] managing editor of the journal *Voprosy Natsionalizma* and another leading ethno-nationalist theoretician, this momentous turning-point in history must be regarded as a blessing in disguise. Such anti-imperial ideas have led the ethno-nationalists into a bitter struggle with the Eurasianists and other empire-nostalgics, whom the national democrats derisively call '*impertsy*'. According to Konstantin Krylov, leader of the National-Democratic Party until his untimely death in 2020, the conflict between these two groups has reached a level of 'open hatred' and 'a war of extinction' (Krylov 2011a, 3).

In this fierce ideological battle, the ethno-nationalists can celebrate a number of defections from the *impertsy* camp to theirs. Sergei Sergeev confesses that he himself had been deluded by Eurasianist ideas before he converted to ethno-nationalism. The change of heart among some former leaders of the National Salvation Front is remarkable. For instance, Ilia Konstantinov, identified by Vera Tolz (1998, 272) as the mastermind behind the establishment of the Front, now sympathises with the ethno-nationalists. Konstantinov remains a member of one of the smaller empire-saving parties[8] but that is primarily for the sake of old friendships.[9] Viktor Alksnis, a former leader of both 'Soiuz' and the Salvation Front, has also shifted sides. In an article tellingly entitled 'Farewell empire! (On the eve of a Russian Russia)', Alksnis admitted that 'I have always been and will remain a person with an imperial mind-set and to me it has been painful to accept that my Great Imperial Idea has died.' However, one has to adapt to new realities, he writes: 'In Russia's transition from empire to nation-state . . . we must take into account the national interests of the state-bearing nation – the Russians' (Alksnis 2007, 42).[10] Thus, while in the 1990s the ranks of the National Salvation Front were filled up to some extent with former 'culturalists' such as Igor Shafarevich and Valentin Rasputin, now the tide seemed to have shifted in the opposite direction, at least temporarily.

The threat against a genuine Russian nation-state, as the new ethno-nationalists see it, does not emanate from the side of the *impertsy* only. They are fighting on two fronts, the other being the battle to dispel the illusions of Tishkov's civic nation-state model. The Tishkovian nation-state has no ethnic kernel, the nationalists complained.

Kirill Benediktov claims that the most important task for contemporary Russian nationalists is to regain legitimacy for the '*russkii*' concept and to fight back against the term *rossiiane*' ('Russkii natsionalizm' 2010, 6). Aleksandr Khramov (2013, 229) criticises Tishkov for believing that in nation-building 'only the civic component is important – as if all citizens of Russia automatically make up a civic nation. In reality, without a common culture no self-identification as a nation is possible,' Khramov insisted. Sergei Sergeev (2010, 208) looked forward to the day when Tishkovianism will take its place in the graveyard of discarded pseudo-scientific ideas.

Konstantin Krylov (2012) mockingly called the current Russian Federation *Erefiia* ('RF-iia'), while another national democrat, Pavel Sviatenkov, claims that not only in the RSFSR but also in the Russian Federation the Russians have been deprived of a nation-state. For members of one of the smaller Russian ethnic groups, such as the Avars, it can make sense to say both 'I am an Avar' and 'I am a *rossianin*', Sviatenkov claims. In that case, 'Avar' means ethnicity and *rossianin* citizenship, 'but for a Russian, such a phrase is devoid of meaning' (Sviatenkov 2010, 3–4). Sviatenkov accepts that a common *rossiiskii* identity is possible, but on one indispensable condition only: 'if it is coupled to the recognition of a state status for the Russian people, Russia as the national state of Russians' (Sviatenkov 2010, 6). The nationality (that is, ethnicity) entry in Russian passports was deleted from the passports, while the official designation of the state remained 'multinational' (*mnogonatsional'nyi*) (Aktürk 2012). Just when the non-Russians gained their national states, the Russians had bowed out of theirs twice over, Russian ethno-nationalists asserted; first they lost the USSR; now Russia was not 'their' state either.

However, in contrast to Alexander Sevastianov's ethnocratic view, for most Russian national democrats a national state for the Russians in Russia both can and ought to be combined with Western-style democracy. This is possible precisely because, with the downscaling of the state from empire to nation-state, there is a much closer fit between the *ethnos* and the *demos*.

The promotion of genuine Western-style democracy is presented as optimal both because of its intrinsic qualities and because it may bring the nationalists to power. Russians constitute the vast majority of Russia's population and, as Krylov explained, in all societies people will tend to vote for the party that best represents their interests. Even so, this is not a matter of opportunistically choosing a system that tilts the outcome to their benefit, Krylov averred. Nationalism and democracy presuppose each other, he argues. This can be seen from European history: the first wave of European nationalism in the nineteenth century was clearly a democratic liberation movement. Therefore, Krylov claimed, the nationalists are the only true democrats in Russia today.[11]

Sergei Sergeev give a number of reasons why democracy is the best system. Again we see how pragmatic and principled thinking is intertwined.

> Firstly, democracy is today the only possible means by which it is possible to legitimize any kind of political regime, irrespective of how we relate to this means. Secondly, the globalization we see in the world today is undemocratic, it works in favor of an anti-traditional world-wide transnational oligarchy. Consequently, traditionalists should not be interested in undermining but strengthening democratic institutions. Thirdly, how many monarchists or communists in Russia are, if they are honest with themselves, ready to forego the level of freedom they enjoy today? Do they really want to return to 1565 [and the rule of Ivan the Terrible] or to 1937 [and Stalin's Great Terror]? And fourthly, in Russia today [ethnic] Russians make up 80 per cent of the population so that the national and the democratic more or less coincide. (Sergeev 2010, xx)

ETHNONATIONALIST RHETORIC IN THE RUSSIAN LEADERSHIP

Writing in April 2014, Igor Zevelev (2014, 3) argued that 'even if ethnonationalism in Russia does not make up an organized political force, it is quite clear that its intellectual influence has been growing in recent years'. While most Russian ethno-nationalists acknowledge that, so far, their impact on Russian public debate has been limited, they noted with considerable satisfaction that some of their ideas and concepts seem to be gradually seeping through the crevices of the Kremlin walls. It would certainly be an exaggeration to claim that Putin and his entourage have adopted ethno-nationalism as their state ideology. Their messages are mixed bags of often disparate signals; official documents and speeches draw on several, sometimes contradictory, discourses, both Russian Federation-civic, Eurasianist and ethno-nationalist. Documents signed by Dmitry Medvedev generally held on to a Tishkovian vision of the state. As long as he was President, Medvedev regularly employed terms like *rossiiskii narod* and *rossiiskaia natsiia* but hardly ever talked about the *russkii narod* (Medvedev 2008; Medvedev 2009). As late as 2011, Medvedev declared that 'it is our task to create a full-fledged *rossiiskaia natsiia* in which the identity of all the peoples who inhabit our country is preserved' (Ria Novosti 2011).

Documents signed by Vladimir Putin also sometimes contain expressions such as *rossiiskaia natsiia*; this is true, for instance, of the December 2012 'Strategy for a nationality policy for the Russian Federation to 2025'. This document had been drafted in the consultative Presidential Council on National Questions, and two prominent members of this council – Valerii Tishkov and Vladimir Zorin – who both had served a stint as Russian minister in charge of nationality questions – must take some credit for having kept ethno-national phrases out of the final version.[12] At one point, for instance, the inclusion of the concept of the Russian people as a 'state-forming nation' had been suggested, but this idea did not find its way into the published text. However, the final version *did* refer to the Russian (*russkii*) people as 'the historically system-creating core' of the Russian state. 'Thanks to the unifying role of the *russkii* people . . . a unique cultural multiformity and a spiritual community of various peoples have been created' (*Strategiia* 2012). This was a far cry from Yeltsin-era rhetoric.

In the run-up to the 2012 presidential elections, Vladimir Putin published a series of newspaper articles on various topics as part of his election campaign. One of these articles, 'On the National Question', was, on the face of it, an attack on Russian ethno-nationalism. Putin denounced what he called 'thoroughly false talk about the *russkie*'s right to self-determination'. The *russkie*, he declared, had exercised their right to self-determination long ago, by creating a polyethnic civilisation held together by a *russkii* cultural core. By dint of the fact that Russia continues to exist, the *russkii* people is therefore *gosudarstvoobrazuiushchii*, the 'state-forming' nation, in that state.

> Historically, Russia is not an ethnic state and not an American melting pot . . . . The Russian experience of state development is unique: we are a multinational society but we are one people. Therefore, attempts to preach the idea of a Russian 'national', monoethnic state contradict our thousand-year-long history. Indeed, it is the fastest path forward towards the destruction of the *russkii* people and *russkii* statehood. (Putin 2012)

To a large extent, Putin was lashing out here against a straw man, since few, if any, Russian ethno-nationalists are in favour of a monoethnic state (Alexander Sevast'ianov being one exception). Instead, what they clamour for is for the current Russian state to be regarded as an expression of '*russkii* statehood' and that the Russian nation should be declared 'state-forming'. Both of these terms, as we saw above, were in fact used by Putin himself in his article. Two of the ethnonationalists' core tenets had then, surprisingly, crept into official Kremlin rhetoric. Leading ethno-nationalist theoretician Oleg Nemenskii (2012, 18) therefore chose to interpret Putin's message not as criticism, but as indirect acceptance of some of their main ideas. Nemenskii maintained that Putin's

> complete rejection of the previous attempt to establish a *rossiiskii* nation, together with his new accentuation of the Russian ethnic dominant element, represents a major shift in official discourse on nationality policy. V. V. Putin's article legitimizes the Russian ethnonym in the official vocabulary.

The very fact that Putin found it necessary to attack them the ethno-nationalists see as confirmation that the Russian leadership recognises the importance of the issues they raise.

DRIVERS BEHIND THE NEW NATIONALISM:
MIGRATION AND MIGRANTOPHOBIA

The shift from Eurasianist to ethnocentric positions among Russian nationalists after 2000, and the growing willingness among Russian liberals to include 'the national question' on their agenda, was remarkable. How can this rapid transformation be best understood? While no phenomenon has only one cause, the crucial factor here seems to be the fact that Russia in the first decade of 2000s became a major recipient of labour migrants from former Soviet republics.

The differences in living standards between Russia and the southern tier of former Soviet republics began to widen drastically and the near-collapse of the economy (with subsequent unemployment and low wages) in many of these countries made people travel to Russia in search for work. A street-sweeper in Moscow could earn far more than most people in, say, Tajikistan. In 2004, the GDP per capita in Tajikistan was only one-fifteenth of that in Russia (Korobkov 2007, 180–1). Initially, the typical 'guest worker' was a young male who came alone and sent remittances to his family back home; later, many women also arrived. In 2007 remittances were estimated to constitute 42 per cent of Tajikistan's GDP (Human Rights Watch: 2009, 12), making Tajikistan one of the countries in the world where remittances have the largest impact on the GDP level.

Since there are no visa requirements for citizens from most member states of the Commonwealth of Independent States (CIS)[13] in Russia, migrants could enter the country legally – but in order to work, they needed a work permit, which might be almost impossible to obtain. The official work quotas were fluctuating but generally far too small to meet demand and supply, so very many of the Central Asians ended up working illegally, often for unscrupulous employers who paid them a pittance, with no contract.

How many illegal workers there were in Russia is anybody's guess, with estimates from around 2010 varying between a few millions and 10 million, or more. According to official statistics, the number of migrants who work legally in Russia were about 3 million, while the number of labour migrants without a work permit was estimated by some to be anywhere up to 15 million, with 6 or 7 million a more realistic figure (Myhre 2014, 20). The real numbers, however, were less important for the new nationalism discourse in Russia than the perception that the country was being inundated by people who were not only culturally alien but also dangerous (Schenk 2018). Migrants were rumoured to be behind a disproportionate share of crimes committed in Russian cities, and manipulated or even fictitious crime statistics were quoted as proof (Blakkisrud and Kolstø 2018, 218–21). Moreover, in the new migration debate few distinctions were made between migrants from Central Asia, who are foreign nationals, and North Caucasians, who are Russian citizens (Alexseev 2010). Opinion polls showed that xenophobic attitudes were on the rise in the Russian population in general, and in Moscow in particular (Kolstø 2013a). Thus, the new migration issue clearly was one important factor among others that could explain why the ethnification of Russian nationalism picked up speed after the turn of the millennium and not earlier.

The 'old' Russian nationalists, the Eurasianists, had few solutions to offer for such a situation. They wanted to integrate the former Soviet republics as much as possible with Russia and would like to keep the borders open. 'Well', the national democrats retorted, 'here you see the result: our country is taken over by non-assimilating Asians.' The flip-side of the national democrats' European credo was their insistence that Russia should turn its back on Asia and keep the Asians out. Their demand that Russia introduce visa regimes for migrants from Central Asia resonated extremely well with the Russian population. This demand was fiercely resisted by the Putin regime – if introduced, it would reduce the leverage Russia has in that region. Geopolitical concerns won out in the Kremlin. The visa scheme, however, was so popular that in the 2013 mayoral election campaign in Moscow all candidates, even Putin-backed front-runner Sergei Sobianin, espoused it. The 'national–liberal' candidate, Aleksey Navalny, however, could present that demand with far greater credibility, since the nationalists were the ones who first put it on the national political agenda, and also pushed it hard when there was no election campaign under way. Navalny's dexterous handling of the migration issue was probably a major reason behind his remarkably good showing in these elections, in which he garnered no less than 27 per cent of the vote (Kolstø and Blakkisrud 2018).

Visa regimes for foreign nationals from certain countries are not illiberal as such: it all depends on how they are intended to function in practice. Here, many national-democrats come down on the harsh side. Some insisted that all migrant workers currently living in Russia should be deported and apply for re-entry from home. Even more restrictive was Alexander Khramov, who argued that labour migrants should be isolated as much as possible from the local population:

Special dormitories should be built for them with the necessary infrastructure – shops, barber shops, and brothels – all of which should be
served by their compatriots. Such a system has been tried out in Persian
Gulf countries which use migrant labor from Asia extensively. When
their work visa expires (for instance, after one year), the migrants should
be obliged to leave the country. (Khramov 2011, 63–4)

Other national-democrats proposed taking Israel's use of Palestinian labour
from the West Bank as a model. It seems ironic that the national-democrats,
who insisted that Russia ought to emulate Europe as much as possible, should
look not to the EU but to the Middle East for migration regimes.

Popular Russian Ethno-Nationalism

Based on results from a 2013 Levada survey, Boris Dubin (2014, 15) claimed
in 2014 that the nationalism of the majority of Russians today is state-oriented
and not ethnic. It is somewhat difficult to see how he drew that conclusion since
much of the survey results, which he himself cited, pointed in another direction.
Thus for instance, Dubin found that 66 per cent supported (more or less strongly)
the slogan 'Russia for Russians (*russkie*)' while 61 per cent expressed negative
attitudes towards Caucasians and immigrants from Central Asia (Dubin 2014, 9
and 12). A ROMIR survey from the same year, in May 2013, conducted under
the auspices of the NEORUSS project at the University of Oslo, which I led,
also confirmed that ethnocentric and xenophobic attitudes were strong among
the Russian public. When we asked the same question about the slogan 'Russia
for Russians (*russkie*)', we saw slightly less support than Levada but it was still
quite high: 59.3 per cent. It should be emphasised, as pointed out above, that the
meaning of the word *russkie* is in flux; in certain contexts it is being understood
as encompassing more than just ethnic Russians. When asked about this, 25 per
cent of our respondents did indeed explain that, to them, *russkie* meant 'all citizens of the Russian Federation', while 30 per cent ticked the option for 'mostly
but not exclusively ethnic Russians'. Only 39 per cent thought it meant 'ethnic
Russians only'. Thus, the elusive quality of the word *russkie* must be taken into
account when we interpret such survey results.

Even so, some of the responses in the ROMIR survey must be characterised as remarkably ethnocentric, even ethnocratic: thus, for instance, as much
as 73.9 per cent agreed 'fully' or 'basically' with the statement that 'Russians
(*russkie*) ought to be given priority at appointments to higher positions in
the state'. Even more remarkable was support for the view that 'the Russian
(*russkii*) people ought to play the leading role in the Russian (*rossiiskii*) state':
47.4 per cent fully agreed, in addition to another 34.6 per cent who basically
agreed. These attitudes are incompatible with a civic nation-state idea in which
all citizens have equal opportunities.

In the 2013 ROMIR survey, these ethnocentric attitudes were accompanied by strong scepticism towards migrants and other people who are perceived as being culturally alien. Some 60.5 per cent believed that Islam represents a threat to social stability and Russian culture, while more than half declared that Chechens, Chinese and Roma represent cultural values that are incompatible with a Russian way of life. The same assessment was given by a large minority to Kyrgyz (39 per cent), Tajiks (46.8 per cent) and Azerbaijanis (44.3 per cent). These groups are strongly represented among the labour immigrants in Russian cities. A total of 43 per cent believed that many migrants come not to do honest work, but to steal from Russians and to weaken the Russian people. Close to a half thought that *all* migrants – not only those without proper work permits – ought to be deported back to their home countries, along with their children.[14]

In November 2014 our research team was able to assess the effect of the Crimean annexation on popular attitudes towards nationalist issues by conducting a follow-up survey to the May 2013 poll (Alexseev and Hale 2016). With many of the same questions (plus some new ones directly related to the Crimea issue), this repeat survey gave us a unique opportunity to assess how this momentous event impacted on Russian attitudes towards the national question. The numbers revealed overwhelming support for this action: more than four-fifths supported Crimea's incorporation into the Russian state. When we asked whether the respondents were in favour of further territorial expansion, however, support was *lower* in 2014 than in the 2013 survey. This seemed to indicate that, in the view of the majority of Russians, snatching Crimea from Ukraine was fine, on the whole, but this ought to be a one-off operation. Russian state-focused nationalists who hankered for a restoration of the Empire would find little solace in our survey.

A comparison of responses to certain questions in the two surveys suggested that support for nationalist stances were on the rise. For instance, while 77 per cent of the sample in 2013 regarded ethnicity as an important factor in the choice of a marriage partner for oneself or a relative, this number had increased to 86 per cent eighteen months later. However, on most other questions the opinions expressed through the survey were remarkably stable. If 64 per cent of respondents expressed complete or partial endorsement of the slogan 'Russia for Russians' in 2013, this number had increased by only two percentage points the year after. Support for the view that *russkie* should enjoy a privileged position in Russia remained equally high – around 75 per cent – while about half of the respondents continued to believe that *russkie* ought to play the leading role in the state. Roughly the same numbers as in 2013–23 per cent versus 24 per cent – also fully supported the position that all migrants ought to be deported back to their home countries. Ethnocentric attitudes, therefore, remained more or less unchanged at a high level.

Based on these figures, Mikhail Alexseev and Henry Hale drew the conclusion that the annexation of Crimea did not lead to any 'rallying round the flag' in Russia, simply because Russian nationalism was already extremely strong. At the same time, the surveys suggested that attitudes towards the state authorities, and in particular towards the President, had changed significantly after Crimea: while only 40 per cent of all respondents in 2013 declared that they would vote for Putin, by November 2014 this number had increased to a hefty 68 per cent (Alexseev and Hale 2016, 198). Thus, while people's nationalist perceptions remained more or less unchanged, the Crimean operation and the nationalist rhetoric that accompanied it had raised the popularity of the nation's leader significantly. Against this background, Alexseev and Hale (2016, 217) suggested that 'Putin appears to have tapped into these [nationalist] sentiments, rather than engendering them through his actions and the Kremlin's public relations campaign.'

At the same time as Putin stepped forward as champion of the national cause, he clamped down on the nationalistic opposition. Several nationalist leaders were arrested on dubious charges: for instance, in 2016 the leader of the 'Russkie' movement, Alexander Belov, was sentenced to seven and a half years in a penal colony, while the next year his collaborator, Dmitry Demushkin, was incarcerated for two and half years (Verkhovsky 2018, 144–5). After Crimea, the Russian nationalist movement appeared to be at a low ebb. The radical nationalists behind the annual Russian Marches were able to mobilise only a fraction of the number of people they had managed to bring into the streets only a few years earlier (Yudina and Alperovich 2014). In 2014, probably no more than around 3,000 demonstrators participated, less than half than the year before. To make things even worse for the nationalists, they were now divided into two groups – those for and those against the secessionist movement in Eastern Ukraine – who organised separate marches ('Russian March' 2014). The next year, 2015, the decline continued, and no more than about 1,500 people combined turned up on the two rival marches ('Moscow-2015' 2015).

As Alexander Verkhovsky explains, however, the harsher repression of the Russian nationalists was only part of the explanation for this downturn. The rank-and-file nationalists were also abandoning the movement for other reasons. In 2011–12 several nationalist leaders, such as Alexander Belov, Konstantin Krylov and Vladimir Tor, had decided to make common cause with the Western-oriented liberals in the opposition and participate in joint anti-Putin demonstrations (see Chapter 9). This decision did not sit well with many of their followers, who detested the liberals even more than they hated Putin. Later, the Euromaidan revolution in Ukraine caused further unrest and schisms among the Russian nationalists: some of them sympathised with the attempt to topple the corrupt Ukrainian President, Viktor Yanukovich, while others noted with dismay that most of the demonstrators on the Maidan square wanted to move Ukraine closer to Europe and further away from Russia (Horvath 2015).

In an ironic twist of history the Russian nationalists could now observe that one of their most important demands was now being fulfilled: after around 2014 a large part of the 'guest workers' in Russia returned to their homelands, but this was not a result of anything the Russian nationalists had done. Instead, it stemmed from the downturn in the Russian economy which followed in the wake of Western sanctions and Russian counter-sanctions after the Crimean annexation, as well as from lower oil prices. The nationalists could not really celebrate the exodus of the Central Asians as their triumph; instead, it deprived them of one of their main rallying cries.

The most important reason for the setback of the Russian nationalist movement after 2014 seems to be the fact that Putin had now donned the nationalist mantle himself. When the President became the foremost banner carrier of the 'Russian cause', it made less sense for the nationalists to demonstrate against him. What we could observe, then, was a demobilisation of nationalism in Russia at the societal level, at the same time as it was being activated at the state level. The state not only 'tapped into' Russian societal nationalism – it also 'drained' it. Russian political scientist Emil Pain (2018) sees a historical pattern here: in times when the Russian state does not feel that it needs nationalism as a legitimation base for its own purposes, various groups of autonomous nationalists have – more than the liberal opposition – been allowed to operate, and seem to have served as a safety valve for social frustration. However, in times of turbulence and official usage of nationalist propaganda, the state tolerates no competitors. Figuratively speaking, state nationalism and societal nationalism in Russia are connected vessels: when the state vessel fills up, the other empties (Kolstø and Blakkisrud 2018).

CONCLUSIONS

In the Tsarist Empire, ethnic Russians did not dominate, either demographically or politically. In the 1897 census, the share of Great Russians in this state was only 44 per cent, and Russians did not enjoy any particular prerogatives such as privileged access to jobs in the civil service. Educated members of some non-Russian groups, such as Germans and Poles, were far more likely to land an attractive job in the state apparatus (Kappeler 1993). Many Russians were, no doubt, proud to be subjects of the Tsar and identified with the state, but this was a dynastic state, and certainly not 'their' 'nation-state' in any sense. Certain elements of a Russification policy were introduced in the last decades of the Empire, but this affected the life of the non-Russians more than the Russians.

In territorial terms the Soviet Union represented a continuation of the Russian Empire. While the nationality policy of the Bolsheviks differed radically from the one pursued by the Tsars, it was no more conducive to the formation of a Russian national identity. The federal structure of the Soviet Union gave all the major non-Russian nationalities an ethnic homeland which bore their name and also, to some extent, their cultural imprint. In all Union republics and autonomous republics education was available in the titular language, at least in elementary school, if not necessarily at higher levels. Titulars were also overrepresented in top jobs in the republics in both party and government structure (Hodnett 1979). All Soviet citizens carried with them at all times their internal passport, in which their *natsionalnost'* (read: ethnic identity) was fixed as the so-called fifth point. This meant that non-Russians living in other parts of the country, having a personally ascriptive identity that corresponded with one of the republics, would also naturally identify with this federal unit.

All of this was different for the ethnic Russians. The first 'R' in the RSFSR was not 'russkii' but 'rossiiskii', and this vast conglomerate republic was not intended to be, or to be understood as, a homeland for ethnic Russians. As a federation in itself with a large number of ethnically defined subunits, the RSFSR was, in a sense, a copy of the Soviet Union writ small; however, it lacked some basic attributes of the Union republics, such as a separate party organisation or its own branch of the Academy of Sciences, as it was felt that this would duplicate the respective Soviet structures and be redundant (Kolstø 2000, 194–8). At the same time, Russian language schools and cultural institutions were available throughout the Soviet Union. For these reasons, Russians, to a much larger degree than non-Russians, would identify with the USSR as a whole, not with any particular geographical area (Kolstø 1999b). To be Russian was, in a sense, an unmarked quality, the opposite of being 'ethnic' (Brubaker 1996, 49). This was also reflected in Russian nationalism, which for the most part was focused on state strength and state size. Hardly any Russian nationalists at the time would contemplate a truncation of state territory.

Only when the Soviet Union unravelled during perestroika did the RSFSR become, for the first time, a serious contender for the loyalty and identity of ethnic Russians. But also, in its new incarnation as the Russian Federation, it was officially a multiethnic state and not a 'nation-state'. Valerii Tishkov made a resolute attempt to develop a civic Russian nation-state model, which virtually all Russian nationalists find lacklustre and anaemic. Their alternative visions for a Russian state idea, however, point in two very different directions. On the one hand, quite a few still hang on to a statist or imperial nation concept, while on the other, 'the new Russian nationalists' prioritise ethnic culture and the interests of ethnic Russians over state grandeur. Finally, some also try to combine an imperialist and an ethnic national idea and end up with what I have called supremacist nationalism here. This means that, in the post-Soviet debate on the future of the Russian national idea, all four boxes in my typology of nationalisms are populated. Even so, some of them are more crowded than others and gain new recruits in interlopers from the other positions. The supremacists are a small and dwindling minority, certainly in the Russian population, but also among professed nationalists. This leaves us with three contenders who fight for the hearts and minds of the Russians, as well as for influence over the political leadership.

An ethnification of popular attitudes among the Russian public can be evidenced from opinion polls fed primarily by growing migrantophobia. For a number of reasons the Russian state authorities hesitated to embrace the new ethnic rhetoric. For one thing, playing the ethnic card must be assumed to antagonise the non-Russian part of the population (see Alexseev 2016). For the purposes of national consolidation, a civic nation idea seems more promising, and indeed elements of a *rossiiskii* nation concept are still evident in Putin's speeches. However, if this idea does not stir any feelings and fails to attract people to the state, it does not serve its purpose.

The benefit of Eurasianism for the Kremlin is that it can provide ideological underpinnings for a foreign policy aimed at expanding Russian influence in 'the near abroad'. Symptomatically, Putin's pet project of an Eastern mini-EU that would include as many as possible of the former Soviet republics is called the 'Eurasian Union'. The downside of this policy is that it does not provide any answers to what a large and increasing number of Russian see as a major problem: the alleged inundation of Russia by 'culturally alien' migrants from other parts of the former Soviet Union. Precisely this problem swelled the ranks of the ethno-nationalists. This reorientation of Russian nationalism brought it into line with the migrantophobia-driven nationalism evident in Western Europe and North America.

Putin's nationalist messaging has been pointing in very different, often seemingly contradictory, directions. To be sure, from around the onset of his third term, Putin appeared to be switching from adopting the Yeltsinite '*rossiiskii*' nation-building terminology to increasingly using '*russkii*'. The first clear indication of this was his pre-election article on the nationality question, where he referred to ethnically Armenian and German citizens of Russia as 'Russian (*russkie*) Armenians' and 'Russian (*russkie*) Germans' (Putin 2012). This was followed up and even accentuated in his other addresses after the Crimean annexation (see Putin 2014a; Putin 2014b). Seemingly, Putin was adopting if not the agenda, then at least the terminology of the ethno-nationalists. However, just as that conclusion began to seem logical, Putin gave the go-ahead to draw up a law defining the *rossiiskii* nation (*rossiiskaia natsiia*) (Teper 2018, 85). What are we to make of this?

While several interpretations are possible, I suggest that, rather than revealing confusion or vacillation in the Kremlin, this can be seen as an attempt to eradicate the difference between *russkii* and *rossiiskii*. That may not be quite as radical as it sounds. Most languages do not make a lexical distinction between an ethnic and a civic designation of the nation. Neither the paradigmatic 'ethnic' case – German – or the paradigmatic 'civic' case – French – has more than one word to describe the 'national'. The Russian language, on the other hand, not only allows for a distinction between those two aspects, it also makes it impossible for Russian speakers *not* to choose one of the two words, *russkii* or *rossiiskii*, when they talk or write. There is no 'neutral' term to describe Russianness. The only way to fuse those two aspects therefore seems to be to use the two terms interchangeably, until they are, in the end, understood as expressing the same meaning (just as the two designations of the state, 'Russia' and the 'Russian Federation', do in practice).

Seen from this perspective, the language games of the Kremlin's nation-building strategy can be regarded as attempts to make Russia a 'normal' nation-state like Germany and France. While, as pointed out above, German and French nation-building have historically been informed by very different principles, more recently this distinction has been gradually fading. Contemporary French nationalism focuses very much on the need to permeate the entire population with French culture and to teach all citizens to speak proper French; German nationalists created their own unified nation-state in the late nineteenth century – later modified several times – with which they identify keenly (Brubaker 1998). Today, therefore, it is probably more accurate to speak of a common French–German, or simply civic–cultural, 'European' nation model, which, it can be argued, the Russian leadership is attempting to emulate – at least on the rhetorical level.

We should note one major caveat, however: modern European nation-states that identify 'the nation' with the culture, language, citizens and territory of the state no longer question the state borders, not even in cases when compact groups of co-ethnics reside outside the borders of the nation-state. Germany, for example, a country that has experienced dramatic truncations of the state's territory over the last century, does not harbour irredentist aspirations today. For the first couple of decades after the breakup of the Soviet Union, it also seemed as if Russia would follow that path, but the annexation of Crimea belied those expectations. Deeds speak louder than words, and as long as Russia continues to hold on to and justify Crimea's annexation with nationalist rhetoric, it is of minor importance whether this rhetoric is interpreted as 'imperialistic' or 'ethnic': in either case, it is clearly not 'civic'. Therefore, the annexation is not only a watershed in modern European history, but also, we argue, a major barrier to Russia's nation-state transformation.

NOTES

1. Even if he did not use that term himself.
2. For other models of Russian nationalism, highlighting other aspects, see Yanov 1978; Carter 1990, 138–9; Tuminez 2000; and Tolz 1998.

3. A few other dissident nationalists in the 1970s and 1980s can also be put down as ethno-nationalists, including Vladimir Balakhonov (Szporluk 1989, 25–6) and Sergei Soldatov (Dunlop 1983, 250).
4. Author's interview, Moscow, November 2013. When I later asked Tishkov whether he believed that Putin's talk about a 'divided' Russian (*russkii*) nation undermined the *rossiiskii* nation-state concept, he denied that.
5. Author's interview, Moscow, October 2013.
6. Author's interview with Konstantin Krylov, leader of the National-Democratic Party, Moscow, October 2013.
7. Author's interview, October 2013.
8. Sergei Baburin's Party of National Revival, 'Narodnaia Volia'.
9. Author's interview in Moscow, October 2013.
10. Alksnis is an ethnic Latvian.
11. Author's interview with Krylov, Moscow, October 2013.
12. Author's interview with Tishkov and Zorin in Moscow, November 2013.
13. The membership of the CIS has contracted and expanded several times but currently includes, in addition to Russia, Armenia, Azerbaijan, Belarus, Kazakhstan, Kyrgyzstan, Moldova, Russia, Tajikistan and Uzbekistan.
14. For survey results see 'Outcomes' 2013.

7

THE ST GEORGE RIBBON AND THE IMMORTAL REGIMENT: NEW SYMBOLS AND RITUALS IN RUSSIAN REGIME-LEGITIMATION

State-sponsored national symbols provide nodal points around which the people can develop a common political identity (Kolstø 2006). States need the support of the overwhelming majority of the population in order to survive in the long run. As Margaret Canovan has argued, a state that fails to garner this kind of support will eventually be supplanted by one that does (Canovan [1996] 1998, 22).

State leaders normally prefer to present their symbols as having been part of the national tradition since time immemorial. However, as Eric Hobsbawm and Terence Ranger (1992) have pointed out, no tradition has 'always' existed; there is a particular starting point in time, surprisingly often of very recent provenance. Since recently created state symbols are not covered by historical patina, their mystique is more fragile than is the case with older symbols. The emotional link between the symbol and the nation cannot be taken for granted; the magician's sleight-of-hand is more difficult to hide. Even so, new symbols and traditions are constantly designed, some eventually establishing themselves while others fade into oblivion.

The crucial test of the success of a national symbol is whether it can unite the people and bolster their loyalty towards the state. Here I examine one recently created symbol, the ribbon of St George, which, for the last fifteen years, has been promoted as a symbol of the Soviet victory in World War II – or the 'Great Fatherland War', as the Russians prefer to call it. From a modest start in 2005, this victory has become a major societal and political event, involving millions of participants in various activities in the weeks leading up to Victory Day, 9 May (Beliaev 2010). In 2015, on the seventieth anniversary of the end of the war, orange-and-black-striped St George ribbons were distributed to and worn by millions of Russians, in addition to thousands of people in dozens of other countries. It is a moot question whether wearing the ribbon is mandatory or voluntary during the victory celebrations, but most evidence suggests that the vast majority of the Russian population has taken the symbol to its heart; there is, however, one clear exception to this and that is the Western-oriented, liberal opposition. They tend to reject the ribbon since it is a symbol not only of the victory over the Nazis but also, and increasingly, an emblem of the Putine regime. To the current state powers, this does not represent any problem – quite the contrary: it symbolically highlights who are 'with us' and who are 'against us', and since the Kremlin has managed to appropriate the sacred war legacy, the political opposition can be branded as unpatriotic, if not traitors to the nation.

The new ribbon tradition is interwoven with another recently created ritual, the 'Immortal Regiment', in which relatives of deceased war veterans walk through the cities bearing photographs of their dear ones. The marchers and often also the photographs are adorned with St George ribbons. To an even greater degree than the St George ribbon itself, the Regiment draws ordinary Russian citizens directly into the victory celebrations, in ways that strengthen the ties between the political leadership and the population.

The theoretical literature on nation-building highlights two aspects of the capacity of symbols and rituals to produce social cohesion: the internal and the external perspective. While the first focuses on relations *within* groups, the other understands group cohesion as a function of the contrast with other groups through the erection of *group boundaries*. These two aspects are not mutually exclusive and my examination of the St George ribbon shows that one and the same symbol may be seen to perform both tasks at the same time. It may obscure ideological and cultural differences between some subgroups in the community – while also excluding and erecting boundaries against others.

Barth's concept of the boundary, I argue, can be extended to the study not only of national and ethnic groups but also to social groups *within* the putative nations (Bourdieu 1991, 120–4). It can fruitfully be employed to a study of contentious politics among various groups who engage in struggles to define 'the nation' – what Hutchinson (2005) calls 'cultural wars'.

In this chapter I chronicle the short but eventful history of the ribbon of St George as a newly invented state symbol in Russia, focusing on its ability to unite the population. I discuss why this particular symbol was chosen, by whom and why, the reactions to it, and how its meaning has been constantly changing.

Picking Symbols from an Almost Empty Toolbox?

In his blog on the website of the Ekho Moskvy radio station, the commentator Boris Vishnevskii wrote in 2015 that, from being a 'a symbol of unity', the St George ribbon has turned into 'a symbol of discord' (Vishnevskii 2015). If this is correct, it should perhaps regarded as a failure, since the main purpose of any state symbol is precisely to unite the population. However, I will argue that it has, in fact, been extremely successful, not least because it has become a symbolic bone of contention. It unites the vast majority of the Russian population, who identify with the ribbon, and at the same time excludes those small sections of society that stand in opposition to the powers that be, whom Putin and his entourage have concluded it is better to excise from the national body rather than try to woo on board.

Russia has a chequered political history, punctuated by revolutions and counter-revolutions. Today, the symbols of each period in the country's past have their aficionados and detractors. While many Russian nationalists and imperialists draw on imagery from both the prerevolutionary and postrevolutionary periods, Tsarist symbols continue to be anathema to diehard communists while communist symbols are abhorred by most Orthodox believers. The main public holiday in the Soviet period, the celebration of the October Revolution on 7 November, was discontinued during Boris Yeltsin's years in power, and attempts to establish alternative 'national days' proved less than successful (Smith 2002). The official 'Russia Day' on 12 June does not count for much in Russian society, while the 'Day of National Unity', 4 November, has been seized upon by right-wing nationalists seeking to turn its official message on its head: the main slogan during their 'Russian Marches' is 'Russia for [ethnic] Russians', a clear provocation to non-Russian minorities (Verkhovsky 2016, 92–6).

The Yeltsin administration failed to achieve consensus in the political elite on the national symbols for the new Russia. Neither the reintroduction of the white–blue–red tricolour nor the attempt to resurrect Mikhail Glinka's patriotic melody as a national anthem achieved the necessary votes in the Duma to become official state symbols; in the end, they were sanctioned into law by presidential decree (Kolstø 2004). However, symbols that are foisted upon a reluctant population are inevitably unable to fulfil their most important task: to unite people and give them a common purpose and identity.

Shortly after having taken office as president, Putin brought the thorny issue of national symbols back to the table and managed to steer it through parliament. His packet solution was a compromise: the white–blue–red tricolour was retained as the country's flag, while the new national anthem is a refashioned version of the Soviet anthem, and the Tsarist symbol, the two-headed eagle, adorns the country's coat of arms. The words of the anthem are new but written by the same author, Sergei Mikhalkov, a popular author of children's books who had penned the original version during World War II. While some dissidents denounce the anthem as Stalinist (Shevtsova 2003, 144–6), it has been almost universally embraced in Russian society: Putin had hit upon an important source of regime support. Evidently, he and his advisers concluded that victory in the war should be tapped even deeper for political legitimation, and preferably in ways that had no strong associations with Stalinism.

The major contribution of the Soviet Union to the defeat of Nazi Germany is indisputable; in absolute figures, Soviet war losses were incomparably greater than those of any other combatant nation. While the Stalin regime after 1946 no longer celebrated 9 May as a national holiday and Khrushchev introduced a low-key commemoration only, under Brezhnev the Soviets leaders did whatever they could to extract legitimacy from the Great Victory, and from the mid-1960s 9 May was celebrated each year with considerable fanfare (Laruelle 2021, 29). As in some other countries, not least in France, a huge military parade inspected by the state leaders was the main feature of the celebrations, but there were also numerous local celebrations throughout the country. Even so, Christel Lane points out, this public ritual was more decentralised and restrained than the other two major Soviet holidays – International Workers' Day on 1 May and the October Revolution on 7 November (Lane 2010, 143).

In 1965, Victory Day was officially instituted as a public holiday. Celebrations normally started the day before, with a ceremony at the various workplaces – the *kollektivy*. Early the next morning the townspeople gathered around the local war memorial for a wreath-laying ceremony. The honour guard was usually made up of three generations, as a relay of memory. A standard ingredient in the ceremony would be a rollcall of the dead, and for each name a Pioneer youngster would step forward and declare: 'he died the death of the brave' (Lane 2010, 145). A brass band would play, a poem would be recited, and there would be a one-minute silence. War veterans would be in attendance, wearing all of their medals.

The Soviet Union always celebrated Victory Day one day after the rest of Europe, a tradition which has been retained in Russia. Technically, this resulted from the time difference between Moscow and continental Europe; when the German surrender was signed on 8 May in Berlin, it was already past midnight in the Soviet capital. Gradually, this calendar difference acquired a symbolic subtext: the USSR had fought its own, parallel, war with Nazi Germany – the Great Fatherland War – or 'VOV' as a Russian acronym. The Soviet war effort was rarely referred to as part of the 'Second World War'. While World War II started on 1 September 1939, the Great Fatherland War began nearly two years later, with the German invasion of the USSR on 22 June 1941.

In the late Soviet period there was some evidence that enthusiasm for the victory celebrations was flagging – in particular, the younger generations were not taking it to heart. An entire ten-day period at the beginning of May – starting with

International Workers' Day on 1 May and ending with Victory Day – was more or less a continuous holiday season, mainly celebrated with vodka and good food on family picnics. On that day, 'they' (the state leaders) were doing 'their things' in the public arena, things which did not necessarily concern 'ordinary people'. The Putin regime was determined to change this aloofness: a new, officially sanctioned version of history-writing returned victory in the Great Fatherland War to the centre of regime legitimation (Bækken and Enstad 2020).[1]

The first St George ribbons were worn by ordinary Russians in 2005. The ribbon is modelled on a high-ranking order instituted by the Stalin regime in 1942. It has the same colours as the Soviet medal but a different name: the Soviet prototype was called 'Order of the Guard' (*gvardeiskii orden*). Its colours – orange and black – are said to symbolise fire and gun-smoke. The Order itself, as well as various kinds of ornamentation in orange and black, featured on numerous wartime and postwar posters and postcards (see Figures 7.1 and 7.2; see e.g. Lex undated).[2]

Why was the new commemorative ribbon introduced under Putin called 'St George' (*georgievskii*) and not '*gvardeiskii*'? An Order of St George 'for service and valour' had been instituted by Catherine the Great in 1769, and clearly Stalin was deliberately drawing on associations with this order when he introduced his own.[3] However, he had not only changed the name, but also readjusted the image somewhat: the original St George order had been yellow and black, or occasionally golden and black, while the orange colour was introduced by the communists (Krechetnikov 2014) (see Figure 7.3).

Figure 7.1 Soviet New Year stamp showing the Moscow Kremlin, and stamp with St George ribbon, 1985. © Kingarion / Shutterstock.comshutterstock_179592530.jpg.

Figure 7.2 'Krasnoi armii – slava!', by L. F. Golovanov. 1 ruble 50 Russian postage stamp, 2000. Shutterstock_380429167.jpg.

Figure 7.3 Tsarist order of St George, Galereia S.ART. All rights reserved.

In this way the Soviets managed to signal both continuity and change with the prerevolutionary symbolism. In a strikingly similar manner the new commemorative St George ribbon introduced under Putin eclectically combines elements from both previous periods: the name is taken from the Tsarist order and the colour nuances from the Soviet Army emblem (Eliseev 2015).

Moreover, the Order of St George was used also by General Vlasov's Russian Liberation Army, which fought on the side of the Axis Powers during the final years of World War II. Thus, the emblem can be associated with three very different political systems: tsarism, communism and fascism. Hardly anyone in Russia draws a line from the Vlasovites to today's St George ribbon[4] – but that is done in other post-Soviet states.

Most observers take it for granted that the St George commemorative ribbon was introduced into Russian political imagery by state fiat. This may or may not be correct: but if it is, that is not something the authorities will readily admit to. Officially, it is claimed that the initiative for the ribbon campaign (or 'action' – *aktsiia*) was 'spontaneous' (*stikhiino*), meaning that it emanated from society and not from the state authorities ('Lentochka nashei' 2010). The roots of the action may be traced back to the 'Student Community' (*Studencheskaia obshchina*) civil society organisation; their original objective was to keep the memory of the Victory alive among younger generations. Explained political scientist Mikhail Savva:

> Much has been said about the broken bond between the generations in our country, and that is indeed true. And no one had so far come up with a better means of restoring this connection than this joint work towards a common goal. (2006)

According to the article on *Studencheskaia obshchina* in the Russian Wikipedia, this is 'one of the few social youth organizations in [Moscow] which is financially and politically independent' ('ROOSPM' undated). However, this information should probably be taken with a pinch of salt, as the Wikipedia editors have equipped the article with a warning that it looks suspiciously like a public relations piece. Be that as it may, we can conclude that the story about the civil society origins of the ribbon symbol is a vital part of the 'action' itself (Timofeychev 2018).

The target group of the St George action has been expanded: no longer an educational programme aimed at youth only, it reaches out to all Russian citizens at home and abroad – indeed, to anyone anywhere who wants to pay tribute to the Soviet war effort. The main slogans are 'Thank you, granddad, for the Victory' and 'I remember – I am proud.'

The students in 'Student Community' apparently needed some informational structures through which to disseminate their campaign message, and contacted Natalia Loseva at the RIA Novosti news agency. Since RIA Novosti is an official agency of the Russian state, Loseva is unlikely to have agreed to participate in this endeavour without the consent of her superiors.[5] Loseva maintains that the ribbon was launched as a reaction to the nihilism of the previous epoch that followed the dissolution of the Soviet Union: 'it is difficult for a society to be healthy without emotional and historic pillars to lean on . . . It seems the ribbon filled the niche of healthy pride' (Timofeychev 2018).

Iulia Latynina (2015) insists that the timing of the first ribbon campaign was not fortuitous: it was launched after the Orange Revolution in Ukraine, and must be seen as a deliberate attempt to forestall any 'colour revolution' in Russia. Even the orange colour was purloined from the Maidan activists, she claims. While this is an intriguing interpretation, there is little evidence to support it. We can also note that the campaign had a rather long fuse before it exploded into the mega-event it has become today. Not until 2007 – during the third year of the campaign – was the ribbon officially worn by Vladimir Putin and Dmitry Medvedev for the first time (see Figure 7.4) ('Lentochka nashei' 2010).

From a relatively modest start, the campaign has grown in size and significance. While 800,000 ribbons were manufactured in 2005 (Poroshina 2007) and 6 million in 2006, by 2010 6 million copies did not suffice to cover demand

Figure 7.4 Dmitrii Medvedev (left) and Vladimir Putin (right), Moscow, Russia – 9 May 2014: celebration of the sixty-ninth anniversary of Victory Day (World War II) on Red Square. © ID1974 / Shutterstock.com shutterstock_201699974.jpg.

even in Moscow city alone. It became necessary to introduce restrictions on how many ribbons each individual could pick up at the distribution points: a limit of three was imposed (Beliaev 2010). Various sponsors – commercial and official – financed the production of the ribbons, which were sewn at textile factories all around the country. In 2015 one textile mill in Kazan alone rolled out no less than 10,000 km of ribbon (Antonov 2015).

Activist groups in several cities have produced supersized ribbons, aimed at getting into the *Guinness Book of Records*: a 3.5 m × 50 m specimen made of one seamless piece of cloth was produced in Simferopol in Crimea in 2009 ('Samaia bol'shaia' 2009), but this was outdone two years later when citizens of the Moldovan capital, Chisinau, produced a 360 m-long ribbon (Miller 2012, 96). In Stavropol in southern Russia in 2013 local citizens could proudly exhibit a 500 m long ribbon (Emel'ianova 2013)[6] but this record was beaten in 2020 when 500 volunteers carried a 2,100 m² ribbon around the Rzhevsk war memorial ('U Rzhevskogo' 2020). In 2008 ribbons were distributed in thirty countries ('Lentochka nashei' 2010), and then in more than sixty countries the next year (Beliaev 2010). In 2019 Immortal Regiment events were held in 115 countries, with a total participation of 850,000, in addition to 10 million marchers in Russia ('Bessmertnyi polk' 2020). An even larger manifestation would no doubt have taken place in 2020 during the seventy-fifth anniversary, but due to the coronavirus situation that year's event had to be organised online (Bobylev 2020) (Figure 7.5).

Figure 7.5 Action in memory of the Immortal Regiment. People carry a large St George ribbon, symbol of solidarity, Krasnoyarsk, Russia, 9 May 2019. shutterstock_1392840929.jpg.

To explain the success of the campaign, commentators note how the ribbon 'ties' people together. While the campaign has occasionally been used to collect money to support veteran organisations, *Rossiiskaia gazeta* avers that this is not its chief purpose: 'The main thing in the campaign, of course, is not money, but its spirit, the idea – to unite the nation around the Great Victory' (Ivanova 2008). Summing up the second campaign in 2006, *Rossiiskaia gazeta* argued that 'a country on the rise is in need of symbols of national unity':

> [The ribbon] not only unites us with our recent past, but also with each other. To be reminded about our civil unity by means of the St George ribbon is extraordinarily important. Far too many dividing lines run through the Russian nation – from differences in income levels, to different political viewpoints and different nationalities. (Savva 2006)

In *Kommersant*, Elizaveta Surnacheva (2015) wrote, 'the Victory has turned out to be the main if not the only "spiritual tie" (*skrepa*) of Russian statehood'. Similarly, an unsigned editorial in *Nezavisimaia gazeta* in April 2015 maintained that 'the victory in the Great Fatherland War, the 70th anniversary of which Russia is celebrating next week, remains one of the very few symbols that can unite citizens with different convictions, attitudes towards the authorities, and social status' ('Velikaia Pobeda' 2015). Leading sociologist and pollster Lev Gudkov claims that Victory Day is 'the only opportunity for the nation to assert itself. There are no other foundations left for national pride' ('V-Day' 2015). Such sentiments seem to be an important part of the reason why the St George ribbon was chosen as a rallying symbol for the regime. Listeners to the radio station Ekho Moskvy were told that the St George ribbon had been concocted 'as a symbol of the only event in the history of our Fatherland able to unite the entire country – the victory' (Vishnevskii 2015). And finally, according to three journalists in *Komsomol'skaia Pravda*, the St George ribbon is 'perhaps the only symbol of the victory which can unite the entire people' (Shokareva et al. 2011). The authors of these remarkably similar assessments span the entire spectrum of political orientations in Russia, from Putinists who gladly pin the ribbon on to their chests, to oppositionist who scorn it as a symbol of subservience to an authoritarian regime. A common premise for them all seems to be that national unity in Russia cannot be taken for granted. It is a sensitive plant that must be cultivated tenderly, lest it wither away. The ribbon of St George is one of the few tools left in the authorities' gardening kit.

A VICTIM OF ITS OWN SUCCESS? THE ST GEORGE RIBBON FROM POPULARITY TO *POSHLOST'*

Unlike the red poppies worn by the British on Remembrance Day, St George ribbons are not sold for charity but distributed for free.[7] It is explicitly stated in the charter of the St George action that it shall be 'non-commercial' ('Georgievskaia lentochka' undated). Many Russian private firms and shops, however, have not resisted the temptation to try to profit from the St George craze. This has been done in various ways, either by designing commercials adorned with ornamentation in orange and black, or by charging a certain sum for the ribbons they have available. There is a fine line between expressing support for this patriotic action and enriching oneself unreasonably from it. In several cities, self-appointed patriotic vigilantes have taken it upon themselves to determine where that line is to be drawn, and have pilloried in the press those shops and firms that, in their view, have overstepped it (Khokhlov and L'vov 2015; Polygaeva 2015). As one zealot expressed it, 'To make a trade of something which is practically speaking a sacred item (*sviatynia*) is unethical' (Semenova 2015). A pharmacy in Krasnoyarsk gave away St George ribbons for free, but only to customers who bought medicine for a minimum of 350 roubles; this was censured as lacking in good taste (Shokareva et al. 2011). And wrapping up salad or liver in orange and black paper is denounced as *poshlost'*, an almost untranslatable word with a meaning somewhere between 'vulgarity' and 'banality' (Shokareva et al. 2011).

Even worse, designs in orange and black have been used to decorate commodities like cheap vodka (Kirsheva and Valiulina 2015). The most egregious case of this kind involved a firm that provided public bio-toilets with orange/black stripes (see Figure 7.6). Posing as a People's Tribune, Vladimir Zhirinovskii proposed making illegal any use of Victory symbols in advertising – a move opposed by spokespersons for private business, who argued that 'patriotism should not be banned' (Polygaeva 2015).

Figure 7.6 Public toilets with the St George ribbon. Galereia S.ART.

However, not only business but also ordinary people have contributed to the trivialisation of the St George action, at least in the opinion of some purists. While the ribbon was originally supposed to be pinned on to the lapel, it soon turned up on suitcase handles and children's prams, as well as on cars, not only attached to the car aerial or inside the front window, but also on licence plates. Some 'concerned citizens', particularly of the older generation, perceived impudence when they saw the ribbon used as shoelaces, as body art, around dogs' necks or attached in abundance all over the body (see Figures 7.7 and 7.8) (Simokhina 2011). Some self-appointed guardians of St George ribbon ethics accepted this as an expression 'not of base motives, but simply a lack of taste', while others warned against turning Victory Day into a preposterous piece of buffoonery (Kriviakina 2015). According to some critical voices, 'a massive theatre of the absurd is unfolding before our eyes, which has nothing to do with the Victory which we are commemorating on 9 May' (Vishnevskii 2015). Psychiatrist Andrei Bil'zho found reason to warn against turning the St George action into 'a mass psychosis' ('Situatsiia' 2015).

If the 'offender' of the unwritten St George code of conduct was known to be an oppositional, condemnation was particularly harsh – as when Ksenia Sobchak, a prominent anti-Putin liberal, posted pictures of herself on Instagram in a bikini, the lower part of which was orange-and-black striped (Sukhanova 2015).

Figure 7.7 St George ribbon as shoelaces. Galereia S.ART. All rights reserved.

Figure 7.8 St George ribbon in abundance on girls' clothing. Galereia S.ART.
All rights reserved.

However, the wrath of the bigots has also descended upon inoffensive minors who have involuntarily attracted attention. In April 2015, a video clip of some dancing schoolgirls in Orenburg created a nationwide scandal. They were dressed up as bees that chased away Winnie the Pooh and saved their honey, but someone concluded that not only were they making indecent movements with the lower parts of their bodies – so-called twerking – but their costumes were even sewn of orange-and-black-striped cloth ('Iunie "pchelki"' 2015). The local state prosecutor took responsibility and opened an investigation into the matter (Boiko 2015). However, at this point, some *bona fide* patriots concluded that the moral panic of these sticklers itself threatened to turn the St George action into a farce. High-profile nationalist Egor Kholmogorov reminded the public that the natural colours of bees are in fact orange and black ('Publitsist Egor' 2015). In the end, the case was closed without anyone being punished by the authorities ('SK otkazalsia' 2015).

TYING THE RIBBON TO THE STATE JUGGERNAUT

When Stephen Norris reported in 2011 on the 65th Victory celebrations in Russia, his analysis focused on the widespread concern in the country that the commemoration was threatened by distasteful business exploitation (Norris 2011). By 2015, the commercial issue had moved to the background: the major controversy now concerned the intimate connection between the victory celebrations and support for the Putinist regime.

Officially, the action is to be not only non-profit, but also emphatically non-political ('Georgievskaia lentochka' undated). However, the concept of 'political' is defined rather narrowly in Russia: it pertains to party politics only. The actions of state authorities are not regarded as 'political': what they do is 'statecraft'. The state could not and should not stay out of the ribbon campaign: the authorities have assisted the organisers in various ways – and have themselves been helped by the action, no doubt a major motivation. Thus, the official organ of the Russian government – *Rossiiskaia gazeta* – explained to its readers that the 'St George action is non-political' but in the very same article also reported that the ribbons were disseminated abroad with the active assistance of Russian embassies and diplomatic personnel (Ivanovskaia 2012). As a Foreign Ministry spokesperson explained, 'the preservation of historical memory is one of the vectors of our foreign policy . . . . Therefore we provide support for this symbolic action' (Kolybalov 2015).

The link between the authorities and the ribbon of St George is more than a matter of the regime lending a helping hand to the action. Tanks and other military vehicles adorned with orange and black stripes symbolise the military power of the contemporary Russian state just as much or more than they commemorate the war (see Figure 7.9). Increasingly, the ribbon has become a symbol not only of patriotism and of honouring the veterans of the Great Fatherland War, but also of supporting the Putin regime. The slide towards such politicisation became particularly acute in 2015, with accounts of state employees in the provinces who were threatened with dismissal unless they wore the St George ribbon, and of pupils reported to the police because they came to school without it (Vishnevskii 2015). In May 2015, journalist Anton Orekh on Ekho Moskvy opined that the St George ribbon had originally been a brilliant idea. In the first years, it was worn mainly by young people chanting 'I remember, I'm proud' and it all seemed very sincere. However,

> the celebration has become increasingly bureaucratic and lifeless, and the man in the street is almost indifferent to it . . . . The ribbon has become a code symbol for devotion to the authorities and the president. And even if his ratings have reached cosmic heights, I see far fewer ribbons in the streets now that I did even as recently as last year. (Orekh 2015)

Orekh's observation of a decreasing number of ribbons on public display may or may not be correct – other Russians would probably dispute it. However, it does point to an inherent dilemma for the Putin regime. As argued above, it has been essential to present the action as a civil society initiative, and not just another campaign foisted upon society from above. Only if it is perceived as

Figure 7.9 Military parade dedicated to Victory Day in World War II on 7 May 2014 in Moscow. Kingarion Shutterstock 193037834.

an expression of independent, sincere and voluntary support can it provide the regime with legitimacy. But in authoritarian societies, genuinely independent support is difficult to sustain.

A brief excursion into the parallel phenomenon of the 'Immortal Regiment' can illustrate this point. Just like the ribbon of St George, the 'Immortal Regiment' is a recently invented tradition, and is similarly claimed to have emanated from outside the corridors of power. However, while in the case of the St George ribbon this claim rests on somewhat shaky ground, few will deny that the Immortal Regiment was initially a genuine grassroots undertaking. The tradition originated in the Siberian city of Tomsk in 2012 at the initiative of some journalists at a local TV station, TV-2, which at the time was not only independent but also regarded as clearly oppositional (later, the station was taken over by regime-loyal owners) (see Okara 2015).[8] As with the St George action, the bylaws of the Regiment state that it is 'non-commercial and non-political'; further, it is 'a non-governmental, civil society initiative'; and finally, 'The Regiment cannot be personalized by any one individual, not even the most respected one' ('Ustav polka' undated). This seems to be a rather transparent reference to Putin, and a warning to the authorities not to try to take over the enterprise.

The 'Regiment' consists of columns of people who walk down one of the main thoroughfares of a city carrying photographs of their loved ones who fought in the Great Fatherland War.[9] Superficially, the event may seem to have associations to Soviet-era parades, when pictures of Marx, Lenin and Stalin were carried in solemn procession on 1 May and 7 November. This, however, is probably not the most relevant parallel. Importantly, the photographs carried in the 'regiment' marches do not represent 'the powers', but a relative of the participants themselves. Therefore, a funeral cortege or a church procession is probably a more apt comparison. It has been pointed out that the marches often resemble religious processions, in which the photos of the veterans are sometimes mixed with icons and saints (Obukhov 2016),[10] and they have been described as a Durkheimian-style 'civil religion' ritual (Linchenko and Golovashina 2019, 67).

Due to its semi-private character, the 'Immortal Regiment' has been somewhat less susceptible than the St George ribbon campaign to attempts at a 'hostile takeover' on the part of the authorities. Even so, an urge to do so apparently lingers among Putin ideologists. The influential pro-Kremlin journalist Nikolai Starikov, for instance, writing in his *LiveJournal* blog, deplored how 'instead of celebrating this day as a day of unity and Victory, it is developing into millions of instances of private mourning' (Starikov 2015). Therefore, in Starikov's view, the Regiment march does not serve to bolster state patriotism sufficiently.

The 2015 Immortal Regiment was a spectacular success, surpassing all prognoses. On the seventieth anniversary of the victory in World War II that year, between 350,000 and 500,000 people, according to various estimates, participated in Moscow ('V aktsii' 2015), more than double or treble the number that had originally signed up (see Figure 7.10) ('Okolo 150' 2015). A total of 12 million people participated in 120 different Russian towns and cities, in addition to marches organised abroad (Zhdanov 2015) In 2016 marches took place in forty different countries (Vasil'chenko 2016), and in eighty countries in 2019, according to Russian Wikipedia. A few critical voices denounced the marches as 'a cynical, coarse propaganda parade' (Mel'nikov 2015), and a week after the march a number of photos were published on the Internet, showing heaps of discarded Regiment placards near public rubbish bins. Allegedly, this showed that participants in the marches had been paid to carry portraits of people they did not know and did not care about, and therefore they disposed of the placards unceremoniously as soon as the march was finished. On the other hand, Oleg Lur'e, a former journalist at *Novaia gazeta*, speculated that the photos were fake and the entire story a hoax, intended to discredit the Regiment. The placards, he believed, had probably been produced after the march by the same people who posted the photos on the Internet (Lur'e 2015). In some cases, however, the explanation turned out to be rather mundane: some local organisers of

Figure 7.10 The Immortal Regiment marches on. Moscow celebrates the seventieth Victory Day anniversary on 9 May 2015. © Alexander Kuguchin / Shutterstock.com.

the Immortal Regiment marches had, with the best intentions, produced placards of veterans who had no surviving relatives and handed them out to people who wanted to participate in the march but had no relatives who fought in the war. After the march, nobody had made sure that these photos were collected and discarded of properly (Interfaks 2015; Bilalutdinov 2016). However, in some other cases the origin of some of these portrait piles remained obscure, and the chairman of the interregional council of the Immortal Regiment, Sergei Lapenkov, reported them to the local public prosecutor. Interestingly, he argued that the discarded photos might qualify as a violation of the Russian penal code 'since the St George ribbon is depicted on them' ('Sozdateli "Bessmertnogo polka"' 2015). Evidently, while the photos themselves were 'private' and abuse of them of no concern to the state, the ribbon is official and desecration of it is regarded as a far more serious matter – indeed, an offence against the state.

In any case, most commentators – including those from the anti-Putin opposition – accepted the marches as genuine expressions of affectionate memory. On Ekho Moskvy, Anton Orekh remarked, 'Personally, I have no doubts about the sincerity of the "Immortal Regiment". This is very different from the Putin rallies to which the multitudes are ushered or bused in' (Orekh 2015). However, just as the St George ribbon had, in his view, become the symbol of 'hysterical semi-officialdom (*ofitsioz*)', he feared something similar could happen with the Regiment.

These apprehensions were not unfounded. Two Russian researchers maintain that the Immortal Regiment has contributed to the greater influence that the official politics of memory has on local memories of the Russian families, 'which were often in opposition to the images of the past broadcast by the state' (Linchenko and Golovashina 2019, 66). They report that, in larger Russian cities, participation of schoolchildren in the marches is encouraged but not obligatory, but in rural schools, 'participation of all pupils and their families is strictly obligatory' (Linchenko and Golovashina 2019, 67) Refusal leads not only to reprimanding of the students but also to public censure.

In an interview with Russian TV, Putin emphasised that the initiative for the march 'was born not in offices or in administrative structures, but in the hearts of people' ('Vladimir Putin' 2015). This seemed to send the message that he would respect the independence of this civil initiative, but the original Tomsk organisers were not reassured. In May 2015 they sent a letter to President Putin in person, expressing concerns that the All-Russian Popular Front, a 'GONGO'[11] established in 2011 at the behest of Putin himself, was trying to take their organisation under its umbrella and, indeed, to control it (Kozlov and Korchenkova 2015; Kozenko 2015). And indeed, in 2015, a rival organisation with almost the same name, 'The Immortal Regiment of Russia', with links to the All-Russian Popular Front, was established and took over the marches in Moscow and some other cities (Fedor 2017, 315–18). Since then, two parallel Immortal Regiment structures have existed. In 2015, for the first time, the Moscow march ended at Red Square, perhaps the most potent architectural symbol of Russian state power (Protsenko 2015). Here, the marchers were met by Vladimir Putin, who walked with them for the final steps, carrying a photograph of his father (see Figure 7.11). Julie Fedor concludes that the Immortal Regiment was being instrumentalised 'to appropriate the Red Army's war dead, and the emotions they evoke, in the service of an authoritarian vision of the future of Russia and the region' (Fedor 2017, 309).

Uniting the Russian Nation – and Isolating the Russian State

Russian oppositionists hold that the politicisation of the St George ribbon divides the Russian nation. In May 2015 Boris Vishnevskii claimed that 'no perfidious enemy could have changed the perception of the symbol of Russian military honour more mercilessly than the Russian authorities themselves have done over the last year' (Vishnevskii 2015). The St George ribbon has become 'a badge of belonging to the Putinite majority' (Okara 2015), a 'litmus test of loyalty', and for that reason produces societal schism (*raskol*) ('Kak sokhranit' 2015). Liberals point out that the ribbon is used as a sign of recognition among participants in pro-regime flash-mobs attacking opposition rallies (Pozniakov 2015).

According to an unsigned editorial in *Nezavisimaia gazeta* in April 2015,

> The black and orange has become an attribute to rallies against 'fifth columnists' and liberals. This is something new. Now the citizen is pushed towards a position where he along with the memory of the war also

Figure 7.11 Russian President Vladimir Putin (centre) holds a portrait of his father as he takes part in the Immortal Regiment march during Victory Day celebrations in Moscow on 9 May 2015. © Shutterstock_310498208.jpg

accepts a very concrete political programme, specifically, a stigmatization of the West and Kiev. If he does not do that, and remains, for instance, a liberal, a westernizer, opposed to the annexation of Crimea, then that means that he has not taken on board the lessons of the war, that he is not worthy of the feats of our fathers and grandfathers. ('Velikaia Pobeda' 2015)

Opinion polls show that the overwhelming majority of the population support the St George ribbon campaign and have warm feelings towards it. *Rossiiskaia gazeta* reported in 2013 that, while among people of twenty-four years and younger 62 per cent approved unequivocally of the campaign, among those of forty-five years and older this figure rose to 74 per cent. Roughly 12 per cent of those interviewed had negative attitudes towards the ribbon; among them, only 6 per cent were 'categorically' against it (Dobrynina 2013).

A poll from 2015 conducted by the highly respected Levada Institute showed that as much as 85 per cent had watched the Victory Parade in Red Square on 9 May; 78 per cent liked it, a mere 5 per cent did not. Only 6 per cent of the respondents were unaware of the 'Immortal Regiment' phenomenon; no more than 3 per cent had a negative opinion of it. The vast majority, 89 per cent,

STRATEGIC USES OF NATIONALISM AND ETHNIC CONFLICT

were positive ('Sdvig' 2015). Another survey from 2014 reported by *Kommersant* showed that a staggering 94 per cent of those interviewed appreciated the St George ribbon, 82 per cent 'with no qualifications'. Valerii Fedorov, director-general of the (government-owned) polling institute VTSIOM, pointed out that 82 per cent was remarkably similar to the popularity levels recorded for Vladimir Putin after the Crimean annexation. In Fedorov's view, this was no coincidence: 'with Putin's 84 per cent popularity ratings, the correlation of forces between the pro-ribbon and the anti-ribbon people could be quite easily predicted' (Surnacheva 2015).

Assuming that the polling data are basically correct,[12] the Putin regime seems to have won acceptance among the populace for the view that the St George ribbon campaign is a genuine expression of pride in Russia's victory in World War II, and that the current powerholders in the Kremlin are the legitimate custodians of this honourable legacy. Supporting the ribbon and supporting Putin are two sides of the same coin, and those who distance themselves from the St George ribbon campaign should be ostracised from the Russian nation. Furthermore, it can be argued that, by their vehement reactions against the St George ribbon, some oppositionists are themselves contributing to this ostracism. They not only attack the regime, but also taunt ordinary Russians who participate in the campaign. For instance, Andrei Pozniakov writes, 'in the current situation, to put on the St George ribbon for the sake of the celebration is very much like wearing a swastika after a series of Jewish pogroms, and arguing that this is a sign of sun, summer and light' (Pozniakov 2015). Besides being somewhat far-fetched, that comparison is unlikely to boost recruitment to the anti-ribbon camp. Similarly, Sergei Zaporozhskii claims that the whistling and dancing of grandchildren whose grandfathers fought in the war reminded him of 'a witches' Sabbath of brainless demons'. Further: 'their billboards with St George ribbons and patriotic inscriptions often contain grammatical errors' (Zaporozhskii 2015). Such attempts to show that 'we of the opposition are better educated and more cultured than you' will inevitably serve only to drive the anti-Putin opposition deeper into isolation.

During his first two presidential terms of office, Putin clearly tried to appeal to as many segments of the Russian population as possible, and also the pro-Western and pro-democracy liberals. With his third term came a major shift in Kremlin strategy. A new ideology of 'traditional values' was concocted, including stringent opposition to homosexuality, with a flurry of draconian new laws rushed through parliament in the spring and summer of 2012, severely curtailing any kind of opposition activity (Flikke 2015; Suslov and Uzlaner 2020). The Putin regime had clearly concluded that it could do without the support of the liberals, who, in any case, were irredeemably lost to 'the national cause' (Hale 2016). Trying to woo them back was futile – but they could be included in the nation-building strategy in another way, as an internal enemy and a contrast agent.

However, while the St George ribbon campaign can be said to have had the desired effects *within* Russia, the same cannot be said about its fallout abroad, particularly not in the other former Soviet republics. Here, too, the same message that resonates within Russia is received loud and clear: enthusiasm for the ribbon and support for the Putin regime amount to the same thing. For precisely this reason, attempts are being made throughout the post-Soviet space to curtail or even prohibit public display of the ribbon.

For obvious reasons, opposition towards the St George ribbon has been most vociferous in Ukraine (see Chapter 9), but attacks on the ribbon have occurred in virtually all of Russia's neighbour states. In May 2014, Russian actress Lidia Fedoseeva-Shukshina told reporters that when she had arrived at the Finnish border with a St George ribbon on her blouse, she had been exposed to a particularly thorough search ('Georgievskaia lentochka' 2014). Crossing Russia's borders in either direction may often be a time-consuming affair, but this time the 'victim' felt that she had to speak about it at a press conference. In nearby Estonia, Russian veterans who tried to bring some dozen ribbons into the country had them confiscated at the border (Akhmetzhanova 2014). An Estonian employee of the Norwegian oil company Statoil (now Equinor) was taken to the office of her boss for an 'educational conversation' when she was seen wearing a St George ribbon. The company explained that it 'does not encourage the demonstration of political views at the workplace' ('Georgievskaia lentochka' 2015).

In Latvia, one MP announced plans to introduce a bill in the Saeima which would make it illegal to wear the ribbon in public places; repeat offenders could be given a €700 fine or fifteen days behind bars (Ermolaeva 2015b). The fact that this politician had no party affiliation and apparently also no support for his proposal did not prevent the Russian press, including the official government organ *Rossiiskaia gazeta*, from writing several stories about it (Ermolaeva 2015c). A more serious attempt was made in Moldova in June 2014 to introduce a ban on the St George ribbon and impose a fine of the equivalent of 200 US dollars on offenders (Gamova 2014).

Even so, some Russians continue to go to the 'near abroad', and sometimes clearly in order to provoke reactions. In spring 2015 a group of aggressively pro-Putin Russian bikers, the Night Wolves, celebrated the seventieth anniversary of the Victory by touring neighbouring countries, and got into a squabble in Tbilisi with a senior citizen who tried to tear their ribbons off their chests. When her mobile phone fell to the ground and broke during the tiff, the bikers and not the woman were charged with misconduct, confirming Russian suspicions that Russians always have the burden of proof weighted against them ('Rossiiskikh baikerov' 2015).

Many of the 'incidents' recorded above were so minor that the Russian media, one might think, could well have ignored them without neglecting their journalistic duties as normally understood. Therefore, the fact that they so often chose to devote space to them is significant in itself. They seem to be parts of a master narrative of Russia as a besieged fortress: Russians everywhere abroad – and particularly in the 'near abroad' – are a vulnerable and persecuted group. This narrative can be interpreted as an element in a nation-building strategy, albeit with definite costs. As noted, identity-building is relational and contrastive. A strong 'we' is premised on the construction of a strongly differentiated 'Other'. In this case, 'the Other' encompasses virtually the entire outside word. A cohesive Russian national unity is bought at the expense of increasing isolation from the international community.

Apparently, some Russian firms believe that they may suffer from a harsher international business climate by being associated with the St George ribbon. The leading business newspaper *Kommersant* observed that most of the official sponsors of the St George ribbon campaign are small or medium-sized companies, and speculated that larger firms that were more dependent on export kept away, fearing that association with the campaign could create image problems for them abroad (Surnacheva 2015). Some firms allegedly even hesitated at first to buy ribbons for their employees, but evidently concluded that the potential damage which could be incurred vis-à-vis the Russian authorities by refusing was greater than reduced profits abroad.

In the official Russian media, victory in the Great Fatherland War is always presented as a result of a Herculean effort on the part of all the Soviet nations, not only the Russians. However, the Putin era has seen some subtle changes in that regard. The Victory is ever more closely associated with the Russian state, and the introduction of the St George ribbon symbolises that turn. The provenance of this symbol is indisputably Russian, and state leaders in other post-Soviet countries feel that they need their own imagery in order to highlight their national contribution to the victory (Gamova 2015). Unsurprisingly, Ukraine has taken the lead here. In 2014 Ukraine stopped using the St George ribbon altogether and introduced a red poppy instead (Novikova 2014; 'Kiev otkazalsia' 2014). Despite Ukrainian claims that it is a 'European' symbol, the red poppy is used only in the British Isles, and not on 8 May but on Remembrance Day, 11 November. Furthermore, its roots go back to World War I, not II. The Ukrainian change of symbols is clearly intended to signal not only that a clean break is being made with the Soviet past but also that Ukraine is a 'European country', a point made abundantly clear by switching to 8 May as the day of commemoration.

Not only Ukraine but virtually all post-Soviet countries, including some of Russia's closest allies, have felt increasingly uneasy about the St George ribbon as a common victory symbol (Karney and Sindelar 2015). Kyrgyzstan and Kazakhstan now celebrate victory under their national colours – red and yellow in Kyrgyzstan and light blue in Kazakhstan ('V Kazakhstane' 2015). In most Central Asian countries the Russian embassies are no longer allowed to distribute ribbons during the victory celebrations, as they used to do prior to 2014. The rationale behind this hardened attitude in this part of the former Soviet Union is sometimes different from the reasons given in other post-Soviet states: in Kyrgyzstan, the ribbon is associated with the aggression of the Russian Empire against the Kyrgyz population in 1916 when they rose up against the mobilisation of Kyrgyzs for non-combat duty in the Russian army during World War I ('Tsveta i tsvety' 2017). Similarly, in Turkmenistan, people remember that Russian soldiers who participated in the colonial war against the Turkmens in the early 1880s were awarded the Order 'For Victory at Geok Tepe' with the same colours as the Order of St Georg (Kim 2015). The storming of the last Turkmen stronghold, the Geok Tepe fortress, which resulted in more than 2,000 deaths – including women and children – is a national trauma in Turkmenistan today. This illustrates that not only the Stalinist connotations of the St George ribbon but also the Tsarist legacy may be highly problematical.

President Aleksandr Lukashenko's St George ribbon conundrum in Belarus is noteworthy. He evidently felt that he had ended up between the hammer and the anvil: on the one hand, he did not want to antagonise his powerful Russian partner in their common Union-State; on the other hand, his nation-building strategy increasingly focused on Belarusian national themes and symbols. As late as in 2013, customers in some Belarusian supermarkets received a St George ribbon for free together with their receipts ('Belorusskie oppozitsionery' 2014), but by the next year this practice was increasingly frowned upon. Clearly, this change of attitude was connected to the use of the St George ribbon in the war in Eastern Ukraine, which the Belarusian authorities did not want to be associated with (Smok 2014; ch. 9 in this volume). So, in 2015, a new national Victory ribbon was introduced: red and green – the colours of the Belarusian flag – with an apple blossom appended. However, Lukashenka himself and his closest entourage during the Victory celebrations did not wear 'pure' apple blossom ribbons, but opted for a hybrid version: half of it was orange and black, while the other half was the new red and green Belarusian ribbon, replete with the apple flower (see Figure 7.12) (Mozheiko 2015). This episode graphically illustrated how sensitive the symbol issue has become in Russia's relations with other CIS countries, and how important it is for state leaders in neighbouring countries not to make any false steps.

Conclusions

The ribbon of St George is semantically open and ambiguous, as are all symbols. Our understanding of it is based entirely on our knowledge of how it has been used earlier, and our assumptions about the intentions of those who are using it today. The colours of Ksenia Sobchak's bathing suit were the same that many hyper-patriotic Russians dressed in, but the regime-loyal Russians

Figure 7.12 Lukashenko with his youngest son, Nikolai, Minsk 2015.
Galereia S.ART. All rights reserved

reacted very negatively in the first instance and not in the second. That should warn us against trying to interpret symbols on the basis of their design or colours.[13] Their message, as Anthony Cohen has noted (Cohen [1985] 2008), is entirely 'in the minds of their beholders'.

Some national symbols may be so old and well established that their origins are difficult to trace, so they may come to be seen as a 'natural' part of the nation (Hobsbawm and Ranger 1992). This is not the case with recently introduced symbols: it is much easier to examine why, how and by whom they were installed. The Russian St George ribbon campaign is one such case.

While the visibility of the St George ribbon in Russian Victory celebrations increased every year since it was introduced in 2005, with a peak in 2015, during the seventieth anniversary of the Victory,[14] this symbol became a major emblem of the current Russian regime only in Putin's third term. This turn was clearly connected to two events – the massive anti-regime demonstrations in winter 2011–12, and the Ukrainian crisis and the Donbas war (2014–) (see Chapters 8 and 9). In the first case, the ribbon was used as a distinguishing mark vis-à-vis the pro-Western opposition; in the second, as a rallying standard in an undeclared war against a neighbouring state. In both cases it has proved its usefulness to the full.

Many Russian oppositionists regard the St George ribbon with good reason as a tool of 'political technology' (see e.g. Latynina 2014). Authoritarian state leaders strenuously try to equate support for the country with loyalty towards the regime (Arvidsson and Blomquist 1987; Lane 2010, Ch. 9; Kubik 1994; Guibernau 2013), and it is not difficult to see how this symbol is being manipulated by Russian authorities for both community-building purposes and regime legitimation at the same time. On the one hand, the ambiguous quality of the ribbon symbol makes it possible to sell it to different ideological groups in Russian society, ranging from conservatives, monarchists and Orthodox believers to communists and Soviet nostalgics. Presenting it as harkening back to Tsarist times *and* to World War II at the same time was clearly intentional and highly successful.[15]

No doubt, a Russian national victory symbol could have been constructed and framed in such a way to appeal to the third major ideological group in Russian society – the liberals – too. Instead, we see that in recent years the ribbon symbol has erected an identity boundary between mainstream Russian society and this group. The liberals are so few in number and so firmly set in their anti-Putin ways that Kremlin ideologists seem to have concluded that it would be hopeless to recruit them as a support group for the regime. But, paradoxically, in this way they may also contribute inadvertently to Russian nation-building and political consolidation: as a contrasting foil for those defined as the in-group. Anti-Putin liberals can be portrayed as carriers of alien, dangerous and un-national ideas that are threatening to the Russian nation. Writes Boris Vishnevskii in *Ekho Moskvy*:

> From being a sign of military valour [the St George ribbon] has been turned into a symbol of loyalty towards the Putin regime and to Putin personally. It has become a symbol of patriotism on display rather than of genuine patriotism. A symbol of a besieged fortress since, as the Kremlin-controlled TV media are trying to assure us, Russia is surrounded by enemies on all sides and all of the besieged people must rally around the leader. And those who fail to do so are traitors, defectors, and fifth columnists. (Vishnevskii 2015)

The ribbon symbol is being used as a potent weapon in a 'cultural war' within the nation. Julie Fedor emphasises that while the Immortal Regiment is focused on remembering a past war, for the pro-Kremlin camp it is also used as an effective tool to combat 'domestic enemies' in present-day Russia (Fedor 2017, 334). However, it takes two to tango: both the in-group and the out-group contribute to the boundary-based construction of communal identity. Some anti-Putin oppositionists, with their harsh attacks not only on the symbol but also on those who wear it, actively contribute to this boundary-building.

While the St George ribbon in Russian domestic politics functions as a litmus test for regime support, it also marks Russia off from the outside world.

When political leaders in neighbouring countries, fearing a Russian cultural neo-imperialism, refuse to use a shared but Russian-made victory symbol and introduce their own instead, Russians learn that 'the world out there' is a hostile place and it is time to rally around their leader.

Notes

1. A detailed 'historical–cultural standard' for patriotic education for use in all schools has been launched. See <http://histrf.ru/ru/biblioteka/book/istoriko-kul-turnyi-standart> (last accessed 19 July 2021).
2. The medal 'For Victory Over Germany', which virtually all Soviet soldiers received, was also in orange and black.
3. In Orthodox hagiography St George is referred to as 'St George the Victorious' (*Pobedonosets*). On the breast of the double-headed eagle on the Russian coat of arms he is depicted slaying the dragon.
4. An exception is the leftist journalist Alexander Nevzorov, who is highly critical of the St George ribbon. See 'Tvorcheskii vecher' 2014.
5. According to one version, the idea to launch the St George ribbon campaign originated with Natalia Loseva. See e.g. 'Georgievskaia lentochka' 2009 and Timofeychev 2018.
6. A major intention in manufacturing this gargantuan ribbon was to demonstrate interethnic harmony in the restive North Caucasian region. The ribbon was produced by students from all the seven federal subjects in the North Caucasian Federal *Okrug* as a token of interethnic brotherhood.
7. Even so, many Muscovites have experienced how the young people who distribute ribbons in the streets clearly expect to receive a 'donation'.
8. In an alternative version, the march was five years older, and originated with a pensioner in the city of Tiumen', Gennadii Ivanov, who organised what he called 'a parade of victors'. See Grishina 2015. Ivanov claims that idea came to him in a dream. Apparently, his original initiative petered out, and the Immortal Regiment was reinvented five years later.
9. They do not necessarily have to have died in the war.
10. It raised some eyebrows when Natalia Poklonskaia, a prominent nationalist, carried an icon of Nicholas II in the Immortal Regiment in her hometown of Simferopol. See 'Poklonskaia proshla' 2016.
11. GONGO = government-organised non-governmental organisation.
12. Some respondents may have thought it safer or more convenient to respond in a way they assumed the pollsters would like, a common methodological problem with opinion polls even in democratic countries (cf. the so-called 'Bradley effect').
13. For an example of an infelicitous attempt to measure the 'visual syntax' of national symbols see Cerulo 1993.
14. An even larger manifestation would no doubt have taken place in 2020, during the seventy-fifth anniversary, but due to the coronavirus situation that year it had to be an online event for the most part.
15. It should be noted, however, that some communists reject the St George ribbon as a Tsarist symbol that, in their view, has nothing to do with Stalin's Order of the Guards. See e.g. Ivachev 2011.

8

COLLABORATION BETWEEN NATIONALISTS AND LIBERALS IN THE RUSSIAN OPPOSITION, 2011–2013

In the winter of 2011–12, Russia was rocked by massive anti-regime demonstrations, larger than at any other time since the collapse of the Soviet Union. A noteworthy new element in the mobilisation of the opposition was collaboration between groups with very different ideological profiles and agendas: radical leftists, Western-oriented, liberal centrists and right-wing nationalists. Earlier, these people had distrusted each other deeply, and indeed, continued to do so to a large degree even as they stepped on to the same podiums and addressed mixed crowds of their followers. What made it possible for them to bury the hatchet temporarily and unite in a common struggle was a shared hostility to, if not to say hatred of, the Putin regime, and the ability to define the few common slogans and memes to agree on. Their demands were simple, such as 'for honest elections' and 'the Putin regime must go', and they shared a common emblem, a White Ribbon. As with all symbols, it could be given different interpretations: it stood for both 'purity' against the 'dirty' politics of the powers-that-be, and also unity among the oppositionists. In this chapter I focus on the relationship between the nationalists and liberals in particular and on what made it possible for them to forget old animosities.

Smaller demonstrations were organised almost immediately after the ill-fated 4 December parliamentary elections. They protested against fraud in the recent Duma elections as well as against the 'castling' when Dmitrii Medvedev and Vladimir Putin decided to switch jobs as President and Prime Minister. This arrangement, announced on 24 September, was seen as a pre-emptive move that deprived the people of a genuine choice in the presidential elections in March the next year. The turning point, however, was 10 December, when Moscow woke up to the largest anti-regime demonstration since the heady days of perestroika. The massive turnout on that day, along with demonstrations on 24 December and 4 February – with between 60,000 and 130,000 participants – showed that Russian politics had suddenly changed in unexpected ways.

Importantly, on these days marches were held not only in the capital but in many other cities as well – a nationwide mobilisation (Greene 2014). The anti-Putin opposition managed to maintain pressure on the Putin–Medvedev 'tandem' regime with frequent demonstrations throughout the winter and spring. Initially, the authorities seemed uncertain about how to react. Not only did they, for the first time in years, grant permission to hold huge demonstrations in central Moscow, close to the Kremlin; they even gave them (selective) coverage in the national, regime-controlled media. Further, Medvedev announced some concessions, like the reintroduction of popular elections of governors in the Russian Federation subjects. Presidential elections, however, proceeded as planned in March, and once installed in office in May, Putin launched a counter-offensive. In summer 2012, the Duma passed a barrage of restrictive laws which not only nullified the half-hearted liberalisation earlier in the year but tightened control over civil society to a higher degree than ever since the fall of the communist regime. Smaller demonstrations were held in several cities throughout 2012, and a new, smaller cycle of protest commenced in spring 2014 against the annexation of Crimea – but the momentum for change had clearly passed. Instead of ushering in a more liberal regime, the demonstrations achieved the exact opposite: greater authoritarianism.

Even if the Russian 'winter of discontent' proved only passing, it was a game-changer that raises several crucial questions. How was possible to unite the many disparate elements in the Russian opposition in the same demonstrations, and to invite people of very different persuasions to march together? The ease with which the regime managed to curb the mobilisation and reintroduce 'normalcy' is also puzzling. Neither question has a simple one-dimensional answer; different dynamics were activated, influencing each other. Here I focus on one aspect only: the collaboration between liberals and Russian nationalists. These two groups had a long history of distrust, even antagonism, but in the 2011/12 opposition cycle, their leaders stood shoulder to shoulder on the podium, addressing the crowds below. Nicu Popescu, a perceptive observer of Russian politics, described this new alliance as 'one of the most striking and unexpected features of these events' (Popescu 2012, 46). He speculated that the 'Russian democrats' flirtation with nationalism, which is evolving into a marriage of convenience, could prove to be either an elixir of life or the kiss of death' (Popescu 2012, 46). And Andreas Umland, an expert on the Russian far-right movement, asked, 'could Russia's ultranationalists subvert pro-democracy protests?' (Umland 2012). Thus, the liberal–nationalist alliance may be seen as a factor behind either the (initial) success or the (subsequent) failure of the mass mobilisation, or both – or of no consequence.

In this chapter I employ social movement theory, examining what it can tell us about the assets and drawbacks of creating broad alliances across ideological chasms. Three concepts of social movement theory are especially pertinent here: master frames, ideologies and bridge-builders. In addition, I introduce a concept of my own: 'bridge-wreckers', a social movement equivalent to 'spoiler'.

Social movement theory maintains that mass demonstrations cannot be sustained for long without some kind of formalised organisation (McAdam et al. 1996). Indeed, as part of the new climate of collaboration within the Russian opposition, deliberate efforts were made to channel the new activism into a structured framework. This resulted in the decision in June 2012 to establish a 'Coordination Council of the Opposition', with elections held on 20 October. However, while quite innovative – with open, Internet-based elections – this Council fared no better than the demonstrations, and fell prey to infighting and acrimonious disputes.

The final section of this chapter focuses on public perceptions in Russia of the opposition and its various ideological strands. This part is based on a new survey, commissioned by our research team in September/October 2014. The results of this survey may offer a basis for qualified speculation about the effects of liberal–nationalist cooperation in the Russian protest movement.

Merits and Perils of Broad-Based Coalitions Across Ideological Lines: 'Master-Frames', 'Ideologies' and 'Bridge-Builders'

In social movement theory, 'frames' are 'the specific metaphors, symbolic representations, and cognitive cues used to render or cast behavior and events in an evaluative mode and to suggest alternative modes of action' (Zald 1996, 262). They are interpretive schemata that simplify and condense the outside world by selectively punctuating and encoding objects, situations, events, experiences and sequences of actions within one's present or past environment (Snow and Benford 1992, 137).

However, different segments within a movement often disagree over tactics and goals. Frames are therefore contested – not only externally, by countermovement actors, bystanders, and state officials who oppose the movement, but also *within* the movement, as leaders and cadre debate alternative goals and visions (Zald 1996, 261). Such internal disagreements may be overcome if the various parts of the movement can agree on some overarching general frame, often referred to as 'master-frames', a term coined by David Snow and Robert Benford in 1992. In their understanding, master-frames perform the same function as movement-specific collective action frames, but on a larger scale, making it possible for activists from different ideological and cultural backgrounds to work for a common goal (Snow and Benford 1992, 138–9).

Several ideological strands were discernible within the anti-Putin movement. Here I focus on the mutual perceptions and collaboration between two groups only, the Western-leaning liberals and the Russian nationalists. On many issues their worldviews differed sharply and the scope for tension and disagreement was considerable. However, as Anthony Oberschall (1997, 26) has pointed out, ideological differences do not necessarily represent insurmountable barriers to collaboration in social movements. For instance, the massive, nationwide and sustained mobilisation in the USA against the Vietnam War in the late 1960s showed successful broad-spectrum cooperation, involving pacifist Quakers, peace activists of various other faiths and denominations, mothers for peace, Vietnam veterans against the war, draft resisters, students for a democratic society, small and radical-leftist groups, and many others. Still, as history shows, persuading adherents of different ideological groups to march together under a common banner is rarely easy.

The relationship between frames and ideologies has been studied theoretically by Oliver and Benford (2005) and by Westby (2005). On the surface, they note, ideologies and master-frames may be seen as equivalent: both are broad configurations of ideas, within which more specific ideas are included. However, they also indicate some important differences: master-frames lack the elaborate social theory and normative value systems that characterise full-blown ideologies (Oliver and Benford 2005, 193 and 197–8).

Snow and Benford (2005, 209) describe ideologies as '*a cultural resource for framing activity*' (emphasis in the original). However, while ideology may function as the glue *within* a single organisation, the relationship between ideologies and a master-frame that spans several movements is more complicated. As argued by David Westby, they may, in fact, work at cross-purposes:

1. Movements frequently have internal schismatic struggles over ideology.
2. The various forms of collaboration in movements often engender contentious ideological variants.
3. There may be differences regarding the primacy of particular aspects of the ideology.
4. The movement may march under an eclectic banner of more than one single distinct ideology. (Westby 2005, 219)

In a meta-study of social movement coalitions, Holly McCammon and Nella Van Dyke (2010, 294) note that various causal processes go into the creation of such alliances. A comparison of twenty-four studies showed that a commonality of ideology and the availability resources very often combined to produce successful coalitions, indicating that 'organizations typically need to be integrated ideologically before they are willing to work together to stage protest events'. Ideological and cultural differences can prevent coalition work even if there are abundant resources and political allies. Still, McCammon and Van Dyke found that ideological commonality did not appear in the causal combinations in all successful alliances.

The contributions in Bystydzienski and Schacht (2001) and Van Dyke and McCammon (2010), on the politics of coalition-building in social movements, find an array of external and internal factors that facilitate success or failure. An important factor is the importance of agency. As Reese, Petit and Meyer explain, 'grievances and political opportunities, by themselves, do not produce a massive protest movement; organizers do' (Reese et al. 2010, 274). Therefore, 'In the final analysis, the study of coalitions must examine the key personnel who actually pull organizations into coalition activity. It is they who carry out the mundane, but necessary task of interorganizational outreach' (Reese et al. 2010, 274).

Bell and Delaney found that, in the mobilisation efforts they studied, interpersonal dynamics served as impediments to coalition-building efforts: they were 'rife with tensions created by intergroup animosity and lack of trust' (Bell and Delaney 2001, 67). In successful coalitions, particularly important roles were played by what Reece et al. (Reese et al. 2010, 271 and 278–9) call 'movement crossovers', 'brokers' and 'bridge-builders': people with authority who belong to multiple movements and networks, and can negotiate among them.

As such, the deep internal ideological differences should indicate that the anti-Putin mobilisation in the winter of 2011/12 had only a slim chance of holding together in the long run. However, Van Dyke and McCammon hold that ideological congruence is not *required* for a coalition to form:

> unusual circumstances (such as a threat) may lead groups to ignore or downplay ideological differences to work together to confront a serious and common challenge . . . The combination of a common political threat side-by-side with a political opportunity may allow groups to overcome significant differences in beliefs and values to band together to resist potential harm to their interests. (Van Dyke and McCammon 2010, 307–8)

Elena Zdravomyslova has studied the massive protest cycle in the Soviet Union during perestroika which managed to topple the communist regime. She emphasises the key role of symbols in the framing process. 'Symbolism developed by SMs [social movements] condense the meaning of frames' (Zdravomyslova 1996, 125). By the time Mikhail Gorbachev took over as General Secretary, certain aspects of the communist ideology, such as the rhetoric of justice and equality, were still deeply rooted in mass consciousness, but 'the communist symbols and clichés [had] become void of meaning and did not find popular response'.

In order to delegitimate the official ideology the pro-democracy social movements developed 'alternative symbolism which was aggressive in style and confrontational in content' (Zdravomyslova 1996, 124). She argues that the symbols served as the basis of group consciousness, solidarity and a sense of belonging. At the same time, they appeared to be powerful resources that promoted participation in collective action. Hundreds of thousands took to the streets all over the Soviet Union in a sustained cycle of protest over several years, and in the end, the entire edifice of the communist system collapsed.

In the winter of 2011–12, a new political opportunity seemed to be opening up to topple an undemocratic regime, and the protesters clearly hoped to repeat the success of thirty years earlier. They managed to mobilise broadly across the entire ideological spectrum, uniting very disparate groups under a few rather general slogans and symbols. The master-frame that united the various factions in the mass demonstrations against the fraudulent Duma elections can be formulated as follows: 'The current Russian regime is illegitimate.' This was a statement that was more about the political system they wanted to get rid of than about what they wanted to put in its place. As one of the nationalists maintained, 'the time has come to unite. To unite FOR something will be very difficult – practically impossible. Therefore, it is necessary to unite AGAINST – against dishonest elections, against falsifications, against the corrupt and inefficient powers. Finally, against Putin!' (Epifantsev 2012).

As discussed in the previous chapter, since 2005 the St George ribbon had been a major legitimising symbol for the Putin regime, and in the opposition too a ribbon emblem became the most important, if not to say the only, unifying symbol: in this case, a White Ribbon. Like its regime-loyal counterpart, the White Ribbon was a new symbol, conceived, in fact, on the eve of the demonstrations. It is a bit unclear exactly who came up with the idea first; it seems that it was 'blowing in the wind' (Samsonova 2011).[1] It first appeared as an Internet meme in October 2011, some two months before the December elections and before the first street demonstrations. It quickly caught on and engendered little opposition within the anti-Putin movement. It was designed, or at least widely understood, as standing in opposition to the St George ribbon. Historian Aleksei Miller relates that he has observed on a Moscow street a girl with a White Ribbon on one plait and the St George ribbon on the other (Miller 2012, 3–4), but that seems to be a rare exception. For most Russians it was a matter of either/or: you were for Putin or against him. To BBC's Russian Service, wearers of the White Ribbon explained that 'it is a visual marker of my protest' and 'it displays my civic position' (Vasileva 2011), and the threshold for expressing protest with a ribbon was lower than that for participating in a demonstration. 'A rally can gather no more than a hundred thousand, I think, but millions can wear the ribbon' ('Rastushchim v Rossii' 2011).

As with the St George ribbon, the choice of colour seems to have been determined by a desire to unite ideologically disparate elements. In the demonstrations, nationalists, leftists and liberals marched under their own flags: black–gold–white for the nationalists; red for the leftists and white–blue–red for the Westernising liberals. To signal unity among them, the organisers came upon the idea of a White Ribbon since 'white is the sum of all colours' (Ovchinnikov 2011). The official media, however, often preferred to refer to it with another color – orange – in order to suggest that it was a belated attempt at a so-called colour revolution in Russia of the kind that had toppled so many post-Soviet regimes in 2003–2005 (see e.g. Arsiukhin 2012). Finally, white was associated with, on the one hand, purity, andon the other, with winter and snow, and the 2011–12 protest cycle soon became known as 'the snow revolution'.

LIBERAL–NATIONALIST COLLABORATION IN THE RUSSIAN OPPOSITIONAL MOVEMENT: A BRIEF HISTORICAL OVERVIEW

For most of the Yeltsin period, the Westernising democrats in Russia supported the regime while the nationalists opposed it. This changed a few years into the new millennium, when Yeltsin's hand-picked successor, Vladimir Putin, showed increasingly authoritarian tendencies. Several former ministers from Yeltsin's various governments, like Boris Nemtsov and Mikhail Kasianov, as well as defectors from the pro-regime United Russia party like Vladimir Ryzhkov, shifted to the 'anti-system' [*nesistemnaia*] opposition.

At the time, the two most prominent oppositionist leaders were the former chess champion, Garri Kasparov, from the 'democratic camp', and Eduard Limonov, leader of the National Bolshevik party, from the 'leftist/imperialist/ nationalist' camp. Limonov's concerns for democracy were, at best, weakly developed, and it seemed unlikely that he would find common ground with democrats like Kasparov. Nevertheless, the two worked closely together in the rather incongruous movement 'The other Russia' (*Drugaia Rossiia*), which made waves with its resolve to face down the Russian riot police.

As pointed out in Chapter 6, at the beginning of Putin's second term, a new generation of Russian nationalists came to the fore. Less concerned with state grandeur, they focused narrowly on the interests of ethnic Russians, which, as they saw it, were threatened by the influx of non-Russian labour migrants from the other post-Soviet states. In 2005, 'Movement Against Illegal Immigration' (DPNI), together with other like-minded movements, began to organise annual 'Russian Marches' in Moscow and other cities on 4 November, attracting thousands of participants. This was possible because, at that time, the Russian authorities treated nationalists and liberals in the opposition very differently. While even minuscule gatherings of liberals were routinely broken up by the police, the nationalists – sometimes after some hassling – were generally permitted to march. Therefore, the fact that the nationalists were able to mobilise far larger crowds than the liberals was not necessarily an indication of their greater popularity among the population at large.

In late 2010, one year before the mass protest movement commenced, the attitude of the state authorities towards the new nationalists hardened markedly. The immediate trigger was a huge gathering on 11 December of rowdy youth, who chanted nationalist slogans in Manezh Square just behind the Kremlin. The increasingly jittery authorities now tried to bring the extreme nationalists under control: as a result, DPNI was banned. They retaliated by moving from a semi-tolerated/semi-loyal position into hard opposition. Other Russian ethno-nationalists too – in particular, the 'Russian Societal Movement' (*Russkoe obshchestvennoe dvizhenie*, or ROD), the precursor of the National-Democratic Party –adopted a harsh anti-Putin stance. They held that the Russian state under Putin failed to take sufficient consideration of the needs of ethnic Russians, tolerated a criminal regime in Chechnya under Ramzan Kadyrov, and let too many Central Asian migrants into the country.

The nationalists' new-found rejection of the Putinist regime paved the way for cooperation with liberals in the opposition. In the mass demonstrations of winter/spring 2011/12 several Russian nationalists addressed the crowds – including Aleksandr Belov-Potkin from the banned DPNI and Konstantin Krylov and Vladimir Tor from ROD. However, that did not mean that all tensions and disagreements between the liberals and the nationalists had been smoothed out.

THE RUSSIAN WINTER OF DISCONTENT – NATIONALIST PARTICIPATION

The Russian liberal newspaper *Novaia gazeta* has carried minute-by-minute descriptions of most of the major demonstrations in Moscow in 2011/12, both summaries of the speeches delivered from the podium and reports from the atmosphere among the multitudes on the squares. On 10 December its journalist reported that at 2.20 pm 'nationalists with imperial flags arrived at Revolution Square. Asked about how they reacted to the fact that most of those who took part in the demonstration did not share their views, they responded that now this is not important: "The main thing is to unite and get rid of the country's regime of thieves".' ROD leader Konstantin Krylov was quoted as saying that 'this is the beginning of the Russian Revolution' ('Miting na Bolotnoi' 2011).

The willingness of the nationalists to accept other people's views, however, had clear limits. At the next major manifestation fourteen days later, at Andrei Sakharov Square on 24 December, it was reported that many of them heckled and booed[2] speakers not to their liking, including the former high-society celebrity Ksenia Sobchak. There were also more or less open altercations among liberal and nationalist speakers at the podium. For instance, nationalist leader Vladimir Tor sardonically deplored having to take the floor right after Putin's former Minister of Finance, the liberal Aleksei Kudrin. When Tor went on to declare that 'Russia has to become a free, national, democratic state of the Russian (*russkii*) people,' he was met by the same kind of heckling that his followers in the crowd had directed against liberal speakers. Taking the microphone right after Tor, the strongly anti-nationalist liberal Vladimir Ryzhkov announced that he, in fact, had a better slogan than Tor: instead of 'Russia for Russians' he was in favor of 'Russia for everyone' ('Miting na prospekte 2011).

A group of anarchists in the crowd shouted 'Down with fascism!' Shortly thereafter, when some nationalists tried to enter the podium, a tense situation arose. In his address to the rally, the nationalist Krylov tried to reconcile people's differences and cool down the hotheads. He insisted that he was very happy to see them all there, both leftists and rightists, including all those who had booed. Krylov's slogan was 'one for all and all for one!' ('Miting na prospekte' 2011; see also 'Za chestnye' 2011; 'Miting 24' 2011).[3]

More demonstrations were held throughout the spring of 2012. The numbers of participants gradually declined but remained in the five-digit range. Liberals, socialists and nationalists walked in separate columns, and were allowed to frame their protest as they saw fit. They had their own symbols, placards and flags: red or red/black flags for the socialists and anarchists, white–blue–red for the liberals and black–gold–white for the nationalists. The last of these, originally a symbol of the Tsarists and imperialists, had later been adopted as a common symbol for Russian nationalists of all hues, including the ethno-nationalists. The only symbol common to all participants was the White Ribbon.

Some of the organisers were concerned that different flags were not enough to distinguish the various groups from each other in the marches, and suggested that the separate columns should be divided by a space of some 10 to 15 m. In the end, however, it was decided to leave the organisation of the columns to the participants themselves (Markedonov and Reznik 2012).

When the demonstrators arrived at the designated meeting places, the various ideological groups positioned themselves in different parts of the square: nationalists, fittingly, to the right, socialists to the left. In this way they were able to promote the same cause together while keeping their separate identities, without too much squabbling.

At all times there was considerable distrust and tension among the various factions. The nationalist leaders did not always manage to control 'their' part of the demonstration, and there was often destructive behaviour. While a certain number of nationalist leaders were represented among the speakers on the podium on most occasions, on 10 March there were none – and 200 nationalists left the rally in protest (Alperovich et al. 2013).

A mechanism for negotiating differences between liberals, leftists and nationalists in the opposition was already established by late 2011, when the rightists and leftists jointly promoted the idea of establishing ideology-based quotas in the organising committee, the 'Citizens' Council'. In addition to a general, non-ideological group of thirty people, an equal number were appointed in three ideological caucuses – liberal, leftist and nationalist – with ten members in each (Alperovich et al. 2013).

Meeting places and the sizes of the demonstrations were negotiated with the city authorities. Throughout March, the rallies, not only in Moscow but also in most other cities, had received official sanction in advance. However, once Putin had been elected President on 4 March, the federal Russian authorities introduced a harder, and much more confrontational line. The eve of Putin's inauguration, 6 May, proved to be the turning point. The demonstration that day had also been sanctioned, but nevertheless resulted in violent clashes with the police. Several hundred people were arrested and some were given prison sentences of up to several years.

The window of opportunity for public manifestations, which had opened in December the year before, was now closing, and the anti-system opposition sought new forums for channelling their protests and coordinating their activities. This was the backdrop for the initiative to establish the 'Coordinating Council of the Opposition' in June 2012. In the Internet-based elections to this council everyone was invited to vote for their preferred candidates in one of four categories or 'caucuses' [*kurii*]: 30 members of the Council would be elected on a common 'general civic' [*obshchegrazhdanskii*] list, while 15 seats were set aside for oppositionists who were known to represent a particular ideological colour. Leftists, centrists (liberals) and nationalists had five seats each. This arrangement was reminiscent of the separate quotas in the Citizens' Council in the 'street phase' of the protests in the winter, but the ideological quotas were now proportionately smaller – 15 members of a body of 45 rather than 30 out of 60 (Epifanova 2012a).[4] At the same time, it was possible for nationalists, as for everybody else, to run for election in the 'common' or 'general-civic' category too. Competition in the 'general-civic' caucus was harder: roughly six people ran for each seat in this caucus, as against an average of two in the ideological caucuses (Kuz'menkova 2012). There was a fee of 5,000–10,000 rubles for registering as a candidate (Zheleznova 2012). A few nationalists, like the highly controversial but influential neo-Nazi leader and anti-gay activist Maksim Martsinkevich ('the Hatchet'), who was very popular among the extreme right, were denied registration in the 'general-civic' caucus, although in theory it was to be open to all (Kuz'menkova 2012).

At the first elections to the Coordinating Council, held in October 2012, some 80,000 people availed themselves of the possibility to vote (Greene 2014, 215). No known nationalists made it into the 'general-civic' caucus, even though several known nationalists were running (Alperovich et al. 2013; Epifanova 2012b; Kuz'menkova 2012). The dismal performance of the nationalists when they were exposed to open competition indicated that they had less support among the grassroots anti-Putin opposition than many had expected

(Lipskii 2012). The winners in the nationalist caucus were two of the speakers from Bolotnaia Square and Sakharov Square, Vladimir Tor and Konstantin Krylov, together with three lesser-known figures.[5] Two of the organisers of the 'Russian Marches', Aleksandr Belov-Potkin and Dmitrii Demushkin, ran unsuccessfully in the nationalist caucus.

Whereas the Council had been intended to showcase how the opposition could carry out constructive work and collaborate across ideological divides, it achieved the opposite. Almost from the start it was paralysed by lack of consensus and willingness to compromise, and several prominent members soon withdrew. In the end, the Council no longer had a quorum and could not pass any decisions.[6] Even so, an executive commission led by nationalist Vladimir Tor took the initiative to convoke a second Council – which fared little better.

The establishment of special ideological caucuses had been controversial from the start. Kseniia Sobchak had argued that it contravened general democratic principles (Ivashkina 2012), and in a commentary in the liberal newspaper *Novaia gazeta*, journalist Andrei Kolesnikov later opined that the opposition had made a mistake by inviting the nationalists into their ranks and thus giving them an official mandate. Even if the rhetoric of the new Russian nationalists had been drained of its most radical language, they still had a hidden agenda that went against the principles and goals of the rest of the opposition, Kolesnikov claimed. The fact that the new Russian nationalists were currently dressed up in 'respectable forms' should not fool anyone, he maintained (Kolesnikov 2012).

Bridge-Builders . . .

As we saw in the section on social movement theory, the presence of credible bridge-builders with a broad appeal is seen as essential for the establishment of successful movement coalitions. In the anti-regime mobilisation of 2011/12 several such bridge-builders were active. Most famous, and probably also most influential, was blogger and corruption fighter Aleksei Navalny. He had a background in the legally registered social-democratic Yabloko Party, but had been expelled in December 2007 for nationalist deviations (Voronkov 2012, 215–23). Earlier that year, he had established a new movement called 'Narod' together with nationalists like the popular writer Zakhar Prilepin from the National Bolshevik Party. 'Narod' espoused both nationalist and democratic ideas (Kolstø 2014, 128; Laruelle 2014d).

Navalny regularly attended the 4 November 'Russian Marches' and addressed their rallies on several occasions. At the same time, he retained his democratic credentials, and prominent liberals like novelist Boris Akunin (2012) vouched for him. Indeed, Navalny was one of the few opposition leaders who could appeal to people in all camps. During the preparations for the demonstrations on 4 February 2012 he opposed the division of the marchers into separate 'columns'. Rhetorically, he asked: 'and which column do you think I should walk in – among the nationalists or the liberals?' (Girin et al. 2012). As Navalny himself and many others saw it, he incarnated the absurdity of splitting the demonstrators into separate ideological camps. Writing in February 2014, the journalist Grigorii Revzin in *Ekho Moskvy* argued that the mission of Aleksei Navalny was to reconcile 'the White Ribbon people' with 'the Russian March' people. 'The Ukrainian experience shows clearly that without such unity it is impossible to prevail over the ruling regime. But if it is achieved, the chances for victory grow sharply' (Revzin 2014).

Navalny was not the only bridge-builder in the opposition: the leading ethno-nationalist ideologue Konstantin Krylov can also be described using that term. His Russian Social Movement (ROD) would soon evolve into a new nationalist party, pointedly called the National-Democratic Party. Krylov fully realised that 'democracy' is an extremely elastic word which can be taken to mean very many different things, but he insisted that his own vision of democracy was identical to the Western, European model.[7] Yet, he was also one of the co-organisers of the annual 'Russian March', where far less democratic slogans could be heard. Navalny (2013), however, had written on his *LiveJournal* blog that it was the moderating efforts of Krylov and other members of the National-Democratic Party that had made it possible for him to participate in these marches (see also Moen-Larsen 2014).

Finally, mention should be made of a third important bridge-builder. Garri Kasparov, an old hand from the anti-Putin opposition, had substantial experience in navigating among its various factions. As mentioned, he had collaborated with Eduard Limonov in the 'Other Russia' alliance in the early 2000s, and took this tolerant attitude with him into the 2011–12 cycle of protest. On 28 January 2012, he participated at a meeting held in the Russian Union of Writers' building in Moscow, where the nationalists discussed whether they should continue to take part in the anti-Putin demonstrations. Kasparov took the floor with a speech that clearly played to audience sentiments: among other things, he castigated Putin for having returned to China the Damanski islands in the Amur river, 'where the blood of Soviet soldiers has been spilled'. This made Putin 'an enemy of Russia' ('Kasparov vystupil' 2012).

Kasparov's intervention at the meeting was well received by the majority. Both 'old' nationalists like Sergei Baburin and most 'new' nationalists – including Aleksandr Belov, Konstantin Krylov, Egor Kholmogorov, Boris Mironov and Vladimir Tor – agreed that it was necessary to 'maintain constant dialogue with the leftists and the liberals since their interests in these movements for the most part coincide' ('Garry Kasparov' 2012). In his *LiveJournal* blog Krylov acknowledged that 'some people from the liberal camp' did not want to see them at the rally. 'However, our principled position is to take part in and support joint civic manifestations. Simply because we are nationalists: we want to be together with the people – and consequently have to be where the people are' (Krylov 2011b).

While social movement theory focuses on the role of bridge-builders, less attention has been paid to the converse phenomenon, what we might call 'bridge-wreckers', or 'spoilers'. The concept of the spoiler is well established in election studies and in the field of international relations, but is also important for understanding the dynamics of social movements. In the Russian anti-systemic opposition in 2011/12, the attempts of bridge-builders to create broad coalitions were actively resisted by people and groups who did whatever they could to tear them apart.

At the nationalist strategy meeting on 28 January 2012, mentioned above, veteran Russian nationalist Aleksandr Sevast'ianov also participated. Returning home, he wrote on his *LiveJournal* blog that the meeting had left him 'in an abominable mood'. Sevast'ianov was adamantly opposed to any kind of alliance with Russian liberals, whom he regarded as 'enemies of the people, our MAIN adversaries; in leading positions among them we find revanchists whose most cherished reveries are to return Russia back to the times of Yeltsin'. Those nationalists who wanted to collaborate with the liberals reminded him of the Russian Nazi collaborators, the Vlasovites, during World War II: they had tried to topple Stalin's regime by supporting Hitler. But 'plague can never be cured by cholera' (Sevast'ianov 2012).

Interestingly, some Russian nationalists who did participate in the anti-Putin demonstrations also adopted a hard-nosed rhetoric towards the liberals. In advance of the 24 December demonstrations, Aleksandr Belov-Potkin appealed to the DPNI members to turn out in great numbers in order to put their stamp on the demonstrations. The initiators of the rally, he claimed, were a handful of former Yeltsinites who had been removed from power and now wanted to see as few nationalists as possible in the crowd: 'The liberals who pillaged the country in the 1990s are thirsting for revenge and are leading separate negotiations with the Kremlin. In exchange for squelching the people's protest they hope to be offered seats around the feeding-trough.' Therefore, the liberals would do whatever they could to throw a spanner into the nationalists' works, Belov claimed. They had ordered the Russian mass media – allegedly under their control – to ignore them or present them as *provocateurs*. But these tactics should not be allowed to succeed: the nationalists must turn up *en masse* at the Sakharov Square rally (Belov 2011).

A considerable number of nationalists were indeed present at the 24 December demonstrations, and several of their leaders – including Belov himself – were allowed to address the audience, belying his claim that the liberals were doing what they could to marginalise the nationalists. But Belov's war cry hardly prepared the ground for a fruitful collaboration between liberals and nationalists. Vladimir Tor, who likewise addressed the crowd, also cast aspersions on the liberal organisers: it was important that the massive wave of the people's protest should not 'be privatised by the scum [*pena*] left over from the Yeltsin flood' (quoted in Vezhin 2011). In a commentary in the *Nezavisimaia gazeta* newspaper, journalist Savelii Vezhin (2011) speculated that the nationalists might become 'a serious problem' to those liberals who attempted to play with them.

Up to a point, Belov and Tor were right: some liberal leaders indeed did not want to have anything to do with them. When it became clear that nationalists would participate in the 4 February rally at Bolotnaia, some veterans of the Democratic Movement, like Valeriia Novodvorskaia and businessman Konstantin Borovoi, decided to organise their own march on the same day. Boris Nemtsov called this a provocation, to which Borovoi replied that it was indeed his aim to split the democratic coalition. If Nemtsov and Co. carried on with their plans to arrange a rally together with fascists and communists, he would spend twice as much to denounce them to the public as they would spend on the rally (Allenova 2012). The official newspaper of the Russian government, *Rossiiskaia gazeta*, informed its readers that Borovoi's meeting was well equipped, and participants there would be taken good care of. He had ordered 4,500 litres of tea and forty boilers, and received permission for a gathering of 30,000 people ('Goriachaia subbota' 2012). Obviously, the authorities had nothing against a schism among the anti-Putinists, and *Rossiiskaia gazeta*'s rather broad coverage of Borovoi's meeting plans might be interpreted as a deliberate attempt to drive a wedge between them and wean potential participants away from Bolotnaia (Oates and Lokot 2013).[8] In the end, according to the organisers themselves, 1,000 people turned up at Novodvorskaia's and Borovoi's alternative gathering – according to the police, there were no more than 150 (Egorov and Petrov 2012).

If Novodvorskaia and Borovoi may be dismissed as rather marginal figures, it was significant that some leaders of the liberal PARNAS party, *in casu* Vladimir Ryzhkov, were also extremely sceptical of any kind of hobnobbing with the nationalists. In an interview with *Novaia gazeta* in September 2012, Ryzhkov explained that it would be impossible to criticise Putin for acting in contravention of the Constitution as long as the opposition allowed into their ranks people who respected basic constitutional rights no more than he did. 'The nationalists go against one of the most basic premises of the Constitution – the equality of all people before the law, irrespective of their nationality or creed.' Ryzhkov claimed that, originally, there had been no nationalists on the organisational committee, 'but they came and sat down at the table. We did not chase them away although we did not formally include them either. How did they get the floor at the rallies? Under pressure from certain committee members' (Masiuk 2012). As Ryzhkov made clear on numerous occasions, by 'certain members' he meant Navalny, first and foremost. Ryzhkov's co-chairs in PARNAS, however – Boris Nemtsov and Mikhail Kasianov – appreciated the effect of Navalny's charisma and were willing to gloss over ideological differences with him, and with other nationalists (Epifanova 2014). In St Petersburg, the conflict between the party purists in PARNAS and those party leaders who were willing to collaborate with moderate nationalists such as Navalny was particularly acute.[9] In the end, adherents of broad-based coalitions got the upper hand in that city too.

THE REGIME'S COUNTER-ATTACK

The authorities seem to have been at a loss to find the best way to react, and various representatives of the regime chose different tactics. Putin-loyal movements organised a number of counter-demonstrations, often to coincide with the opposition rallies. Their main slogans were 'We have something to lose', 'We oppose the orange plague' and 'Vladimir Putin and nobody else' ('Serdtsu ne prikazhesh' 2012; Smyth et al. 2013, 27). Regime-loyal media claimed that the crowds supporting Putin were larger than those organised by his detractors, which on several occasions may well have been true (Arsiukhin 2012). However, there are also many reports about pro-regime demonstrators being paid or coerced into participating, and bussed into Moscow from faraway regions (Smyth et al. 2013, 29).

Some prominent members of the United Russia party – which the demonstrators pilloried as 'a party of scoundrels and thieves' – accepted that there were indeed some rotten apples in their midst which ought to be thrown out. They organised a group called 'United Russia for honest elections' and began to wear White Ribbons themselves (Razmakhnin 2011).[10] Their initiative was not supported by the party leadership, however, and seems to have been abandoned rather quickly.

Vladimir Putin attempted to discredit the demonstrators by comparing their White Ribbon with a contraceptive (Gazeta.ru 2011; see also video in Putin 2011). Disingenuously, he claimed that when he saw the White Ribbon on the clothes of the protesters for the first time, he believed that they were wearing a condom. He had assumed that their rally was a campaign against AIDS, a disease, he remarked, which was of particular concern for young people. However, the sarcasm backfired on him: the oppositionists turned up in the next demonstration with placards proudly declaring that, in contrast to the President, they knew the difference between a ribbon and a contraceptive. The inventor of the White Ribbon, Elena Tikhonova, confidently predicted that, as a result of Putin's remarks, the movement would only grow stronger (Samsonova 2011).

The vehemence of some of the attacks on the White Ribbon suggests that the authorities perceived the 'snow revolution' as a serious challenge. Somewhat surprisingly, these attacks also continued after the momentum of the protest movement had waned. As late as October 2012 – one year after the launch of the ribbon campaign – the United Russia MP Alexander Sidiakin brought a White Ribbon with him to the lectern of the Duma and demonstratively trampled on it. By doing so, he declared, he was acting in the same way as the opposition was acting against his country. In his assessment, the White Ribbon was 'a symbol of capitulation and treason, it is an imported revolution which foreign political technologists are trying to press upon us' (Raibman 2012).[11]

The head of the cultural department in the Moscow city administration, Sergei Kapkov, explained on Russian TV that to wear a White Ribbon publicly could be considered a 'provocation'. He stopped short of issuing a formal ban against it but insinuated that the ribbon could easily be perceived by ordinary, law-abiding citizens as an affront and lead to brawls (Osharov 2013). The subtext of his message seemed to be that if the demonstrators were attacked on public transport, they themselves were to blame.

One of the most irate attacks on the White Ribbon was published in the communist daily *Pravda*, although the Communist Party was not a direct target of the snow revolution. A video posted on *Pravda*'s webpage drew a preposterous parallel between the white symbol and the armbands worn by guards in Nazi concentration camps, and the shape of the ribbon was allegedly reminiscent of a runic letter worn by the soldiers in an SS tank division on their uniforms (Pravda 2012). This outrageous claim was repeated on various websites.

Grassroots Support for the Anti-Putin Nationalists

How many sympathisers did the nationalists have at grassroots level? Here we must distinguish between those who actually participated in the demonstrations in 2011/12 and those who might have joined the opposition if the composition of its leadership had been different and the demonstrations had been framed differently. The latter question inevitably draws us into speculative terrain, but a survey which we commissioned in the autumn of 2014 allows some tentative conclusions.

During the 24 December demonstrations at Sakharov Square, which marked the peak of the anti-Putin opposition, both the Levada Center and VTsIOM conducted polls among the participants ('Kto vyshel' 2011; 'Mitinguiushschie' 2011). Their findings more or less coincided. The crowd was predominantly (60–64 per cent) male, with a remarkably high percentage of people with higher education – 62–70 per cent, far above the average Russian level. And while four out of five Russians get most of their news from television, the main source of information for 70 per cent of the demonstrators was the Internet. Far from representing a cross-section of the Russian population, the demonstrators were clearly an elite group.

Levada asked respondents to state their political position, among ten options. Five of these – anarchist, 'antifa', 'new left', communist and Social Democrat – could be qualified as 'leftist'; together, they were chosen by roughly 30 per cent of the respondents. Another 69 per cent declared that they were either 'democrats' or 'liberals', while only 3 per cent presented themselves as 'conservatives' or 'national patriots' (6 per cent) ('Kto vyshel' 2011).[12] VTsIOM asked in an open-ended question about the respondents' reasons for coming to the rally, and none of the answers they gave can be seen as distinctly 'nationalist'. As to which of the slogans heard at the rally they agreed with, a mere 1 per cent supported 'a more sensible migration policy'; no other matter typically associated with nationalist positions was recorded.

Respondents were also asked by Levada to name the party they would vote for in a hypothetical election to the state Duma, in which non-registered parties were also allowed to participate. One out of four would have voted for Yabloko and 11 per cent for the communists, with PARNAS garnering 10 per cent. Finally, 2 per cent chose the alternative 'a party of Russian nationalists (Aleksandr Belov/Dmitrii Rogozin)' – again, less than a ringing endorsement for an explicitly nationalist agenda among those who wanted to get rid of the Putin regime. However, 19 per cent expressed a willingness to vote for 'Aleksei Navalny's new party', so a combination of liberalism, populism and nationalism – a sort of 'nationalism light' – may be seen as having support in the crowd. Moreover, Navalny himself was more popular than his party: 36 per cent claimed that they trusted him, as against 3 per cent and 2 per cent who trusted the nationalist leaders Aleksandr Belov and Vladimir Tor, respectively. It seems that nationalists were better represented on the podium than among the people below.[13]

How was the protest movement perceived by the Russian population at large – specifically, by the citizens of Moscow and St Petersburg, where the largest demonstrations took place? To shed light on these questions we commissioned a survey in September/October 2014, with 1,000 respondents nationwide and additional boost surveys in three major cities, each with 600 respondents: Moscow, St Petersburg and Ekaterinburg. The reason behind this selection was that we expected to find a higher number of demonstration participants in the cities than in the country at large, but this was not the case: roughly 3.5 per cent of our respondents reported that they had taken part in anti-regime demonstrations, either once (2 per cent) or several times (1.5 per cent). Surprisingly, Moscow reported the lowest turnout: 1 per cent and 2 per cent, respectively; however, with such low figures the margin of error is too great to permit any firm conclusions.

At the same time, 26–27 per cent in our polls expressed the view that 'Russia is not a democracy', and 30–32 per cent deemed that the December 2011 parliamentary elections had not been free and fair. (The March 2012 presidential elections were perceived as slightly better: only 25 per cent saw them as unfair.) This might indicate that there was a reservoir of resentment and opposition in the Russian population which the organisers of the 2011/12 demonstrations were able to tap into only to a very small degree.

Asked to state their own political affiliation, only 11 per cent nationwide described themselves as 'democrats'; an additional 5 per cent chose 'liberals' (5 per cent). The number of self-declared democrats was somewhat higher in Moscow (16.5 per cent), and particularly so in St Petersburg (26.5 per cent). Interestingly, Ekaterinburg was the city with the lowest percentage of self-declared democrats (7.3 per cent) but with the highest percentage of participants in the winter demonstrations (5.3 per cent), indicating that there was no necessary link between democratic convictions and anti-Putin activism.

We also asked people whether or not they regarded the demonstrations as a lawful democratic attempt to express a political opinion, or as an attempt to remove the legitimate authorities by unlawful means. Some 36.6 per cent nationwide and 43–44 per cent in the cities said they regarded the demonstrations as lawful. As to why they believed people took to the streets, we had the responses shown in Table 8.1 (participants could choose several options):

Table 8.1: 'In your view, the demonstrations were organized ...' (%)

	Nationwide	Moscow	St Petersburg	Ekaterinburg
To protest against election fraud in the December 2011 elections	35.9	23.5	41.8	20.1
To protest against 'castling' – the decision that Putin should become President and Medvedev Prime Minister	22.6	23.0	38.2	11.8
To protest against falling living standards	22.4	25.3	22.2	17.4
To protest against the uncontrolled immigration of 'guest workers'	9.1	15.7	8.8	12.1
Because they were paid by somebody	23.6	38.8	29.0	17.4
Other reasons	2.4	1.8	2.0	1.7
Don't know	21.6	20.7	12.8	41.0

We see that respondents in St Petersburg, the city with the highest percentage of self-declared democrats, more than the others tended to view the demonstrations as a manifestation of democratic aspirations. All over the country, a significant minority saw the state's migration policy as at least one of the reasons why people were turning out in the streets – from 9 per cent (St Petersburg) to 16 per cent (Moscow). This, as we saw above, did not reflect the realities: among of those polled during the demonstrations only 1 in 100 supported slogans in favour of 'a more sensible migration policy'. The fact that Muscovites, to a higher degree than others in our poll, focused on the migration issue as an explanatory factor behind the demonstrations probably reflects the prominence of that issue in the public debate in the capital (Tolz and Harding 2015; Blakkisrud and Kolstø 2018).

Furthermore, we see that a substantial number of respondents in our survey assumed the demonstrators to be venal, driven by pecuniary motives. This was corroborated by responses to another question, where we asked about whom they assumed had organised the demonstrations. Responses were distributed as shown in Table 8.2. Respondents could choose several options.

When we asked in a follow-up question those who had answered 'agents from foreign countries' who these agents might be, they split into two roughly equal groups: one half responded 'Western pro-democracy NGOs and governments' and the other 'the CIA and/or other Western intelligence services'. Cross-tabulations showed that self-declared 'patriots' and 'nationalists' were not overrepresented among those who saw some nefarious force behind the demonstrations.

Finally, respondents were asked to describe how they saw the ideological colouring of the demonstrations (see Table 8.3). Evidently, many Russians have fuzzy notions about what the 2011/12 demonstrators actually wanted. This is shown both by the high percentage of 'don't knows' and also by the even spread of answers among the other response options. Somewhat more people assumed

Table 8.2: 'In your view, who took the initiative to organise the protests after the 2011/12 elections?' (%)

	Nationwide	Moscow	St Petersburg	Ekaterinburg
Political parties	39.7	44.0	47.5	36.6
The citizens themselves	27.5	29.0	34.3	16.8
Agents from foreign countries	19.2	24.0	17.0	13.5
Non-governmental organisations	8.2	13.7	10.3	9.3
Social networks	7.1	6.8	4.2	4.5
Hard to say	24.7	22.0	14.5	37.4

Table 8.3: 'In my view, the demonstrations were basically ...' (%)

	Nationwide	Moscow	St Petersburg	Ekaterinburg
A liberal-democratic anti-government manifestation	12.4	12.7	13.8	11.6
A nationalist anti-government manifestation	9.8	7.7	7.3	3.0
A leftist anti-government manifestation	9.0	13.2	10.5	5.5
A broad-based coalition of all the above	17.3	16.2	16.7	14.6
An incoherent manifestation with very unclear political goals	18.3	21.8	22.2	18.6
Don't know	33.2	28.5	29.5	46.7

that the organisers were pursuing a liberal, democratic agenda, but quite a few respondents saw the rallies as a nationalist or a leftist manifestation.

Finally, when we asked people to state their political position, only 10 per cent in our poll described themselves as 'democrats'; 3 per cent were 'nationalists' and a hefty 35 per cent identified themselves as 'patriots'. It would be a mistake, however, to see the 'patriots' as potential oppositionists who might have been nudged into joining the demonstrations if nationalist slogans had been more prominent in them. In official Russian terminology 'nationalism' is a four-letter word, whereas 'patriotism' is a civic duty. Generally speaking, only people who oppose the Putin regime use 'nationalism' as a label of self-identification. This came out clearly when we cross-tabulated political orientation with trust in various political figures. On a scale from 1 to 10, only 1.4 per cent of the 'nationalists' gave Vladimir Putin a score of 10 – but as much as 42.3 per cent of the 'patriots' did so.[14] Clearly, in Russia 'patriotism' expresses a (positive) attitude not only towards the nation, but also towards the regime, so simply beefing up the nationalist slogans in the marches would not have swelled the ranks of the demonstrators.

CONCLUSIONS

Social movement theory sees broad-based coalitions as one route to success, and this was the path taken by the organisers of the anti-Putin demonstrations in winter 2011/2012. All those who opposed the Putin regime and the undemocratic elections that kept him and his entourage in power were welcome to participate in the marches and rallies. Most evidence indicates that this broad alliance was not the outcome of strategic decisions. While the original initiators behind the rallies hailed from the ranks of the liberals, nationalists responded to the call to participate, as did other people, bringing their banners and symbols with them. The liberal organisers saw no reason to turn them away, at least not as long as they refrained from trying to obstruct the rallies. However, that was exactly what many of the nationalists did. At the rallies, they excelled in heckling speakers they did not like, and occasionally also tried to storm the podium. As observed by the SOVA Analytical Center, 'originally, the ultra-right intended not merely to participate, but to take the initiative away from the hated liberals and leftists who, in their opinion, usurped the protest'. In practice, however, 'they had to settle for the role of extras, who, also, never received a particularly warm welcome from the rest of the opposition' (Alperovich et al. 2013).

The main point which linked all the factions in the Bolotnaia and Sakharov Square demonstrations was their rejection of, even repulsion towards, the Putin regime. It would go against the democratic convictions of the liberals to screen participants ideologically. The broad base of the coalition reflected a sense of moral decency more than any tactical deliberations. In addition, as pointed out by Aleksandr Verkhovsky, a keen observer of the contemporary Russian nationalist movement, it would have been technically almost impossible to chase them away from the rather spontaneously organised rallies. The opposition had no 'cut-off point' for ideological stances which they might have regarded as unacceptable at their meetings. Verkhovsky (2012) also speculates that, for a moderate nationalist like Navalny, it was important to include less moderate nationalists in the gatherings in order to show that he was not an extremist himself, thereby strengthening his own position in the movement as a 'centrist'.

Stanislav Minin believes that the real winners of the broad-based collaboration in the anti-regime opposition were the nationalists. In his view, the fact that they were given their own quota on the Coordinating Council proved that the liberals needed them, but for the nationalists themselves the Council and the rallies were just 'temporary platforms' which granted them access to a larger audience than before. 'Whether or not they managed to increase their number of adherents [during the protest movement] is another question, but it was a chance, and a good one at that' (Minin 2012).

For the nationalist leaders, however, their success in being accepted into the broader opposition movement was a Pyrrhic victory at best. Scepticism towards, if not to say hatred of, the liberals was deep-seated among the rank and file in the nationalist movement and many of them saw the fraternising of some of the most prominent nationalists with pro-Western liberals as a betrayal. This seems to have a weakened the nationalist movement from within.

The Russian 'winter of discontent' never developed into a spring; at most, it can be characterised as a 'thaw'. Moreover, the political climate in Russia after this thaw has been colder than before it started. We can note, however, that already before the authorities introduced new and draconian anti-demonstration and anti-opposition laws in June 2012, this cycle of the protest movement was coming to an end.

The willingness of Russian liberals and right-wing nationalists to set aside old grudges in a concerted effort to topple the regime was, in all likelihood, a major factor behind the early successes of the mobilisation. However, it was precisely this new, all-embracing alliance that proved to be the weak point in their strategy in the long run.

The anti-Putin protesters did many things right. For instance, the selection of the White Ribbon as a unifying symbol, it seems, was in many ways felicitous, but it turned out to be too thin and fragile to tie the disparate elements of the opposition together. Moreover, as Zdravomyslova (1996) points out, while the communist symbols and clichés were widely discredited by the mid-1980s, the Putin regime had been rather resourceful in devising new symbols and rituals that seem to resonate well among large swaths of the population. As discussed in the previous chapter, by means of the St George ribbon and the Immortal Regiment the Putin regime managed to tap into the sacred memory of victory over Nazism and present itself as the legitimate custodian of this legacy. In the duel between the orange–black and the white ribbons, the former has carried the day. This battle does indeed divide the Russian nation, but it is not split into two halves of equal size. The supporters of the White Ribbon remain a minority.

Notes

1. At least two people have been credited with coming up with the idea of the White Ribbon: Elena Tikhonova (see Samsonova 2011) and Arsen Revazov.
2. Or, more precisely, whistled: the Russian equivalent of booing.
3. The slogan was promoted by Navalny, while earlier it was known as a slogan of football hooligans; of course, it refers back to Dumas's *Three Musketeers*.
4. The nationalist parties held what they call their 'primaries' prior to the council elections to decide which nationalists should run in their caucus.
5. Nikolai Bondarik, Igor Artemov and Daniil Konstantinov. Konstantinov was serving a prison sentence for murder on what were widely regarded as trumped-up and politically motivated charges. Prevented from participating in the Council, he was represented by his father, old-time nationalist Ilia Konstantinov. Author's interview with Konstantinov, Moscow, October 2011.
6. Author's interview with Vladimir Tor, October 2011.
7. Author's interview with Krylov in Moscow, October 2013.
8. However, I have not been able to find any signs of a systematic smear campaign in *Rossiiskaia gazeta* or other pro-regime newspapers. During spring 2012, coverage of the anti-system opposition seems to have been more balanced than most times before and after. I have not studied television coverage, but this has been done by Oates and Lokot (2013), who found that reporting on Channel One was particularly unsympathetic.

9. Author's email exchange with Andrei Pivovarov, leader of the winning faction in the St Petersburg chapter of PARNAS, 15 November 2014.
10. Among them were prominent social figures such as sociologist Olga Kryshtanovskaia.
11. The fact that the website of the White Ribbon campaign was on an American Internet provider was seen as evidence that the initiative behind it came from abroad. See Steshin 2011.
12. Respondents could choose several options.
13. Alperovich et al. (2013) estimate that the greatest numbers of nationalist participants were registered at the demonstration on 4 February – when around 900 people could be identified as nationalists. Later, the figures declined precipitously: no more than 100 nationalists in Pushkin Square on 5 March, and 300 in Novy Arbat on 10 March. The 6 May demonstrations at Bolotnaia – which led to clashes with the police – were generally ignored by the nationalists. On this occasion around 100 activists from the 'Greater Russia' party showed up, only to turn away in protest before the march started, to show their contempt for the entire undertaking.
14. Figures for the other categories were 3.1 per cent for 'liberals'; 0.3 per cent for 'leftists'; 8.5 per cent for 'democrats'; and 3.8 per cent for 'communists'.

9

CRIMEA VERSUS DONBAS:
RUSSIAN NATIONALIST REACTIONS

The Putin regime has proved particularly apt at co-opting various kinds of nationalism and using them as tools of legitimation. As I point out in Chapter 8, many Russian nationalists joined the opposition against Putin during the massive anti-regime demonstrations in 2011/12. Although Putin managed to consolidate the situation when he returned to the presidency in May 2012, that was initially achieved primarily by coercive methods that alienated large parts of the population. Two years later, however, support for the regime increased when the annexation of Crimea was carried out under explicit nationalist slogans: Crimea was presented as 'ancient Russian land', and as the cradle of the Russian Church, since Vladimir the Great, who made Orthodoxy the state religion in the Kiev state, had been baptised there.

It would be simplistic to explain the annexation of Crimea as a mere ploy to tap into Russian patriotic sentiments. The motives behind this surprise move were varied: the severe deterioration of relations with the West as well as disappointment at Ukraine's perceived 'defection' to the Western camp. Even so, the return of Crimea to Russia could indeed appeal to the two major strands of Russian nationalists normally at loggerheads with each other: the 'imperialists' and the 'ethno-nationalists'. Those who wanted to see the Russian/Soviet Empire restored saw this territorial expansion as a first step in that direction, whereas the ethno-nationalists gleefully noted that Putin presented this action as a necessary move for reuniting 'the divided Russian nation'. In that way, he managed to steal the thunder from all his nationalist opponents in one fell swoop.

The nationalist euphoria did not last long. In the war in Eastern Ukraine, which commenced shortly thereafter, Russia-supported rebels were pitted against Ukrainian forces, resulting in thousands of casualties. Russia intervened surreptitiously, and failed to engage decisively. Many nationalists saw this is a betrayal of the Russian cause and withdrew the backing they had given to Putin shortly before. This turn of events shows how fickle the support of true-believer nationalists can be, but also how dexterous state leaders can pull nationalism out of the hat and then put it back in again, without unleashing a backlash, leaving the nationalists and not the regime isolated. In a consolidated authoritarian regime like Russia, nationalism is one strategy which may be administered to the population in carefully measured doses.

An important instrument in the strategy to muster support for the war in Donbas was the the St George ribbon. As described in Chapter 7, by 2014 this symbol had already been used for a number of years to boost the legitimacy of the Putin regime by linking the current power-holders in Moscow to the victory in World War II; now the affection engendered by the sacred memory of the suffering and heroic exploits seventy years ago was transplanted a second time, to rally the nation around the new, undeclared war in Eastern Ukraine. In this chapter I analyse how the nationalist segment of the public attempted to interpret and evaluate the fast-evolving Ukrainian scene, in particular the Crimean annexation and the war in Eastern Ukraine.[1]

Close on the heels of the Euromaidan revolution in late February followed the appearance of the 'little green men' in Crimea, with formal Russian annexation of the peninsula on 18 March. Before the impact of this momentous event could be fully digested, insurrections broke out in the Donbas, soon escalating to fully-fledged war with thousands of casualties. The carnage was punctuated by cease-fires that raised short-lived hopes which were soon dashed. Russian TV showed footage of maimed Russian speakers by their devastated homes in East Ukrainian towns and hamlets, stirring up Russians in Russia, who immediately – not least on nationalist websites – engaged in the classic Russian debates 'Kto vinovat'? (Who is to blame?) and 'Chto delat'?' (What should be done?).

The Crimean takeover was justified in the Kremlin with use of nationalist rhetoric not previously heard from the Putinist team. Initially, this rhetoric paid off, boosting Putin's popularity ratings to unprecedented levels and, with a few notable exceptions, also endearing him to nationalistically inclined Russians (Alexseev and Hale 2016). As pointed out in Chapter 6, Putin could now present himself at the same time as the foremost defender of ethnic Russians abroad as well as of Russia's national interests, making it possible to present himself as 'the biggest nationalist in Russia' (Putin 2014c).

The war in Eastern Ukraine antagonised the nationalist segment of the Russian public that had been won over by the Kremlin only months earlier. The Kremlin's nationalist framing of the Crimean annexation hinted that not only Russians on the peninsula but also Russian speakers elsewhere in Ukraine were discriminated against and had a legitimate right to rebel. While the Crimean takeover was clearly engineered from Moscow,[2] the causes behind the Donbas rebellion are more contested. Some commentators have maintained that the war in Eastern Ukraine was part of the Kremlin's original plan, whether in order to secure a land bridge to Crimea or to destabilise the Ukrainian state (see e.g. Shekhovtsov 2014). Others hold that the initiative was local: insurgents acting on their own presented Putin and his team with a *fait accompli* (Kudelia 2014; Sakwa 2015, 180–1).[3] They were emboldened by the successful, bloodless takeover of the Crimean peninsula to attempt similar coups themselves. Andrew Wilson, in his *The Ukraine Crisis* (2014), admits that we do not know much about Putin's frequently shifting strategy, but surmises that 'Putin's original strategy may have been to build up the separatists' authority to force Kyiv to negotiate with him. But the local population was allowing the tail to wag the dog' (Wilson 2014, 133). Putin 'rode the tiger of the Russian nationalism which had been unleashed' (Wilson 2015). If so, Russia had allowed itself to be dragged into a war not of its own making and over which it had only limited control.

Faced with the choice of abandoning the separatists to their own fate, intervening openly in the warfare on their side, or clandestinely supporting them with weaponry and manpower, the Kremlin chose the third course. This strategy created difficulties at home. While virtually all Western observers and politicians are convinced about Russia's active involvement in the Donbas, the official version about Russian detachment was widely believed at home. To show the world that Russia is not an aggressor, the Putin regime has been presenting itself as reacting rather than acting: it is not calling the shots. Russia's involvement came late, was limited and intermittent, never officially recognised by the Kremlin, and unable to enforce a military solution.

THE ROLE OF NATIONALISM IN PUTIN'S STRATEGY

Prior to the Crimean annexation Putin had made only limited use of nationalism, for several reasons. First, most of the main Russian opposition parties were actively playing the nationalist card and would probably be able to outbid the Putin regime in a game of nationalistic competition. Second, while adopting a strongly nationalist stance might endear Putin to parts of the electorate, it would certainly alienate others – in Russia, as elsewhere, nationalism is a potentially divisive issue (Hale 2016). And third, there exists not *one* brand of nationalism in Russia but many, which are often at cross-purposes. As discussed in Chapter 6, the major distinction runs between the ethno-nationalists and the 'imperial nationalists' (or '*impertsy*'). While the former are primarily concerned about the rights and interests of ethnic Russians, the '*impertsy*' focus on strong Russian statehood, increased Russian influence abroad, and even territorial expansion of the Russian state. Finally, as long as the economy was performing well and the regime was favourably compared to the chaotic Yeltsin years, Putin could surf high popularity polls without experimenting with nationalist rhetoric.

All this was to change, however. True, Russia weathered the 2008 financial crisis reasonably well, but the ensuing economic slowdown jeopardised the tacit social contract, whereby the populace, in return for increasing living standards, allowed the Kremlin to rule through manipulated elections and other undemocratic means. Hundreds of thousands of demonstrators took to the streets to protest against the rigged Duma elections of December 2011, and Putin's popularity ratings took a downturn. These events apparently convinced him that he had lost the support of the urban, liberal intelligentsia, so he sought to appeal to other voter groups – the rural, the religious, the conservative and the anti-Western. The Kremlin launched a campaign for the defence of 'traditional values', opposition to 'non-traditional relations between sexes' and other kinds of 'cultural miasma' from the West (Laruelle 2016b). The strategy worked reasonably well, and it is in this light that the nationalistic rhetoric used to justify the annexation of Crimea should be seen (Wilkinson 2014; Hale 2016; Bluhm and Brand 2019).

This is not to say that the Crimean invasion was conducted in order to prop up domestic support for Putin. No doubt there were also other important reasons, like the perceived need to keep the Sevastopol naval base under secure Russian control, and the gut feeling that Russia had been slighted by the West ever since the fall of the Berlin Wall; this, the Russian leadership believed, gave them a moral right to act unilaterally in Crimea, as the West had done in Kosovo and Iraq (see e.g. Tucker 2014). Moreover, the Kremlin could feel confident that the Crimean 'land grab' would be applauded by the Russian public. It was ideally suited as a nationalist strategy, since it could appeal to *both* main strands of current Russian nationalism at the same time. It was hailed by the ethno-nationalists as protecting allegedly threatened ethnic Russians abroad, *and* welcomed by the imperial nationalists as a first step towards the 'resurrection of the Russian Empire' (Prokhanov 2014b). For a while, many Russian nationalists who had previously been solidly entrenched in the anti-Kremlin opposition became fervent supporters of the Putin regime.

THE BIFURCATED RUSSIAN NATIONALIST SCENE

The various movements normally subsumed under the common designation of 'Russian nationalism' represent a far more variegated phenomenon than what is often assumed. As noted, the major fault-line runs between the imperialists and the ethno-nationalists. It is no doubt true that some nationalists use arguments that are both ethnocentric and oriented towards empire restoration, and it may therefore be difficult to place them squarely in one of the two camps. Even so, the leading ideologues on each side regard each other as bitter enemies

(Krylov 2011a, 3). In addition, there are significant disagreements and squabbles within each of these two camps.

As pointed out in Chapter 6, most (but not all) Russian ethno-nationalists present themselves as democrats. The nation-state they yearn for is a democracy – in contrast to the kleptocratic oligarchy which, they claim, now rules in the Kremlin. A number of unregistered ethno-nationalist proto-parties (most of which have later been banned or have ceased to exist for other reasons) had the word 'democratic' in the name: Konstantin Krylov's National-Democratic Party (NDP), Il'ia Lazarenko's National-Democratic Alliance (NDA) and Vladimir Milov's 'Democratic Choice' (DV). Naval'ny's People's Alliance (NA) and Valerii Solovei's 'New Force' (NS) could also be classified as national-democratic.

The ethno-nationalists abhor the attempts of the Yeltsin period to construct a supranational *rossiiskii* identity rather than a nation-state built around the ethnic Russian (*russkii*) people. They are also deeply concerned about what they see as a deluge of non-Slav labour migrants from Central Asia and elsewhere, allegedly threatening the Russian cultural identity of Russia's towns and cities (migration from Orthodox countries such as Ukraine, Belarus and Moldova is more acceptable to them). The majority of ethno-nationalists also reject the Putin regime and belong to the 'hard', 'non-systemic' opposition. This aspect of their programme flows from the first. While Putin is clearly a Russian *state-builder*, he has not been a *nation-builder* in the ethnic sense. The ethno-nationalists see him as a proponent of a *rossiiskii* state idea: indeed, in his very first substantive political statement – the Millennium article from December 1999 – he never once employed the term *russkii*, using '*rossiiskii*' even about Russian culture and Russian values (Putin 1999). Putin's failure to promote a Russian (*russkii*) nation-state also shone through in his pet project – the Eurasian Union, an attempt to create a kind of Eastern counterpart to the EU among former Soviet republics. In order to entice as many post-Soviet leaders as possible into joining this union, Putin consistently disregarded all calls to introduce a visa regime for Central Asian citizens. The Russian ethno-nationalists see such a visa regime as essential for controlling the influx of culturally alien 'guest workers' from 'the near abroad'. Only one prominent ethno-nationalist – the voluble and media-savvy Egor Kholmogorov – broke ranks with the anti-Putin front. For this, he was rewarded with invitations to numerous talk-shows in the official Russian media.[4]

In the 1990s, most of the imperialist phalanx of the Russian nationalist movement had been sharply opposed to the power-holders in the Kremlin. Some, like Ziuganov's Communist Party, belonged to the left of the political spectrum; others, like Zhirinovskii's 'Liberal Democratic Party of Russia' (LDPR), were regarded as rightists/populists. These leftists and the rightists shared an obsession with geopolitics and Soviet nostalgia: what they longed for from the Soviet days was not necessarily the societal or economic model, but the huge and powerful Soviet state. They blamed the breakup of that state on the rise of ethnic nationalism in the non-Russian republics, and on the Yeltsin clique for having abetted this variety of nationalism, so diametrically opposite to their own.

Both the communists and Zhirinovskii's 'Liberal Democrats' eventually found their role in the post-Soviet political system as a loyal – some would say 'pocket' – opposition, each with its own niche in the Russian political marketplace. After the turn of the millennium they were regularly dismissed as 'spent forces', men of the past. The more vital and innovative part of the imperial movement could be found outside the Duma, around intellectuals and quasi-intellectuals like Aleksandr Prokhanov and Aleksandr Dugin. Prokhanov has been around for a long time: as editor of the hard-hitting opposition newspaper *Den'* ('The Day') he was a leading ideologue behind the failed putsch against Gorbachev in August 1991. In 1993 his paper was closed down, only to reappear as *Zavtra* ('Tomorrow'). Prokhanov, a remarkably prolific writer, is also an organiser of imperialist initiatives, like the Izborskii Club – a conservative debate forum established in 2012. The club has been very active during the Ukrainian crisis, even opening a branch in Donetsk (Laruelle 2016a).

Aleksandr Dugin comes from a rather different background. He started in the neo-fascist movement 'Pamiat' during perestroika; later he collaborated with Eduard Limonov in the National Bolshevik Party (NBP) before establishing his own Eurasian movement in 2001 (Shenfield 2001; Laruelle 2008). Dugin is an active member of the Izborskii Club. What unites the various factions of the club is their state-focused nationalism, apocalyptic thinking, obsession with geopolitics and opposition to the Western world, including Western values such as democracy.

After Putin's ascent to the presidency, most imperial nationalists recognised him as a competent leader who was prepared to implement at least parts of their programme. The fact that his attempt to establish closer political and economic ties among post-Soviet states was launched under the name of a 'Eurasian' Union was taken as evidence of this. While they never completely lost their independence, the imperialists moved increasingly closer to official positions as the Putin regime became more authoritarian and less oriented towards cooperation with the West. Only one leading imperialist nationalist – Eduard Limonov, Dugin's former comrade in the National Bolshevik Party (NBP) – continued to distrust and attack the Putin regime. Limonov moved closer to a pro-Putin stance under the impact of the massive anti-Kremlin protests in the winter of 2011–12, in which he did not participate.

Both ethno-nationalists and imperialists in the Russian nationalist opposition have been active in promoting the Donbas rebel cause, through the construction and dissemination of the 'Novorossia' mythology (Laruelle 2016a). I begin by examining the attitudes of the ethno-nationalists, first towards the

Crimean annexation and then to the war in Eastern Ukraine. Next, I do the same for the imperial nationalists.

THE ETHNO-NATIONALISTS AND THE RUSSIAN ANNEXATION OF CRIMEA: NAZI-STYLE ANSCHLUSS OR NATIONALIST TRIUMPH?

The incorporation of Crimea into the Russian Federation caught the Russian ethno-nationalists in a double bind. On the one hand, they had always professed solidarity with Russian diaspora groups in 'the near abroad' – indeed, they had long recommended that Russian communities in the former Soviet republics should be allowed to conduct referenda on unification with Russia, very much along the lines followed in Crimea and Donbas in spring 2014.[5] On the other hand, they deeply distrusted the intentions of Vladimir Putin and his coterie, and their commitment to democratic principles also left them in a predicament. From a democratic point of view the Crimean referendum – conducted under military occupation– was hardly reassuring. Here the nationalists with the most liberal inclinations took a resolute stance against the annexation; others wavered for a while before opting for a position of support, while a third group welcomed the Crimeans into the Russian embrace more or less unreservedly.

The most prominent liberal nationalist in the Russian opposition, Aleksei Naval'nyi, rejected the annexation of the Crimean Peninsula. In Budapest in 1994, he pointed out, Russia had promised to respect the territorial integrity of Ukraine (Navalny 2014). Moreover, since Russia strongly condemned Western military intervention in the Kosovo–Serbian conflict, it should refrain from committing similar acts. The official Russian justification for the annexation – that the rights of Russians in Crimea were threatened – was 'a fib and a provocation concocted in the Kremlin'. After all, the Russian language ruled supreme on the peninsula. If the Russian authorities were genuinely concerned about the plight of Russians in the near abroad, they would have acted when hundreds of thousands of Russians were driven out of Uzbekistan and Tajikistan in the 1990s – but they did not (Eliseev 2014).

The leader of the Democratic Choice party, Vladimir Milov, had previously served as Deputy Minister of Energy and could speak with some authority when he claimed that the annexation of Crimea would result in a huge drain on the Russian state budget. He also, like Navalny, pointed out that no Ukrainification was under way in Crimea: 'In fact, in our own Muslim republics, de-russification is proceeding much faster.' While the people of Eastern Ukraine may sympathise with Russia and dislike nationalists from Western Ukraine, 'that does not in any way mean that they burn with desire to be trampled underfoot by Putin's dictatorship' (Milov 2014).

The leader of the National-Democratic Alliance, Ilia Lazarenko, was no less acerbic in his denunciation of the Crimean land grab. In his view, it was an unmitigated disaster; the prestige of Russia would suffer as a result. Having behaved like a bandit, Russia would now suffer the consequences – economic sanctions and total international isolation. Moreover, this expansion of state and territory would bring no benefits for ethnic Russians: under the current regime, Russia is a concentration camp, to which the Crimean annexation would only add a new barrack (Lazarenko 2014a).

In the National Democratic Party (NDP), many activists participated in the Crimea debate, adopting sometimes rather different attitudes. The party chairman, Konstantin Krylov, claimed that Russia has an undisputable historical right to Crimea; he also held that the principle of 'territorial integrity of states' should not be fetishised. Crimea had been illegally torn from Russia under the communist dictatorship. However, Krylov, as always, was not concerned about *state* rights, but with the interests of *ethnic Russians*. For Russians in Ukraine, reunification with Russia – or 'Anschluss', as he referred to it – would hardly be a blessing. Rescuing them from the danger of Ukrainification would only move them from the frying pan into the fire – into the captivity of the terroristic Moscow regime. Krylov believed that Russia was 'absolutely justified' in moving troops into Crimea as part of a humanitarian effort to protect the Russians living there from Ukrainification – but *not* in order to facilitate annexation (Krylov 2014).

The editor of the NDP webpage, Mikhail Beliaev, pointed out that even if Putin now regularly referred to the peninsula as '*russkii*', Russian authorities also strongly underlined the multiethnic character of its population. Beliaev particularly disapproved of the concessions made to the Crimean Tatars. Their language would acquire official status and they would be allotted specific quotas in the regional parliament.[6] 'The Russians in Crimea will soon enough learn what it means to live in a feudal state with totalitarian manners . . . They have a long period of painful disenchantment with the Russian Federation and with Putin ahead of them' (Beliaev 2014).

However, many of Beliaev's fellow party-members did indeed yield to the sirens' song from the Kremlin loudspeakers. Aleksandr Khramov maintained that Crimea is dear to Russian nationalists, not because of geographical or economic interests – indeed, these interests could well suffer as a result of unification. The important thing is that the majority of the people living there are ethnic Russians. 'The inclusion of Crimea into Russia, therefore, is not an act of "imperial aggression", but a reconstitution of the Russian national body which has been cut into pieces by the Soviet bureaucrats' (Khramov 2014).

Pavel Sviatenkov, a journalist with close links to the National-Democratic Party, waxed lyrical about the Crimean annexation: for the first time in decades, the interests of the Russian authorities and the national interests of Russians coincided, he claimed. Not since Iurii Gagarin's flight into space had Russians felt such national elation. 'This means that the Russians are returning to history'

(Sviatenkov 2014). NDP activist Oleg Nemenskii also hailed the severance of Crimea from Ukraine. Crimea, he mused, could become a bridgehead of the Russian movement, and fill some of the same role for Russian speakers in Ukraine as Galicia was playing for the Ukrainian-speakers (Nemenskii 2014a).

In internal NDP debates on the Crimean Question, the enthusiasts of unification with Russia eventually prevailed. Even Konstantin Krylov, who had derisively described the annexation as 'Anschluss', made a turnabout. No state could forever accede to an arrangement which was based on manifest injustice, he now maintained. The fact that the Ukrainian authorities were so easily reconciled to loss of the peninsula indicated that they had always assumed that this scenario would materialise. 'The reunification of Crimea with Russia at precisely this time and precisely in the way it took place was the best possible outcome' (Krylov 2015). Krylov averred that his principled opposition to the Putin regime remained intact.

Putin had used a wide range of arguments to justify the inclusion of Crimea into the Russian Federation – historical and cultural, as well as alleged precedents in the West's behaviour towards Kosovo, Iraq and other places. His exploitation of the nationalist rhetoric in the 18 March speech, however, was unmistakable (Tsygankov 2015, 294). Russian ethno-nationalists zoomed in on one particular argument: Putin had claimed that 'the Russians (*russkie*) have become one of the largest, if not *the* largest, divided nation in the world' (Putin 2014a). In Putin's earlier texts the term '*russkii*' had taken on various different connotations – political, cultural and historical (see e.g. Putin 2012). In this particular case, however, the sentence makes sense only if the word is understood as an ethnical designation. The Russian ethno-nationalists rejoiced: Putin had adopted their terminology, perhaps also their worldview (Nemenskii 2012). Valery Solovei noted that Putin, on 18 March, used the word '*russkii*' no fewer than twenty-seven times. The plans for a Eurasian Union had been replaced by the vision of 'a Russian world'. This was 'an ideological innovation' (quoted in Piper 2014).[7] To Solovei (2014)[8] this signalled that Putin was *not* resurrecting the Empire, as the *impertsy* claimed, but instead building a Russian national state. That did not necessarily mean that Putin himself was thinking in those categories, Solovei continued. On the contrary, for the Putin regime, Russian nationalists had been and remained its main adversaries. 'I know perfectly well how lamentable and even terrible the situation of Russians in Russia is. But I also know that history moves in the most capricious ways. The most unexpected forces and people can become its instruments' (Solovei 2014).

The Euromaidan revolution had significantly boosted the influence of the radical-right and extremist elements in Ukrainian politics, jeopardising the fragile unity of the Ukrainian nation, Solovei argued. It was this situation that Putin had exploited in an 'adventurous undertaking bordering on true greatness' with his campaign to reunite Crimea with Russia. Says Solovei,

> I am a liberal, a democrat, and a nationalist. I reject Putin's regime. But I am a *Russian* liberal, democrat, and nationalist. . . . To me, what has taken place is not an annexation, but the return to the historical bosom of our motherland of a part that had been torn away. (Solovei 2014)

It was hypocritical of the West to object to the presence of Russian soldiers on the peninsula when the referendum took place. 'I will remind you, that the West recognized elections in both Afghanistan and Iraq as legitimate and democratic in spite of the fact that there were significant military contingents in these countries and even an ongoing war.'[9]

While Solovei remained preoccupied with the democratic credentials of the annexation, other Russian ethno-nationalists regarded this as a secondary issue. Egor Kholmogorov (2006) had long been an active advocate of Russian meddling in Ukrainian affairs. In a strongly worded 'Open letter to the Ukrainians' about the possibility of war, he advised them not even to think about recapturing the peninsula by military means:

> Your propaganda is trying to fool you into believing that Russians (*rossiiane*) are not prepared to die for Putin and his imperial mania. [This propaganda] is lying. There *are* no *rossiiane*, but there are *russkie*, and *russkie* are in complete agreement among themselves, that Crimea is Russian soil. Russian people are living there, and to reunite Russians with Russians is worth fighting for. (Kholmogorov 2014a)

Aleksandr Sevast'ianov, the 'patriarch of Russian ethno-nationalism', expressed himself in a similarly bellicose vein. As early as 5 March he claimed that the turmoil in the Crimea provided all the necessary preconditions for a civil war in Ukraine, and it would be a crime for the Russians not to avail themselves of this unique historical opportunity. Russian interference could be justified as a wholly humanitarian action. Russia had only to wait for NATO to give some support to Western Ukraine as a signal to lend a helping hand to the people in the East:

> For us – for Russia, for the Russians – there is no other solution to the Ukrainian problem than the division of Ukraine and reunification between Russia and the southeastern regions (the Left Bank, Novorossiia and Crimea). Not within the framework of *rossiiskii* neoimperialism, but in the framework of a *russkii* national state, based on the internationally recognised principle of reunification of divided nations. (Sevast'ianov 2014a)

To sum up: the attitudes of Russian ethno-nationalists towards the Crimean annexation were remarkably diverse, from complete rejection to exuberance.

Their reactions followed a fairly straightforward pattern: even if they all presented themselves as democrats, their understanding of precisely what is meant by democracy differs considerably. In general, the more 'ethnic rights' trump 'democratic rights' in the thinking of Russia's ethno-nationalists, the more difficult it has been for them to maintain their defences against Putinism. This shines through clearly in the thinking of Aleksandr Sevast'ianov:

> Russians in general, and Russian nationalists in particular, must take as their starting point not the interests of Putin's Russia, but the interests of the eternal, one and only true Russia. There is no other Russia. That is not to say that we hold no grudges against the Kremlin, or against the Russian Orthodox Church. But now in this fatal, decisive moment in the history of our people, these grudges must be put aside. Proceeding from this position we must stand together with Putin as long as Putin stands together with Novorossiia and Crimea. Today, the president of Russia has adopted a position that deserves our *utmost and unqualified support*. (Sevast'ianov 2014a, emphasis added)

RUSSIAN ETHNO-NATIONALISTS AND THE BLOODSHED IN EASTERN UKRAINE

In his 18 March speech Putin (2014a) claimed that the rights of Russians, not only in Crimea but also in 'Southeastern' Ukraine, were threatened. Although this is not necessarily to be understood as encouraging the people in Donbas to revolt, this is nevertheless how it was interpreted in many parts of Eastern Ukraine. Anti-Maidan movements had been established there after Yanukovich's ousting, shortly after the Crimean takeover and armed takeovers of public buildings commenced in several eastern and southern cities. Russian nationalists who had cheered while Crimea was annexed saw no reason for not supporting the 'militiamen' (*opolchentsy*) on the Ukrainian mainland. However, while Putin could brag that the Crimean operation had been conducted without military clashes and with no loss of human life, Donbas followed a very different script.

The war in Eastern Ukraine earned the Kremlin no new friends while it antagonised some of its most ardent supporters among the nationalists. Predictably, both Naval'nyi and the Democratic Choice party castigated Putin for having achieved nothing except turning the Ukrainian people into inveterate Russophobes (Navalny 2014; 'Zaiavlenie' 2014). They believed that Putin had engineered the East Ukrainian uprising in order to distract Russian public opinion from pressing problems at home and to boost his popularity ratings. But, they continued, that would come to naught. Whereas Crimea was almost hallowed territory to many Russians, Donbas had none of its sacred aura, Milov maintained (Kriukova and Liamets 2015). Putin had acted scandalously and incompetently. As a result, thousands of Russians (*rossiiane*) were dying ('Zaiavlenie' 2014).

Il'ia Lazarenko simply stated that no 'Russian' (*russkii*) Spring[10] had taken place in Eastern Ukraine. Instead, what could be observed was a series of neo-Soviet mutinies with the support of the Russian state, aimed at instigating civil war. Lazarenko (2014b) based this view on the fact that the People's Republics of Donetsk and Lugansk had been proclaimed in the name of their 'multiethnic population', not in the name of the '*russkii*' people.

While these oppositionists concluded that Russia should not have interfered in the East Ukrainian debacle at all, virtually all other ethno-nationalists criticised the Kremlin for the exact opposite reason: Russia was not supporting the rebels *enough*. Seeking to convince world opinion that Russia had clean hands in Donbas, Putin has reportedly claimed that if he instructed the Russian army to capture Kyiv, it could do so in a matter of weeks ('Putin claims' 2014). While this was no doubt true, it did not prove that Russia was not involved at all, and virtually all outside observers remained unconvinced about Russia's detachment. Among Russian nationalists, on the other hand, official assurances about the country's lack of involvement in the conflict led to accusations of letting down ethnic brethren.

The official Russian position was that Ukraine ought to be federalised, not dismembered. Many Russian nationalists saw this as a betrayal. On his Facebook page, Konstantin Krylov wrote 'Russia has never questioned and will never question that Donbass belongs to Ukraine . . . Putin is UKRAINE'S MOST IMPORTANT FRIEND' (2014, capitalisation in original). This was not intended as a compliment. Krylov saw no connection between support for the insurgents and support for Putin – a view shared by the Donbas militiamen themselves, he claimed (Kulikov 2014).

Another NDP activist, Oleg Nemenskii, pointed out that 'when the inhabitants of Donbass – Donetsk Rus' – united in protest, they reckoned with a Crimean scenario'. The future 'separatists' did not expect war – thinking that when they congregated on the squares, occupied administrative buildings and advanced legal demands, some 'polite people' would arrive and no one would dare to oppose 'the will of the people' (Nemenskii 2014b).[11] Nemenskii drew the conclusion that Russia bore deep responsibility for the situation in Donbas since the popular resistance there had been instigated by the Crimean precedence; and he issued an ominous warning: 'Donbas is currently at the center of the people's attention, at the very heart of our identity. Defeat in Donbas can in my view jeopardise our entire future as a country' (Nemenskii 2014b).

Egor Kholmogorov was an enthusiastic supporter of the 'Novorossia' concept and visited Donetsk to demonstrate his solidarity. He was particularly close to the self-appointed commander Igor Strelkov (the *nom de guerre* of Igor Girkin), who soon became immensely popular among the Russian public (see e.g. Nepogodin 2014; Pain 2016).[12] Strelkov never openly challenged Putin's authority, but remained a maverick who was not completely under the Kremlin's control. Like a latter-day Garibaldi, he and his band of insurgents attacked and occupied Slaviansk and established their headquarters there; when they later had to abandon the city in July 2014, Kholmogorov pointed the finger at Moscow. If Russia had sent in 'peacekeepers' in April, the Ukrainian army would have been unable to launch their counter-offensive and the situation in Slaviansk would have been resolved 'without any bloodletting and to everybody's satisfaction'. Kholmogorov did not attack Putin directly but talked nebulously about a 'fifth column' in Moscow ('Kholmogorov' undated). When Putin agreed to a ceasefire on 5 September 2014, in Minsk, Kholmogorov expressed deep dissatisfaction. 'People are sitting in Odesa and Kharkov waiting for the liberators to come . . . To abandon Donbas now would be senseless, and stupid, have no purpose, and be morally uncomfortable. We are too deeply involved' ('Bol'shoe interv'iu' 2014). Already in May Kholmogorov had written on his Facebook page, 'if Putin today lets Donbass down, then immediately cleansing with [Ukrainian] military aviation will commence, and in the space of two years the United States and the EU will force him to return Crimea to Ukraine. I will refrain from any comments about the revenge that will then be meted out on Putin personally' (2014b).

Aleksandr Sevast'ianov also reconsidered in June the 'unconditional' support for Putin which he had expressed in March. He still commended the President for having chopped off Crimea 'brilliantly, with surgical precision', in an operation of high-class political handicraft (Sevast'ianov 2014b). However, the Kremlin's latest behaviour had left him bewildered. If Russia left the rest of Ukraine in the hands of the 'Banderites', in order to appease them and the West which stands behind them, then the country would suffer new strategic defeats tomorrow and be forced to hand back Crimea too:

> To keep Crimea but leave Novorossiia in the hands of Ukraine?! To put the question in this way can only be called idiotic and schizophrenic. And still, this is how it is being formulated by Minister of Foreign Affairs Sergei Lavrov and this is what [Kremlin advisor Vladislav] Surkov and his emissaries in the Donbass are working for. **So the main question arises: whom are you with, President?** The question hangs in the air, and every TV watcher asks himself about this every day as he sees the suffering of peaceable citizens of Donetsk and the courage of the militiamen. (Sevast'ianov 2015, bold in original)

In spring 2014 various Russian nationalists proffered unsolicited advice to the Kremlin on how to proceed after the successful Crimean operation. When this advice was not heeded, the tone of their Internet postings became increasingly shriller over the summer, coupled with predictions about the dire consequences of ignoring them. From there, it was only a small step to accusing the Russian leadership of betrayal – *predatel'stvo*. This was something that the disappointed East Ukrainian rebels were prepared to do. As Richard Sakwa (2015, 164–5) has observed, 'the Donbass resistance movement now turned into fierce critics of Putin, accusing him of betrayal and worse'. Russian nationalists, also among the imperialists, increasingly listened more to the messages coming from rebel-controlled Eastern Ukraine than to those from the Kremlin.

The Imperialist Opposition: The Crimean Operation as Putin's Eminent Statesmanship

At an early stage, the opposition parties in the Duma gave Putin *carte blanche* to intervene in Ukrainian politics. Communist Party leader Ziuganov (2014) called Euromaidan 'a political Chernobyl', with 'far worse consequences than the nuclear one'. While he sanctimoniously averred that nobody planned to interfere in Ukrainian internal affairs, 'we are obliged to defend our fellow countrymen, our citizens and national and state interests, using all means known to this world . . . The Banderovites shall not rule in Crimea and Sevastopol.' Zhirinovskii (2014), for his part, accompanied Putin to Yalta in Crimea to celebrate the annexation there, and declared that after this spectacular feat Putin ought to be given the honorary titles 'supreme leader' and 'Emperor'.

Prokhanov (2014b) also lauded the Crimean annexation: in (literally) flowery language he rejoiced, 'Crimea is again with Russia. What happiness, light, exultation! In every Russian soul gardens are blossoming.' Of course, the West would hate Russia for it, but that was as it should be: Western hatred for Russia was centuries-old and would not change (Prokhanov 2014e). Prokhanov compared Putin's speech of 18 March 2014, to Josef Stalin's celebrated toast to the Russian people on Victory Day 1945: on both occasions people had leapt to their feet, embraced and kissed each other. 'Even the president himself had tears in his eyes.' This was 'a revenge and a rebuttal for the catastrophe of 1991'.

If Prokhanov was now singing the praises of Putin, it was because not he but Putin himself had changed, the writer maintained: earlier, 'no one had been able to seal my mouth, but a number of my statements and judgments had seemed too extravagant, too offensive. Now they are being pronounced in St George's hall [in the Kremlin] by Putin himself' (Prokhanov 2014a). Thus, when Prokhanov described Putin as 'the greatest political leader in Russia and the world', this was largely an expression of self-congratulation. Prokhanov also allowed himself to give interpretations of Putin's statements which the President might not be quite comfortable with. In his Crimean speech, Prokhanov wrote, Putin had claimed that 'the rivers of Western hatred against Russia flow from the insuperable, deep chasm that divides the Western and Russian worldviews and creeds' (2014b).

Aleksandr Dugin used similarly strong language. He claimed that what the world had seen in the Crimean operation was 'the true Putin who had arrived at the Russian truth', a leader who had 'torn off his balaclava . . . . We have seen nothing like this before.' All of Putin's previous speeches had been muddled, but this time it was not a gesture, not a PR campaign . . . 'No, this is a strategy which explains the past and points the direction towards the future' (Dugin 2014c). The Crimean annexation marked the end of the early Putin and the beginning of the mature Putin era. If Putin had initially tried to combine liberalism with patriotism, and play by rules set by the West, nobody could any longer cling to the illusion that Russia was a European country. 'Liberalism and the West are not only a competitor, but an enemy of Russia' (Dugin 2014b).

Like Prokhanov, Dugin arrogated to himself the prerogative to explain to the world – and to Putin – what the essence of Putin's policy was. Already on 17 March – on the eve of Putin's Crimea speech – he published a commentary which proclaimed that 'Crimea is not important any longer. What is important is Novorossiia.' This was accompanied by an illustration showing a train with a locomotive named 'Crimea' pulling railroad cars labelled 'Donetsk', 'Lugansk', 'Khar'kov', 'Odessa' and so on – altogether eleven *oblasts* (counties) in the south and east of Ukraine (Dugin 2014a).

The greatest turnabout involved the formerly staunch anti-Putinist Eduard Limonov. While his so-called 'sermons' had earlier been brimming with scorn for the Russian President, on 6 March he attacked his former allies in the Russian opposition for their failure to welcome Crimea into Russia. 'You, sirs, are blinded by hatred against one person – VVP [= Putin] – and ignore the will of two million people in Crimea and the will of the Donbas population' (Limonov 2014a).

Russian ethno-nationalists and imperialists, then, supported the Crimean takeover for very different reasons. While the former group saw it as necessary for defending ethnic Russians, the imperialists regarded it as a first step towards the resurrection of the Russian Empire (Prokhanov 2014e). Another noteworthy difference: whereas the Crimean operation gave rise to fierce debate within the ethno-nationalist camp, I am not aware of any important imperialist figures who had qualms about lending their propagandistic support to it.

THE IMPERIALISTS AND THE DONBAS: 'MR. PRESIDENT:
LISTEN TO RUSSIAN VOICES OF AGONY!'

Even if virtually all Russian imperialists after the Crimean annexation fell into line behind Putin and his strategy, they wanted to dictate to him the content of that strategy. When he failed to take the message or prevaricated, their admonitions and pleas grew increasingly desperate.

Limonov's new-found infatuation with Putinism quickly soured. In May 2014 he observed that in the EU and United States people were convinced that the uprisings in Donetsk and Lugansk had been organised by Russia, but Russians knew better: the local people had rebelled without any help from Russia – even, regrettably, without any kind of encouragement. 'It's extremely good that Crimea has been accepted into Russia, but deeply execrable that [Russia] doesn't want to take in Donbass where hundreds of our brethren are perishing' (Limonov 2014b). In July, Limonov (2014c) cried out: 'Kremlin, why do you keep silent? Do you believe that we really will forgive you your silence and your yawning when this very morning people are perishing in Donbass?'

In May, Dugin too began to feel that the Kremlin's policy was not following his particular script. When Putin did not recognise the referenda on independence in the Donetsk and Lugansk 'republics' on 11 May, Dugin (2014d) blamed this on the influence of a sixth column in Putin's entourage. 'All the traitors who are nestling in the shadow of Putin have been brought into combat readiness. They understand that with [the successful establishment of the Donetsk People's Republic] they will meet their end – structurally, personally, and class-wise' (Dugin 2014e). The hero from Slaviansk, Igor Strelkov, Dugin described as a lonely, righteous knight who had single-handedly taken on an entire country, Ukraine, with no support from his own political authorities in Russia. 'One against the traitors in Moscow. One against the Kremlin' (Dugin 2014f). Dugin studiously avoided making any direct attacks on Putin, but the myth about 'the captive in the Kremlin', surrounded by 'sixth columnists', was becoming increasingly threadbare. Even if it were true, it would mean that Putin was not in control, not the strong leader he ought to have been.

In mid-May, the military situation in rebel-held Eastern Ukraine was controlled by local field commanders over whom Putin had scant influence. This forced him, according to Pavel Baev (Baev 2014, 77), to back off and at the very last moment call home battle-ready soldiers who had been brought to the Russian–Ukrainian border. The rebels despaired, and so did their supporters in Moscow. In June, Dugin came close to pointing his finger directly at Putin. Although Putin had averred that he would never allow any fully-fledged Ukrainian military operation against the peaceful population in southeastern Ukraine, that was precisely what was happening. There was still no reason to panic, Dugin assured his readers, but Russia was losing the initiative: 'We clearly see the first signs of a betrayal of national interests' (Dugin 2014g). This posting on *Vkontakte* – a Russian Facebook imitation – of 4 June 2014 seems to have been the straw that broke the camel's back in terms of Kremlin patience. A few weeks later, on 27 June, Dugin announced that he had been fired from his position as professor at the Moscow State University as a reaction against his position on the *Novorossiia* issue. This was bitterly ironic since he and Strelkov were 'Putin's most loyal supporters. We are his fervent followers' (Dugin 2014h).

A sharp change in the political course of Russia had taken place, Dugin claimed. Putin at the time of the return of Crimea to Russia and Putin half a year later were two different people. Externally he was the same, but he was no longer able to act as freely as before. Putin was bound, hand and foot; he was disoriented and misinformed, and had been subjected to some kind of blackmail. 'It is clear as day that the people who today decide the Kremlin's policy towards Novorossia are acting not only against Novorossia, and not only in the interests of the West, but against Putin personally.' America's hirelings in Russia were concocting a plot against him, a new Maidan on Russian soil: 'In order to topple Putin, Novorossiia must fall, just as Novorossiia must be rescued in order to strengthen him' (Dugin 2014i). However, Dugin could muster no evidence to substantiate this conspiracy theory.

Among the other leading imperialist ideologues, Prokhanov clung desperately to his pro-Putinist position. In July, while the fighting in Donbas was in full swing, he declared that he did not see any major faults in Russia's policy towards Ukraine. Crimea had been snatched 'from under the noses of the Nazi generals', and Putin was the guarantor that this would not be reversed. If he were to fall ill or be toppled, then the revanchists would return to power in Russia (Prokhanov 2014c). Therefore, task number one for the enemies of Russia was to break Putin's will. When Prokhanov was rebuked in a call-in radio programme in August for supporting the Kremlin, he explained that he did not do so because he was on its payroll – he was not – but because Putin's downfall would be 'a colossal catastrophe': if the Donbas militiamen fled to Russia, that would unleash a chain reaction of defeat. Luckily, Prokhanov maintained, the Russian President had crossed the Rubicon: after the annexation of Crimea there was no turning back for him. In the West he was ostracised, presented as a monster and compared to Hitler. He had no choice but to go on fighting together with the Donbas rebels (Prokhanov 2014d). However, one of the radio listeners was not satisfied with this explanation. He pointed out that Russian Foreign Minister Sergei Lavrov had told the insurgents that they should be prepared to live together with the Ukrainians in one state, while Putin personally had urged them to postpone their referenda on independence. The listener believed that 'Putin and those who fight for the interests of Russia in Novorossia have parted ways.' To a large degree, Prokhanov accepted this assessment, but added that it was based on deficient knowledge about the situation. 'Putin operates under severely brutal circumstances which we do not understand, circumstances that force him to act as he does' (Prokhanov 2014d). This somewhat cryptic explanation was quite in line with Prokhanov's general mysticism: some people have esoteric insight into secrets hidden to ordinary people.

However, as the war dragged on and the casualties kept piling up with no victory in sight, Prokhanov's hope against all hope was wearing increasingly thin. Asked by a journalist from *Komsomol'skaia Pravda* in February 2015 why Donbas was still not part of Russia, he explained that 'at the time of the *coup d'état* on the Maidan the Russian state was strong and robust enough to annex Crimea, but it lacked the energy and the might, even the motivation, to capture anything more'. But it was terrible even to contemplate what might happen to Novorossia if it were handed back to the Ukrainians: 'Firstly, avengers (*karateli*) will arrive and finish off the entire Donbas population, and then Ukraine will be transformed into a consolidated, mighty NATO bridgehead.' Finally, for the Russians in Russia, 'betrayal of Novorossia will be a gigantic moral tragedy' (Gamov 2015). Here, Prokhanov uttered the ominous word 'betrayal', which would resonate ever more loudly on nationalist websites.

Prokhanov's newspaper, *Zavtra*, published desperate pleas for support for the Donbas rebels. After the tragic events in Odesa on 3 May 2014, when more than forty Donbas sympathisers died in a fire while some pro-Ukrainian demonstrators outside apparently prevented them from escaping from the building where they were trapped (Kramer 2014; Sakwa 2015, 97–9), a certain Sergei Sokurov wrote an open letter to the Russian President. He reminded Putin that at a press conference in March he had promised, as a last resort, to use 'all available means' to defend Russian citizens in Ukraine, 'if the people ask for it'. Perhaps there were no legal grounds for calling the death groans of the wounded defenders of the barricades in the Donbas cities a 'plea', and perhaps the forty victims in Odesa were not a sufficiently large group to be counted as grounds for military intervention – 'but in that case I, as a person who has always voted for you, ask: can you please publish specific answers to the questions posed to you at that press conference: exactly how many appeals are needed? How much blood must flow?' (Sokurov 2014).

Maksim Kalashnikov (2014a), a journalist and a member of the Izborskii Club, maintained that even to hold the Donbas would be too little: the entire historical region of Novorossia, from Luhansk to the border of Romania, would have to be liberated. In an interview with the web journal *Nakanune. ru* Kalashnikov pointed out that when some Russian troops finally arrived in Donbas in August, this did not lead to an all-out war with the West: the West was a paper tiger, and from the very beginning Russia could and should have acted much more decisively.

Now Donbas was being slowly strangled, becoming a new Somalia, Kalashnikov lamented. A protracted war of attrition is in the interests of Ukrainian President Poroshenko, who could wait while the 'bony hand' of famine, cold and social barbarisation gripped Donbasian throats. Donbas society was already slowly falling apart; it had become dangerous to walk alone in the streets of Donetsk. To say that Donbas has been 'abandoned' by Russia was, in Kalashnikov's view (2014b), too mild an expression: it had been 'flushed down the toilet'. If Dugin was correct in claiming that he had been fired from his university position because of his pro-*Novorossia* stands, we may wonder why

Kalashnikov does not appear to have suffered in any way for his even more vituperative language.

The St George Ribbon as an Instrument of Nationalist Mobilisation – On Both Sides of the Frontline

Prior to the Crimean annexation and the outbreak of the war in 2014, attitudes towards the St George ribbon in Ukraine were quite relaxed, and in some Russian-speaking regions many people took part in various ribbon actions. In 2009, residents of Simferopol in Crimea produced a 53 m-long ribbon, and the next year the city of Odesa hoped to get into the *Guinness Book of Records* by carrying a 6 × 142 m ribbon down the famous Potemkin Steps. In addition, 400,000 smaller ribbons were distributed in the city and the environs (see Figure 9.1) ('Odessity poshili' 2010; 'Odessa: Potemkinskuiu' 2010). As late as in 2013, a St George ribbon action was organised in the city of Kharkov, with about 150,000 ribbons handed out (Khar'kovchanam 2013). Not all Ukrainians were equally enthused by the ribbon, but there were no attempts to disrupt these celebrations.

All this changed abruptly in spring 2014. Rebels in Eastern Ukraine, as well as nationalists in Russia, harnessed the immense popularity of the St George

Figure 9.1 A huge ribbon of St George is presented on the Potemkin Steps for Victory Day, 8 May 2010, in Odesa, Ukraine. © Slav Bukhal / Shutterstock.com.

ribbon[13] in the propaganda war against the Ukrainian authorities (Matveeva 2018, 198–9). Victory Day is celebrated perhaps even more intensely in Crimea than in Russia proper (see Figure 9.2). Ever since the 'little green men' took over the peninsula, posters and billboards decorated in orange and black stripes have cropped up in towns and hamlets throughout this new Russian Federation subject. In the self-proclaimed Donetsk and Lugansk People's Republics, it is one of the most important symbols. Symptomatically, 'the hero of Slaviansk', Igor Strelkov-Girkin, and his girlfriend are shown on the Internet in outfits made of rather garish orange and black-striped material (see Figure 9.3) ('Igor' Strelkov' 2014).

The Donetsk People's Republic has instituted a St George order of valour for militiamen who distinguished themselves in the ongoing war (see Figure 9.4). Since 2015, 7 December has been celebrated in the *de facto* state as the Day of the St George ribbon. This gives the *de facto* state authorities two occasions each year on which they can organise St George festivities ('V Donetske' 2018). On these days, they roll out their 300 m-long ribbon and carry it through central Donetsk. The head of the state, Denis Pushilin, explains to the multitude of

Figure 9.2 Celebrating the sixty-ninth anniversary of Victory Day and seventieth anniversary of the liberation of Sevastopol from the fascists. Seamen in Sevastopol 2014. © Jiinna / Shutterstock.com.

Figure 9.3 Igor Strelkov-Girkin with fiancée in black and orange outfits. Galereia S.ART. All rights reserved.

listeners that 'every strong state should have their symbols and we have ours' ('Svyshe' 2018):

> for the residents of Donbass, the St George Ribbon is a symbol of the Great Victory, a symbol of the valour, courage and bravery of our people. In 2014, it acquired for us a special significance, becoming a link between generations, a demonstration of the solidarity and unity of the Russian world.
> The defenders of the Donetsk People's Republic, attaching the St George ribbon to their uniform and weapons, repulsed the enemy, and defended the freedom and independence of our country. And each of our victories proves that we are descendants of victors. ('Pozdravlenie' 2019)

It goes without saying that when the semiotics of the ribbon were transferred in this way from the victory in 1945 to the recent war on the Ukrainian side, it could no longer be tolerated by the Kyiv-loyal population. In April 2014 the press secretary of the pro-European Ukrainian party UDAR burned a ribbon on the Eternal Flame in Odesa, and in Kharkiv a policewoman was apparently dismissed from her job in February 2015 for pinning the St George

Figure 9.4 The modern order of St George of the Donetsk People's Republic.

symbol to her chest (Rakitina 2014; Gorelova 2015). In Lviv, the Ukrainian weekly *Vsia vlast'* reported, a man was roughed up for wearing the ribbon on 9 May the same year ('Vo L'vove' 2015).

A curious incident – but one indicative of the increasingly jittery atmosphere in Ukraine – centred around reactions when the April 2015 issue of the Ukrainian edition of the French fashion magazine *Elle* appeared on the streets, the front cover showing the American actor Michelle Williams wearing an orange-and-black striped dress. Although the same cover had been used on the British edition of the magazine the month before, persistent rumours claimed that the Kremlin was behind this alleged Russian propaganda stunt (Tubol'tseva 2015). The French publishers were finally pressured to withdraw the issue and change the cover (Ermolaeva 2015a). The Russian media gleefully reported on such incidents as proof of Ukrainian nationalist folly.

In the Ukrainian conflict, the St George ribbon is presented as both a fascist and an anti-fascist symbol. As a Russian supporter of the rebels explained, 'In 2014, Russian volunteers for the first time since the Great Victory fought the resurgent neo-Nazism – and they did it under the banners of St George's colours' (Birov 2014). In Donbas, it is explained that not only did Soviet soldiers fight against Nazi Germany under its colours but 'in our time the St George ribbon embodies the victory of our Donetsk Republic over Ukrainian neo-fascism' (Gusar 2018). Conversely, in the rest of Ukraine the ribbon is often portrayed as a fascist symbol – partly since it had, as pointed out above (Chapter 7), also been used by the anti-Soviet Russian Liberation Army. A huge billboard outside Lviv in Western Ukraine showed a St George ribbon arranged as a swastika. The text announced: 'the Vlasovite ribbon is a symbol of the occupier. Everyone who carries it is an enemy of Ukraine' (see Figure 9.5). In December 2014, an exhibition in Kyiv of 'the hundred best patriotic posters' showed several images where the ribbon was associated with fascism (see Figure 9.6) ('Ubei "kolorada"' 2014).

Even the serious daily *Zerkalo Nedeli*, reporting on a pro-Russian rally in Kharkiv in May 2014, claimed that the demonstrators carried 'Nazi symbols'. To substantiate this claim, it explained that the demonstrators 'held in their hands the orange-black flag, which was used by Gen. Vlasov's Russian Liberation Army when fighting on the side of Hitler during the Second World War' ('Kruglyi stol' 2014).

In May 2017, the Ukrainian Parliament adopted a law prohibiting public display of the St George ribbon. First-time offenders can be fined up to

Figure 9.5 Billboard outside Lviv, Ukraine: 'The Vlasovite ribbon is a symbol of the occupier. Everyone who carries it is an enemy of Ukraine.'

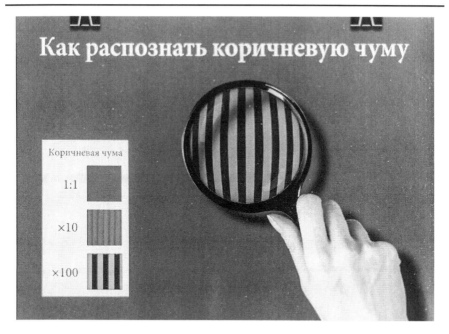

Figure 9.6 'How to recognize the brown plague.' Photo by V. V. Mihailov, copyright Politnavigator News Agency.

100 US dollars while repeat offenders can be given fifteen days' administrative incarceration. President Petro Poroshenko explained that the St George ribbon 'is not a symbol of the Second World War, but of aggression against Ukraine 2014–17. Wearing these ribbons, hitmen are killing our warriors day and night . . . With its actions, Russia has herself outlawed the ribbon' ('Poroshenko ob"iasnil' 2017). Enforcement of this ban has led to some incidents, such as when a German citizen who arrived in Kyiv by plane with a St George ribbon on her backpack was turned back on the border and sent back to Berlin ('Pogranichniki ne pustili' 2020).

The insurgents – and by extension, everyone sympathising with them – are regularly referred to in Ukraine as 'Colorado beetles' – *kolorady* (see e.g. 'V Khar'kove' 2014; Pokal'chuk 2014). This contemptuous moniker, which reduces the enemy to a harmful insect, is based on the fact that this beetle, known to invade gardens and destroy food crops, has orange and black stripes. Just as the real Colorado beetles should be ruthlessly exterminated, no mercy ought to be shown towards the human *kolorady* (Figure 9.7).

When pro-Russian and pro-Ukrainian activists clashed in Odesa on 2 May 2014 (see above), a fire broke out as the pro-Russians sought shelter inside the city's trade union building. More than forty people perished, while, according

Figure 9.7 'Warning against Colorado beetles'. Photo by V. V. Mihailov, copyright Politnavigator News Agency.

to the *New York Times*, demonstrators outside chanted 'burn, *kolorady*, burn!' (Kramer 2014; see also Sakwa 2015). The impression this tragedy made on the Russian public can hardly be exaggerated. The dehumanising connotations of the *kolorady* epithet were regarded as conclusive proof of the callousness of Ukrainian nationalists.

In fact, this odious label was apparently concocted in Russia by anti-Putin oppositionists and then exported to Ukraine. In an interview with the radio station Ekho Moskvy, diehard anti-Putin oppositionist Konstantin Borovoi claimed authorship of the expression, together with his close collaborator, Valeriia Novodvorskaia ('Bez durakov' 2015). Other sources claim that Russian publicist Alexander Nevzorov was the first to use this expression, in June 2013 (Belov 2016, 403). Moreover, some of the most insulting anti-Russian posters at the exhibition of 'patriotic art' in Kiev were produced by a Russian artist from Perm, who later sought political asylum in Ukraine ('Avtor plakata' 2014; 'Permskii khudozhnik' 2014).

Opposition to the St George ribbon has grown perceptively stronger in Russia after 2014 precisely due to its connection to the war in Eastern Ukraine (see e.g. Surnacheva 2015). Iuliia Latynina mused: 'in which war is the St George ribbon actually a victory symbol? The only war which I know to have been fought under the black and orange flag is the undeclared war in Donbas' (Latynina 2015). On the eve of the victory celebrations in 2015, an art exhibition was organised in Moscow called 'We won!' The title of the exhibition was clearly ironical, its message strongly critical towards the Russian authorities and not least towards what the organisers perceived as a cynical capitalisation of the memory of the war for political purposes. One of the artefacts depicted was a meat-mincer, which was fed by green plastic soldier figurines: out of this kitchen utensil came long strips of orange and black ribbon – clearly a reference to the 'little green men' who, in March 2014, invaded Crimea prior to the peninsula's incorporation into Russia, as well as to the role Russian soldiers had been playing in the undeclared war in Donbas (see Figure 9.8). The Russian police closed down the exhibition ('Politsiia razgromila' 2015).

CONCLUSIONS

Marlene Laruelle has described (2014a) the Donbas situation as a Pandora's box that the Kremlin has been struggling to close, worried that the Russian nationalist junta in Eastern Ukraine might turn against them: 'Donbass is a mess not only for Kyiv but also for Moscow.' Such prognoses are commonly linked to assumptions about how the Russian population will react to the economic hardships when the Western sanctions and the Russians counter-sanctions begin to bite. But some observers also believe that Putin's usage of nationalism, in words and deeds, may backfire. Writing in summer 2014, political analyst Nikolai Petrov surmised that,

Figure 9.8 Petr Vois and Liza Savolainen, 'Meat mincer', 2015. Exhibited in 'My pobedili' at Galereia S.ART, Moscow, 7 May to 7 September 2015.

by 'playing the chauvinist card', the Putin regime may 'enhance the danger of an uncontrolled development of Russian nationalism and its pressure on the powers-that-be. Society has been administered a strong narcotic' (Petrov 2014, 59). The Kremlin regime might in this scenario end up like the sorcerer's apprentice, who knew how to make the broom fetch water – but not how to stop it. Senior researcher Mikhail Aleksandrov at the Moscow State University of International Relations expressed the view that 'Russia's non-involvement in the military conflict in Ukraine may have catastrophic consequences' (Polubota 2014). Igor Torbakov at Uppsala University for his part asked, 'how forceful can Putin be, if a large number of nationalists are not behind him?' (Torbakov 2015, 445).

The Putin regime, however, does not stand or fall with support from the professed nationalists. The names of many of them are quite well known – in particular some of the *impertsy* – but that does not mean that Russians identify with them, let alone see themselves as their followers.

Researchers are almost unanimous in regarding the inclusion of nationalist tropes and themes in Putin's speeches and in Kremlin propaganda around 2014 as 'utilitarian' and 'instrumental' (Teper 2016, 12; Laruelle 2015c, 94–5). It allowed him to hijack the nationalist agenda (Frolov 2014). Writing in summer 2014 political scientist-cum-nationalist Valery Solovei remarked that

> indeed, our society has recently been warmed up rather strongly on the patriotic rhetoric emanating from the authorities. Now people are somewhat at a loss: 'We promised to help [the insurgents], so why are we idling'? However, I do not think that the authorities will find it difficult to solve this problem. In the course of 2–3 months they will smoothly lower the temperature in the rhetoric around the events in Ukraine and change the informational agenda. Society as a whole will accept that.

Seven years later, this prognosis still seems to hold water. Russian nationalism has bounced back several times in the past and may well do so in the future, but with his Crimea gambit Putin had provided an object lesson in how to use nationalism against nationalists.

NOTES

1. For reactions of the Russian nationalists to the Euromaidan revolution, readers are referred to Robert Horvath's brilliant survey, 'The Euromaidan and the crisis of Russian nationalism' (2015).
2. Ukrainian President Viktor Yanukovich fled on 21 February 2014, and six days later the first units of soldiers without insignia forced their way into the Crimean Parliament and government buildings. See Gol'ts 2014, 46. Marlène Laruelle believes that Putin 'personally made the decision to annex Crimea against the advice of those close to him, including the ministers of foreign affairs and defense' (Laruelle 2014b, 274).
3. Opinion polls show that, before the Euromaidan revolution, roughly one-third of the population of Donbas supported separatism and unification with Russia (Kuzio 2015, 163).
4. Author's interview with Kholmogorov, October 2013.
5. Author's interview with NDP leader Vladimir Tor, October 2013.
6. This early promise was later reneged upon.
7. The 'Russian world' (*russkii mir*) is a policy concept with several aspects and possible interpretations. In a broad sense, it denotes all who speak Russian and/or love Russian culture and literature; in a narrower sense, it pertains to all parts of the former Soviet Union where Russians continue to live (in reality, virtually the entire post-Soviet space). In 2007 the Kremlin established a 'Russian World Foundation' as a public diplomacy instrument. See Laruelle 2015b. For a different perspective, which more strongly underlines the spiritual message of the Russian world concept as it is used by the Russian Orthodox Church, see Petro 2015.

8. The page was later removed from the web, but Solovei has confirmed the content and that this remains his view. Personal communication with Valery Solovei, 18 December 2015.

9. The author's personal communication with Solovei, 20 March 2014.

10. 'Russian Spring' (*russkaia vesna*) is the term, apparently coined by Egor Kholmogorov, that is commonly used in Russian nationalist discourse to describe the anti-Kyiv mobilisation and occupation of public buildings in East Ukrainian cities in March and April 2014.

11. 'Polite people' is a Russian euphemism for the Russian soldiers, with balaclava helmets and no insignia, who 'suddenly' appeared in Crimea prior to the Russian takeover. This was the Russian equivalent of the Western term 'little green men'.

12. According to Nepogodin, in the summer of 2014 Strelkov's name figured on the Russian Internet just as often as 'Vladimir Putin'.

13. See Chapter 7.

BIBLIOGRAPHY

Absattarov, Raushanbek. 1996. 'Mezhetnicheskaia konsolidatsiia i obsh-chegrazhdanskii patriotism' [Interethnic consolidation and general civil patriotism], *Mysl'*, Almaty, 3: 2–6

Afanas'ev, Valerii Vladimirovich. 2009. 'Konsteptsiia tsivilizatsii Samuela Khantingtona' [Samuel Huntington's concept of civilisation], in Afanas'ev, Vladimir Vladimirovich, ed., *Rossiia i Evropa: Natsii v epokhu globalizatsii* [Russia and Europe: Nations in the Epoch of Globalization]. Moscow: MGU, pp. 146–56

Agurskii, Mikhail. 2003. *Ideologiia natsional-bol'shevizma* [The Ideology of National Bolshvism]. Moscow: Algoritm

Akhmetzhanova, Kseniia. 2014. 'Na granitse s Estoniei u veteranov otobrali georgievskie lenty' [St George ribbons taken away from veterans at the Estonian border], *Komsomol'skaia Pravda*, 11 May. Available from: <http://www.spb.kp.ru/online/news/1732000/> (last accessed 31 May 2020)

Aktürk, Şener. 2012. *Regimes of Ethnicity and Nationhood in Germany, Russia and Turkey*. Cambridge: Cambridge University Press

Akunin, Boris. 2012. 'Razgovor s politikom' [Conversation with a politician], *Akunin's livejournal blog*, 3 January. Available from: <http://borisakunin. livejournal.com/49763.html> (last accessed 30 March 2021)

Alexseev, Mikhail. 2010. 'Fear has wide eyes: Why do Russians see some migrant minorities as more numerous than others?', in Laruelle, Marlène, ed., *Russian Nationalism and the National Reassertion of Russia*. New York: Routledge, pp. 167–84

Alexseev, Mikhail. 2016. 'The USSR 2.0: Russia's ethnic minorities and expansionist ethnic Russian nationalism', in Kolstø, Pål and Blakkisrud, Helge, eds, *The New Russian Nationalism: Imperialism, Ethnicity and Authoritarianism 2000–15*. Edinburgh: Edinburgh University Press, pp. 160–91

Alexseev, Mikhail and Hale, Henry. 2016, 'Rallying round the leader more than the flag: Changes in Russian nationalist public opinion 2013–14', in Kolstø, Pål and Blakkisrud, Helge, eds, *The New Russian Nationalism: Imperialism, Ethnicity and Authoritarianism 2000–2015*. Edinburgh: Edinburgh University Press, pp. 192–220

Alksnis, Viktor. 2007. 'Proshchai, imperiia (nakanune russkoi Rossii)' [Farewell, empire (On the eve of the Russian Russia)], *Apologiia Natsionalizma, Strategicheskii Zhurnal*, Moscow: Institut natsional'noi strategii, 3: 19–28

Allenova, Olga. 2012. '"Biznes protiv etogo soiuza": Konstantin Borovoi, predprinimatel', politik' ['The business is against this union': Konstantin Borovoi, entrepreneur, politician], *Kommersant*, 23 January. Available from: <https://www.kommersant.ru/doc y/1856997> (last accessed 31 May 2020)

Alperovich, Vera, Yudina, Natalia and Verkhovsky, Aleksandr. 2013. 'The ultra-right on the streets with a pro-democracy poster in their hands or a knife in their pocket: Xenophobia and radical nationalism in Russia, and efforts to counteract them in 2012', *Sova, Center for Information and Analysis*, 26 April. Available from: <https://www.sova>center.ru/en/xenophobia/reports-analyses/2013/04/d26972/ (last accessed 31 May 2020)

Andersen, Erik André. 1999. *An Ethnic Perspective on Economic Reform: The Case of Estonia*. Aldershot: Ashgate

Anderson, Benedict. [1983] 1991. *Imagined Communities: Reflections on the Origin and Spread of Nationalism*. London: Verso

Anderson, John. 1997. *The International Politics of Central Asia*. New York: Manchester University Press

Antane, Aina and Tsilevich, Boris. 1999. 'Nation-building and ethnic integration in Latvia', in Kolstø, Pål, ed., *Nation-Building and Ethnic Integration in Post-Soviet Societies*. Boulder, CO: Westview, pp. 63–152

Antonov, Kirill. 2015. 'V Kazani vypustiat 10 tysiach kilometrov georgievskoi lenty' [In Kazan' 10,000 km of St George ribbon will be produced], *Kommersant*, 4 March. Available from: <http://www.kommersant.ru/doc/2679616> (last accessed 31 May 2020)

Armstrong, John A. 1955. *Ukrainian Nationalism 1939–1945*. New York: Columbia University Press

Armstrong, John A. 1976. 'Mobilized and proletarian diasporas', *The American Political Science Review*, 70, 2: 393–408

Armstrong, John A. 1982. *Nations Before Nationalism*. Chapel Hill: University of North Carolina Press

Aronson, I. Michael. 1990. *Troubled Waters: The Origins of the 1881 Anti-Jewish Pogroms in Russia*. Pittsburgh: University of Pittsburgh Press

Aronson, I. Michael. 2004. 'The anti-Jewish pogroms in Russia in 1881', in Klier, John Doyle and Lambroza, Shlomo, eds, *Pogroms: Anti-Jewish Violence in Modern Russian History*. Cambridge: Cambridge University Press, pp. 44–61

Arsiukhin, Evgenii. 2012. 'Na miting protiv "oranzhevoi revoliutsii" prishlo bol'she liudei, chem na Bolotnuiu' [More people attended the rally against the 'Orange Revolution' than the rally at Bolotnaia], *Komsomolskaja pravda*, 4 February. Available from: <http://kp.ru/daily/25829/2804832/> (last accessed 25 April 2021)

Arutiunian, Iurik. 1992. *Russkie: Etnosotsiologicheskie ocherki* [Russians: Ethnosociological Essays]. Moscow: Nauka

Arvidsson, Claes and Blomqvist, Lars Erik, eds. 1987. *Symbols of Power: The Esthetics of Political Legitimation in the Soviet Union and Eastern Europe*. Stockholm: Almqvist & Wiksell International

Averin, I. A. 1995. 'Ural'skoe kazachestvo v Kazakhstane: Istoriia i sovremennaia etnopoliticheskaia situatsiia' [Ural Cossacks in Kazakhstan: History and the present ethnopolitical situation], in *Sreda, kul'tura v usloviiakh obshchestvennykh transformatsii* [Environment and Culture under Conditions of Social Transformation]. Moscow: Carnegie, pp. 159–66

Avis, George. 1987. *The Making of the Soviet Citizen: Character Formation and Civic Training in Soviet Education*. London: Croom Helm

Avrutin, Eugene M. 2007. 'Racial categories and the politics of (Jewish) difference in late Imperial Russia', *Kritika: Explorations in Russian and Eurasian History*, 8, 1: 13–40

Avrutin, Eugene M. 2010. *Jews and the Imperial State: Identification Politics in Tsarist Russia*. Ithaca, NY: Cornell University Press

'Avtor plakata'. 2014. 'Avtor plakata "Ubei kolorada!" poprosit ubezhishche na Ukraine' [The author of the poster 'Kill a Colorado-beetle!' seeks asylum in Ukraine], *Vpered, Rossia!*, 12 December. Available from: <http://вперёдроссия.рф/blog/43967517248/Avtor-plakata-%22Ubey-kolorada!%22-poprosit-ubezhischa-na-Ukrayine> (last accessed 31 May 2020)

Bækken, Håvard. 2021. 'Patriotic disunity: Limits to popular support for militaristic policy in Russia', *Post-Soviet Affairs*, 37, 3: 261–75

Bækken, Håvard and Enstad, Johannes Due. 2020. 'Identity under siege: Selective securitization of history in Putin's Russia'. *Slavonic and East European Review*, 98, 2: 321–44

Baev, Pavel. 2014. 'Geopolitika samoizoliatsii', *Pro et Contra*, May–August: 73–86

Balakrishnan, Gopal. [1996] 2012. *Mapping the Nation*. London: Verso

Barghoorn, Frederick. 1956. *Soviet Russian Nationalism*. Westport, CT: Greenwood Press

Barghoorn, Frederick. 1980. 'Four faces of Soviet Russian ethnocentrism', in Allworth, Edward, ed., *Ethnic Russia in the USSR*. New York: Pergamon Press, pp. 55–66

Barkashov, Aleksandr. 1993. 'Natsionalizm ili patriotism? O neizbezhnosti natsional'noi revoliutsii' [Nationalism or patriotism? On the inevitability of a national revolution], *Russkii poriadok*, 2, February: 1–2

Barker, Rodney S. 2001. *Legitimating Identities: The Self-Presentation of Rulers and Subjects*. Cambridge: Cambridge University Press

Barth, Fredrik, ed. [1969] 1998. *Ethnic Groups and Boundaries: The Social Organization of Cultural Difference*. Prospect Heights, IL: Waveland Press, pp. 9–38

Bassin, Mark, Glebov, Sergey and Laruelle, Marlène, eds. 2015. *Between Europe & Asia: The Origins, Theories and Legacies of Russian and Eurasianism*. Pittsburgh: University of Pittsburgh Press

Bassin, Mark and Pozo, Gonzalo. 2017. *The Politics of Eurasianism: Identity, Popular Culture and Russia's Foreign Policy*. London: Rowman and Littlefield

Beiner, Ronald. 1999. *Theorizing Nationalism*. Albany: State University of New York Press

Beissinger, Mark R. 2002. *Nationalist Mobilization and the Collapse of the Soviet State*. Cambridge: Cambridge University Press

Bekus, Nelly. 2010. *Struggle over Identity: The Official and the Alternative 'Belarusianness'*. Budapest: Central European University Press

Beliaev, Dmitrii. 2010. 'Sviazannye odnoi tsel'iu: V Rossii nachalas' aktsiia "Georgievskaia lentochka"' [Tied together by a common aim: In Russia the St George ribbon event has begun], *Rossiiskaia gazeta*, 24 April. Available from: <http://m.rg.ru/2010/04/23/lentochka.html> (last accessed 31 May 2020)

Beliaev, Mikhail. 2014. 'Pro Krym bez illiuzii' (About Crimea without illusions), *Livejournal*, 12 March. Available from: <http://rosndp.org/pro-krim-bez-illyuzij.htm> (last accessed 17 December 2015, no longer available)

Bell, Sandra J. and Delaney, Mary E. 2001. 'Collaborating across difference: From theory and rhetoric to the hard reality of building coalitions', in Bystydzienski, Jill M., and Schacht, Steven P., eds, *Forging Radical Alliances Across Difference: Coalition Politics for the New Millennium*. Lanham, MD: Rowman & Littlefield, pp. 63–76

'Belorusskie oppozitsionery'. 2014. 'Belorusskie oppozitsionery prizyvaiut GAI borot'sia s georgievskimi lentochami' [Belarusian oppositionists call for the traffic police to fight against the St George ribbons], *Novaia gazeta*, 29 September. Available from: <https://novayagazeta.ru/articles/2014/09/29/61358-171-stop-imperiya-187> (last accessed 31 May 2020)

Belov, Aleksandr. 2011. 'Natsionalisty na obshchegrazhdanskom mitinge 24 dekabria. Obrashchenie Aleksandra Belova' [Nationalists on the general civil rally 24 December. Appeal by Aleksander Belov], 19 December. Available from: <https://www.dpni.org/articles/vazhnoe/28187/> (last accessed 1 June 2020)

Belov, Vadim. 2016. 'Nekotorye leksicheskie protsessy v rossiiskom politicheskom diskurse (na materiale rossiiskikh Internet-gazet) [Some lexical processes in the Russian political discourse (based on Russian Internet newspapers)]', *Zeitschrift für Slavische Philologie*, 72, 2: 383–411

Benz, Wolfgang. 2004. *Was Ist Antisemitismus?* Munich: C. H. Beck

Bereza, Borislav. 2020. 'Voina tsivilizatsii. Chem Ukraina otlichaetsia ot Rossii' [Clash of civilizations. What distinguishes Ukraine from Russia?], *NV*, 24 February. Available from: <https://nv.ua/opinion/ukraina-rossiya-voyna-chem-otlichayutsya-gosudarstva-novosti-ukrainy-50071985.html> (last accessed 25 April 2021)

'Bessmertnyi polk' [Immortal Regiment]. 2020. Available from: <https://www.may9.ru/events/bessmertnyj-polk/> (last accessed 25 April 2021)

'Bez durakov' 2015. 'Bez durakov' [Frankly speaking], *Ekho Moskvy*, 9 May. Available from: <http://echo.msk.ru/programs/korzun/1544308-echo/> (last accessed 31 May 2020)

Bilalutdinov, Azat. 2016. 'Die Gedenkinitiative "Unsterbliches Regiment" zwischen Gesellschaft und Politik', in Mischa Gabowitsch, Cordula Gdaniec and Ekaterina Makhotina, eds, *Kriegsgedenken als Event: Der 9. Mai 2015 im postsozialistischen Europa*. Paderborn: Ferdinand Schöningh, pp. 126–40

Birov, Eduard. 2014. 'Kogo Pugaet Georgievskaia Lentochka?' *Stiag*, 12 May. Available from: <www.Stjag.Ru/Index.Php/2012-02-08-10-29-37/Item/36112-Кого-Пугает-Георгиевская-Ленточка?.html> (last accessed 26 July 2021)

Blakkisrud, Helge and Kolstø, Pål. 2018. '"Restore Moscow to the Muscovites": Othering "the migrants" in the 2013 Moscow mayoral elections', in Kolstø, Pål and Blakkisrud, Helge, eds, *Russia Before and After Crimea: Nationalism and Identity, 2010–17*. Edinburgh: Edinburgh University Press, pp. 213–15

Bluhm, K. and Brand, M. 2019. '"Traditional values" unleashed: The ultra-conservative influence on Russian family policy', in Bluhm, K. and Varga,

M. eds. *New Conservatives in Russia and East Central Europe*. London: Routledge, pp. 223–44

Blum, Douglas. 2006. 'Official Patriotism in Russia: Its Essence and Implications', *PONARS Policy Memo No. 420*. Available from: <http://ponarseurasia.com/sites/default/files/policy-memos-pdf/pm_0420.pdf> (last accessed 25 April 2021)

Bobylev, Sergei. 2020. 'Istoriia aktsii "Bessmertnyi polk" v Rossii i mire. V etom godu iz-za pandemii aktsiia proidet v onlain-rezhime' [The history of the "Immortal Regiment" event in Russia and world-wide. This year the event will take place online], *TASS*, 8 May. Available from: <https://tass.ru/info/8428801> (last accessed 25 April 2021)

Bohr, Annette. 1989. 'Violence erupts in Uzbekistan', *Report on the USSR*, 16 June, 23–6

Boiko, Aleksandr. 2015. 'Sledstvennyi komitet usmotrel razvrat v tantse orenburgskikh "pchelok"' [The investigating committee looked into the lewdness of the dance of the 'bees' in Orenburg], *Komsomol'skaia Pravda*, 14 April. Available from: <http://www.kp.ru/daily/26366/3247977/> (last accessed 31 May 2020)

'Bol'shoe interv'iu'. 2014. 'Bol'shoe interv'iu o Novorossii, Russkoi Vesne, Strelkove kak aktere i samom sebe kak bloggere' [Extensive interview about New Russia, the Russian Spring, Strelkov and himself as a blogger], Interview with Egor Kholmogorov, 18 September. Available from: <https://holmogor.livejournal.com/6621155.html> (last accessed 30 March 2021)

Bourdieu, Pierre. 1991. *Language and Symbolic Power*. Oxford: Polity Press

Brandenberger, David. 2002. *National Bolshevism: Stalinist Mass Culture and the Formation of Modern Russian National Identity 1931–1956*. Cambridge, MA: Harvard University Press

Brass, Paul R. [1991] 1996. *Ethnicity and Nationalism: Theory and Comparison*. New Delhi: Sage

Bremmer, Ian and Welt, Cory. 1996. 'The trouble with democracy in Kazakhstan', *Central Asian Survey*, 15, 2: 179–200

Breslauer, George and Dale, Catherine. 1997. 'Boris Yeltsin and the invention of a Russian nation-state', *Post-Soviet Affairs*, 13, 4: 303–32

Breuilly, John. [1982] 1985. *Nationalism and the State*. Chicago: University of Chicago Press

Bronner, Stephen Eric. 2003. *A Rumor about the Jews: Antisemitism, Conspiracy and the Protocols of Zion*. New York: Oxford University Press

Brown, Bess. 1991. 'Ten months after the Dushanbe riots', *Report on the USSR*, 3, 4 January, 32–4

Brubaker, Rogers. 1996. *Nationalism Reframed: Nationhood and the National Question in the New Europe*. Cambridge: Cambridge University Press

Brubaker, Rogers. [1998] 1999. 'Myths and misconceptions in the study of nationalism', in Hall, John, ed., *The State of the Nation: Ernest Gellner and the Theory of Nationalism*. Cambridge: Cambridge University Press, pp. 132–68

Brubaker, Rogers. 2004. *Ethnicity Without Groups*. Cambridge, MA: Harvard University Press

Brudny, Yitzhak M. 2000. *Reinventing Russia: Russian Nationalism and the Soviet State 1953–1991*. Cambridge, MA: Harvard University Press

Brutskus, Iudel'-Leib. 1904. 'Evreiskii vopros v Russkoi pechati' [The Jewish question in the Russian press], *Evreiskaia Zhizn'*, 3: 198–212

Budnitskii, Oleg. 2002. 'Jews, pogroms, and the White Movement: A historiographical critique', *Kritika*, 2, 4: 751–2

Bystydzienski, Jill M. and Schacht, Steven P. 2001. *Forging Radical Alliances Across Difference: Coalition Politics for the New Millennium*. Lanham, MD: Rowman & Littlefield

Calhoun, Craig. 2007. *Nations Matter: Culture, History and the Cosmopolitan Dream*. Abingdon: Routledge

Canovan, Margaret. [1996] 1998. *Nationhood and Political Theory*. Cheltenham: Edward Elgar

Carrère d'Encausse, Hélène. 1979. *Decline of an Empire*. New York: Newsweek Books

Carrère d'Encausse, Hélène. 1992. *The Great Challenge: Nationalities in the Bolshevik State*, 1917–1930 (transl. N. Festinger). New York: Holmes and Meier

Carrère d'Encausse, Hélène. 1993. *The End of the Soviet Empire: The Triumph of the Nations*. New York: Basic Books

Carter, Stephen. 1990. *Russian Nationalism: Yesterday, Today, Tomorrow*. New York: St Martin's Press

Cerulo, Karen A. 1993. 'Symbols and the world system: National anthems and flags', *Sociological Forum*, 8, 2: 243–71

Chernoiarov, Ivan. 1890. *Zhidy. Ocherk ikh proiskhozhdeniia, izvrashchenie verovaniia, tselei i tainy* [Jews: An Outline of their Origin, Religious Distortions, Aim and Secrets]. St Petersburg: Tipografiia Doma prizreniia Maleletnykh Bednykh

Chikovani, Nino. Undated. 'Georgia on the crossroad of civilizations', *International Association of Caucasology*. Available from: <http://www.nplg.gov.ge/caucasia/messenger/eng/n3/summary/27.htm> (last accessed 30 March 2020)

Chua, Amy. 2003. *World on Fire: How Exporting Free Market Democracy Breeds Ethnic Hatred and Global Instability*. New York: Doubleday

Cohen, Abner. [1974] 1976. *Two-Dimensional Man: An Essay on the Anthropology of Power and Symbolism in Complex Societies*. Berkeley: University of California Press

Cohen, Anthony. 1994. 'Boundaries of consciousness, consciousness of boundaries', in Vermeulen, Hans, and Covers, Cora, eds, *The Anthropology of Ethnicity: Beyond Ethnic Groups and Boundaries*. Amsterdam: Het Spinhuis

Cohen, Anthony, ed. 2000. *Signifying Identities: Anthropological Perspectives on Boundaries and Contested Values*. London: Routledge

Cohen, Anthony. [1985] 2008. *The Symbolic Construction of Community*. London: Routledge

Cohen, Robin. 1997. *Global Diasporas: An Introduction*. London: UCL Press

Connor, Walker. 1984. *The National Question in Marxist–Leninist Theory and Strategy*. Princeton, NJ: Princeton University Press

Connor, Walker. 1994. *Ethnonationalism: The Quest for Understanding*. Princeton, NJ: Princeton University Press

Connor, Walker. 2004. 'Nationalism and political illegitimacy', in Conversi, Daniele. ed., *Ethnonationalism in the Contemporary World: Walker Connor and the Study of Nationalism*. London: Routledge, pp. 24–49

'Convention No. 169'. 1989. 'Convention No 169'. *International Labour Organization*. Available from: <http://www.ilo.org/dyn/normlex/en/f?p=NORMLEXPUB:12100:0::NO:12100:P12100_ILO_CODE:C169> (last accessed 30 May 2020)

Conversi, Daniele. 1995. 'Reassessing current theories of nationalism: Nationalism as boundary maintenance and creation', *Nationalism and Ethnic Politics*, 1, 1: 73–85

Conversi, Daniele. 1999. 'Nationalism, boundaries, and violence', *Millennium* 28, 3: 553–84

Conversi, Daniele. 2004. 'Conceptualizing nationalism: An introduction to Walker Connor's work', in Conversi, Daniele, ed., *Ethno-nationalism in the Contemporary World: Walker Connor and the Study of Nationalism*. London: Routledge, pp. 1–23

Conversi, Daniele. 2007. 'Mapping the field: Theories of nationalism and the ethnosymbolic approach', in Leoussi, Athena and Grosby, Stephen, eds, *Nationalism and Ethnic Symbolism: History, Culture and Ethnicity in the Formation of Nations*. Edinburgh: Edinburgh University Press, pp. 16–30

Conquest, Robert. 1967. *Soviet Nationalities Policy in Practice*. London: The Bodley Head

Côté, Isabelle and Mitchell, Matthew. 2017. 'Deciphering 'Sons of the Soil' conflicts: A critical survey of the literature', *Ethnopolitics*, 16, 4: 333–51

Dave, Bhavna. 1996. 'A new parliament consolidates presidential authority', *Transition*, 2, 6: 33–7

Dave, Bhavna. 2007. *Kazakhstan: Ethnicity, Language and Power*. London: Routledge

Demidov San-Donato, Pavel. 1883. *Evreiskii Vopros v Rossii* [The Jewish Question in Russia]. St Petersburg: Tipografiia M. M. Stasiulevicha

Demushkin, Dmitrii et al. 2004. 'Uroki russkogo natsionalizma' [Lessons about Russian nationalism]. Available from: <http://www.demushkin.com/page3.php (last accessed 30 June 2016, no longer available)

Deutsch, Karl. 1996. *Nationalism and Social Communication: An Inquiry into the Foundations of Nationality*. Cambridge, MA: MIT

de Waal, Thomas. 2003. *Black Garden: Armenia and Azerbaijan through Peace and War*. New York: New York University Press

Dima, Nicholas. 1991. *From Moldavia to Moldova: The Soviet-Romanian Territorial Dispute*. Boulder, CO: East European Monographs

Dobrynina, Ekatarina. 2013. 'Rossiianam nravitsia aktsiia "Georgievskaia lentochka"' [Russians like the St George ribbon campaign], *Rossiiskaia gazeta*, 2 May. Available from: <http://www.rg.ru/2013/05/02/lentochka-site.html> (last accessed 31 May 2020)

Dokuchaeva, Aleksandra. 1994. 'Eshche raz o iazyke, i ne tol'ko o nem . . .' [Once more about the language, and not only about that], *Vedi respublika Kazakhstan*, December

Dontsov, Dmytro. [1921] 1957. *Pidstavy nashoy polityky* [The Foundations of Our Politics]. New York: no publisher given

Dorpema, Marc. 2021. 'Abkhazia: Recasting 'ethnic' war', *Europe-Asia Studies*, Ahead Of-Print, 1–18. Available from: <https://doi-org.ezproxy.uio.no/10.1080/09668136.2021.1884663> (last accessed 25 April 2021)

Drobizheva, Leokadia. 1998. 'Russian ethnonationalism', in Drobizheva, Leokadia, Gottemoeller, Rose, McArdle Kelleher, Catherine and Walker, Lee, eds, *Ethnic Conflict in the Post-Soviet World: Case Studies and Analysis*. Armonk, NY: M. E. Sharpe, pp. 129–47

Dubin, Boris. 2014. 'Natsionalizm v Rossii: obshchestvennye nastroeniia i gosudarstvennaia politika' [Nationalism in Russia: Public sentiments and government policy], *Pro et Contra*, 18: 6–18

Dubnov, Simon. 1975. *History of the Jews in Russia and Poland from the Earliest Times to the Present Day*. Vol. 2. New York: Ktav Publishing House

Dugin, Aleksandr. 2014a. 'Zdravstvui, Krym! Vperedi bitva za Novorossiiu' [Welcome, Crimea! The battle for New Russia awaits], *Otdelnyi divizion*, 17 March. Available from: <http://odivizion-ru.livejournal.com/205356.html> (last accessed 30 March 2021)

Dugin, Aleksandr. 2014b. 'Ukraina v velikoi voine kontinentov' [Ukraine in the Great War of the Continents], *Evrazia*, 25 March. Available from: <http://evrazia.info/article/4774> (last accessed 17 December 2015)

Dugin, Aleksandr. 2014c. 'Segodnia my uvideli nastoiashchego Putina, kotoryi prishel k russkoi istine' [Today we saw the real Putin who has come to the Russian truth], *Nakanune.ru*, 17 April. Available from: <http://www.nakanune.ru/articles/18908/> (last accessed 30 March 2021)

Dugin, Aleksandr. 2014d. 'Rozhdenie Novorossii' [The birth of Novorossiia], *Evrazia*, 19 May. Available from:< http://evrazia.info/article/4805> (last accessed 17 December 2015)

Dugin, Aleksandr. 2014e. 'Za Akhmetova grud'iu vstala rossiiskaia "shestaia kolonna"' [The Russian sixth column stood up for Akhmetov], *Nakanune.ru*, 21 May. Available from: <https://www.nakanune.ru/news/2014/05/21/22353563/> (last accessed 17 December 2015)

Dugin, Aleksandr. 2014f. 'Prizrak poruchika: nashe imia Strelkov' [The ghost of a lieutenant: Our name is Strelkov], *Evrazia*, 25 May. Available from: <http://evrazia.info/topic/16/> (last accessed 30 March 2021)

Dugin, Aleksandr. 2014g. From his *Vkontakte* page, 4 June. Available from: <http://vk.com/wall18631635_2898> (last accessed 30 March 2021)

Dugin, Aleksandr. 2014h. 'Uspekhi shestoi kolonny. Moia lichnaia plata za Novorossiiu' [The Success of the Sixth Column: What I personally had to pay for Novorossiia], from his *Facebook* page, 27 June. Available from: <https://www.facebook.com/alexandr.dugin/posts/804580389552003> (last accessed 30 March 2021)

Dugin, Aleksandr. 2014i. 'Protiv Putina gotovitsia zagovor' [They are planning a conspiracy against Putin], *Nakanune*, 3 October. Available from: <https://www.nakanune.ru/articles/19518/> (last accessed 30 March 2021)

Duncan, Peter J. S. 2000. *Russian Messianism: Third Rome, Revolution, Communism and After*. London: Routledge

Dunlop, John B. 1983. *The Faces of Contemporary Russian Nationalism*. Princeton, NJ: Princeton University Press

Dunlop, John B.1985. *The New Russian Nationalism*. New York: Praeger

Dunlop, John B. 1993. *The Rise of Russia and the Fall of the Soviet Empire*. Princeton, NJ: Princeton University Press

Durkheim, Emile. [1912] 2008. *Elementary Forms of Religious Life*. Oxford: Oxford University Press

Dzhokhadze, Avto. 2007. 'Rossiia glazami gruzina' [Russia in the eyes of a Georgian], *Gruzia Online*, 19 April. Available from: <http://www.apsny.ge/society/1177005060.php> (last accessed 8 November 2008)

Dzhunusova, Zhalnylzhan. 1996. *Respublika Kazakhstan: President. Instituty Demokratii* [Republic of Kazakhstan: President. Institutions of Democracy]. Almaty: Zhety Zhargy

Edelman, Murray. [1964] 1985. *The Symbolic Uses of Politics*. Urbana: University of Illinois Press

Egorov, Ivan and Petrov, Vitalii. 2012. 'Miting na prospekte Sakharova sobral 150 chelovek' [150 people showed up at a rally at Sakharov Square], *Rossiiskaia gazeta*, 2 February. Available from: <http://www.rg.ru/2012/02/04/poklon-site.html> (last accessed 31 May 2020)

Elagin, Andrei Sergeevich. 1993. *Kazachestvo i Kazach'i voiska v Kazakhstane* [The Cossacks and the Cossack Hosts in Kazakhstan]. Almaty: 'Kazakhstan'

Elgenius, Gabriella. 2011a. *Symbols of Nations and Nationalism: Celebrating Nationhood*. New York: Palgrave Macmillan

Elgenius, Gabriella. 2011b. 'The politics of recognition: Symbols, nation building and rival nationalisms', *Nations and Nationalism*, 17, 2: 396–418

Eliseev, Igor'. 2015. 'Kak i kogda poiavilis' georgievskaia i gvardeiskaia lentochki' [How and when did the St George and the Guard ribbons appear?], *Rossiiskaia gazeta*, 6 May. Available from: http://m.rg.ru/2015/05/07/lentochka.html (last accessed 31 May 2020)

Eliseev, Stanislav. 2014. 'Naval'nyi: Martovskie tezisy, ili razviornutaia pozitsiia po Ukraine i Krymu' [Navalnyi: The March theses, or a detailed statement about Ukraine and Crimea], *Republic.ru*, 12 March. Available from: <http://slon.ru/fast/russia/navalnyymartovskie-tezisy-ili-razvernutaya-pozitsiya-po-ukraine-i-krymu-1069397.xhtml> (last accessed 30 March 2021)

Emel'ianova, Svetlana. 2013. 'Iz Stavropolia Georgievskaia lenta otpravilas' po strane' [From Stavropol the St George ribbon has been sent around the country], *Rossiiskaia gazeta*, 29 April. Available from: <http://www.rg.ru/2013/04/29/reg-skfo/pobeda.html> (last accessed 31 May 2020)

Epifanova, Mariia. 2012a. 'Kandidaty v koordinatory' [The candidates for the Coordination council], *Novaia gazeta*, 21 September. Available from: <https://novayagazeta.ru/articles/2012/09/20/51525-kandidaty-v-koordinatory> (last accessed 1 June 2020)

Epifanova, Mariia. 2012b. 'Debaty daiut mandaty' [Debates lead to mandates], *Novaia gazeta*, 24 October. Available from: <https://novayagazeta.ru/articles/2012/10/24/52031debaty-dayut-mandaty?print=true> (last 1 June 2020)

Epifanova, Mariia. 2014. 'Nazrel otkrovennyi muzhskoi rasgovor: Vnutri obedinennoi partii RPR- PARNAS sereznyi krisis. Udastia li uberech ee ot raskola?' [It's time for a serious talk man-to-man: There is a serious crisis inside the United People's Freedom's Party-PARNAS], *Novaia gazeta*, 31 January. Available from: <www.novayagazeta.ru/politics/62036.html> (last accessed 30 June 2016, no longer available)

Epifantsev, Andrei. 2012. 'Oshibki oppozitsii' [The mistakes of the opposition], *APN*, 27 February. Available from: <https://www.apn.ru/publications/article26056.htm> (last accessed 25 April 2021)

Eriksen, Thomas Hylland. 1993. *Ethnicity & Nationalism: Anthropological Perspectives*. London: Pluto Press

Ermolaeva, Nadezhda. 2015a. 'Ukrainskii Elle pomenial oblozhku nomera iz-za ugroz natsionalistov' [Ukrainian Elle changed the cover of one of its issues due to nationalist threats], *Rossiiskaia gazeta*, 24 April. Available from: <http://www.rg.ru/2015/04/24/elle-site-anons.html> (last accessed 31 May 2020)

Ermolaeva, Nadezhda. 2015b. 'V Latvii predlozhili sazhat' v tiurmu za noshenie georgievskoi lentochki' [Proposal in Latvia to throw people in jail for wearing St George ribbons], *Rossiiskaia gazeta*, 6 May. Available from: <http://www.rg.ru/2015/05/06/latvia-site-anons.html> (last accessed 31 May 2020)

Ermolaeva, Nadezhda. 2015c. 'Seim Latvii rassmotrit predlozhenie o zaprete georgievskoi lentochki' [The Saeima will discuss proposal to ban St George ribbons], *Rossiiskaia gazeta*, 13 May. Available from: <http://www.rg.ru/2015/05/13/latvia-site-anons.html> (last accessed 31 May 2020)

Fearon, James, and Laitin, David. 2010. 'Sons of the Soil, Migrants, and Civil War', *World Development* 39, 2: 199–211

Fedor, Julie. 2017. 'Memory, kinship, and the mobilization of the dead: The Russian state and the "Immortal Regiment movement"', in Julie Fedor, Markku Kangaspuro, Jussi Lassila and Tatiana Zhurzhenko, eds, *War and Memory in Russia, Ukraine and Belarus*. London: Palgrave, pp. 307–44

Feoktistov, Aleksandr. 1992. *Russkie, Kazakhi i Altai* [Russians, Kazakhs and Altai]. Moscow/Ust'-Kamenogorsk: Al'fa i Omega

Fish, Steven. 2014. 'The end of the Putin mystique', *Washington Post*, Monkey cage, 3 April. Available from: <https://www.washingtonpost.com/news/monkey-cage/wp/2014/04/03/the-end-of-the-putin-mystique/> (last accessed 26 July 2021)

Flikke, Geir. 2015. 'Resurgent authoritarianism: The case of Russia's new NGO legislation', *Post-Soviet Affairs*, 32, 2: 1–29

Frolov, Vladimir. 2014. 'Crimea helped Putin hijack the nationalists', *The Moscow Times*, 13 April. Available from: <https://www.themoscowtimes.com/2014/04/13/crimea-helped-putin-hijack-the-nationalists-a33899> (last accessed 30 March 2021)

Fuller, Elizabeth and Bohr, Annette. 1989. 'Chronology of ethnic disturbances in Transcaucasia and Central Asia', *Report on the USSR*, 1: 16–18

Gabdrafikov, Il'dar. 1998. *Respublika Bashkortostan: Model' etnologicheskogo monitoringa* [The Republic of Bashkortostan: Model for Ethnological Monitoring]. Moscow: Institut Etnologii i Antropologii

Gagnon, Valère Philip. 1997. 'Ethnic nationalism and international conflict: The case of Serbia', in Brown, M. E., Coté Jr, O. R., Lynn-Jones, S. M.

and Miller, S. E., eds, *Nationalism and Ethnic Conflict*. Cambridge, MA: MIT Press, pp. 132–68

Gagnon, Valère Philip. 2004. *The Myth of Ethnic War: Serbia and Croatia in the 1990s*. Ithaca, NY: Cornell University Press

Galiev, Anuar, Babakumarov, Erzhan, Zhansugurova, Zh. and Perushaev, A. 1994. *Mezhnatsional'nye otnosheniia v Kazakhstane. Etnicheskii aspekt kadrovoi politiki* [Interethnic Relations in Kazakhstan. Personnel Policy from an Ethnic Perspective]. Almaty: Institut Razvitiia Kazakhstana

Gamov, Aleksandr. 2015. 'Aleksandr Prokhanov: Donbass predavat' nel'zia. Esli eto sluchitsia, Rossii ne pomogut nikakie antikrizisnye mery' [Aleksandr Prokhanov: We cannot betray Donbas. If that should happen, no anti-crisis measures can help Russia], *Komsomolskaia pravda*, 13 February. Available from: <http://www.kp.ru/daily/26341/3224169> (last accessed 30 March 2021)

Gamova, Svetlana. 2014. 'V Moldavii mogut shtrafovat' za georgievskuiu lentochku' [In Moldova, people may be fined for St George ribbons], *Nezavisimaia gazeta*, 6 June. Available from: <http://www.ng.ru/cis/2014-06-06/2_moldavia.html> (last accessed 31 May 2020)

Gamova, Svetlana. 2015. 'Georgievskaia lenta stala simvolom raskola Sodruzhestva Nezavisimykh Gosudarstv' [The St George ribbon has become a symbol of a schism in the Commonwealth of Independent States], *Regnum*, 29 April. Available from: <https://regnum.ru/news/polit/1920388.html> (last accessed 01 June 2020)

'Garry Kasparov'. 2012. 'Garry Kasparov kak lider russkikh natsionalistov' [Garry Kasparov as a leader of Russian nationalists], *Russkaia Narodnaia Liniia*. Available from: <http://ruskline.ru/news_rl/2012/02/02/garri_kasparov_kak_lider_russkih_nacionalistov/> (last accessed 31 May 2020)

Gatrell, Peter. 1986. *The Tsarist Economy 1850–1917*. London: B. T. Batsford

Gazeta.ru. 2011. 'Putin pro belye lentochki kak simvol "tsvetnoi revoliutsii": pokhozhi na kontratseptivy' [Putin about White Ribbons as a symbol of a 'Colour Revolution': They look like contraceptives], 15 December, *Gazeta.ru*. Available from: <https://www.gazeta.ru/news/lenta/2011/12/15/n_2135786.shtml> (last accessed 25 April 2021)

Geisler, Michael E., ed. 2005. *National Symbols, Fractured Identities: Contesting the National Narrative*. Hanover: University Press of New England

Gellner, Ernest. [1964] 1972. *Thought and Change*. London: Weidenfeld & Nicholson

Gellner, Ernest. [1983] 1990. *Nations and Nationalism*. Oxford: Basil Blackwell

'Georgievskaia lentochka'. Undated. 'Georgievskaia lentochka' [St George ribbons], *Kodeks aktsii*. No longer available

'Georgievskaia lentochka'. 2009. '"Georgievskaia lentochka" prevrashchaetsia v instrument piara i aksessuar odezhdy' [The St George ribbon is being turned into an instrument of public relations and a clothing accessory'], *Gazeta.ru*. 8 May. Available from: <http://www.gazeta.spb.ru/152358-0/> (last accessed 31 May 2020)

'Georgievskaia lentochka'. 2014. 'Georgievskaia lentochka Lidii Fedoseevoi-Shukshinoi vyzvala allergiu u finskikh pogranichnikov' [Lidiia Fedoseeva-Shukshina's St George's ribbon caused an allergic reaction among Finnish border guards], *Komsomol'skaia Pravda*, 11 May. Available from: <http://kompravda.eu/online/news/1734111> (last accessed 31 May 2020)

'Georgievskaia lentochka'. 2015. 'Georgievskaia lentochka na grudi sotrudnitsy kompanii Statoil napugala v Estonii politika i biznesmena' [St George ribbon on the breast of an employee of Statoil company in Estonia frightened a politician and businessman], *Komsomol'skaia pravda*, 8 May. Available from: <http://www.kp.ru/online/news/2050541/> (last accessed 31 May 2020)

Gessen, Iulii. 1906. *O zhizni Evreev v Rossii* [About the Lives of Jews in Russia]. St Petersburg: No publisher given

Giller, Boris and Shatskikh V. 1993. 'Russkoiazychnye v Kazakhstane: Opredelenie berega' [Russian-speaking people in Kazakhstan: Where to go], *Karavan*, 24 December

Girin, Nikita, Murtazin, Irek and Artemova, Anna. 2012. 'Esli boiatsia moroza-ottepeli ne budet' [Without frost there will not be thaw], *Novaia gazeta*. Available from: <http://www.novayagazeta.ru/politics/50620.html> (last accessed 30 June 2016, no longer available)

Gitelman, Zvi. [1988] 2001. *A Century of Ambivalence: The Jews of Russia and the Soviet Union, 1881 to the Present*. Bloomington: Indiana University Press

Giuliano, Elise. 2005. 'Do Grievances Matter in Nationalist Mobilization? Evidence from Russia's Republics, 1989–94'. Paper Presented to the Association for the Study of Nationalities Annual Convention, Columbia University

Giuliano, Elise. 2006. 'Secessionism from the bottom up', *World Politics*, 58, 2: 276–310

Giuliano, Elise. 2011. *Constructing Grievance: Ethnic Nationalism in Russia's Republics*. Ithaca, NY: Cornell University Press

Goble, Paul A. 1995. 'Three faces of nationalism in the Former Soviet Union', in Kupchan, Charles, ed. *Nationalism and Nationalities in the New Europe*. Ithaca, NY: Cornell University Press, pp 122–35

Goldstein, Jonah and Rayner, Jeremy. 1994. 'The politics of identity in late modern society', *Theory and Society*, 23, 3: 367–84

Gol'ts, Aleksandr. 2014. 'Chetvertoe vziatie Kryma' [The fourth conquest of Crimea], *Pro et Contra*, May–August: 45–56

Goode, J. Paul. 2018. 'Everyday patriotism and ethnicity in today's Russia', in Kolstø, Pål and Blakkisrud, Helge, eds, *Russia Before and After Crimea:*

Nationalism and Identity, 2010–17. Edinburgh: Edinburgh University Press, pp. 258–81

Gorelova, Mariia. 2015. 'V Khar'kove sotrudnitsu militsii uvolili za georgievskuiu lentochku' [In Kharkiv a policewoman with a St George ribbon was fired], *Komsomol'skaia pravda*, 24 February. Available from: <http://www.kp.ru/online/news/1983170/> (last accessed 31 May 2020)

Gorenburg, Dmitrii. 2003. *Minority Ethnic Mobilization in the Russian Federation.* Cambridge: Cambridge University Press

Gosudarstvennaia Duma. 1999. *Federal"nyi zakon o gosudarstvennoi politike Rossiiskoi Federatsii v otnoshenii sootechestvennikov za rubezhom* [Federal Law on the State Policy of the Russian Federation on Relations with Compatriots Abroad]. 5 March. Available from: <http://pravo.gov.ru/proxy/ips/?docbody=&nd=102059567> (last accessed 31 May 2020)

Gosudarstvennaia programma 'Narody Bashkortostana', (kontseptsiia) [State Program 'The People of Bashkortostan', (Concept)]. 1999. Ufa: Akademiia nauk Respubliki Bashkortostan

Govorun, Kirill. 2015. 'Interpretiruia "russkii mir": Slozhnoe obshchestvo' [When interpreting 'the Russian world': A complicated community], *Russkii zhurnal*, 6, October. Available from: <http://www.russ.ru/Mirovaya-povestka/Interpretiruya-russkij-mir> (last accessed 13 March 2018)

Greene, Samuel A. 2014. *Moscow in Movement: Power and Opposition in Putin's Russia.* Stanford, CA: Stanford University Press

Grishina, Viktoriia. 2015. '"Bessmertnyi polk" pridumal tiumenskii pensioner' [The Immortal Regiment was invented by a pensioner from Tiumen´], *Komsomol'skaia Pravda*, 11 May. Available from: <http://www.kp.ru/online/news/2051662/> (last accessed 31 May 2020)

Guboglo, Mikhail. 1993. *Perelomnye gody: Mobilizirovannyi lingvilizm* [Turning Years: Mobilised Linguism]. Moscow: Tsimo

Gubolgo, Mikhail, ed. 1994. *Perelomnye gody, iazykovaia reforma – 1989* [Turning Years, Language Reform – 1989]. Moscow: Tsimo

Guboglo, Mikhail. 1998. *Iazyki Etnicheskoi Mobilizatsii* [Languages of Ethnic Mobilisation]. Moscow: Shkola 'Iazyki Russkoi Kultury'

'Goriachaia subbota'. 2012. 'Goriachaia subbota: 4 fevralia v Moskve proidet 4 mitinga' [A hot Saturday: On 4 February four rallies will take place in Moscow], *Rossiiskaia gazeta*, 2 February. Available from: <http://www.rg.ru/2012/02/02/subbota.html> (last accessed 31 May 2020)

Guibernau, Montserrat. [2007] 2011. *The Identity of Nations.* Cambridge: Polity Press

Guibernau, Montserrat. 2013. *Belonging: Solidarity and Division in Modern Societies.* Cambridge: Polity Press

Gusar, Aleksandr. 2018. 'V Donetske otprazdnovali Den' Georgievskoi lenty' [St George Ribbons' Day was celebrated in Donetsk], Politnavigator,

7 December. Available from: <https://www.politnavigator.net/v-donecke-otprazdnovali-den-georgievskojj-lenty.html> (last accessed 30 March 2021)

Hale, Henry E. 2000. 'The parade of sovereignties: Testing theories of secession in the Soviet setting', *British Journal of Political Science*, 30, 1: 31–56

Hale, Henry E. 2016. 'How nationalism and machine politics mix in Russia', in Kolstø, Pål and Blakkisrud, Helge, eds, *The New Russian Nationalism: Imperialism, Ethnicity and Authoritarianism 2000–2015*. Edinburgh: Edinburgh University Press, pp. 221–48

Hall, John A., ed. 1998. *The State of the Nation: Ernest Gellner and the Theory of Nationalism*. Cambridge: Cambridge University Press

Hechter, Michael. 1975. *Internal Colonialism: The Celtic Fringe in British National Development, 1536–1966*. London: Routledge and Kegan Paul

Hirsch, Francine. 2005. *Empire of Nations: Ethnographic Knowledge and the Making of the Soviet Union*. Ithaca, NY: Cornell University Press

Hobsbawm, Eric. 1991. *Nations and Nationalism Since 1780*. Cambridge: Cambridge University Press

Hobsbawm, Eric and Ranger, Terence. 1992. *The Invention of Tradition*. Cambridge: Cambridge University Press

Hodnett, Grey. 1979. *Leadership in the Soviet National Republics*. Oakville, Ontario: Mosaic Press

Horowitz, Donald. 1985. *Ethnic Groups in Conflict*. Berkeley: University of California Press

Horvath, Robert. 2015. 'The Euromaidan and the crisis of Russian nationalism', *Nationalities Papers*, 43, 6: 819–39

Hosking, Geoffrey. 1997. *Russia: People and Empire 1552–1917*. Cambridge, MA: Harvard University Press

Hosking, Geoffrey. 1998. 'Empire and nation-building in late Imperial Russia', in Hosking, Geoffrey and Service, Robert, eds, *Russian Nationalism, Past And Present*. London: Macmillan, pp. 19–33

Human Rights Watch. 2009. *Are you Happy to Cheat us? Exploitation of Migrant Construction Workers in Russia*, Report, February. Available from: <https://www.hrw.org/sites/default/files/reports/russia0209web_0.pdf> (last accessed 2 May 2021)

Huntington, Samuel. 1991. *The Third Wave: Democratization in the Late Twentieth Century*. Norman: University of Oklahoma Press

Huntington, Samuel. 1993. 'The clash of civilizations?', *Foreign Affairs* 72: 22–49

Huntington, Samuel. 1996. *The Clash of Civilizations and the Remaking of World Order*. London: The Free Press

Huntington, Samuel. 1999. *Tsivilisatsioonide kokkupõrge ja maailmakorra ümberkujundamine*. Tartu: Fontes.

Hutchinson, John. 2005. *Nations as Zones of Conflict*. London: Sage

Huttenbach, Henry R., ed. 1990. *Soviet Nationality Policies: Ruling Ethnic Groups in the USSR*. London: Mansell

Hüttermann, Jörg. 2000. 'Der Avancierende Fremde: Zur Genese von Unsicherheitsfahrungen und Konflikten in einem Ethnisch Polarisierten und Socialräumlich Benachteiligten Stadtteil', *Zeitschrift für Soziologie*, 29, August: 275–93

Iarmonkin, Valentin. 1894. *Evreiskii vopros* [The Jewish Question]. St Petersburg: Tipografiia ministerstva putei soobshcheniia

'Igor' Strelkov' 2014. 'Igor' Strelkov zhenilsia na grazhdanke Ukrainy' [Igor Strelkov got married to a woman who is a Ukrainian citizen], *SPR*, 18 December. Available from: <http://www.spr.ru/novosti/2014-12/igor-strelkov-zhenilsya-na-grazhdanke-ukraini.html> (last accessed 31 May 2020)

Ingram, Alan. 1999. '"A nation split into fragments": The Congress of Russian Communities and Russian nationalist ideology', *Europe-Asia Studies*, 51, 4: 687–704

Interfaks. 2015. 'Foto s vybroshennymi plakatami "Bessmertnogo polka" v Priamur'e ob'iasnili nedorabotkoi koordinatorov' [The photos with discarded placards from the Immortal Regiment in Priamur'e was explained as a result of the coordinators' sloppy work], *Interfaks*, 14 May. Available from: <http://www.interfax.ru/russia/441747> (last accessed 19 July 2021)

'Iunie "pchelki"'. 2015. 'Iunie "pchelki v georgievskikh lentakh" ispolnili eroticheskii tanets' [Young 'Bees in St George ribbons' performed an erotic dance], *Moskovskii komsomolets*, 13 April. Available from: <http://www.mk.ru/print/article/1206505/> (last accessed 31 May 2020)

Ivachev, Aleksandr. 2011. 'Georgievskaia lentochka: ocherednoi obman?' [St George ribbons: Just another deception?], *The Communist Party of the Russian Federation*, 5 May. Available from: <https://www.rbth.com/history/328240-st-georges-ribbon> (last accessed 25 April 2021)

Ivanova, Elena. 2008. 'Pamiat' ognennogo tsveta' [A fire-coloured memory], *Rossiiskaia gazeta*, 12 May. Available from: <http://www.rg.ru/2008/05/12/reg-kuban/georglenty.html> (last accessed 31 May 2020)

Ivanovskaia, Natal'ia. 2012. 'Ia pomniu, ia gorzhus': Georgievskie lentochki vnov' opoiasali mir' [I remember and I'm proud: St George ribbons once again girdle the world], *Rossiiskaia gazeta*, 24 April. Available from: <http://m.rg.ru/2012/04/23/georgsite.html> (last accessed 31 May 2020)

Ivashkina, Dar'ia. 2012. 'Sobchak vystupila protiv kvot na vyborakh v Koordinatsionnyi sovet oppozitsii' (Sobchak spoke out against electoral quotas for the Coordination Council of the opposition], *Komsomol'skaia Pravda*, 17 September. Available from: <http://www.kp.ru/online/news/1248797/> (last accessed 31 May 2020)

Jenkins, Richard. 1996. *Social Identities*. London: Routledge

Jones, Ellen and Grupp, Fred. 1984. 'Modernisation and ethnic equalisation in the USSR', *Soviet Studies* 36, 2: 159–84

Judge, Edward H. 1992. *Easter in Kishinev: Anatomy of a Pogrom*. New York: New York University Press

Kaiser, Robert J. 1994. *The Geography of Nationalism in Russia and the USSR*. Princeton, NJ: Princeton University Press

Kaiser, Robert J. 1995. 'Nationalizing the work force: Ethnic restratification in the newly independent states', *Post-Soviet Geography*, 36, 2: 87–111

Kaiser, Robert J. and Chinn, Jeff. 1995. 'Russian–Kazakh relations in Kazakhstan', *Post-Soviet Geography* 36, 5: 257–73

'Kak sokhranit'. 2015. 'Kak sokhranit' podlinnyi den' pobedy' [How to preserve the authentic Victory Day], Interview with Gennadii Bordiugov, *Ekho Moskvy*, 2 May. Available from: <http://echo.msk.ru/programs/victory/1540158-echo/> (last accessed 31 May 2020)

Kalashnikov, Maksim. 2014a. 'Novorossiia – zavtrashniaia real'nost' [New Russia – the reality of tomorrow], *Zavtra*, 29 May. Available from: <http://www.zavtra.ru/content/view/novorossiya-zavtrashnyaya-realnost/> (last accessed 30 March 2021)

Kalashnikov, Maksim. 2014b. 'Ia by ne nazval eto "sdachei". Novorossiiu prosto spustili v unitaz' [I would not call it surrender. New Russia was just spoiled down in the toilet], *Nakanune.ru*, 12 September. Available from: <http://www.nakanune.ru/articles/19440/> (last accessed 30 March 2021)

Kappeler, Andreas. 1993. *Russland als Vielvölkerreich. Entstehung, Geschichte, Zerfall*. Munich: C. H. Beck

Karklins, Rasma. 1984. 'Ethnic politics and access to higher education: The Soviet case', *Comparative Politics*, 16, 3: 277–94

Karklins, Rasma. 1986. *Ethnic Relations in the USSR: The Perspective from Below*. Boston: Unwin Hyman

Karney, Ihar and Sindelar, Daisy. 2015. 'For Victory Day, post-Soviets show their colors – just not orange and black', *RFE/RL*, 7 May. Available from: <http://www.rferl.org/content/victory-day-st-george-ribbon-orange-and-black/26999911.html> (last accessed 31 May 2020)

'Kasparov vystupil'. 2012. 'Kasparov vystupil na forume natsionalistov' [Kasparov spoke at a nationalist forum], *Natsional'nyi aktsent*, 30 January. Available from: <http://nazaccent.ru/content/3644-kasparov-vystupil-na-forume-nacionalistov.html> (last accessed 31 May 2020)

Kaufman, Stuart J. 2001. *Modern Hatreds: The Symbolic Politics of Ethnic War*. Ithaca, NY: Cornell University Press

Kautsky, Karl. 1906. *Evreiskie Pogromy i Evreiskii Vopros* [Jewish Pogroms and the Jewish Question]. No place given: Novy Mir

Kel'ner, Viktor. 2004. 'Russkaia intelligentsiia i "Evreiskii Vopros" v nachale XX v. (Antisemitizm, Iudofiliia. Asemitizm)' [The Russian intelligentsia and the 'Jewish Question' at the beginning of the twentieth century. (Antisemitism, judofilia, asemitism)], *Paralleli*, 4–5: 73–86

Kenez, Peter. 2004. 'Pogroms and white ideology in the Russian civil war', in Klier, John Doyle and Lambroza, Shlomo, eds, *Pogroms: Anti-Jewish Violence in Modern Russian History*. Cambridge: Cambridge University Press, pp. 293–313

Kertzer, David I. 1988. *Ritual, Politics and Power*. New Haven, CT: Yale University Press

Khakimov, Rafail' [Khakim, Rafail']. 1993. *Sumerki imperii: K voprosu o natsii i gosudarstve* [Empire at Nightfall: On the Question of the Nation and the State]. Kazan': Tatarskoe knizhnoe izdatel'stvo

'Khar'kovchanam razdadut'. 2013. 'Khar'kovchanam razdadut' po simvolu Pobedy' [All people in Kharkov will get the victory symbol], 23 April, *Kharkovskie izvestiia*. Available from: <http://izvestia.kharkov.ua/online/20/1135873.html> (last accessed 30 March 2021)

Khasanov, Bakhytzhan. 1996. 'Priniatie zakona o iazykakh – mirovoi standart razvitiia iazykov' [The law on languages marks a world standard in the development of languages], *Kazakhstanskaia Pravda*, 29 November

Khazanov, Anatoly. 1995. *After the USSR: Ethnicity, Nationalism, and Politics in the Commonwealth of Independent States*. Madison: University of Wisconsin Press

Khokhlov, Oleg and L'vov, Iurii. 2015. 'Kak Pobeda stala dvigatelem torgovli' [How the victory became a motor of commerce], *Kommersant*, 11 May. Available from: <http://www.kommersant.ru/doc/2713642> (last accessed 31 May 2020)

Kholmogorov, Egor. 2006. *Zashchitit li Rossiia Ukrainu* [Will Russia Defend Ukraine?]. Moscow: Evropa

Kholmogorov, Egor. 2014a. 'Otkrytoe pis'mo ukraintsam' [Open letter to the Ukrainians]. Available from: <http://holmogor.livejournal.com/6196638.html> (last accessed 30 March 2021)

Kholmogorov, Egor. 2014b. *Facebook*, 26 May. Available from: <http://www.svoboda.org/contentlive/liveblog/25399831.html> (last accessed 18 December 2015, no longer available)

'Kholmogorov o vstreche'. Undated. 'Kholmogorov o vstreche so Strelkovym' [Kholmogorov about his meeting with Strelkov], *Livejournal*. Available from: <https://kolokoll.livejournal.com/449849.html> (last accessed 30 March 2021)

Khramov, Aleksandr. 2011. *Katekhizis natsional-demokrata* [A Catechism of a National Democrat]. Moscow: Skimen'

Khramov, Aleksandr. 2013. 'Mozhet li nationalist byt' liberalom?' [Is it possible for a nationalist to be a liberal?], *Voprosy natsionalizma*, 13: 222–30

Khramov, Aleksandr. 2014. 'Prisoediniaia Krym, Rossiia vozlagaet na sebia otvetstvennost' za russkikh' [By annexing Crimea Russia takes responsibility for Russians], *Svobodnaia pressa*, 13 March. Available from: <http://svpressa.ru/politic/article/83647/> (last accessed 30 March 2021)

'Khronologiia aktsii'. 'Khronologiia aktsii protesta protiv fal'sifikatsii vyborov v Rossii (2011–2012)' [The protests against the falsification of the Russian elections (a chronological resume 2011–2012)], *Wikipedia*

'Kiev otkazalsia'. 2014. 'Kiev otkazalsia ot georgievskoi lentochki kak simvol Dnia Pobedy' [Kiev refuses to use St George ribbons as a symbol of Victory Day], *TASS*, 6 May. Available from: <http://tass.ru/mezhdunarodnaya-panorama/1168788> (last accessed 31 May 2020)

Kim, Alexander. 2015. 'St George's ribbons and their dubious symbolism in post-Soviet Central Asia', *Eurasia Daily Monitor*, 12, 86 (7 May). Available from: <https://jamestown.org/program/st-georges-ribbons-and-their-dubious-symbolism-in-post-soviet-central-asia/> (last accessed 25 April 2021)

Kimberley, Marten. 2014. 'Vladimir Putin: Ethnic Russian nationalist', *The Washington Post*, Monkey cage, 19 March. Available from: <http://www.washingtonpost.com/blogs/monkey-cage/wp/2014/03/19/vladimir-putin-ethnic-russian-nationalist/> (last accessed 17 December 2015)

King, Charles and Melvin, Neil. 1999. *Nations Abroad: Diaspora Politics and International Relations in the Former Soviet Union*. Boulder, CO: Westview Press

Kirkpatrick, Jeane J. 2013. 'The modernizing imperative: Tradition and change', in *Foreign Affairs. The Clash of Civilizations? The Debate: 20th Anniversary Edition*. New York: Foreign Affairs

Kirsheva, Irina and Valiulina, Svetlana. 2015. 'V krasnoiarskom supermarkete prodaiut deshevuiu vodku, pereviazannuiu georgievskoi lentockhoi' [A Krasnoiarsk supermarket sells cheap vodka with the St George ribbon tied around the bottle], Komsomol'skaia pravda, 28 April. <Available from: http://www.kp.ru/daily/26372/3253933/> (last accessed 31 May 2020)

Klier, John Doyle. 1986. *Russia Gathers Her Jews: The Origins of the 'Jewish Question' in Russia, 1772–1825*. Dekalb: Northern Illinois University Press

Klier, John Doyle, 1995. *Imperial Russia's Jewish Question 1855–1881*. Cambridge: Cambridge University Press

Klier, John Doyle. 2004. 'Russian Jewry on the eve of the pogroms', in Klier, John Doyle and Lambroza, Shlomo, eds, *Pogroms: Anti-Jewish Violence in Modern Russian History*. Cambridge: Cambridge University Press, pp. 3–12

Klier, John Doyle and Lambroza, Shlomo. 2004. 'The pogroms of 1881–1884', in Klier, John Doyle and Lambroza, Shlomo, eds, *Pogroms: Anti-Jewish Violence in Modern Russian History*. Cambridge: Cambridge University Press, pp. 39–42

'Klimpush-Tsintsadze'. 2017. 'Klimpush-Tsintsadze: Ukraina – forpost evropeiskikh tsennostei' [Klimpush-Tsintsadze: Ukraine – an outpost of European values], *Ukrinform*, 28 August. Available from: <https://www.ukrinform.ru/rubric-polytics/2294079-klimpuscincadze-ukraina-forpost-evropejskih-cennostej.html> (last accessed 25 April 2021)

Koberidze, Nodar. 2008. 'Ruseti – sashoi borot'ebisa' [Russia – the womb of evil], *Saerto Gazeti* [The Common Newspaper], August, 8. Available from: <http://kardu.wordpress.com> (last accessed 13 March 2018)

Kohn, Hans. 1971. *Nationalism, Its Meaning and History*. New York: D. Van Nostrand

Kołakowski, Leszek. 1978. *Main Currents of Marxism*, I–III (translated from the Polish by P. S. Falla). Oxford: Clarendon Press

Kolesnikov, Andrei. 2012. 'Tor na grani fola' [Tor is on the edge of foul], *Novaia gazeta*, 3 December. Available from: <https://novayagazeta.ru/articles/2012/12/03/52588-tor-na-grani-fola?print=true> (last accessed 1 June 2020)

Kolstø, Pål. 1995. *Russians in the Former Soviet Republics*. London: Hurst & Co

Kolstø, Pål. 1998. 'Anticipating demographic superiority: Kazakh thinking on integration and nation building', *Europe-Asia Studies*, 50, 1: 51–69

Kolstø, Pål, ed. 1999a. *Nation-Building and Ethnic Integration in Post-Soviet Societies: An Investigation of Latvia and Kazakstan*. Boulder, CO: Westview Press

Kolstø, Pål. 1999b. 'Territorialising diasporas: The case of Russians in the former Soviet Republics', *Millennium*, 28, 3: 607–31

Kolstø, Pål. 2000. *Political Construction Sites: Nation-Building in Russia and the Post-Soviet States*. Boulder, CO: Westview Press

Kolstø, Pål, ed. 2002. *National Integration and Violent Conflict in Post-Soviet Societies:The Cases of Estonia and Moldova*. Lanham, MD: Rowman and Littlefield

Kolstø, Pål. 2003. 'Nation-building and language standardisation in Kazakhstan', in Cummings, S., ed., *Oil, Transition and Security in Central Asia*. London: Routledge, pp. 119–30

Kolstø, Pål. 2004. 'Nation-building in Russia: A value-oriented strategy', in Kolstø, Pål and Blakkisrud, Helge, eds, *Nation-Building and Common Values in Russia*. Lanham, MD, Boulder, CO, and New York: Rowman & Littlefield, pp. 1–28

Kolstø, Pål. 2005a. 'Russian diaspora', in *Immigration and Asylum from 1900 to the Present*, Vol. 1. Santa Barbara: ABC Clio, pp. 531–7

Kolstø, Pål. 2005b. 'Introduction: Assessing the role of historical myths in modern society', in Kolstø, Pål, ed., *Myths and Boundaries in South-Eastern Europe*. London: C. Hurst & Co., pp. 1–34

Kolstø, Pål. 2006. 'National symbols as signs of unity and division', *Ethnic and Racial Studies*, 29, 4: 676–701

Kolstø, Pål. 2008.'Nationalism, ethnic conflict, and job competition: Non-Russian collective action in the USSR under perestroika', *Nations and Nationalism*, 14, 1: 151–69

Kolstø, Pål. 2011. 'Beyond Russia becoming local: Trajectories of adaption to the fall of the Soviet Union among ethnic Russians in the former Soviet Republics', *Journal of Eurasian Studies*, 2, 2: 153–63

Kolstø, Pål. 2013a. 'Moscow: City of xenophobia', *Transition Online 25 July*. Available from: <http://www.tol.org/client/article/23876-moscow-city-of-xenophobia.html> (last accessed 31 May 2020)

Kolstø, Pål. 2013b. 'Faulted for the wrong reasons: Soviet institutionalisation of ethnic diversity and Western (mis)interpretations', in Cordell, Karl, Agarin, Timofei and Osipov, Aleksandr, eds, *Institutional Legacies of Communism: Change and Continuities in Minority Protection*. Abingdon: Routledge, pp. 31–44

Kolstø, Pål. 2014. 'Russia's nationalists flirt with democracy', *Journal of Democracy*, 25, 3: 120–34

Kolstø, Pål. 2015. 'John Armstrong: Typologies and grand narratives', *Nations and Nationalism*, 21: 177–81

Kolstø, Pål. 2016. '"Western Balkans" as the new Balkans: Regional names as tools for stigmatisation and exclusion', *Europe-Asia Studies*, 68, 7: 1245–63

Kolstø, Pål, 2019. 'Is imperialist nationalism an oxymoron? Anthony Smith memorial lecture', *Nations and Nationalism*, 25, 1: 18–44

Kolstø, Pål and Blakkisrud, Helge, eds. 2004. *Nation-building and Common Values in Russia*. Rowman & Littlefield

Kolstø, Pål and Blakkisrud, Helge. 2013. 'Yielding to the Sons of the Soil: Abkhazian democracy and the marginalization of the Armenian vote', *Ethnic and Racial Studies*, 36, 12: 2075–95

Kolstø, Pål and Blakkisrud, Helge. 2018. 'Introduction: Exploring Russian nationalisms', in Kolstø, Pål and Blakkisrud, Helge, eds, *Russia Before and After Crimea Nationalism and Identity, 2010–17*. Edinburgh: Edinburgh University Press, pp. 1–22

Kolstø, Pål and Malkova, Irina. 1997. 'Is Kazakhstan being Kazakhified?', *Analysis of Current Events*, 9

Kolstø, Pål and Rusetskii, Aleksandr. 2012. 'Power differentials and identity formation: Images of self and other on the Russian–Georgian boundary', *National Identities*, 14, 2: 139–55

Kolybalov, Arkadii. 2015. 'Lentochka vidna iz kosmosa' [The ribbon can be seen from space], *Rossiiskaia gazeta*, 22 April. Available from: <http://www.rg.ru/2015/04/22/lentochka-site.html> (last accessed 31 May 2020)

Kongress demokraticheskikh sil Kazakhstana 3–4 dekabria 1998 goda [Congress of the Democratic Forces of Kazakhstan 3–4 December 1998]. 1999. Moscow: no publisher given

Konstitutsiia respubliki Bashkortostan [Constitution of the Republic of Bashkortostan]. 1995. Ufa: Prezidium Verkhovnogo Soveta Respubliki Bashkortostan

Korobkov, Andrei V. 2007. 'Migration trends in Central Eurasia: politics versus economics', *Communist and Post-Communist Studies*, 40, 2: 169–89

Koroteeva, Viktoria. 2000. *Ekonomicheskie interesy i natsionalizm* [Economic Interests and Nationalism]. Moscow: Russkii Gosudarstvennyi Gumanitarnyi Universitet

Kosven, Mark. 1904. 'K voprosu o vysshem obrazovanii Russkikh Evreev' [On the question of higher education for Russian Jews], *Evreiskaia Zhizn'*, 7: 161–9

Kozenko, Andrei. 2015. '"Bessmertnyi polk" popal v okruzhenie' ['The "Immortal Regiment" is surrounded], *Meduza*, 30 April. Available from: <https://meduza.io/feature/2015/04/30/bessmertnyy-polk-popal-v-okruzhenie> (last accessed 31 May 2020)

Kozlov, Viacheslav and Korchenkova, Natalia. 2015. '"Bessmertnyi polk" ne khochet v shtat' ['The "Immortal Regiment" does not want to be a part of the state bureaucracy], *Kommersant*, 29 May. Available from: <http://kommersant.ru/doc/2736209> (last accessed 31 May 2020)

Kramer, Andrew E. 2014. 'Ukraine's reins weaken as chaos spreads', *New York Times*, 4 May. Available from: <http://www.nytimes.com/2014/05/05/world/europe/kievs-reins-weaken-as-chaos-spreads.html> (last accessed 30 March 2021)

Kravchenko, Volodymyr. 2019. 'Why didn't the antemurale historical mythology develop in the early 19th century Ukraine?', in Berezhnaya, Liliya and Hein-Kircher, Heidi, eds, *Rampart Nations, Bulwark Myths of East European Multiconfessional Societies in the Age of Nationalism*. New York: Berghahn, 207–40

Krawchenko, Bohdan. 1985. *Social Change and National Consciousness in Twentieth-Century Ukraine*. New York: St Martin's Press

Krechetnikov, Artem. 2014. '"Lenta razdora": pochemu simvol Pobedy razdelil obshhestvo' [A ribbon of discord: Why the symbol of victory divides society] BBC online, 8 May. Available from: <https://www.bbc.com/russian/russia/2014/05/140508_st_george_ribbon_history> (last accessed 26 July March 2021)

Kriukova, Svetlana and Liamets, Sergei. 2015. 'Vladimir Milov: Putin – ne v adekvate' [Vladimir Milov: Putin is inadequate], *Ukrainskaia Pravda*, 27 January. Available from: <http://www.epravda.com.ua/rus/publications/2015/01/27/523756/> (last accessed 30 March 2021)

Kriviakina, Elena. 2015. 'Ne prevrashchaite Den' Pobedy v balagan' [Do not turn Victory Day into a farce], *Komsomol'skaia Pravda,* 23 April. Available from: <http://www.kp.ru/daily/26371.4/3252273/> (last accessed 31 May 2020)

Krokodil. 1989, issue 34

'Kruglyi stol' 2014. 'Kruglyi stol natsional'nogo edinstva v Khar'kove piketiruiut liudi s vlasovskimi flagami" [A roundtable of national unity in Kharkiv is being picketed by people with Vlasov flags], *Zerkalo nedeli*, 17 May. Available from: <http://zn.ua/UKRAINE/kruglyy-stol-nacionalnogo-edinstva-v-harkove-piketiruyut-lyudi-svlasovskimi-flagami-145262_.html> (last accessed 31 May 2020)

Krylov, Konstantin. 2011a. 'Umeret' ili pomuchit'sia? K sporam o liberalizme, imperstve, i russkom natsionalizme' [To die or to suffer? On the disputes about liberalism, the empire and Russian nationalism], *Voprosy natsionalizma*, 6: 3–9

Krylov, Konstantin. 2011b. 'Torzhestvennym tonom. "Govoriu ot sebia, no za vsekh"' [With a solemn tone 'The words are mine, but I speak for everyone'], *Krylov's blog*, 17 December. Available from: <http://krylov.cc/prnt.php?id=9345&c=p> (last accessed 31 May 2020)

Krylov, Konstantin. 2012. 'Erefiia kak politicheskaia realnost' ['Erefiia' as a political reality], in *Russkie vopreki Putinu*. Moscow: Algoritm

Krylov, Konstantin. 2014. 'O pozitsii po ukrainskomu voprosu' [About our position on the question of Ukraine], *Russkii obozrevatel'*, 4 March. Available from: <www.rus-obr.ru/blog/29883> (last accessed 30 March 2021)

Krylov, Konstantin. 2015. *Zapis' iz Feisbuka* [Transcription from Facebook], 7 April, 09:47. Available from: <http://krylov.cc> (last accessed 17 December 2015)

'Kto vyshel'. 2011. 'Kto vyshel na prospekt Sakharova 24 dekabria?' [Who went out on Sakharov Prospekt on 24 December?], *Novaia gazeta* 28 December. Available from: <https://novayagazeta.ru/articles/2011/12/28/47587-kto-vyshel-na-prospekt-saharova-24-dekabrya> (last accessed 1 June 2020)

Kubik, Jan. 1994. *The Power of Symbols Against the Symbols of Power: The Rise of Solidarity and the Fall of State Socialism in Poland*. University Park: Pennsylvania State University Press

Kudelia, Serhiy. 2014. 'Domestic sources of the Donbas insurgency', *PONARS Eurasia Policy Memo*, no. 351, 29 September

Kulikov, Anton. 2014. '"Russkii marsh" protiv "Russkoi vesny"?' [The Russian march against 'The Russian Spring'?], *Pravda.ru*, 10 October. Available from: <http://www.pravda.ru/politics/parties/other/10-10-2014/1230494-rusmarsh-0/> (last accessed 30 March 2021)

Kundera, Milan. 1984. 'The tragedy of Central Europe', *New York Review of Books*, 31, 7 (26 April): 33–8

Kuzio, Taras. 2015. 'Competing nationalisms, Euromaidan, and the Russian-Ukrainian conflict', *Studies in Ethnicity and Nationalism*, 15, 1: 157–69

Kuz'menkova, Ol'ga. 2012. 'Ot "zvezd" do sumashedshikh: Zavershilos' vydvizhenie kandidatov v Koordinatsionnyi soviet oppozitsii' [All from 'stars' to madmen: The nomination process of candidates for the coordinative council of the opposition is finished], *Gazeta.ru*, 17 September. Available from: http://www.gazeta.ru/politics/2012/09/17_a_4774933.shtml> (last accessed 31 May 2020)

Laitin, David. 1991. 'The national uprisings in the Soviet Union', *World Politics*, 44, 1: 139–77

Lambroza, Shlomo. 2004. 'The pogroms of 1903–1906', in Klier, John Doyle and Lambroza, Shlomo, eds. *Pogroms: Anti-Jewish Violence in Modern Russian History*. Cambridge: Cambridge University Press, pp. 195–247

Landau, Jacob M. and Kellner-Heinkele, Barbara. 2001. *Politics of Language in the Ex-Soviet Muslim State*. Ann Arbor: University of Michigan Press

Lane, Christel. 2010. *The Rites of Rulers: Ritual in Industrial Society: The Soviet Case*. Cambridge: Cambridge University Press

Laqueur, Walter. 1993. *Black Hundred: The Rise of the Extreme Right in Russia*. New York: HarperCollins

Laqueur, Walter. 2006. *The Changing Face of Anti-Semitism: From Ancient Times to the Present Day*, Oxford: Oxford University Press

Laruelle, Marlène. 2008. *Russian Eurasianism: An Ideology of Empire*. Baltimore: Johns Hopkins University Press

Laruelle, Marlène, ed. 2009. *Russian Nationalism and the National Reassertion of Russia*. London: Routledge

Laruelle, Marlène. 2014a. 'Is anyone in charge of Russian nationalists fighting in Ukraine?', *The Washington Post*, Monkey cage, 26 June. Available from: <http://www.washingtonpost.com/blogs/monkey-cage/wp/2014/06/26/is-anyone-in-charge-of-russian-nationalists-fighting-in-ukraine/> (last accessed 30 March 2021)

Laruelle, Marlène. 2014b. 'Russian nationalism and Ukraine', *Current Affairs*, October: 272–7

Laruelle, Marlène. 2014c. 'Russkii natsionalizm kak oblast' nauchnykh issledovanii' [Russian nationalism as a field of scientific research], *Pro et Contra*, 18: 54–72

Laruelle, Marlène. 2014d. 'Alexei Navalny and challenges in reconciling "nationalism" and "liberalism"', *Post-Soviet Affairs*, 30, 4: 276–97

Laruelle, Marlène. 2015a. 'Russia as a "divided nation", from compatriots to Crimea: A contribution to the discussion on nationalism and foreign policy', *Problems of Post-Communism*, 62: 88–97

Laruelle, Marlène. 2015b. 'The "Russian world": Russia's soft power and geopolitical imagination', *Center on Global Interests*, Washington DC, May. Available from: <http://globalinterests.org/wp-content/uploads/2015/05/FINAL-CGI_Russian-World_Marlene-Laruelle.pdf> (last accessed 31 May 2020)

Laruelle, Marlène. 2016a. 'The three colors of Novorossiya, or the Russian nationalist mythmaking of the Ukrainian crisis', *Post-Soviet Affairs*, 32, 1: 55–74

Laruelle, Marlène. 2016b. 'Russia as an anti-liberal European civilisation', in Kolstø, Pål and Blakkisrud, Helge, eds, *The New Russian Nationalism: Imperialism, Ethnicity and Authoritarianism, 2000–2015*. Edinburgh: Edinburgh University Press, pp. 275–97

Laruelle, Marlène. 2021. *Is Russia Fascist? Unraveling Propaganda East and West*. Ithaca, NY: Cornell University Press

Laruelle, Marlène and Siegert, Jens. 2013. 'Xenophobia and migrants', *Russian Analytical Digest*, 141, 23 December

Lasswell, Harold. 1935. *Politics: Who Gets What, When, How*. New York: McGraw-Hill

Latynina, Iuliia. 2014. 'Georgievskaia lentochka – eto vam ne flaer' [The St George ribbon shouldn't be used as a flyer], *Novaia gazeta*, 12 May. Available from: <https://novayagazeta.ru/articles/2014/05/12/59525-georgievskaya-lenta-151-eto-vam-ne-flaer> (last accessed 1 June 2020)

Latynina, Iuliia. 2015. 'Kod dostupa' [Entrance code], *Ekho Moskvy*, 2 May. Available from: <http://m.echo.msk.ru/interview/detail.php?ID=1541010> (last accessed 31 May 2020)

Lauristin, Marju and Vihalemm, Peeter, eds. 1997. *Return to the Western World: Cultural and Political Perspectives on the Estonian Post-Communist Transition*. Tartu: Tartu University Press

Lawaty, Andreas. 2015. 'The figure of "*antemurale*" in the historiography at home and in exile', in Zadencka, Maria, Plakans, Andrejs and Lawaty, Andreas, eds, *East and Central European History Writing in Exile 1939–1989*. Leiden/Boston: Brill, pp. 360–74

Lazarenko, Il'ia. 2014a. 'Prisoedinenie Kryma dlia Rossii velikii minus' [The annexation of Crimea is a great minus for Russia], *Vkontakte*. Available from: <http://vk.com/video-25801613_168203407> (last accessed 30 March 2021)

Lazarenko, Il'ia. 2014b. 'Donetskaia mnogonatsionaliia' [Multinationalist Donetsk], *Rufabula*, 9 May. Available from: <http://rufabula.com/author/ ilya-lazarenko/1> (last accessed 30 March 2021)

'Lentochka nashei'. 2010. 'Lentochka nashei pamiati. Istoriia aktsii "Georgievskaia lentochka"" [A ribbon for our memory: The history of the 'St George Ribbon Action'], *Argumenty i fakty*, 27 April. Available from: <http://www.aif.ru/society/history/17737> (last accessed 31 May 2020)

'Leonid Kuchma'. 1994. 'Leonid Kuchma prinial prisiagu narodu Ukrainy i pristupil k ispolneniiu svoikh obiazannostei' [Leonid Kuchma took the oath to the people of Ukraine and took up his duties], *Rabochaia gazeta Ukrainy*, 21 July, 1

Le Rider, Jacques. 2008. 'Mitteleuropa, Zentraleuropa, Mittelosteuropa: A mental map of Central Europe', *European Journal of Social Theory*, 11, 2: 155–69

Lewis, Bernard. 1982. *The Muslim Discovery of Europe*. New York: W. W. Norton & Company

Lewis, Robert, Rowland, Richard and Clem, Ralph. 1976. *Nationality and Population Change in Russia and the USSR: An Evaluation of Census Data, 1897–1970*. New York: Praeger

Lex, Albert. 2015. 'Lozh' o georgievskoi lente' [Lies about the St George ribbon], *LiveJournal blog*, 20 April. Available from: <http://albert-lex. livejournal.com/28216.html> (last accessed 31 May 2020)

Limonov, Eduard. 2014a. 'Vy prizyvaete ne meshat' karateliam zagnat' krymskii narod opiat' v ukrainskii lager' [You ask us not to prevent the punishers from once again closing up the people of Crimea in a Ukrainian prison], *Livejournal*, 6 March. Available from: <http://limonov-eduard.livejournal. com/446033.html> (last accessed 30 March 2021)

Limonov, Eduard. 2014b. 'Vystuplenie na Triumfal'noi ploshchadi' [Speech on Triumph Square], *Livejournal*, 31 May. Available from: <http:// limonov-eduard.livejournal.com/490535.html> (last accessed 30 March 2021)

Limonov, Eduard. 2014c. 'Kreml', ty chego molchish' [Kremlin, why are you silent?], *Livejournal*, 5 July. Available from: <https://nashenasledie. livejournal.com/3111537.html> (last accessed 30 March 2021)

Linchenko, Andrei and Golovashina, Oxana. 2019. '"With tears upon our eyes?": Commemorations of Victory Day in the Great Patriotic War in the school practice in the Soviet Union and Russia', *Journal of Social Science Education*, 18, 1: 56–80

Lipskii, Andrei. 2012. 'Sozdan protoparlament' [A proto-parliament is created], *Novaia gazeta*, 24 October. Available from: <http://www.

novayagazeta.ru/politics/55088.html> (last accessed 30 June 2016, no longer available)

Liutostanskii, Ippolit. 1880. *Ob upotreblenii Evreiami Khristianskoi krovi dlia religioznykh tselei* [The Jews; Use of Christian Blood for Religious Purposes], 2 vols. St Petersburg: Obshchestvennaia Pol'za

Loginova, Natalia. 1995. 'Sotsial'no-psikhologicheskaia adaptatsiia russkikh v suverennom Kazakhstane' [Socio-psycholocial adaptation of Russians in sovereign Kazakhstan], *Mysl'*, Almaty, 7: 37–42

Löwe, Heinz-Dietrich. 1978. *Antisemitismus und Reaktionäre Utopie: Russischer Konservatismus im Kampf gegen den Wandel von Staat und Gesellschaft, 1890–1917*. Hamburg: Hoffmann und Campe

Lur'e, Oleg. 2015. '"Bessmertnyi polk". Tekhnologiia feikov i bol'shie den'gi' ["The Immortal Regiment": Fake technology and big money], *Ekho Moskvy*, 11 May. Available from: <http://echo.msk.ru/news/1547186-echo.html> (last accessed 31 May 2020)

Mach, Zdzisław. 1993. *Symbols, Conflict, and Identity: Essays in Political Anthropology*. New York: State University of New York Press

Malešević, Siniša. 2004. *The Sociology of Ethnicity*. London: Sage

Malešević, Siniša. 2019. *Grounded Nationalisms*. Cambridge: Cambridge University Press

Mannheim, Karl. 1936. *Ideology and Utopia*. London: K. Paul, Trench, Trubner & Co

Markedonov, Lev and Reznik, Irina. 2012. 'Svernuli s Sadovogo: Orgkomitet aktsii 4 fevralia ne soglasilsia ukhodit' iz tsentra' [They turned off from the Garden Ring: The organizational committee of the 4 February event did not agree to leave the centre], *Gazeta.ru*, 24 January. Available from: <http://www.gazeta.ru/politics/elections2011/2012/01/24_a_3972625.shtml> (last accessed 31 May 2020)

Marples, David R. 1999. *Belarus: A Denationalized Nation*. Amsterdam: Harwood Academic

Martin, Terry. 2001. *An Affirmative Action Empire: Nations and Nationalism in the Soviet Union, 1923–1939*. Ithaca, NY: Cornell University Press

Masiuk, Elena. 2012. 'Vladimir Ryzhkov: "Na shtykakh, kak govoril Napoleon, neodobno sidet"' [Vladimir Ryzhkov: 'It's uncomfortable, as Napoleon said, to sit on bayonets'], *Novaia gazeta*, 10 September. Available from: <https://novayagazeta.ru/articles/2012/09/06/51323-vladimir-ryzhkov-171-na-shtykah-kak-govoril-napoleon-neudobno-sidet-187-avtorskaya-versiya?print=true> (last accessed 1 June 2020)

Matveeva, Anna. 2018. *Through Times of Trouble: Conflict in Southeastern Ukraine Explained from Within*. Lanham, MD: Lexington Books

Mayall, James. 1990. *Nationalism and International Society*. Cambridge: Cambridge University Press

McAdam, Doug, McCarthy, John D. and Zald, Mayer N., eds. 1996. *Comparative Perspectives on Social Movements: Political Opportunities, Mobilizing Structures, and Culture Framings*. Cambridge: Cambridge University Press

McAdam, Doug, Tarrow, Sidney and Tilly, Charles. [2001] 2008. *Dynamics of Contention*. Cambridge: Cambridge University Press

McCammon, Holly J. and Van Dyke, Nella. 2010. 'Applying qualitative comparative analysis to empirical studies of social movement coalition formation', in Van Dyke, Nella and McCammon, Holly J., eds, *Strategic Alliances: Coalition Building and Social Movements*. Minneapolis: University of Minnesota Press, pp. 292–315

McGarry, John and O'Leary, Brendan, eds. 1993. *The Politics of Ethnic Conflict Regulation: Case Studies of Protracted Ethnic Conflicts*. London: Routledge

Medvedev, Dmitrii. 2008. 'Poslanie Federal'nomu Sobraniyu Rossiiskoi Federatsii' [Address to the Federal Assembly of the Russian Federation], 5 November. Available from: <http://www.kremlin.ru/transcripts/1968> (last accessed 24 April 2021)

Medvedev, Dmitrii. 2009. 'Poslanie Federal'nomu Sobraniyu Rossiiskoi Federatsii' [Address to the Federal Assembly of the Russian Federation], *Kremlin*, 12 November. Available from: <http://www.kremlin.ru/transcripts/5979> (last accessed 31 May 2020)

Mel'nikov, Aleksei. 2015. 'Prizrachnyi polk' [A regiment of ghosts], *Ekho Moskvy*, 9 May. Available from: <http://aleks-melnikov.livejournal.com/317210.html >(last accessed 31 May 2020)

Melvin, Neil. 1995. *Russians Beyond Russia: The Politics of National Identity*. London: Royal Institute of International Affairs

Mikhal'chenko, Nikolai. 2016. *Velikii tsivilizatsionnyi vzryv na rubezhe XX–XXI vekov* [The Great Civilizational Explosion at the Turn of the 21st Century]. Kyiv: Parlamentskoe izdatel'stvo

Miller, Aleksei. 2012. 'Izobretenie traditsii' [The Invention of Tradition], *Pro et contra*, May–June: 94–7

Milne, Robert. 1981. *Politics in Ethnically Bipolar States: Guyana, Malaysia, Fiji*. Vancouver: University of British Columbia Press

Milov, Vladimir. 2014. 'Ukraina: pochemu tak poluchilos' i v chem uroki dlia Rossii' [Ukraine: Why things turned out as they did and what Russia can learn from it], *Republic.ru*, 24 March. Available from: <http://slon.ru/world/milov_pro_ukrainu_1060888.xhtml> (last accessed 30 March 2021)

Minin, Stanislav. 2012. 'Liberal-natsionalizm, ili dve golovy odnogo protesta' [National liberalism, or two heads of the same protest], *Russkii zhurnal*, 2 November. Available from: <http://www.russ.ru/Mirovaya-povestka/Liberal-nacionalizm-ili-dve-golovy-odnogo-protesta> (last accessed 31 May 2020)

Mirsky, Georgiy I. 1997. *On Ruins of Empire: Ethnicity and Nationalism in the Former Soviet Union*. Westport, CT: Greenwood Press

'Miting na Bolotnoi'. 2011. 'Miting na Bolotnoi ploshchadi. Onlain-transliatsiia sobytii' [Rally at Bolotnaia Square. Online translation of the events], *Novaia gazeta*, 10 December. Available from: <https://novaya-gazeta.ru/articles/2011/12/10/47274-10-dekabrya-miting-na-bolotnoy-ploschadi-onlayn-translyatsiya-sobytiy> (last accessed 1 June 2020)

'Miting na prospekte'. 2011. 'Miting na prospekte Akademika Sakharova (Videotransliatsiia. Zapis')' [Rally on the Sakharov Prospekt (video translation, transcription)], *Novaia gazeta*, 24 December. Available from: <https://novayagazeta.ru/articles/2011/12/24/47532-24-dekabrya-miting-na-prospekte-akademika-saharova-videotranslyatsiya-zapis> (last accessed 1 June 2020)

'Miting 24'. 2011. 'Miting 24 dekabria: 72-protsentnaia kvota liberalov' [Rally 24 December: 72 per cent were liberals], *Tolkovatel'*, 24 December. Available from: <http://ttolk.ru/?p=8762> (last accessed 31 May 2020)

'Mitinguishshchie'. 2011. 'Mitinguiushchie v Moskve: Kto, zachem i kak vyshel na prospect Sakharova v subbotu?' [Protestors in Moscow: Who came to Sakharov Prospekt, how, and for what purpose], *VTsIOM*, 27 December, Press-Vypusk 1917. Available from: <http://wciom.ru/index.php?id=459&uid=112274> (last accessed 31 May 2020)

Mitrokhin, Nikolai. 2003. *Russkaia partiia: Dvizhenie russkikh natsionalistov v SSSR 1953–1985* [The Russian Party: The Russian Nationalist Movement in the USSR 1953–1985]. Moscow: Novoe Literaturnoe Obozrenie

Moen-Larsen, Natalia. 2014. '"Normal nationalism": Alexei Navalny, LiveJournal and "the Other"', *East European Politics* 30, 4: 548–67

Mogilner, Marina. 2019. 'Racial purity vs imperial hybridity: The case of Vladimir Jabotinsky against the Russian Empire', in Rainbow, David, ed., *Ideologies of Race: Imperial Russia and the Soviet Union in Global Context*, Montreal: McGill-Queens University Press, pp. 103–31

Mordvinov, Vladimir. 1880. *Tainy Talmuda i Ievrei v Otnoshenii k Khristian-skomu Miru* [Secrets of the Talmud and the Jews in their Relation to the Christian World]. Moscow: Tipografiia F. Iogansona

Morgulis, Mikhail. 1910. 'Bezporiadki 1871 goda v Odesse' [The riots in Odesa in 1871], *Evreiskii Mir*, 2–3: 42–6

'Moscow 2015'. 2015. 'Moscow-2015. The 'Russian' and other nationalist marches', 27 November, *Sova Center for Information and Analysis*. Available from: <https://www.sova-center.ru/en/xenophobia/news-releases/2015/11/d33323/> (last accessed 31 May 2020)

Motyl, Alexander J. 1980. *The Turn to the Right: The Ideological Origins and Development of Ukrainian Nationalism, 1919–1929*. New York: Columbia University Press

Motyl, Alexander J. 1987. *Will the Non-Russians Rebel?* Ithaca, NY: Cornell University Press

Motyl, Alexander J. 1990. *Sovietology, Rationality, Nationality: Coming to Grips with Nationalism in the USSR.* New York: Columbia University Press

Moynihan, Daniel Patrick. 1993. *Pandaemonium: Ethnicity in International Politics.* Oxford: Oxford University Press

Mozheiko, Gennadii. 2015. 'Aleksandr Lukashenko priletel v Moskvu s georgievskoi lentochi' [Aleksandr Lukashenko flew to Moscow with a St George ribbon on his chest], *Komsomol'skaia pravda*, 7 May. Available from: <http://www.kompravda.eu/daily/26378.4/3257216/> (last accessed 31 May 2020)

Myhre, Marthe Handå. 2014. *Labour Migration from Central Asia to Russia – State Management of Migration.* Oslo: NIBR – Norwegian Institute for Urban and Regional Research

Myhre, Marthe Handå. 2018. 'Compatriots into Citizens Policies and Perceptions of Citizenship Acquisition in Post-Soviet Russia', PhD Dissertation, University of Oslo

Nahaylo, Bohdan and Swoboda, Victor. 1990. *Soviet Disunion: A History of the Nationalities Problem in the USSR.* London: Hamish Hamilton

'Narody Bashkortostana' [The peoples of Bashkortostan] 1999. *Gosudarstvennaia programma, (chast' pervaia)* [State program. (Part one)]. Ufa: Akademiia nauk Respubliki Bashkortostan

Nash put': strategicheskie perspektivy razvitiia Rossii v XXI veke [Our Path: Strategic Perspectives on the Development of Russia in the 21st Century] 1999. Moscow: Arktogeia

Nathans, Benjamin. 2004. *Beyond the Pale: The Jewish Encounter with Late Imperial Russia.* Berkeley: California University Press

Natsional'nyi sostav naseleniia SSSR [The National Composition of the Population of the USSR]. 1991. Moscow: Goskomstat

Naval'nyi, Aleksei. 2013. 'Russkii marsh' [The Russian March], *LiveJournal blog.* Available from: <http://navalny.livejournal.com/877154.html?thread=532545634> (last accessed 31 May 2020)

Naval'nyi, Aleksei. 2014. 'Naval'nyi vystupil protiv prisoedineniia Kryma k Rossii' [Navalny spoke out against the Russian annexation of Crimea], *Lenta.ru*, 12 March. Available from: <http://lenta.ru/news/2014/03/12/navalny/> (last accessed 30 March 2021)

Nazarbaev, Nursultan. 1993. *Ideinaia konsolidatsiia obshchestvo – kak uslovie progressa Kazakhstana* [The Ideological Consolidaton of Society as a Condition for the Progress of Kazakhstan]. Almaty: 'Kazakhstan –XXI vek'

Nazarbaev, Nursultan. 1995. *Za mir i soglasia v nashem obshchem dome* [For Peace and Harmony in Our Common Home]. Almaty: 'Kazakhstan'

Nekrich, Aleksandr. 1978. *The Punished Peoples: The Deportation and Fate of Soviet Minorities at the End of the Second World War*. New York: Norton

Nekrich, Aleksandr and Heller, Mikhail. 1986. *Utopia in Power: The History of the Soviet Union from 1917 to the Present* (transl. P. B. Carlos). New York: Summit Books

Nemenskii, Oleg. 2012. 'Nasledie i vybor' [Heritage and choice], *Voprosy natsionalizma*, 9: 17–21

Nemenskii, Oleg. 2014a. 'Ukraine ne udalos' sozdat' obshchegrazhdanskuiu model' identichnosti' [Ukraine did not succeed in creating a general civil model of identity], *Rossiiskii Institut Strategicheskikh Issledovanii*, 28 April. Available from: <https://riss.ru/article/13504/> (last accessed 30 March 2021)

Nemenskii, Oleg. 2014b. 'Reshaetsia v Donbasse' [A solution is in progress in Donbas], *Literaturnaia gazeta*, 18 July. Available from: <https://lgz.ru/article/-27-6470-9-07-2014/reshaetsya-v-donbasse/> (last accessed 30 March 2021)

Nepogodin, Vsevolod. 2014. 'Geroi nashego vremeni' [The hero of our time], *Svobodnaia pressa*, 1 August. Available from: <http://svpressa.ru/t/94172> (last accessed 30 March 2021)

Neumann, Iver B. 1993. 'Russia as Central Europe's constituting Other', *East European Politics and Societies*, 7, 2: 349–69

Neumann, Iver B. 1999. *Uses of the Other: 'The East' in European Identity Formation*. Minneapolis: University of Minnesota Press

Norris, Stephen M. 2011. 'Memory for sale: Victory Day 2010 and Russian remembrance', *The Soviet and Post-Soviet Review*, 38, 2: 201–29

Novikova, Anastasia. 2014. 'Kiev otkazalsia ot georgievskoi lenty kak simvola Dnia Pobedy' [Kiev rejects the St George ribbon as a symbol of Victory Day], *Komsomol'skaia Pravda*, 6 May. Available from: <https://www.kp.md/online/news/1728495/> (last accessed 31 May 2020)

Numanov, Askar and Sidorov, Dmitry. 1989. 'Novy Uzen – The buildup to explosion', *Moscow News*, 27: 5

Oates, Sarah and Lokot, Tetyana. 2013. 'Twilight of the Gods?: How the Internet Challenged Russian Television News Frames in the Winter Protests of 2011–12', Paper prepared for the *Post-Socialist and Post-Authoritarian Communication Working Group International Association for Media and Communication Research Annual Conference*, Dublin, June 2013

Oberschall, Anthony. 1997. *Social Movements: Ideologies, Interests, and Identities*. New Brunswick, NJ: Transaction

'Obrashchenie'. 1992. 'Obrashchenie k grazhdanam Rossii orgkomiteta fronta natsional'nogo spaseniia' [A call to the Russian people from the organizational committee of the National Salvation Front], *Den'*, 11–17 October: 1

Obukhov, Andrei. 2016. 'Poklonskaia sdelala Nikolaia Vtorogo uchastnikom "Bessmertnogo polka"' [Poklonskaia made Nikolai II a participant in the 'Immortal Regiment'], *Moskovskii komsomolets* 9 May. Available from: <https://www.mk.ru/social/2016/05/09/poklonskaya-sdelala-nikolaya-vtorogo-uchastnikov-bessmertnogo-polka.html> (last accessed 25 April 2021)

'Odessa: Potemkinskuiu'. 2010. 'Odessa: Potemkinskuiu lestnitsu nakryla gigantskaja Georgievskaia lenta (foto)' [Odesa: The Potemkin Steps were covered by a gigantic St George ribbon (photo)], *Timer*, 8 May. Available from: <http://timer-odessa.net/news/odessa-potemkinskuyu-lestnicu-nakryla-gigantskaya-georgievskaya-lenta.html> (last accessed 31 May 2020)

'Odessity poshili'. 2010. 'Odessity poshili samuiu bol'shuiu v mire georgievskuiu lentochku' [Odesa residents sewed the world's biggest St George ribbon], Vecherniaia Odessa, 29 April. Available from: <https://m.prichernomorie.com.ua/odessa/monitorings/201004-29/121437.php> (last accessed 30 March 2021)

Okara, Andrei. 2015. 'Den' pobedy kak informatsionnaia duel' Moskvy i Kieva' [Victory Day as an informational duel between Moscow and Kiev], *Ekho Moskvy*, 21 May. Available from: <http://echo.msk.ru/blog/okara/1552514-echo/> (last accessed 31 May 2020)

'Okolo 150'. 2015. 'Okolo 150 tys. chelovek primut uchastie v aktsii "Bessmertnyi polk" –Moskva' [Roughly 150,000 people to take part in the 'Immortal Regiment' action in Moscow], *TASS*, 28 April. Available from: http://tass.ru/obschestvo/1937498 (last accessed 31 May 2020)

O'Leary, Brendan. 2001. 'Instrumentalist theories of nationalism', in Leoussi, Athena, ed., *Encyclopaedia of Nationalism*. New Brunswick, NJ: Transaction, pp. 148–53

Oliver, Pamela E. and Benford, Robert D. 2005. 'What a Good Idea! Ideologies and frames in social movements research', in Johnston, Hank and Noakes, John A., eds, *Frames of Protest: Social Movements and the Framing Perspective*. Lanham, MD: Rowman & Littlefield, pp. 185–204

Olzak, Susan. 1992. *The Dynamics of Ethnic Competition and Conflict*. Stanford, CA: Stanford University Press

Opalski, Magdalena, Tsilevich, Boris and Dutkiewicz, Piotr. 1994. *Appendix to Ethnic Conflict in the Baltic States: The Case of Latvia*. Kingston, Ontario: Canada Communications Group

Orbach, Alexander. 2004. 'The development of the Russian Jewish community, 1881–1903', in Klier, John Doyle and Lambroza, Shlomo, eds, *Pogroms: Anti-Jewish Violence in Modern Russian History*. Cambridge: Cambridge University Press, pp. 137–63

Orekh, Anton. 2015. 'Tabel' o rangakh' [Table of ranks], *Ekho Moskvy*, 17 May. Available from: <http://echo.msk.ru/programs/tabel/1550256-echo/> (last accessed 31 May 2020)

Orshanskii, Il'ia. 1877. *Evrei v Rossii – Ocherki ekonomicheskago i obshchest-vennago byta Russkikh Evreev* [Jews in Russia – An Outline of the Every-day Life of Russian Jews from an Economic and Social Perspective]. St Petersburg: Tipografiia O. I. Baksta

Osharov, Roman. 2013. 'Belye lenty i moskovskie vlasti' [White Ribbons and the Moscow authorities], *Golos Ameriki*, 5 February. Available from: <https://www.golosameriki.com/a/russia-white-ribbon-ban/1597555.html> (last accessed 25 April 2021)

'O simvole'. 1993. 'O simvole griadushchei Rossii' [About the symbol of future Russia], *Russkii poriadok*, 2: 2

Østbø, Jardar. 2017. 'Demonstrations against demonstrations', *Russian Ana-lytical Digest*, 210, 14 November. Available from: <https://css.ethz.ch/content/dam/ethz/specialinterest/gess/cis/center-for-securities-studies/pdfs/RAD210.pdf> (last accessed 25 April 2021)

'Outcomes'. 2013. 'Outcomes', *National Survey* (excel). Available from: <https://www.hf.uio.no/ilos/english/research/projects/neoruss/index.html> (last accessed 31 May 2020)

Ovchinnikov, Aleksei. 2011. 'Tsoi pel, OMON ulybalsia, a Bolotnaia likov-ala: Miting protesta na Bolotnoi ploshchadi v Moskve sobral okolo 50 tysiach chelovek' [Tsoi sang while the riot police smiled and rejoiced: Protest rally in Moscow's Bolotnaia Square attended by 50 thousand], *Komsomol'skaia pravda*, 10 December. Available from: <http://m.spb.kp.ru/daily/25802/2783071/> (last accessed 31 May 2020)

Özkırımlı, Umut, 2005. *Contemporary Debates on Nationalism: A Critical Engagement*. Houndmills, Basingstoke: Palgrave

Pain, Emil. 2014. 'Ksenofobiia i natsionalizm v epokhu rossiiskogo bezvremen'ia' [Xenophobia and nationalism in the age of Russian hard times], *Pro et Contra*, 18: 34–53

Pain, Emil. 2016. 'The imperial syndrome and its influence on Russian nation-alism', in Kolstø, Pål and Blakkisrud, Helge, eds, *The New Russian Nationalism: Imperialism, Ethnicity and Authoritarianism, 2000–2015*, Edinburgh: Edinburgh University Press, pp. 46–74

Pain, Emil. 2018. 'Contemporary Russian nationalism in the historical struggle between "official nationality" and "popular sovereignty"', in Kolstø, Pål and Blakkisrud, Helge, eds, *Russia Before and After Crimea: Nationalism and Identity, 2010–17*. Edinburgh: Edinburgh University Press, pp. 23–49

Pain, Emil and Prostakov, Sergei. 2014. 'Monolikii russkii natsionalizm: ego ideino-politicheskie raznovidnosti v Rossii 2010–2014 gg' [Multifac-eted Russian nationalism: Its ideological and political versions in Russia 2010–2014], *Polis*, 4, July: 96–113

'Permskii khudozhnik'. 2014. 'Permskii khudozhnik uekhal v Ukrainu iz-za dela ob ekstremizme' (Artist from Perm fled to Ukraine due to the case against him about extremism], *Novaia gazeta*, 12 December. Available from: <https://novayagazeta.ru/news/2014/12/12/108622-permskiy-hudozhnik-uehal-v-ukrainu-iz-za-dela-ob-ekstremizme?print=true> (last accessed 1 June 2020)

Pervyi vsemirnyi kurultai Bashkir, 1–2 Iunia 1995. Stenograficheskii otchet [First Global Kurultai of the Bashkirs, 1st–2nd June 1995. Stenographic Report]. 1995. Ufa: Kitap

Petrov, Andrei. 2010. 'Bat'ka otvetil Putinu, vypustiv v efir Saakashvili' [The 'father' (of Belorus) replied to Putin by letting Saakashvili speak on national television], *Svobodnaia pressa*, 16 July. Available from <http://svpressa.ru/society/article/27841/?go=popul> (last accessed 30 March 2020)

Petrov, Nikolai N. 2014. 'Rossiia v 2014-m: skatyvanie v voronku' [Russia in the year of 2014: Falling into a mine-crater], *Pro et contra*, May–August: 57–72

Petro, Nicolai N. 2015. 'Russia's Orthodox soft power', *Carnegie Council*, 23 March. Available from: <http://www.carnegiecouncil.org/publications/articles_papers_reports/727> (last accessed 31 May 2020)

Pilkington, Hilary. 1998. *Migration, Displacement and Identity in Post-Soviet Russia*. London: Routledge

Pinkus, Benjamin. [1988] 1998. *The Jews of the Soviet Union: The History of a National Minority*. Cambridge: Cambridge University Press

Piper, Elizabeth. 2014. '"Patriot's handbook" may give insight into Putin's thoughts', *Global Post*, 9 June. Available from: <https://www.voanews.com/europe/patriots-handbook-may-give-insight-putins-thoughts> (last accessed 30 March 2021)

Pipes, Richard. [1954] 1997. *The Formation of the Soviet Union*. Cambridge, MA: Harvard University Press

'Platforma tatarskogo'. 1991. 'Platforma tatarskogo obshchestvennogo tsentra' [Platform of the Tatar community centre], *Panorama*, 2: 13–27

Plokhy, Serhii. 2017. *Lost Kingdom: A History of Russian Nationalism from Ivan the Great to Vladimir Putin*. London: Allen Lane

'Pochemu belorusy?'. 2017. 'Pochemu belorusy — evropeitsy. Istorik rasklady-vaet vopros po polochkam' [Why Belorusians are Europeans. A historian gives an outline], *Belsat*, 17 February. Available from: <https://naviny.belsat.eu/ru/news/pochemu-belorusy-evropejtsy-istorik-raskladyvayet-vopros-po-polochkam/> (last accessed 25 April 2021)

'Pogranichniki ne pustili'. 2020. 'Pogranichniki ne pustili v Ukrainu inostrantsev, u odnogo iz kotorykh byla georgievskaia lenta' (Ukrainian border guards turned back two foreigners, one of whom was wearing a St George ribbon], *Gordon*, 4 December. Available from: <https://gordonua.com/news/localnews/pogranichniki-ne-pustili-v-ukrainu-inostrancev-u-odnogo-iz-kotoryh-byla-georgievskaya-lenta-1530265.html> (last accessed 30 March 2021)

Pokal'chuk, Oleg. 2014. 'Voina liudei' [War among people], *Zerkalo nedeli*, 22 May. Available from: <https://zn.ua/socium/voyna-lyudey-1-_.html> (last accessed 1 June 2020)

'Poklonskaia proshla'. 2016. 'Poklonskaia proshla v kolonne "Bessmertnogo polka" s ikonoi Nikolaia II' [Poklonskaia attended the event "The Immortal Regiment" with an icon of Nikolai 2nd], *Ria novosti*, 9 May. Available from: <https://ria.ru/20160509/1429702188.html> (last accessed 25 April 2021)

Poliakov, Léon. 1973–6. *The History of Anti-Semitism*. New York: Routledge & Kegan Paul

Poliakov, Léon. 1974. *The Aryan Myth: A History of Racist and Nationalist Ideas in Europe*. New York: Basic Books

'Politsiia razgromila'. 2015. 'Politsiia razgromila vystavku "My pobedili" v Moskve' ['Police broke up the exhibition "We won!" in Moscow'], *BBC*, 8 May. Available from: <http://www.bbc.com/russian/russia/2015/05/150508_moscow_gallery_police> (last accessed 31 May 2020)

Polokhalo, V. et al. 1993. 'Ukraine and Russia in the context of European values', *Politychna dumka*, 1: 139–41

Polubota, Aleksei. 2014. 'Razocharovanie patriotov: kak povliiaet na reiting vlasti otkaz ot vvoda voisk v Donbass' [Disappointing the patriots: How the rejection to send troops into Donbass will affect the rating], *Svobodnaia pressa*. Available from: <http://svpressa.ru/politic/article/91987/> (last accessed 30 March 2021)

Polygaeva, Dar'ia. 2015. 'Patriotizm zakonodatel'no zapretit' nel'zia' [Patriotism should not be outlawed], *Kommersant*, 8 May. Available from: <http://www.kommersant.ru/doc/2723786> (last accessed 31 May 2020)

Popescu, Nicu. 2014. 'Ukraine's impact on Russia', *European Union Institute for Security Studies*, July, no. 32. Available from: <https://www.iss.europa.eu/content/ukraine%E2%80%99s-impact-russia> (last accessed 30 March 2021)

'Poroshenko ob"iasnil'. 2017. 'Poroshenko ob"iasnil, pochemu v Ukraine zapretili "georgievskuiu" lentochku' [Poroshenko explained why St George ribbons are banned in Ukraine], *Segodnia*, 21 May. Available from: <https://politics.segodnya.ua/politics/poroshenko-obyasnil-pochemu-v-ukraine-zapretili-georgievskuyu-lentochku-1022786.html> (last accessed 30 March 2021)

Poroshina, Marina. 2007. 'Gvardii shtof. Georgievskuiu lentu izpol´zuiut dlia reklamy spirtnogo' [A glass flask for the guard: The St George ribbon is used as an advertisement for alcohol], *Rossiiskaia gazeta*, 8 May. Available from: <http://www.rg.ru/2007/05/08/reg-ural/lenta.html> (last accessed 31 May 2020)

Posen, Barry. 1993. 'The security dilemma and ethnic conflict', *Survival*, 35, 1: 27–47

Posner, Daniel N. 2005. *Institutions and Ethnic Politics in Africa*. Cambridge: Cambridge University Press

'Pozdravlenie Glavy' 2019. 'Pozdravlenie Glavy DNR Denisa Pushilina po sluchaiu Dnia Georgievskoi lenty' [Greetings from the head of the Donetsk People's Republic Denis Pushilin on St George Ribbon's Day], *Obschchestvennoe dvizhenie 'Donetskaia Respublika' [The Civic Movement 'The Donetsk Republic'*], 6 December. Available from: <http://oddr. info/pozdravlenie-glavy-dnr-denisa-pushilina-po-sluchaju-dnja-georgievs-koj-lenty/> (last accessed 30 March 2021)

Pozniak, Zenon [*Zianon Pazniak* in Belarusian]. 1993. 'Natsional'noe gosu-darstvo est naivysshaia kul'turnaia i obshchestvennaia tsennost' [A national state is the highest possible cultural and social value], in 'Belorusskii shl-iakh: "Kruglyi stol v redaktsii zhurnala"' [The Belorusian Way: 'Round-table of the Journal's Editorial Office'], *Neman*: 3–43

Pozniak, Zenon [*Zianon Pazniak* in Belarusian].1994. 'O russkom impe-rializme i ego opasnosti' [About Russian imperialism and its dangers], *Narodnaia gazeta*, 15–17

Pozniakov, Andrei. 2015. 'Georgievskie lenty v kazhdyi dom?' [A St George ribbon to every home?], *Ekho Moskvy*, 6 May. Available from: <http:// echo.msk.ru/blog/shoo_ash/1543526-echo/> (last accessed 31 May 2020)

Prager Dennis and Telushkin, Joseph. 2003. *Why the Jews? The Reason for Antisemitism*. New York: Simon and Schuster

Pravda. 2012. 'Belye lentochki – skorbnaia pamiat' o zhertvakh natsizma' [White Ribbons represent a mournful memory of the victims of Nazism], *Pravda*, 3 February. Available from <https://www.pravda.ru/video/politics/1028. html> (last accessed 12 April 2021)

'Programma DPNI'. 2009. 'Programma DPNI' [Program of the Movement Against Illegal Immigration], *DPNI*. Available from: <http://www.dpni. org/articles/dokumenti/13255/> (last accessed 31 May 2020)

'Programma tatarskoi'. 1991. 'Programma tatarskoi partii natsional'noi neza-visimosti (TPNN) "Ittifak"' [Program of the Tatar Party of National Independence (TPNI) 'Ittifak'], *Panorama*, 6: 15–25

Prokhanov, Aleksandr. 2014a. 'Aleksandr Prokhanov schitaet Putina krup-neishim politicheskim liderom Rossii i mira' [Aleksandr Prokhanov sees Putin as the greatest political leader of Russia and the world], *Argumenty nedeli*, 26 March. Available from: <http://argumenti.ru/ politics/2014/03/328155> (last accessed 17 December 2015)

Prokhanov, Aleksandr. 2014b. 'Klevetnikam Rossii' [To those who slander Russia], *Zavtra*, 10 April. Available from: <http://zavtra.ru/content/view/ klevetnikam-rossii/> (last accessed 30 March 2021)

Prokhanov, Aleksandr. 2014c. 'Evoliutsiia maidana' [The evolution of the Maidan revolution], *Izborskii klub*, 14 July. Available from: <http://dynacon.ru/content/articles/3624/> (last accessed 30 March 2021)

Prokhanov, Aleksandr. 2014d. 'Razlozhenie ukrainskoi armii' [The demoralisation of the Ukrainian army], *Izborskii klub*, 4 August. Available from: <http://dynacon.ru/content/articles/3643/> (last accessed 30 March 2021)

Prokhanov, Aleksandr. 2014e. 'Prokhanov: Krym i Donbass – eto vozrozhdenie Rossiiskoi imperii' [Prokhanov: The events in Crimea and in Donbasse represent the revival of the Russian Empire], *Politnavigator*, 31 October. Available from: <https://www.politnavigator.news/prokhanov-krym-i-donbass-ehto-vozrozhdenie-imperii.html> (last accessed 30 March 2021)

Protsenko, Liubov'. 2015. 'Bolee 110 tysiach moskvichei zapisalos' na aktsiiu "Bessmertnyi polk"' [More than 110,000 Muscovites have signed up for the 'Immortal Regiment' action], *Rossiiskaia gazeta*, 22 April. Available from: <http://m.rg.ru/2015/04/22/polk-site.html> (last accessed 31 May 2020)

'Publitsist Egor'. 2015. 'Publitsist Egor Kholmogorov – o posledstviiakh kotorye sleduiut za arkhaizatsiei natsional'noi massovoi kul'tury' [Publicist Egor Kholmogorov on the consequences that follow from an archaization of the national mass culture], *Izvestiia*, 16 April. Available from: <http://izvestia.ru/news/585507#ixzz3juNH89oh> (last accessed 31 May 2020)

'Putin claims'. 2014. 'Putin claims Russian forces "could conquer Ukraine capital in two weeks"', *The Guardian*, 2 September. Available from: <http://www.theguardian.com/world/2014/sep/02/putin-russian-forces-could-conquer-ukraine-capital-kiev-fortnight> (last accessed 30 March 2021)

Putin, Vladimir. 1999. 'Rossiia na rubezhe tysiacheletii' [Russia at the turn of the millennium], *Nezavisimaia gazeta*, 30 December. Available from: <http://www.ng.ru/politics/1999-12-30/4_millenium.html> (last accessed 31 March 2021)

Putin, Vladimir. 2008. 'Gruziia nanesla smertel'nyi udar po svoei gosudarstvennosti' [Georgia inflicted a fatal blow on her own statehood], *Komsomol'skaia Pravda*, 9 August. Available from <http://www.kp.ru/daily/24143/361219> (last accessed 30 March 2020)

Putin, Vladimir. 2011. 'Putin pro belye lentochki' [Putin about the White Ribbons], *YouTube*, 15 December. Available from: <https://www.youtube.com/watch?v=tD-NauE6AGU> (last accessed 18 April 2021)

Putin, Vladimir. 2012. 'Rossiia: natsional'nyi vopros' [Russia: the national question], *Nezavisimaia gazeta*, 23 January. Available from: <http://www.ng.ru/politics/2012-01-23/1_national.html> (last accessed 31 March 2021)

Putin, Vladimir. 2013. 'Interviu Pervomu kanalu i agentstvu Associated Press' [Interview to Chanel 1 and the Associated Press Agency], *Kremlin.ru*, 3 September. Available from: <http://kremlin.ru/events/president/news/19143> (last accessed 30 March 2020)

Putin, Vladimir. 2014a. 'Obrashchenie Prezidenta Rossiiskoi Federatsii' [The Russian President's address], *Kremlin.ru*, 18 March. Available from: <http://kremlin.ru/news/20603> (last accessed 31 March 2021)

Putin, Vladimir. 2014b. 'Poslanie Prezidenta Federal'nomu Sobraniiu' [The President's address to the Federal Assembly], *Kremlin.ru*, 4 December, Available from: <http://kremlin.ru/news/47173> (last accessed 7 March 2015)

Putin, Vladimir. 2014c. 'Zasedanie Mezhdunarodnogo diskussionnogo kluba "Valdai"' [Session at the "Valdai" International Discussion Club]. Available from: <https://www.youtube.com/watch?v=v8UgW9lfZFQ> and <http://kremlin.ru/events/president/news/46860> (last accessed 25 April 2021)

Putin, Vladimir. 2020. 'Ob Ukraine (interv'iu TASS)' [About Ukraine (interview with TASS], *Kreml.ru*, 21 February. Available from: <http://kremlin.ru/events/president/transcripts/62835> (last accessed 25 April 2021)

Raibman, Natal'ia. 2012. 'Edinoross Sidiakin rastoptal beluiu lentu pered polupustoi Gosdumoi' [Member of the United Russia party Sidiakin trampled upon a White Ribbon in front of a half-empty State Duma], *Vedomosti*, 26 October. Available from: <https://www.vedomosti.ru/politics/articles/2012/10/26/deputat_sidyakin_na_plenarnom_zasedanii_obrugal_i_rastoptal> (last accessed 19 July 2021)

Rakhimov, Murtaza. 1998. *Bashkortostan –moia sud'ba* [Bashkortostan is my Fate]. Ufa: Kitap

Rakitina, Anna. 2014. 'Predali plameni. V Odesse radikaly sozhgli georgievskuiu lentochku na Vechnom ogne' [Consigned to the flames: In Odesa radicals burned a St George ribbon in the Eternal flame], *Rossiiskaia gazeta*, 2 April. Available from: <http://m.rg.ru/2014/04/01/lentochka.html> (last accessed 31 May 2020)

'Rastushchim v Rossii'. 2011. 'Rastushchim v Rossii protestam pridumali vizual'noe vyrazhenie: belaia lentochka' [The growing protests in Russia came up with a virtual expression: A White Ribbon], *News.ru*, 7 December. Available from: <https://www.newsru.com/russia/07dec2011/band.html> (last accessed 19 July 2021)

Razmakhnin, Anton. 2011. 'Edinorossy nadeli belye lentochki i trebuiut 'chistok'. Chleny partii vlasti organizovali gruppu "ER za chestnye vybory"' [Members of United Russia put on White Ribbons and demands 'purges'. Members of the ruling party organized the group 'United Russia for Fair Elections'], *Svobodnaia pressa*, 13 December. Available from: <https://svpressa.ru/politic/article/50895/> (last accessed 25 April 2021)

Reese, Ellen, Petit, Christine and Meyer, David. 2010. 'Sudden mobilization: Movement crossovers, and the surprising rise of the U.S. antiwar movement', in Van Dyke, Nella and McCammon, Holly J., eds, *Strategic Alliances: Coalition Building and Social Movements*. Minneapolis: University of Minnesota Press, pp. 266–91

Revzin, Grigorii. 2014. 'O liberalakh i natsionalistakh' [About liberals and nationalists], *Ekho Moskvy*, 23 February. Available from: <http://echo.msk.ru/blog/revzin/1264688-echo/> (last accessed 31 May 2020)

Ria novosti. 2011. 'Rossiiskaia natsiia dolzhna sostoiat' iz samobytnykh narodov – Medvedev' [The Russian nation should consist of indigenous peoples – Medvedev], *Ria novosti* 11 February. Available from: <http://ria.ru/politics/20110211/333366199.html> (last accessed 31 May 2020)

Riasanovsky, Nicholas V. 1952. *Russia and the West in the Teaching of the Slavophiles*. Gloucester, MA: Peter Smith

Riasanovsky, Nicholas V. 1959. *Nicholas I and Official Nationality in Russia, 1825–1855*. Berkeley: University of California Press

Roeder, Philip G. 1998. 'Liberalization and ethnic entrepreneurs in the Soviet successor states', in B. Crawford and R. D. Lipschutz, eds, *The Myth of 'Ethnic Conflict': Politics, Economics, and 'Cultural' Violence*. Berkeley: University of California Press, pp. 78–107

Rogger, Hans. 1966. 'The Beilis case: Anti-Semitism and politics in the reign of Nicholas II', *Slavic Review*, 25, 4: 615–29

Rogger, Hans. 1986. *Jewish Policies and Right-Wing Politics in Imperial Russia*. Berkeley: University of California Press

'ROOSPM'. Undated. 'ROOSPM "Studencheskaia obshchina"' [Regional Social Organization for Social Support to Young People 'Students' society'], *Wikipedia*. No longer available

Ross, Marc Howard. 2009. *Culture and Belonging in Divided Societies: Contestation and Symbolic Landscapes*. Philadelphia: University of Pennsylvania Press

'Rossiia, Gruziia'. 2008. 'Rossiia, Gruziia i pravoslavnaia tsivilizatsiia' [Russia, Georgia and the Orthodox civilisation], *Russkii obozrevatel'*, 20 August. Available from: <http://www.rus-obr.ru/opinions/531> (last accessed 25 April 2021)

'Rossiiskikh baikerov'. 2015. 'Rossiiskikh baikerov zastavili v Tbilisi sniat' georgievskie lenty' [In Tbilisi Russian bikers were forced to take off their St George ribbons], *RIA Novosti*, 2 May. Available from: <http://ria.ru/world/20150502/1062182387.html> (last accessed 31 May 2020)

Rossov, S. 1907. *Evreiskii Vopros* [The Jewish Question]. St Petersburg: no publisher given

Rothschild, Joseph. 1981. *Ethnopolitics: A Conceptual Framework*. New York: Columbia University Press

Rowley, David G. 2000. 'Imperial versus national discourse: The case of Russia', *Nations and Nationalism*, 6, 1: 23–42

Rudling, Per Anders. 2013. 'The return of the Ukrainian far right. The case of VO Svoboda', in Wodak, Ruth and Richardson, John E., eds, *Analyzing Fascist Discourse: European Fascism in Talk and Text*. London: Routledge, pp. 228–55

Rumer, Boris Z. 1990. *Soviet Central Asia: 'A Tragic Experiment'*. Boston: Unwin Hyman

Rutkovskii, Aleksandr. 2008. 'Do i posle Ioseliani' [Before and after Ioseliani], *Ezhenedel'nik 2000*, 43, 24–9 October. Available from: <http://sir-michael.ru/zakkurapiya/postsovetskoe-prostranstvo/gruziya/do-i-posle-ioseliani/> (last accessed 8 November 2016)

'Russian March'. 2014. '"Russian March" 2014 in Moscow: For and against Novorossiya', 13 November, *Sova Center for Information and Analysis*. Available from: <https://www.sova-center.ru/en/xenophobia/news-releases/2014/11/d30652/> (last accessed 31 May 2020)

'Russkie voiska'. 2008. 'Russkie voiska manevriruiut bliz Tbilisi' [Russian troops are maneuvering not far from Tbilisi], *Kavkazcenter* 16 August. Available from: <http://kavkazcenter.com/russ/content/2008/08/16/60293.shtml> (last accessed 30 March 2020)

'Russkii natsionalizm'. 2010. 'Russkii natsionalizm: Teoriia i praktika' [Russian nationalism: Theory and practice], Round table, *Voprosy Natsionalizma*, 2: 2–15

Rywkin, Michael. 1979. 'Central Asia and Soviet manpower', *Problems of Communism*, 28, 1: 1–13

'Saakashvili depicted'. 2006. 'Saakashvili depicted Russia as barbarous tribe of Huns at Economic Forum in Poland', 7 September. Available from: <http://www.regnum.ru/english/700884.html> (last accessed 24 November 2010, no longer available)

'Saakashvili ustanovil'. 2006. 'Saakashvili ustanovil svoe rodstvo s Prometeem' [Saakashvili established his kinship with Prometheus], 14 November. Available from: <lenta.ru/news/2006/11/14/prometeus/> (last accessed 8 November 2008)

Sabikenov, Salakhiden. 1994. 'Natsional'nyi i narodnyi suverenitet. V chem ikh otlichie?' [National and people's sovereignty. What is the difference?], *Mysl'*, Almaty, 4: 9–11

Saganovich, Genad. 1993. ''Russkii vopros' s tochki zreniia Belarusa' [The Russian question from the perspective of a Belarusian], *Narodnaia gazeta*, 30 April

Sakwa, Richard. 2015. *Frontline Ukraine: Crisis in the Borderlands*. London: I. B. Tauris

'Samaia bol'shaia'. 2009. 'Samaia bol'shaia v mire Georgievskaia lentochka sdelana v Simferopole' [The world's biggest St George ribbon made in Simferopol], *RIA Novosti*, 8 May. Available from: <http://ria.ru/society/20090508/170381613.html> (last accessed 31 May 2020)

Samsonova, Tonia. 2011. 'Sozdatel' saita "Belaia Lenta": 'Posle slov Putina nas stanet bol'she' [The creator of the 'White Ribbon' site: 'After Putin's utterings our movement will become bigger'], *Republic*, 15 December. Available from: <https://republic.ru/posts/l/725481> (last accessed 25 April 2021)

Sanina, Anna. 2017. *Patriotic Education in Contemporary Russia: Sociological Studies in the Making of the Post-Soviet Citizen*. Stuttgart: Ibidem

Savva, Mikhail. 2006. 'Mai prodolzhaetsia' [May is continuing], *Rossiiskaia gazeta*, 5 December. Available from: <http://www.rg.ru/2006/12/05/savva.html> (last accessed 31 May 2020)

Schenk, Caress. 2018. 'Anti-migrant, but not nationalist: pursuing statist legitimacy through immigration discourse and policy', in Kolstø, Pål and Blakkisrud, Helge, eds, *Russia Before and After Crimea: Nationalism and Identity 2010–17*. Edinburgh: Edinburgh University Press, pp. 236–57

Scholtbach, Álvaro Pinto and Nodia, Ghia. 2006. *The Political Landscape of Georgia. Political Parties: Achievements, Challenges, and Prospects*. Eburon Delft: Caucasus Institute for Peace, Democracy and Development

Schwartz, Lee. 1990. 'Regional population redistribution and national homelands in the USSR', in H. Huttenbach, ed., *Soviet Nationality Policies*. London: Mansell, pp. 121–61

'Sdvig v storonu'. 2015. 'Sdvig v storonu gordosti i paradnosti. Kak s godami izmenilsia pervonachal'nyi smysl Dnia Pobedy' [Moving closer to pride and parades: How the original meaning of Victory Day has changed over the years], *Lenta.ru*, 20 April. Available from: <http://lenta.ru/articles/2015/04/20/denpobedy/> (last accessed 31 May 2020)

Semenova, Ekatarina. 2015. 'Magazin kroiki i shit'ia v Pushkine vystavil na prodazhu Georgievskie lentochki' [In the city of Pushkin St George ribbons are on sale in an embroidery shop], *Komsomol'skaia pravda*, 22 April. Available from: <http://www.spb.kp.ru/daily/26371.4/3251606/> (last accessed 31 May 2020)

'Serdtsu ne prikazhesh'. 2012. 'Serdtsu ne prikazhesh. Na Poklonnoi gore proshel 100-tysiachnyi "antioranzhevyi" miting' [The heart cannot be commanded. On Poklonnaia Hill there was held an 'Anti-orange' rally with more than a hundred thousand participants', *Lenta.ru*, 5 February, Available from:<https://lenta.ru/articles/2012/02/04/poklonnaja/> (last accessed 25 April 2021)

Sergeev, Sergei. 2010. *Prishestvie natsii?* [The Coming of the Nation?]. Moscow: Skimen'

Seton-Watson, Hugh. 1986. 'Russian nationalism in historical perspective', in Conquest, Robert, ed., *The Last Empire: Nationality and the Soviet Future*. Stanford, CA: Hoover Institution Press, pp. 14–29

Sevast'ianov, Aleksandr. 2008. *Russkii natsionalizm: ego druz'ia i vragi* [Russian Nationalism: It's Friends and Enemies]. Moscow: Russkaia pravda

Sevast'ianov, Aleksandr. 2010. 'Natsional-demokratiia – ne Natsional-sotsializm' [National democracy is not national socialism], *Voprosy natsionalizma*, 2: 119–40

Sevast'ianov, Aleksandr. 2012. 'Slepye vedut slepykh . . . v revoliutsiiu' [The blind are leading the blind . . . into a revolution], *Sevast'ianov's livejournal blog*, 29 January. Available from: <http://a-Sevast'ianov.livejournal. com/10863.html> (last accessed 31 May 2020)

Sevast'ianov, Aleksandr. 2013. 'Razbalansirovka diskursa: Natsional-demokratiia ili national-liberalizm?' [The imbalance of the discourse: National democracy or national liberalism?], *Voprosy natsionalizma*, 13: 201–21

Sevast'ianov, Aleksandr. 2014a. 'UKRAINO, MOIA UKRAINO!' [UKRAINE, MY UKRAINE], *Razumei.ru*, 3 March. Available from: <http://www. razumei.ru/lib/article/2157> (last accessed 30 March 2021)

Sevast'ianov, Aleksandr. 2014b. 'Sud'ba russkogo naroda reshaetsia v Donetske i Luganske' [The fate of the Russian people will be sealed in Donetsk and Lugansk], *APN*, 1 June. Available from: <http://www.apn.ru/publications/article31762.htm> (last accessed 30 March 2021)

Sevast'ianov, Aleksandr. 2015. 'K kakim posledstviiam mozhet privesti sdacha Novorossii banderovskoi Ukraine?' [What may be the consequences of giving up New Russia to Bandera-Ukraine], *Kontseptual*, 12 January. Available from: <http://концептуал.рф/rokovaya-oshibka-putina/print> (last accessed 17 December 2015)

Shanin, Teodor. 1985a. *The Roots of Otherness: Russia's Turn of Century*. Basingstoke: Macmillan

Shanin, Teodor. 1985b. *Russia as a 'Developing Society'*. London: Macmillan

Sheehy, Ann. 1990. 'Russians the target of interethnic violence in Tuva', *Report on the USSR*, 2, 37: 13–17

Shekhovtsov, Anton. 2014. 'The "Ukraine crisis" is a long-planned operation', *Anton Shekhovtsov's blog*, 29 August. Available from: <http://anton-shekhovtsov.blogspot.no/2014/08/the-ukraine-crisis-is-long-planned. html> (last accessed 30 March 2021)

Shenfield, Stephen D. 2001. *Russian Fascism: Traditions, Tendencies, Movements*. Armonk, NY: M. E. Sharpe

Shevel, Oxana. 2011. 'Russian nation-building from Yel'tsin to Medvedev: Ethnic, civic or purposefully ambiguous?', *Europe-Asia Studies*, 63, 2: 179–202

Shevtsova, Lilia. 2003. *Putin's Russia*. Washington DC: Carnegie Endowment for International Peace

Shkandrij, Myroslav. 2015. *Ukrainian Nationalism: Politics, Ideology, and Literature, 1929–1956*. New Haven, CT: Yale University Press

Shmakov, Aleksei. 1897. *Evreiskie rechi* [Speeches on the Jewish Question]. Moscow: Tipografiia A. I. Mamontova

Shmakov, Aleksei. 1906. *Svoboda i Evrei* [Freedom and the Jews]. Moscow: Moskovskaia gorodskaia tipografiia

Shokareva, Tatiana, Khustik, Svetlana and Karpovich, Stanislav. 2011. 'Georgievskie lenty v etom godu prevratili v sposob nazhivy' [This

year the St George ribbon has been turned into a means of profit],
Komsomol'skaia Pravda, 8 May. Available from: <http://www.kem.kp.ru/
daily/25682/841222/?geoid=1> (last accessed 31 May 2020)

Shornikov, Piotr. 1997. *Pokushenie na status* [An Attack on the Status]. Kishinev:
Kishinevskaia Obshchina Rossian

Simokhina, Ekaterina. 2011. 'Georgievskaia lentochka i pilotka: "Pomniu, gorzhus'!" ili "Tak modno"?' [The St George ribbon and the
side-cap: 'I remember, I am proud!' or 'Because it is fashionable?'],
Komsomol'skaia Pravda, 5 May. Available from: <http://m.volgograd.
kp.ru/daily/25681.4/839750/> (last accessed 31 May 2020)

Simon, Gerhard. 1991. *Nationalism and Policy Toward the Nationalities in the
Soviet Union: From Totalitarian Dictatorship to Post-Stalinist Society*.
Boulder, CO: Westview Press

Simonsen, Sven Gunnar. 1996. 'Raising the Russian Question: Ethnicity and
statehood, *russkie* and *Rossiya*', *Nationalism and Ethnic Politics*, 2, 1:
91–110

'Situatsiia'. 2015. 'Situatsiia s georgievskoi lentochkoi blizka k massovomu
psikhozu' [The situation with the St George ribbon is moving closer to
mass psychosis], *Kommersant*, 7 May. Available from: <http://www.kom-
mersant.ru/doc/2723416> (last accessed 31 May 2020)

'SK otkazalsia'. 2015. 'SK otkazalsia vozbuzhdat' delo posle tantsa "pchelok" v
Orenburgskoi oblasti' [The investigating committee [i.e. the State Prosecu-
tor] refused to press charges after the dance of 'the Bees' in the Orenburg
Oblast], *Gazeta.ru*, 18 May. Available from: <http://www.gazeta.ru/social/
news/2015/05/18/n_7204533.shtml> (last accessed 31 May 2020)

Slezkine, Yuri. 1994. 'The USSR as a communal apartment, or how a socialist
state promoted ethnic particularism', *Slavic Review*, 53, 2: 414–52

Slezkine, Yuri. 2004. *The Jewish Century*. Princeton, NJ: Princeton University Press

'Slovo k narodu'. 1992. 'Slovo k Narodu' [A word to the people], *Den'*, no.
29, 57: 1

Smith, Anthony D. [1986] 1991. *The Ethnic Origins of Nations*. Oxford:
Blackwell

Smith, Anthony D. 1991. *National Identity*. Harmondsworth: Penguin

Smith, Anthony D. 1995. *Nations and Nationalism in a Global Era*.
Cambridge: Polity

Smith, Anthony D. 2009. *Ethno-Symbolism: A Cultural Approach*. Abingdon:
Routledge

Smith, Graham, Law, Vivien, Wilson, Andrew, Bohr, Annette and Allworth,
Edward. 1998. *Nation-Building in the Post-Soviet Borderlands: The Politics of National Identities*. Cambridge: Cambridge University Press

Smith, Kathleen E. 2002. *Mythmaking in the New Russia: Politics and Memory
During the Yeltsin Era*. Ithaca, NY: Cornell University Press

Smith, Rogers M. 2004. 'Identities, interests, and the future of political science', *Perspectives on Politics*, 2, 2: 301–12

Smok, Vadzim. 2014. 'Belarus bans St. George's ribbons at V-Day celebrations', *BelarusDigest*, 9 May. Available from: <https://belarusdigest.com/story/belarus-bans-st-georges-ribbons-at-v-day-celebrations/> (last accessed 19 July 2021)

Smolar, Piotr. 2008. 'Saakashvili: "Rossiia nastol'ko uiazmima!"' [Saakashvili: 'Russia is so vulnerable!'], *Inosmi.ru* 21 September. Available from: <http://inosmi.ru/world/20080921/244130.html> (last accessed 30 March 2020)

Smyth, Regina, Sobolev, Anton and Soboleva, Irina. 2013. 'A well-organized play: Symbolic politics and the effect of the pro-Putin rallies', *Problems of Post-Communism*, 60, 2: 24–39

Snow, David A. and Benford, Robert D. 1992. 'Master frames and cycles of protest', in Morris, Aldon D. and Mueller, Carol McClurg, eds, *Frontiers in Social Movement Theory*. New Haven, CT: Yale University Press, pp. 133–56

Snow, David A. and Benford, Robert D. 2005. 'Clarifying the relationship between framing and ideology', in Johnston, Hank and Noakes, John A., eds, *Frames of Protest: Social Movements and the Framing Perspective*. Lanham, MD: Rowman & Littlefield, pp. 205–11

Sobchak, Kseniia. 2015. Foto, *Instagram*, 2 May. Available from: <https://instagram.com/p/2b4JGViCIG/?taken-by=xenia_sobchak> (last accessed 31 May 2020)

Sokurov, Sergei. 2014. 'Prezidentu Putinu – srochnoe pis'mo' [An urgent letter to President Putin], *Zavtra*, 4 May. Available from: <http://zavtra.ru/content/view/prezidentu-putinu-srochnoe-pismo/> (last accessed 30 March 2021)

Solovei, Valery. 2014. 'Natsiia, ne imperiia' [A nation, not an empire], *Novaia sila*, 18 March. Available from: <http://novayasila.org/lenta/news602> (last accessed 8 April 2015)

Solzhenitsyn, Aleksandr. [1973] 1980. 'Letter to the Soviet leaders,' in Solzhenitsyn, Aleksandr, *East and West*. New York: Harper and Row, pp. 75–142

Sombart, Werner. 1913. *The Jews and Modern Capitalism*. New York: E. P. Dutton and Company, Facsimile Edition

Sovetskaia Molodezh. 1990. 4 July

'Sozdateli "Bessmertnogo polka"'. 2015. 'Sozdateli "Bessmertnogo polka" obratilis' v prokuratoru iz-za fotografii s vybroshennymi plakatami' [The creators of "Immortal Regiment" contacted the state attorney about photographs of discarded placards]. *Interfaks*, 12 May. Available from: <http://www.interfax.ru/russia/441228> (last accessed 19 July 2021)

Starikov, Nikolai. 2015. 'Vedet li Bessmertnyi polk k bessmertiu Pobedy' [Will the Immortal Regiment lead to immortality for the victory?], *Blog*.

8 April. Available from: <http://nstarikov.ru/blog/50518> (last accessed 31 May 2020)

'Stenograficheskii otchet'. 2008. 'Stenograficheskii otchet o vstreche s prestavi-teliami obshchestvennykh organizatsii' [Stenographic record from meeting with representatives from public organizations], *Kremlin.ru*, 19 September. Available from: <http://news.kremlin.ru/transcripts/8209> (last accessed 30 March 2020)

Steshin, Dmitrii. 2011. 'Ushi "Beloi lenty" torchat iz Ameriki? Protesty pro-tiv narushenii na vyborakh v rossiiskii parlament byli zaplanirovany davnym-davno' [Are the 'White Ribbons' ears hanging all the way from America? The protests against violations in the elections for the Russian parliament were planned long ago], *Komsomolskaia Pravda*, 8 December. Available from: <https://www.kp.ru/daily/25801.4/2782350/> (last accessed 25 April 2021)

'Strategiia gosudarstvennoi natsional'noi'. 2012. 'Strategiia gosudarstvennoi natsional'noi politiki Rossiiskoj Federatsii na period do 2025 goda' [The national state policy of the Russian Federation until 2025], *Garant*. Available from: <http://www.garant.ru/hotlaw/federal/437675/> (last accessed 31 May 2020)

Strayer, Robert. 1998. *Why did the Soviet Union Collapse? Understanding Historical Change*. Armonk, New York: M. E. Sharpe

Struve, Petr. 1997. 'Dva natsionalizma' [Two types of nationalism], in *Patrio-tika: politika, kul'tura, religiia, sotsializm* [Patriotic Literature: Politics, Culture, Religion, Socialism]. Moscow: Respublika, pp. 164–72

Sukhanova, Irina. 2015. 'Kseniia Sobchak snialas' v bikini tsvetov georgievs-koi lentochki' [Kseniia Sobchak photographed in a bikini in the colours of the St George ribbon], *Komsomol'skaia Pravda*, 16 April. Available from: <http://www.kp.ru/daily/26368.4/3248978/> (last accessed 31 May 2020)

Suny, Ronald. 1993. *The Revenge of the Past: Nationalism, Revolution, and the Collapse of the Soviet Union*. Stanford, CA: Stanford University Press

Suhr, Gerald. 2003. 'Ekaterinoslav city in 1905: Workers, Jews, and violence', *International Labor and Working-Class History*, 64, Fall: 139–66

Surnacheva, Elizaveta. 2015. 'Lentochnyi konveier: kak zarabotat' na patri-oticheskikh chuvstvakh' [A ribbon conveyor: How to make a profit from patriotic emotions], *Kommersant*, 11 May. Available from: <http://www.kommersant.ru/doc/2714479> (last accessed 31 May 2020)

Suslov, Mikhail and Uzlaner, Dmitry, eds. 2020. *Contemporary Russian Conservativism: Problems, Paradoxes and Perspectives*. Leiden/Boston: Brill

Sviatenkov, Pavel. 2010. 'Vozmozhna li rossiiskaia identichnost'?' [Is a Rossiiskaia identity possible?], *Voprosy natsionalizma*, 3: 3–6

Sviatenkov, Pavel. 2012. 'Putin predlagaet Rossii to, chto razrushaet Evropu' [Putin is offering Russia what is destroying Europe], *Voprosy natsionalizma*, 9: 14–16

Sviatenkov, Pavel. 2014. 'Rossiia perestala oshchushchat' sebia koloniei' [Russia does not feel like a colony anymore], *Russkii obozrevatel'*, 26 March. Available from: <http://www.rus-obr.ru/ru-web/30341> (last accessed 30 March 2021)

'Svyshe 10 tysiach'. 2018. 'Svyshe 10 tysiach chelovek sobralis' na glavnoi ploshchadi Donetska na prazdnovanie Dnia Georgievskoi lenty' [More than ten thousand people gathered at the main square of Donetsk to celebrate St George Ribbon's Day], 7 December. Available from: <https://dan-news.info/obschestvo/svyshe-10-tysyach-chelovek-sobralis-na-glavnoj-ploshhadi-donecka-na-prazdnovanie-dnya-georgievskoj-lenty.html> (last accessed 30 March 2021)

Szporluk, Roman. 1989. 'Dilemmas of Russian nationalism', *Problems of Communism*, July–August: 15–35

Taagepera, Rein. 1993. *Estonia: Return to Independence*. Boulder, CO: Westview Press

Tarasov, Stanislav and Ermolaev, Dmitrii. 2008. 'Osennee obostrenie ili geopoliticheskie tezisy Mishiko Saakashvili' [Autumn escalations or the geopolitical theses of Mishiko Saakashvili], *Rossiiskie vesti*, 8–15 October. Available from: <http://rosvesty.ru/1931/interes/?id=1000000230> (last accessed 8 November 2008)

Tarrow, Sidney. [1998] 2011. *Power in Movement: Social Movements and Contentious Politics*. Cambridge: Cambridge University Press

Tatimov, Makash. 1995. 'Vliiane demograficheskikh i migratsionnykh protsessov na vnutripoliticheskuiu stabil'nost' Respubliki Kazakhstan' [The influence of demographic and migration processes on internal political stability], *Saiasat*, 5, November: 18–23

Taylor, Charles, and Gutman, Amy. 1994. *Multiculturalism: Examining the Politics of Recognition*. Princeton, NJ: Princeton University Press

Teper, Yuri. 2016. "Official russian identity discourse in the light of the annexation of Crimea: National or imperial?", *Post-Soviet Affairs*, 32, 4: 378–96

Teper, Yuri. 2018. 'Kremlin's post-2012 national policies: Encountering the merits and perils of identity-based social contract', in Kolstø, Pål and Blakkisrud, Helge, eds. *Russia Before and After Crimea: Nationalism and Identity, 2010–17*. Edinburgh: Edinburgh University Press, pp. 68–92.

Tevzadze, Gigi. 2009. 'Speech at symposium on "Georgia at the crossroads of European and Asian cultures"', *Harriman Institute*, 4 May. Available from: <http://harriman.columbia.edu/files/harriman/01397.pdf> (last accessed 30 March 2020)

Timofeychev, Alexey. 2018. 'St. George's ribbon: How a grassroots initiative became a national project'. *Russia Beyond*. 9 May. Available from: <https://www.Rbth.Com/History/328240-St-Georges-Ribbon> (last accessed 25 April 2021)

Tishkov, Valerii A. 1992. 'Natsiia – to zhe plemia, no tol'sko s armiei' (A nation is like a tribe, only with an army], interview with Marina Shakina, *Novoe Vremia*, 35: 9–12

Tishkov, Valerii A. 1995. 'What is Rossia? Prospects for nation-building', *Security Dialogue*, 26, 1: 41–54

Tishkov, Valerii A. 1997. *Ethnicity, Nationalism and Conflict in and after the Soviet Union: The Mind Aflame*. London: Sage

Tishkov, Valerii A. 2003. *Rekviem po etnosu: Issledovaniia po sotsial'no-kul'turnoi antropologii* [A Requiem on Ethnos: Studies on Socio-Cultural Anthropology]. Moscow: Nauka

Tishkov, Valerii A. 2009. 'I russkii, i rossiiskii' [Both *Russian* and a Russian citizen], *Vestnik rossiiskoi natsii*, 2, 4, April. Available from: <http://www.rosnation.ru/index.php?D¼438&goto¼432> (last accessed 31 May 2020)

Tishkov, Valerii A. 2010. *Rossiiskii narod: Kniga dlia uchitelia* [The Russian People: A Book for Teachers]. Moscow: Prosveshchenie

Tishkov, Valerii A., ed. 2011. *Rossiiskaia natsiia, stanovlenie i etnokul'turnoe mnogoobrazie* [The Russian Nation, Creation and Ethnocultural Variation]. Moscow: Nauka

Tishkov, Valerii A. 2013. *Rossiiskii narod: Istoriia i smysl natsional'nogo samo-soznaniia* [The Russian People: The History and Meaning of National Self-Awareness]. Moscow: Nauka

Todorova, Maria. 2009. *Imagining the Balkans*. Oxford: Oxford University Press

Toft, Monica. 2003. *The Geography of Ethnic Violence*. Princeton, NJ: Princeton University Press

Tolz, Vera. 1998. 'Conflicting "homeland myths" and nation-state building in postcommunist Russia', *Slavic Review*, 57, 2: 267–94

Tolz, Vera. 2001. *Russia: Inventing the Nation*. London: Arnold

Tolz, Vera. 2019. 'Constructing race, ethnicity and nationhood in Imperial Russia: Issues and misconceptions' In Rainbow, David, ed., *Ideologies of Race: Imperial Russia and the Soviet Union in Global Context*. Montreal: McGill-Queen's University Press, pp. 29–58

Tolz, Vera and Harding, Sue-Ann. 2015. 'From "compatriots" to "aliens": The changing coverage of migration on Russian television', *The Russian Review*, 74, 3: 452–77

Torbakov, Igor. 2015. 'A parting of ways? The Kremlin leadership and Russia's new-generation nationalist thinkers', *Demokratizatsiya*, 23, 4: 427–57

Tsygankov, Andrei. 2015. 'Vladimir Putin's last stand: The sources of Russia's Ukraine policy', *Post-Soviet Affairs*, 31, 4, July: 279–303

'Tsveta i tsvety'. 2017. 'Tsveta i tsvety Pobedy. Pochemu sporiat o "georgievs-koi lentochke"' [The flowers and colours of Victory: Why they are quar-relling about the St George ribbon], *Current Time*, 7 May. Available from: <https://www.currenttime.tv/a/28469937.html> (last accessed 19 July 2021)

Tubol'tseva, Natal'ia. 2015. 'Oblozhka zhurnala "Elle" s plat'em tsvetov geor-gievskoi lenty vyzvala skandal na Ukraine' [The cover of Elle with a dress in the colours of the St George ribbon created a scandal in Ukraine], *Komsomol'skaia pravda*, 22 April. Available from: <http://www.kp.ru/daily/26370/3251319/> (last accessed 31 May 2020)

Tucker, Joshua. 2014. 'What is motivating Putin?', *The Washington Post*, Monkey cage, 18 March. Available from: <http://www.washingtonpost.com/blogs/monkey-cage/wp/2014/03/18/what-is-motivating-putin/> (last accessed 17 December 2015)

Tulepbaev, M. 1996. 'Kakogo kachestva kazachestvo?' [Of what quality are the Cossacks?], *Kazakhstanskaia Pravda*, 6 January

Tuminez, Astrid S. 2000. *Russian Nationalism Since 1856: Ideology and the Making of Foreign Policy*. Lanham, MD: Rowman & Littlefield

Tutkevich, Dmitrii. 1906. *Chto Takoe Evrei* [What Are the Jews Like]. Kiev: Tipografiia I. I. Gorbunova

'Tvorcheskii vecher'. 2014. 'Tvorcheskii vecher Nevzorova, v kontsertnom zale u Finliandskogo' [Cultural evening with Nevzorov in the concert hall by the Finland Station], *Nevzorov.TV*, 19 April. Available from: <http://nevzorov.tv/2014/04/tvorcheskij-vecher/> (last accessed 13 August 2015, no longer available)

'Ubei "kolorada"'. 2014. 'Ubei "kolorada"! – v Kieve otkrylas' vystavka "100 luchshikh patrioticheskikh plakatov"' [Kill a 'Colorado bee-tle'! In Kiev an exhibition of the hundred best patriotic posters has opened], 2 December. Available from: <https://www.politnavigator.net/ne-prokhodi-mimo-ubejj-kolorada-v-kieve-otkrylas-vystavka-100-luch-shikh-patrioticheskikh-plakatov-foto.html> (last accessed 1 June 2020)

'Ukraina seichas'. 2014. 'Ukraina seichas nastoiashchii forpost Evropy – Poro-shenko' [Ukraine is now a real outpost of Europe – Poroshenko], *Segod-nia* 1 September. Available from: <http://www.segodnya.ua/ukraine/ukraina-seychas-nastoyashchiy-forpost-evropy-poroshenko-548608.html> (last accessed 1 September 2021)

'Ukraina iavleiaetsia'. 2015. 'Ukraina iavliaetsia forpostom evropeiskoi tsivilizat-sii v borbe za svobodu i demokratiiu – Poroshenko' [Ukraine is an outpost for European civilization in the fight for freedom and democracy], *UNIAN* 29 April. Available from: <http://www.unian.net/politics/1073218-ukraina-yavlyaetsya-forpostom-evropeyskoy-tsivilizatsii-v-borbe-za-svobodu-i-demokratiyu-poroshenko.html> (last accessed 8 November 2016)

Umland, Andreas. 2012. 'Could Russia's ultranationalists subvert pro-democracy protests?', *World Affairs* 19 January. Available from: <https://www.researchgate.net/publication/255720261_Could_Russia's_Ultranationalists_Subvert_Pro-Democracy_Protests> (last accessed 1 June 2020)

'U Rzhevskogo'. 2020. 'U Rzhevskogo memoriala razvernuli samuiu bol'shuiu v mire georgievskuiu lentu' [The world's longest St George ribbon was folded out around the Rzhevsk Memorial], *RIA novosti*, 22 August. Available from: <https://ria.ru/20200822/volontery-1576168455.html?in=t> (last accessed 25 April 2021)

Uspenskii, Nikolai. 2008. 'Nikolai Uspenskii: Gruziny – bratskii narod' [Nikolai Uspenskii: Georgians are a friendly people], *Rusdelfi* 11 August. Available from: <http://rus.delfi.ee/daily/politics/article.php?id=19558690> (last accessed 30 March 2020)

'Ustav polka'. Undated. 'Ustav polka' [The regiment charter], *Moypolk.ru*. Available from: <http://moypolk.ru/ustav-polka> (last accessed 31 May 2020)

Vakar, Nicholas. 1956. *Belorussia: The Making of a Nation: A Case Study.* Cambridge, MA: Harvard University Press

'V aktsii'. 2015. 'V aktsii "Bessmertnyi polk" v Moskve priniali uchastie ne menee 350 tysiach chelovek' [At least 350,000 people participated in the Immortal Regiment action in Moscow], *Ekho Moskvy*, 9 May. Available from: <http://echo.msk.ru/news/1545576-echo.html?=top> (last accessed 31 May 2020)

Van Dyke, Nella and McCammon, Holly J. eds, 2010. *Strategic Alliances: Coalition Building and Social Movements.* Minneapolis: University of Minnesota Press

Vasil'chenko, Elena. 2016. '"Bessmertnyi polk" vyvedet na ulitsy mira bolee 10 millionov chelovek' [The Immortal Regiment leads more than 10 million people into the streets of the world]. *Moskovskii komsomolets*, 8 May. Available from: <http://www.mk.ru/social/2016/05/08/bessmertnyy-polk-vyvedetna-ulicy-mira-bolee-10-millionov-chelovek.html> (last accessed 20 April 2021)

Vasileva, Mariia. 2011. '"Belaia lentochka": nedovol'nye vykhodiat iz seti na ulitsy' [The white ribbon: Those who are disgruntled move from the Internet into the strcets'] *BBC's Russian service*, 8 December. Available from: <https://www.bbc.com/russian/russia/2011/12/111208_white_ribbon_russia> (last accessed 26 July 2021)

'V-Day'. 2015. 'V-Day in Russia evokes national pride at difficult time', *Associated Press*, 7 May. Available from: <https://www.voanews.com/europe/v-day-russia-evokes-national-pride-difficult-time> (last accessed 31 May 2020)

'V Donetske'. 2018. 'V Donetske otprazdnuiut Den' Georgievskoi lenty' [St George Ribbons' Day will be celebrated in Donetsk], RIA Novosti,

7 December. Available from: <https://ria.ru/20181207/1547592203.html> (last accessed 30 March 2021)

'Velikaia Pobeda'. 2015. 'Velikaia Pobeda: deistvitel'no odna i deistvitel'no na vsekh' [The Great Victory: Indeed, it is only one and indeed it is for everyone], *Nezavisimaia gazeta*, 30 April. Available from: <http://www.ng.ru/editorial/2015-04-30/2_red.html> (last accessed 31 May 2020)

Verkhovsky, Alexander. 2009. 'Future prospects of contemporary Russian nationalism', in Laruelle, Marlène, ed., *Russian Nationalism and the National Reassertion of Russia*. London: Routledge, pp. 89–103

Verkhovsky, Aleksandr. 2012. 'Natsionalisty v protestnom dvizhenii – pochemo i kak' [Nationalists in protest movement – why and how], *Sova Analytical Center*, 22 August. Available from: <http://www.sova-center.ru/racism-xenophobia/publications/2012/08/d25142/?print=1> (last accessed 31 May 2020)

Verkhovsky, Aleksander. 2016. 'Radical nationalists from the start of Medvedev's presidency to the war in Donbas – true till death?', in Kolstø, Pål and Blakkisrud, Helge, eds, *The New Russian Nationalism: Imperialism, Ethnicity, Authoritarianism 2000–2015*. Edinburgh: Edinburgh University Press, pp. 75–103

Verkhovsky, Alexander. 2018. 'The Russian nationalist movement at low ebb', in Kolstø, Pål and Blakkisrud, Helge, eds, *Russia Before and After Crimea Nationalism and Identity, 2010–17*. Edinburgh: Edinburgh University Press, pp. 142–62

Vermeulen, Hans and Govers, Cora, eds. 1994. *The Anthropology of Ethnicity: Beyond Ethnic Groups and Boundaries*. Amsterdam: Het Spinhuis

Vezhin, Savelii. 2011. 'Ne prevratitsia li miting v "Russkii marsh"' [Will the rally not turn into a 'Russian March'?], *Nezavisimaia gazeta* 23 December. Available from: <http://www.ng.ru/politics/2011-12-23/1_meeting.html> (last accessed 31 May 2020)

Vishnevskii, Boris. 2015. 'Ot simvola edinstva – k simvolu raz'edineniia' [From a symbol of unity to a symbol of division], *Ekho Moskvy*, 6 May. Available from: <http://echo.msk.ru/blog/boris_vis/1543916-echo/> (last accessed 31 May 2020)

Vishniak, Mark. 1942. 'Antisemitism in tsarist Russia: A study in government-fostered antisemitism', in Pinson, Koppel S., ed., *Essays on Antisemitism*. New York: Conference on Jewish Relations, pp. 79–110

'V Kazakhstane'. 2015. 'V Kazakhstane nachalas' kampaniia protiv georgievskoi lentochki [A campaign has started in Kazakhstan against the St George ribbon], *Vzgliad*, 11 April. Available from: <http://vz.ru/news/2015/4/11/739447.html> (last accessed 31 May 2020)

'V Khar'kove'. 2014. 'V Khar'kove proizoshla potasovka mezhdu Maidanom i Antimaidanom' [A fight broke out in Kharkiv between Maidan and anti-Maidan factions], *Zerkalo nedeli*, 13 July. Available from: <http://

zn.ua/UKRAINE/v-harkove-proizoshla-potasovka-mezhdu-maydanom-i-antimaydanom-148883_.html> (last accessed 31 May 2020)

'Vladimir Putin'. 2015. 'Vladimir Putin prinial uchastie v aktsii "Bessmertnyi polk"' [Vladimir Putin took part in the Immortal Regiment parade], *Youtube*, 9 May. Available from: <https://www.youtube.com/watch?v=S4oMzVhNa60> (last accessed 31 May 2020)

'V Moldove'. 2014. 'V Moldove za noshenie Georgievskoi lentochki budut shtrafovat' na 200 dollarov' [In Moldova people will get a fee of 200 dollars for wearing a St George ribbon], *Komsomol'skaia pravda*, 4 June. Available from: <http://www.kp.md/daily/26239/3121360/> (last accessed 31 May 2020)

Voitkevich, E. 1997. 'Rodina tam, gde glubzhe korni' [Motherland is where you have the deepest roots], *Kazakhstanskaia Pravda*, 31 January

'Vo L'vove'. 2015. 'Vo L'vove izbili muzhchinu s georgievskoi lentoi' [In L'viv a man with a St George ribbon was beaten up], *Vsia vlast'*, 11 May. Available from: <http://www.vv.com.ua/news/90464> (last accessed 31 May 2020)

Voronkov, Konstantin. 2012. *Aleksei Naval'ny: Groza zhulikov i vorov* [Aleksei Navalny: The Threat of Crooks and Thieves]. Moscow: Eksmo

Voslenskii, Mikhail. 1984. *Nomenklatura: Gospodstvuiushchii klass Sovetskogo Soiuza* [The *Nomenklatura*: The Ruling Class of the Soviet Union]. London: Overseas Publications Interchange

Walzer, Michael. 1967. 'On the role of symbolism in political thought', *Political Science Quarterly*, 82, 2: 191–204

Weinberg, Robert. 2004. 'The Pogrom in 1905 in Odessa, a Case Study', in Klier, John Doyle and Lambroza, Shlomo, eds, *Pogroms: Anti-Jewish Violence in Modern Russian History*. Cambridge: Cambridge University Press, pp. 248–89

Weiner, Myron. 1978. *Sons of the Soil: Migration and Ethnic Conflict in India*. Princeton, NJ: Princeton University Press

Weinerman, Eli. 1994. 'Racism, racial prejudice and Jews in late Imperial Russia', *Ethnic and Racial Studies*, 17, 3: 442–95

Westby, David L. 2005. 'Strategic imperative, ideology, and frames', in Johnston, Hank and Noakes, John A., eds, *Frames of Protest: Social Movements and the Framing Perspective*. Lanham, MD: Rowman & Littlefield, pp. 217–36

Wilentz, Sean, ed. [1985] 1999. *Rites of Power: Symbolism, Ritual, and Politics since the Middle Ages*. Philadelphia: University of Pennsylvania Press

Wilkinson, Cai. 2014. 'Putting "traditional values" into practice: The rise and contestation of anti-homopropaganda laws in Russia', *Journal of Human Rights*, 13, 3: 363–79

Wilkinson, Steven I. 2004. *Votes and Violence: Electoral Competition and Ethnic Riots in India*. Cambridge: Cambridge University Press

Wilson, Andrew. 1997. *Ukrainian Nationalism in the 1990s: A Minority Faith*. Cambridge: Cambridge University Press

Wilson, Andrew. 2014. *Ukraine Crisis: What It Means for the West*. New Haven, CT: Yale University Press

Wilson, Andrew. 2015. Interview with the Norwegian Broadcasting Service, 11 June. Available from: <https://tv.nrk.no/serie/urix> (last accessed 17 December 2015)

Wimmer, Andreas. 2013. *Ethnic Boundary Making: Institutions, Power, Networks*. Oxford: Oxford University Press

Yanov, Alexander. 1978. *The Russian New Right: Right-Wing Ideologies in the Contemporary USSR*. Berkeley: Institute of International Studies

Yeltsin, Boris. 1994. 'Poslanie Prezidenta Rossii Borisa El'tsina Federal'nomu Sobraniiu RF: "Ob ukreplenii Rossiiskogo Gosudarstva" 1994 god' [Address of the Russian President Boris Yeltsin to the Federal Assembly of the Russian Federation: 'About the strengthening of the Russian state], *Intelros*. Available from: <http://www.intelros.ru/2007/02/04/poslanija_prezidenta_rossii_borisa_elcina_federalnomu_sobraniju_rf_1994_god.html> (last accessed 31 May 2020)

Yudina, Natalia and Alperovich, Vera. 2014. 'Ukraine upsets the nationalist apple-cart: Xenophobia, radical nationalism and efforts to counteract it in Russia during the first half of 2014', *Sova Center for Information and Analysis*, 6 August. Available from: <https://www.sova-center.ru/en/xenophobia/reports-analyses/2014/08/d30003/> (last accessed 31 May 2020)

'Za chestnye'. 2011. 'Za chestnye vybory. Prodolzhenie' [For fair elections. A continuation], *Interfax*, 24 December. Available from:< http://www.interfax.ru/russia/223525> (last accessed 31 May 2020)

'Zaiavlenie'. 2014. 'Zaiavlenie "Demokraticheskogo vybora" o nedopustimosti rossiiskogo voennogo vmeshatel'stva na Ukraine' [A statement of 'Democratic choice' about the inadmissability of Russian military interference in Ukraine], *Demokraticheskii vybor*, 1 March. Available from: <http://demvybor.ru/declaration/1387-zayavlenie-demokraticheskogo-vybora-o-nedopustimosti-rossijskogo-voennogo-vmeshatelstva-na-ukraine.html> (last accessed 30 March 2021)

'Zakon'. 1992. 'Zakon o korennom narode Respubliki Bashkortostan, (proekt 21 noiabria 1992g.)' [Law about the indigenous people of the Republic of Bashkortostan, (project 21 November 1992)], in Safin, F. G., ed., *Iz khroniki etnicheskoi mobilizatsii. Respublika Bashkortostan* [The Chronicles of Ethnic Mobilization of the Republic of Bashkortostan], Vol. I. Moscow: TsIMO, pp. 124–6

Zald, Mayer N. 1996. 'Culture, ideology, and strategic framing', in McAdam, Doug, McCarthy, John D. and Zald, Mayer N., eds, *Comparative Perspectives on Social Movements: Political Opportunities, Mobilizing*

Structures, and Culture Framings. Cambridge: Cambridge University Press, pp. 261–74

Žanić, Ivo. 2005. 'The symbolic identity of Croatia in the triangle *crossroads–bulwark–bridge*', in Kolstø, Pål, ed., *Myths and Boundaries in South-Eastern Europe*. London: Hurst & Co., pp. 35–76

Zaporozhskii, Sergei. 2015. 'U chertei svoi den' Pobedy (The demons have their Victory day)', *Ekho Moskvy*, 7 May. Available from: <http://m.echo.msk.ru/blogs/detail.php?ID=1544356> (last accessed 26 July 2021)

Zaprudnik, Jan. 1993. *Belarus: At a Crossroads in History*. Boulder, CO: Westview

Zaslavsky, Viktor. 1993. 'Success and collapse: Traditional Soviet nationality policy', in Bremmer, Ian and Taras, Ray, eds. *Nations and Politics in the Soviet Successor States*. Cambridge: Cambridge University Press, pp. 29–42.

Zaslavsky, Viktor. [1982] 1994. *The Neo-Stalinist State: Class, Ethnicity, and Consensus in Soviet Society*. Amonk, NY: M. E. Sharpe

Zdravomyslova, Elena. 1996. 'Opportunities and framing in the transition to democracy: The case of Russia', in McAdam, Doug, McCarthy, John D. and Zald, Mayer N., eds. *Comparative Perspectives on Social Movements: Political Opportunities, Mobilizing Structures, and Cultural Framings*. Cambridge: Cambridge University Press, pp. 122–37

Zevelev, Igor. 2001. *Russia and its New Diasporas*. Washington, D.C.: United States Institute of Peace Press

Zevelev, Igor. 2014. 'Granitsy russkogo mira: transformatsiia natsional'noi identichnosti i novaia vneshnepoliticheskaia doktrina Rossii' [The borders of the Russian world: The transformation of national identity and the new international political doctrine of Russia], *Rossiia v Global'noi Politike*, 27 April. Available from: <http://www.globalaffairs.ru/number/Granitcy-russkogo-mira--16582> (last accessed 31 May 2020)

Ziuganov, Gennadii. 2014. 'Politicheskii chernobyl: Vystuplenie G.A. Ziuganova na plenarnom zasedanii Gosdumy' [The political Chernobyl: Speech of G. A. Ziuganov at the plenary session of the state Duma], *Sovietskaia Rossiia*, 27 February. Available from: <https://kprf.ru/party-live/cknews/128664.html> (last accessed 30 March 2021)

Zhdanov, Anatolii. 2015. '"Bessmertnyi polk" ne khochet v shtat' [The Immortal Regiment does not want to become part of the establishment], *Kommersant*, 29 May. Available from: <http://kommersant.ru/doc/2736209> (last accessed 31 May 2020)

Zheleznova, Mariia. 2012. 'V Shtab oppozitsii voidut liberaly, levye i natsionalisty' [Liberals, leftists and nationalists will join the staff of the opposition], *Vedomosti*, 2 August. Available from: <http://www.vedomosti.ru/politics/news/2429521/vybor_bolotnoj> (last accessed 31 May 2020)

Zhirinovskii, Vladimir. 2014. 'Vystuplenie v Ialte 14 August, Krym: Putin Verk-hovnyi pravitel', Imperator' [Speech at Yalta 14 August, Crimea: Putin is a supreme ruler], *Youtube*, 15 August. Available from: <https://www.youtube.com/watch?v=MVWjMVvX8ic> (last accessed 30 March 2021)

Zhurzhenko, Tatiana. 2018. 'From borderlands to bloodlands', *Transit: Europäische Revue*, 45 (Ukraine—the Unexpected Revolution). Available from: <http://www.iwm.at/read-listen-watch/transit-online/borderlands-bloodlands> (last accessed 13 March 2018)

Zuev, Dennis and Virchow, Fabian. 2014. 'Performing national-identity: The many logics of producing national belongings in public rituals and events', *Nations and Nationalism*, 20, 2: 191–9

INDEX

professional rivalries and anti-Semitism,
15, 30, 31, 34, 35, 36–7, 42, 46–7,
51, 52
unemployment in Central Asia, 15,
55–6, 57, 60, 64
see also migration
Eriksen, Thomas Hylland, 16
Estonia
citizenship requirements, 71–2
opposition to the St George ribbon, 161
ethnic boundary making
antiquitas myth, 19–20, 93
boundary contraction, 19, 22, 113
boundary expansion, 19, 21
boundary maintenance, 17
boundary markers (diacritica), 24, 26
boundary-making within a nation, 3, 142
counter-discourses, 19
diacritica (boundary markers), 16, 17, 93
for identity formation, 16–17, 59
individual agency, 18–19
martyrium myth, 19, 94
as multifaceted, 17–18
myths, symbols and rituals, 22–5, 93
for self- and other-identification, 19,
93, 110
strategic behaviour, 18–19
sui generis myth, 19, 94, 100, 111
in Zambia, 17–18
see also antemurale myth
ethnic conflict
in Central Asia, 56–7, 64, 76
in the former Yugoslavia, 8
globally, 2
labour factor in, 15, 58–61, 62–3, 64–6
over higher education, 66–7
during perestroika, 55, 56
titular/non-titular group power
dynamics, 15
warmongering strategies, 8
see also Anti-Semitism
ethnic entrepreneurs
belief in own ideas, 14
nationalist rhetoric, 2
power struggles of, 12–13
use of ethnic boundaries, 17
use of Russian/titular economic gaps,
13–14
ethnic identities
common-culture approach, 6, 16

under the communist regime, 2
interactions with the Other, 16, 110
role of culture, history and symbols,
3–4, 141, 142
ethnic Russians
dominance in well-paid jobs, 14
status in the non-Russian republics,
74–5
in Tsarist Russia, 38
ethnicity
elites and identity-formation, 6, 7
politicisation of, 6–7, 77
Soviet institutionalisation of, 77–8
ethno-nationalism
the Crimean annexation, 196–200, 204
democratic leanings, 126–7, 128–9, 194
emergence of in Russia, 126–9
imperialist-ethno-nationalist divisions in
Russia, 117, 118, 127–8, 192, 193–4
migrantphobia, 126, 131–3, 138, 194
national democrats, 126–7, 128, 132–3,
174–5, 194
nationalism as, 116–17, 118
opposition to the Putin regime, 194
popular support in Russia, 133–5
russkii concept, 128, 133, 194
shift from statism to, 115
stance on the war in Eastern Ukraine,
200–3
ethno-nationalist rhetoric
efficacy of in titular/non-titular regions,
12, 13
of the Putin regime, 114–15, 126,
129–31, 138, 192–3, 215–17
use by regional leaders in the USSR
under perestroika, 11–12
ethno-symbolism, 3–4, 28–9
Eurasianism, 119–20
Europe
Central Europe, 95, 96
East/West cultural divide, 95–7
Huntington's civilisational division,
96–8

Fearon, James, 90–1
Feoktistov, Aleksandr, 86
Fish, Stephen, 27
flags, 23
former Yugoslavia, 8
functionalism, 5

Saakashvili, Mikheil, 107, 108
Sabikenov, S., 85
Saganovich, Genad, 101
Sergeev, Sergei, 127, 129
Sevast'ianov, Alexander, 127, 128, 130,
    179, 199, 200, 202
Shaimiev, Mintimer, 88
Shevel, Oxana, 118, 125
Shmakov, Aleksei, 50
Shornikov, Petr, 70
Simonsen, Sven Gunnar, 117
Slavic Union, 126
Smith, Anthony, 3, 4, 28
Smith, Rogers, 27
Snow, David, 169, 170
social movement theory
    bridge-builders, 169, 171, 177–9
    bridge-wreckers, 169, 179–81
    coalition-building efforts, 171
    frames, 169
    ideologies, 169, 171
    ideologies-frames relationship, 170–1
    master frames, 169–70, 172
    role of symbols, 171–2
Solovei, Valery, 198–9, 217
Solzhenitsyn, Alexander, 115,
    120, 124
sons of the soil (SoS) conflicts
    arrival time factors, 91
    in Bashkortostan, 76, 81–3
    concept, 75–6
    expectations of in the former Soviet
        republics, 90–1, 92
    in Kazakhstan, 76, 83–8
    korennoi discourse, 74–5, 76
    migrant anxiety, 75–6, 90–1
Soviet Union (USSR)
    dissolution of the state, 3
    ethno-federal structure, 10
    formation, 2
    korenizatsia policy, 9–10
    nationality policies, 9–10, 77
    Russian nationalism, 119–20, 136–7
    Russo-centric Soviet state nationalism
        during WW II, 10–11
    St George ribbon provenance, 25–6,
        145, 146–7
    USSR-focused statism, 122–3
    Victory Day, 9 May, 144–5
    during World War II, 144

St George Order of the Donetsk People's
    Republic, 210, 211
St George ribbon
    anti-Putin liberals and, 142, 152, 159,
        163–4, 165
    as a boundary marker, 26, 161–2
    commercial adoption, 150–3
    dual provenance, 25–6, 145–7, 165
    an emblem of the Putin regime, 26, 142,
        153–5, 158–9, 160–1, 164–5
    and the Immortal Regiment, 26, 142,
        149, 154–5
    opposition to outside Russia, 161–3, 166
    popular adoption of, 141–2, 143, 148–50,
        159–60
    Student Community's initiative, 147–8
    support for in Ukraine 208
    during the war in Eastern Ukraine, 27,
        191, 208–15
    Ukrainian opposition to, 161, 162
    'We won!' art exhibition, 215, 216
    the White Ribbon as opposition to, 26,
        172, 188
Stalin, Joseph, 9, 10
state
    civic nation-state model, 125–6, 128, 129
    dissident statists, 115, 120
    institutions, 25
    state-focused nationalism, 21, 115,
        116–17, 118, 119–20, 122–3
    strategies for identity-building, 4
    use of national symbols, 25
    USSR-focused statism, 122–3
Strelkov-Girkin, Igor, 201–2, 205, 209, 210
Surh, Gerald, 47
Sviatenkov, Pavel, 197–8
symbols
    as boundary markers, 22, 24, 93
    definition, 23
    ethno-symbolism, 3–4, 28–9
    within national identity formation, 3–4,
        141, 142
    national symbols of the Yeltsin era, 143
    rituals and, 23, 24
    rival symbolic repertoires, 24
    Russian national symbols, 25–6,
        143–4, 145
    in social movement theory, 171–2
    symbolic construction of society, 22–3
    of Tsarist Russia, 143

Printed and bound by CPI Group (UK) Ltd, Croydon, CR0 4YY

09/04/2025

01843114-0003